Hands-On RESTful Python Web Services

Second Edition

Develop RESTful web services or APIs with modern Python 3.7

Gaston C. Hillar

BIRMINGHAM - MUMBAI

Hands-On RESTful Python Web Services
Second Edition

Commissioning Editor: Aaron Lazar
Acquisition Editor: Reshma Raman
Content Development Editor: Rohit Singh
Technical Editor: Gaurav Gala
Copy Editor: Safis Editing
Project Coordinator: Vaidehi Sawant
Proofreader: Safis Editing
Indexer: Priyanka Dhadke
Graphics: Alishon Mendonsa
Production Coordinator: Shraddha Falebhai

First published: October 2016
Second edition: December 2018

Production reference: 1221218

Published by Packt Publishing Ltd.
Livery Place
35 Livery Street
Birmingham
B3 2PB, UK.

ISBN 978-1-78953-222-7

www.packtpub.com

To my sons, Kevin and Brandon, and my wife, Vanesa.

– Gaston C. Hillar

`mapt.io`

Mapt is an online digital library that gives you full access to over 5,000 books and videos, as well as industry leading tools to help you plan your personal development and advance your career. For more information, please visit our website.

Why subscribe?

- Spend less time learning and more time coding with practical eBooks and videos from over 4,000 industry professionals

- Improve your learning with Skill Plans built especially for you

- Get a free eBook or video every month

- Mapt is fully searchable

- Copy and paste, print, and bookmark content

Packt.com

Did you know that Packt offers eBook versions of every book published, with PDF and ePub files available? You can upgrade to the eBook version at `www.packt.com` and, as a print book customer, you are entitled to a discount on the eBook copy. Get in touch with us at `customercare@packtpub.com` for more details.

At `www.packt.com`, you can also read a collection of free technical articles, sign up for a range of free newsletters, and receive exclusive discounts and offers on Packt books and eBooks.

Contributors

About the author

Gaston C. Hillar is Italian and has been working with computers since he was 8 years old. Gaston has a Bachelor's degree in computer science (graduated with honors) and an MBA.

Currently, Gaston is an independent IT consultant and a freelance author who is always looking for new adventures anywhere in the world.

He was a senior contributing editor at Dr. Dobb's, and has written more than a hundred articles on software development topics. He has received the prestigious Intel® Black Belt Software Developer award eight times. He has written many articles about Java for Oracle Java Magazine.

Gaston was also a former Microsoft MVP in technical computing. He lives with his wife, Vanesa, and his two sons, Kevin and Brandon.

While writing this book, I was fortunate enough to work with an excellent team at Packt Publishing Ltd, whose contributions vastly improved its presentation. Reshma Raman allowed me to provide her with ideas for developing the second edition of this book and I jumped at the exciting prospect of teaching how to use many popular web frameworks for developing RESTful web services with modern Python 3.6 and 3.7. Rohit Singh helped me realize my vision for this new edition of the book and provided many sensible suggestions regarding the text, the format, and the flow. I would like to thank my technical reviewers and proofreaders for their thorough reviews and insightful comments. I was able to incorporate some of the knowledge and wisdom they have gained during their many years in the software development industry. This book was possible because they provided valuable feedback.

I usually start writing notes about ideas for a book when I spend time at software development conferences and events. I wrote the initial idea for the first edition of this book in San Francisco, California, at Intel Developer Forum 2015. One year later, at Intel Developer Forum 2016, I had the opportunity to discuss the book I was completing with a number of software engineers and incorporate their suggestions in the final drafts of the first edition. I started writing notes for the second edition in San Jose, California, at Sensors Expo 2018.

The entire process of writing a book requires a huge number of lonely hours. I wouldn't be able to write an entire book without dedicating some time to play soccer against my sons, Kevin and Brandon, and my nephew, Nicolas. Of course, I never won a match. However, I did score a few goals.

About the reviewers

Norbert Máté is a web developer who started his career back in 2008. His first programming language as a professional web developer was PHP, before moving on to JavaScript/Node.js and Python/Django/Django Rest Framework. He is passionate about software architecture, design patterns, and clean code. Norbert has reviewed other Django books, including *Django RESTful Web Services*.

Sanjeev Jaiswal is a Computer Graduate from CUSAT with 9 years of industrial experience. He uses Perl, Python, AWS, and GNU/Linux for his day-to-day activities. He is currently working on projects involving penetration testing, source code review, and security design and implementations in AWS and cloud security projects. He is currently learning about DevSecOps and security automation as well. Sanjeev loves teaching engineering students and IT professionals. He has been teaching in his leisure time for the last 8 years. He has written *Instant PageSpeed Optimization* and co-authored *Learning Django Web Development* for Packt Publishing.

Packt is searching for authors like you

If you're interested in becoming an author for Packt, please visit `authors.packtpub.com` and apply today. We have worked with thousands of developers and tech professionals, just like you, to help them share their insight with the global tech community. You can make a general application, apply for a specific hot topic that we are recruiting an author for, or submit your own idea.

Table of Contents

Preface

REST (short for **REpresentational State Transfer**) is the architectural style that is driving modern web development and mobile app development. In fact, developing and interacting with RESTful web services is a required skill in any modern software development job. Sometimes, you have to interact with an existing API and in other cases, you have to design a RESTful API from scratch and make it work with JSON (short for JavaScript Object Notation).

Python is one of the most popular programming languages. Python 3.6 and 3.7 are the most modern versions of Python. Python is open source and multiplatform, and you can use it to develop any kind of application, from websites to extremely complex scientific computing applications. There is always a Python package that makes things easier for you to avoid reinventing the wheel and solve the problems faster. The most important and popular cloud computing providers make it easy to work with Python and its related web frameworks. Thus, Python is an ideal choice for developing RESTful web services. This book covers all the things you need to know to select the most appropriate Python web framework and develop a RESTful API from scratch.

You will work with the latest versions of the four most popular Python web frameworks that make it easy to develop RESTful web services: Flask, Django, Pyramid, and Tornado. Each web framework has its advantages and disadvantages. You will work with examples that represent appropriate cases for each of these web frameworks, in combination with additional Python packages that will simplify the most common tasks. You will learn how to use different tools to test and develop high-quality, consistent, and scalable RESTful web services.

You will write unit tests and improve test coverage for the RESTful web services that you will develop throughout the book. You won't just run the sample code; you will also make sure that you write tests for your RESTful API. You will always write modern Python code and you will take advantage of features introduced in the latest Python versions.

This book will allow you to learn how to take advantage of many packages that will simplify the most common tasks related to RESTful web services. You will be able to start creating your own RESTful APIs for any domain in any of the covered web frameworks in Python 3.6, 3.7, or greater.

Who this book is for

This book is for web developers who have a working knowledge of Python and would like to build amazing web services by taking advantage of the various frameworks of Python. You should have some knowledge of RESTful APIs.

What this book covers

Chapter 1, *Developing RESTful APIs and Microservices with Flask 1.0.2*, begins working with Flask and its Flask-RESTful extension. We will create a RESTful Web API that performs **CRUD** (short for **Create, Read, Update, and Delete**) operations on a simple list.

Chapter 2, *Working with Models, SQLAlchemy, and Hyperlinked APIs in Flask*, expands the capabilities of the RESTful API that we started in the previous chapter. We will use SQLAlchemy as our ORM to work with a PostgreSQL database and we will take advantage of advanced features included in Flask and Flask-RESTful that will allow us to easily organize code for complex APIs, such as models and blueprints.

Chapter 3, *Improving Our API and Adding Authentication to it with Flask*, improves the RESTful API in many ways. We will add user-friendly error messages when resources aren't unique. We will test how to update single or multiple fields with the PATCH method and we will create our own generic pagination class. Then, we will start working with authentication and permissions. We will add a user model and update the database. We will make many changes in the different pieces of code to achieve a specific security goal, and we will take advantage of Flask-HTTPAuth and passlib to use HTTP authentication in our API.

Chapter 4, *Testing and Deploying an API in a Microservice with Flask*, explains how to set up a testing environment. We will install pytest and the necessary plugins to make it easy to discover and execute unit tests, and we will create a new database to be used for testing. We will write a first round of unit tests, measure test coverage, and then write additional unit tests to improve test coverage. Finally, we will learn many considerations for deployment, scalability, and the execution of a Flask RESTful API within a microservice on the cloud.

Chapter 5, *Developing RESTful APIs with Django 2.1*, shows how to start working with Django and Django REST Framework, and we will create a RESTful Web API that performs CRUD operations on a simple SQLite database.

Chapter 6, *Working with Class-Based Views and Hyperlinked APIs in Django 2.1*, expands the capabilities of the RESTful API that we started in the previous chapter. We will change the ORM settings to work with a more powerful PostgreSQL 10.5 database and we will take advantage of advanced features included in Django REST Framework that allow us to reduce boilerplate code for complex APIs, such as class-based views.

Chapter 7, *Improving Our API and Adding Authentication to it with Django,* improves the RESTful API that we started in the previous chapter. We will add unique constraints to the model and update the database. We will make it easy to update single fields with the PATCH method and we will take advantage of pagination. We will start working with authentication, permissions, and throttling.

Chapter 8, *Throttling, Filtering, Testing, and Deploying an API with Django 2.1,* takes advantage of many features included in Django REST Framework to define throttling policies. We will use filtering, searching, and ordering classes to make it easy to configure filters, search queries, and the desired order for the results in HTTP requests. We will use the Browsable API feature to test these new features included in our API. We will write a first round of unit tests, run them with pytest, and then write additional unit tests to improve test coverage. Finally, we will learn many considerations for running Django RESTful APIs on the cloud.

Chapter 9, *Developing RESTful APIs with Pyramid 1.10,* works with Pyramid combined with other useful packages to create a RESTful Web API. We will design a RESTful API to interact with a simple data source. We will define the requirements for our API and we will understand the tasks performed by each HTTP method. We will create the class that represents a surfboard metric and we will use marshmallow to validate, serialize, and deserialize the model. We will write functions to process the different HTTP request methods and we will configure the view handlers.

Chapter 10, *Developing RESTful APIs with Tornado 5.1.1,* works with Tornado to create a RESTful Web API. We will design a RESTful API to interact with slow sensors and actuators. We will define the requirements for our API and we will understand the tasks performed by each HTTP method. We will create the classes that represent a drone and write code to simulate slow I/O operations that are called for each HTTP request method. We will write classes that represent request handlers and process the different HTTP requests and configure the URL patterns to route URLs to request handlers and their methods.

Chapter 11, *Working with Asynchronous Code, Testing, and Deploying an API with Tornado*, explains the difference between synchronous and asynchronous execution. We will create a new version of the RESTful API that takes advantage of the non-blocking features in Tornado combined with asynchronous execution. We will improve scalability for our existing API and we will make it possible to start executing other requests while waiting for the slow I/O operations with sensors and actuators. Then, we will set up a testing environment. We will install pytest to make it easy to discover and execute unit tests. We will write a first round of unit tests, measure test coverage, and then write additional unit tests to improve test coverage.

To get the most out of this book

In order to work with the different samples for Python 3.6 and Python 3.7, you will need a computer with an Intel Core i3 or higher CPU and at least 4GB of RAM. You can work with any of the following operating systems:

- Windows 7 or greater (Windows 8, Windows 8.1, or Windows 10)
- Windows Server 2012 or greater (Windows Server 2016 or Windows Server 2019)
- macOS Mountain Lion or greater
- Any Linux version capable of running Python 3.7.1 and any modern browser with JavaScript support

You will need Python 3.7.1 or greater installed on your computer.

Download the example code files

You can download the example code files for this book from your account at www.packt.com. If you purchased this book elsewhere, you can visit www.packt.com/support and register to have the files emailed directly to you.

You can download the code files by following these steps:

1. Log in or register at www.packt.com.
2. Select the **SUPPORT** tab.
3. Click on **Code Downloads & Errata**.
4. Enter the name of the book in the **Search** box and follow the onscreen instructions.

Once the file is downloaded, please make sure that you unzip or extract the folder using the latest version of:

- WinRAR/7-Zip for Windows
- Zipeg/iZip/UnRarX for Mac
- 7-Zip/PeaZip for Linux

The code bundle for the book is also hosted on GitHub at `https://github.com/PacktPublishing/Hands-On-RESTful-Python-Web-Services-Second-Edition`. In case there's an update to the code, it will be updated on the existing GitHub repository.

We also have other code bundles from our rich catalog of books and videos available at `https://github.com/PacktPublishing/`. Check them out!

Download the color images

We also provide a PDF file that has color images of the screenshots/diagrams used in this book. You can download it here: `https://www.packtpub.com/sites/default/files/downloads/9781789532227_ColorImages.pdf`.

Conventions used

In this book, you will find a number of text styles that distinguish between different kinds of information. Here are some examples of these styles and an explanation of their meaning.

There are a number of text conventions used throughout this book.

`CodeInText`: Indicates code words in text, database table names, folder names, filenames, file extensions, pathnames, dummy URLs, user input, and Twitter handles. Here is an example: "We can include other contexts through the use of the `include` directive."

A block of code is set as follows:

```
html, body, #map {
 height: 100%;
 margin: 0;
 padding: 0
}
```

When we wish to draw your attention to a particular part of a code block, the relevant lines or items are set in bold:

```
[default]
exten => s,1,Dial(Zap/1|30)
exten => s,2,Voicemail(u100)
exten => s,102,Voicemail(b100)
exten => i,1,Voicemail(s0)
```

Any command-line input or output is written as follows:

```
# cp /usr/src/asterisk-addons/configs/cdr_mysql.conf.sample
        /etc/asterisk/cdr_mysql.conf
```

Bold: Indicates a new term, an important word, or words that you see onscreen. For example, words in menus or dialog boxes appear in the text like this. Here is an example: "Clicking the **Next** button moves you to the next screen."

Warnings or important notes appear like this.

Tips and tricks appear like this.

Reader feedback

Feedback from our readers is always welcome. Let us know what you think about this book-what you liked or disliked. Reader feedback is important for us as it helps us develop titles that you will really get the most out of.

To send us general feedback, simply e-mail feedback@packtpub.com, and mention the book's title in the subject of your message.

If there is a topic that you have expertise in and you are interested in either writing or contributing to a book, see our author guide at www.packtpub.com/authors.

Customer support

Now that you are the proud owner of a Packt book, we have a number of things to help you to get the most from your purchase.

Get in touch

Feedback from our readers is always welcome.

General feedback: If you have questions about any aspect of this book, mention the book title in the subject of your message and email us at customercare@packtpub.com.

Errata: Although we have taken every care to ensure the accuracy of our content, mistakes do happen. If you have found a mistake in this book, we would be grateful if you would report this to us. Please visit www.packt.com/submit-errata, selecting your book, clicking on the Errata Submission Form link, and entering the details.

Piracy: If you come across any illegal copies of our works in any form on the Internet, we would be grateful if you would provide us with the location address or website name. Please contact us at copyright@packt.com with a link to the material.

If you are interested in becoming an author: If there is a topic that you have expertise in and you are interested in either writing or contributing to a book, please visit authors.packtpub.com.

Errata

Although we have taken every care to ensure the accuracy of our content, mistakes do happen. If you find a mistake in one of our books-maybe a mistake in the text or the code-we would be grateful if you could report this to us. By doing so, you can save other readers from frustration and help us improve subsequent versions of this book. If you find any errata, please report them by visiting http://www.packtpub.com/submit-errata, selecting your book, clicking on the **Errata Submission Form** link, and entering the details of your errata. Once your errata are verified, your submission will be accepted and the errata will be uploaded to our website or added to any list of existing errata under the Errata section of that title.

To view the previously submitted errata, go to https://www.packtpub.com/books/content/support and enter the name of the book in the search field. The required information will appear under the **Errata** section.

Reviews

Please leave a review. Once you have read and used this book, why not leave a review on the site that you purchased it from? Potential readers can then see and use your unbiased opinion to make purchase decisions, we at Packt can understand what you think about our products, and our authors can see your feedback on their book. Thank you!

For more information about Packt, please visit `packt.com`.

Piracy

Piracy of copyrighted material on the Internet is an ongoing problem across all media. At Packt, we take the protection of our copyright and licenses very seriously. If you come across any illegal copies of our works in any form on the Internet, please provide us with the location address or website name immediately so that we can pursue a remedy.

Please contact us at `copyright@packt.com` with a link to the suspected pirated material.

We appreciate your help in protecting our authors and our ability to bring you valuable content.

Questions

If you have a problem with any aspect of this book, you can contact us at `questions@packtpub.com`, and we will do our best to address the problem.

1
Developing RESTful APIs and Microservices with Flask 1.0.2

In this chapter, we will start our journey toward RESTful Web APIs with Python 3.7 and four different web frameworks. Python is one of the most popular and versatile programming languages. There are thousands of Python packages, and these allow you to extend Python capabilities to any kind of domain you can imagine, such as web development, **Internet of Things** (**IoT**), artificial intelligence, machine learning, and scientific computing. We can work with many different web frameworks and packages to easily build simple and complex RESTful Web APIs with Python, and we can combine these frameworks with other Python packages.

We can leverage our existing knowledge of Python and all of its packages to code the different pieces of our RESTful Web APIs and their ecosystem. We can use the object-oriented features to create code that is easier to maintain, understand, and reuse. We can use all the packages that we are already comfortable with to interact with databases, web services, and different APIs. Python makes it easy for us to create RESTful Web APIs. In addition, lightweight frameworks, such as Flask, are ideal candidates for creating microservices that provide RESTful APIs. We don't need to learn another programming language; we can use the one we already know and love.

In this chapter, we will start working with Flask 1.0.2 and its Flask-RESTful extension, and we will create a RESTful Web API that performs **CRUD** (short for **Create, Read, Update, and Delete**) operations on a simple list. We will establish the baseline to develop microservices that provide a RESTful API with Flask. We will look at the following topics:

- Design a RESTful API that performs CRUD operations in Flask with the Flask-RESTful extension
- Understand the tasks performed by each HTTP method
- Understand microservices
- Work with lightweight virtual environments
- Set up the virtual environment with Flask and its Flask-RESTful extension

- Declare status codes for the responses with an enumerable
- Create the model
- Use a dictionary as a repository
- Configure output fields
- Work with resourceful routing on top of Flask pluggable views
- Configure resource routing and endpoints
- Make HTTP requests to the Flask API
- Work with command-line tools to interact with the Flask API
- Work with GUI tools to interact with the Flask API
- Consume the API with other programming languages

Designing a RESTful API to interact with a simple data source

Imagine that we have to configure the notification messages to be displayed in an **OLED** (short for **Organic Light Emitting Diode**) display wired to an IoT device. The IoT device is capable of running Python 3.7.1, Flask 1.0.2, and other Python packages. There is a team writing code that retrieves string messages that represent notifications from a dictionary and displays them in the OLED display wired to the IoT device. We have to start working on a mobile app and a website that has to interact with a RESTful API to perform CRUD operations with string messages that represent notifications.

We don't need an **ORM** (short for **Object-Relational Mapping**) because we won't persist the notifications on a database. We will just work with an in-memory dictionary as our data source. It is one of the requirements we have for this RESTful API. In this case, the RESTful Web Service will be running on the IoT device; that is, we will run the Flask development service on the IoT device.

 We will definitely lose scalability for our RESTful API because we have the in-memory data source in the service, and therefore we cannot run the RESTful API in another IoT device. However, we will work with another example that is related to a more complex data source that will be able to scale in the RESTful way later. The first example is going to allow us to understand how Flask and Flask-RESTful work together with a very simple in-memory data source.

We have chosen Flask because it is an extremely lightweight framework, we don't need to configure an ORM, and we want to start running the RESTful API on the IoT device as soon as possible to allow all the teams to interact with it. We consider that there will be a website that will be coded with Flask too, and therefore, we want to use the same web micro-framework to power the website and the RESTful Web Service. In addition, Flask is an appropriate choice to create a microservice that can run our RESTful API on the cloud.

There are many extensions available for Flask that make it easier to perform specific tasks with the Flask micro-framework. We will take advantage of Flask-RESTful, an extension that will allow us to encourage best practices while building our RESTful API. In this case, we will work with a Python dictionary as the data source. As previously explained, we will work with more complex data sources in forthcoming examples.

First, we must specify the requirements for our main resource—a notification. We need the following attributes or fields for a notification:

- An integer identifier.
- A string message.
- A **TTL** (short for **Time to Live**), that is, a duration in seconds that will indicate the time the notification message has to be displayed on the OLED display.
- A creation date and time. The timestamp will be added automatically when adding a new notification to the collection.
- A notification category description, such as *Warning* or *Information*.
- An integer counter that indicates the times when the notification message has been displayed on the OLED display.
- A Boolean value that indicates whether the notification message was displayed at least once on the OLED display.

The following table shows the HTTP verbs, the scope, and the semantics for the methods that our first version of the API must support. Each method is composed of an HTTP verb and a scope, and all the methods have a well-defined meaning for all notifications and collections. In our API, each notification has its own unique URL:

HTTP verb	Scope	Semantics
GET	Collection of notifications	Retrieve all the stored notifications in the collection.
GET	Notification	Retrieve a single notification.
POST	Collection of notifications	Create a new notification in the collection.
PATCH	Notification	Update one or more fields for an existing notification.
DELETE	Notification	Delete an existing notification.

Understanding the tasks performed by each HTTP method

Let's consider that `http://localhost:5000/service/notifications/` is the URL for the collection of notifications. If we add a number to the previous URL, we identify a specific notification whose ID is equal to the specified numeric value. For example, `http://localhost:5000/service/notifications/5` identifies the notification whose ID is equal to 5.

 We want our API to differentiate collections from a single resource of the collection in the URLs. When we refer to a collection, we will use a slash (/) as the last character for the URL, as in `http://localhost:5000/service/notifications/`. When we refer to a single resource of the collection, we won't use a slash (/) as the last character for the URL, as in `http://localhost:5000/service/notifications/5`.

We have to compose and send an HTTP request with the following HTTP verb (POST) and request URL (`http://localhost:5000/service/notifications/`) to create a new notification. In addition, we have to provide the JSON key-value pairs with the field names and the values to create the new notification. As a result of the request, the service will validate the values provided for the fields, making sure that it is a valid notification and persists it in the in-memory notifications dictionary. The service will return a 201 Created status code and a JSON body with the recently added notification serialized to JSON, including the assigned ID that was automatically generated by the service to the notification object:

```
POST http://localhost:5000/service/notifications/
```

We have to compose and send an HTTP request with the following HTTP verb (GET) and request URL (`http://localhost:5000/service/notifications/{id}`) to retrieve the notification whose ID matches the specified numeric value in the place where {id} is written. For example, if we use the `http://localhost:5000/service/notifications/23` request URL, the service will retrieve the notification whose ID matches 23 from the dictionary. If a notification is found, the service will serialize the notification object into JSON and return a 200 OK status code and a JSON body with the serialized notification object. If no notification matches the specified ID or primary key, the service will return just a 404 Not Found status:

```
GET http://localhost:5000/service/notifications/{id}
```

We have to compose and send an HTTP request with the following HTTP verb (`PATCH`) and request URL (`http://localhost:5000/service/notifications/{id}`) to update one or more fields for the notification whose ID matches the specified numeric value in the place where `{id}` is written. In addition, we have to provide the JSON key-value pairs with the field names to be updated and their new values. As a result of the request, the service will validate the values provided for the fields, update these fields on the notification that matches the specified ID, and update the notification in the dictionary if it is a valid notification. The service will return a `200 OK` status code and a JSON body with the recently updated notification serialized to JSON. If we provide invalid data for the fields to be updated, the service will return a `400 Bad Request` status code. If the service doesn't find a notification with the specified ID, the service will return just a `404 Not Found` status:

```
PATCH http://localhost:5000/service/notifications/{id}
```

The `PATCH` method will allow us to easily update two fields for a notification—the integer counter, which indicates the times the notification message has been printed, and the Boolean value, which specifies whether the notification message was printed at least once.

We have to compose and send an HTTP request with the following HTTP verb (`DELETE`) and request URL (`http://localhost:5000/service/notifications/{id}`) to remove the notification whose ID matches the specified numeric value in the place where `{id}` is written. For example, if we use the `http://localhost:5000/service/notifications/27` request URL, the service will delete the notification whose ID matches `27`. As a result of the request, the service will retrieve a notification with the specified ID from the dictionary. If a notification is found, the service will ask the dictionary to delete the entry associated with this notification object and the service will return a `204 No Content` status code. If no notification matches the specified ID, the service will return just a `404 Not Found` status.

```
DELETE http://localhost:5000/service/notifications/{id}
```

Understanding microservices

In the last few years, many large and complex applications started shifting from a monolithic architecture to a microservices architecture. Instead of working with large and extremely complex web services, the microservices architecture proposes developing a collection of smaller, loosely-coupled services to implement all the features required by complex applications in a way that enables and simplifies continuous delivery.

RESTful APIs are essential pieces of the microservices architecture, and Python is extremely popular when shifting to this architecture. Each microservice can encapsulate a RESTful API that fulfills a specific and limited purpose. The microservice is self-contained, it is easy to maintain, and it helps to support continuous delivery.

As happens with any architecture, there are several ways to implement the microservices architecture. We will learn to encapsulate a RESTful API developed with Flask and Python into a microservice. This way, we will be able to leverage our skills by developing RESTful APIs and using them as the essential pieces to build self-contained and easy-to-maintain microservices.

Working with lightweight virtual environments

Throughout this book, we will be working with different frameworks, packages, and libraries to create RESTful Web APIs and microservices, and therefore, it is convenient to work with Python virtual environments to isolate each development environment. Python 3.3 introduced lightweight virtual environments and they were improved in subsequent Python versions. We will work with these virtual environments and, therefore, you will need Python 3.7.1 or higher. You can read more about the PEP 405 Python virtual environment, which introduced the `venv` module, at
`https://www.python.org/dev/peps/pep-0405`. All the examples for this book were tested on Python 3.7.1 on Linux, macOS, and Windows.

> In case you decide to use the popular `virtualenv`
> (`https://pypi.python.org/pypi/virtualenv`) third-party virtual
> environment builder or the virtual environment options provided by your
> Python IDE, you just have to make sure that you activate your virtual
> environment with the appropriate mechanism whenever it is necessary to
> do so, instead of following the step explained to activate the virtual
> environment generated with the `venv` module integrated in Python.
> However, make sure you work with a virtual environment.

Each virtual environment we create with `venv` is an isolated environment and it will have its own independent set of installed Python packages in its site directories (folders). When we create a virtual environment with `venv` in Python 3.7 or higher, `pip` is included in the new virtual environment. Notice that the instructions provided are compatible with Python 3.7.1 or greater. The following commands assume that you have Python 3.7.1 installed on Linux, macOS, or Windows.

First, we have to select the target folder or directory for our lightweight virtual environment. The following is the path we will use in the example for Linux and macOS:

```
~/HillarPythonREST2/Flask01
```

The target folder for the virtual environment will be the `HillarPythonREST2/Flask01` folder within our home directory. For example, if our home directory in macOS or Linux is `/Users/gaston`, the virtual environment will be created within `/Users/gaston/HillarPythonREST2/Flask01`. You can replace the specified path with your desired path in each command.

The following is the path we will use in the example for Windows:

```
%USERPROFILE%\HillarPythonREST2\Flask01
```

The target folder for the virtual environment will be the `HillarPythonREST2\Flask01` folder within our user profile folder. For example, if our user profile folder is `C:\Users\gaston`, the virtual environment will be created within `C:\Users\gaston\HillarPythonREST2\Flask01`. Of course, you can replace the specified path with your desired path in each command.

In Windows PowerShell, the previous path would be:

```
$env:userprofile\HillarPythonREST2\Flask01
```

Now, we have to use the -m option, followed by the `venv` module name and the desired path, to make Python run this module as a script and create a virtual environment in the specified path. The instructions vary depending on the platform in which we are creating the virtual environment. Thus, make sure you follow the instructions for your operating system.

Open a Terminal in Linux or macOS and execute the following command to create a virtual environment:

```
python3 -m venv ~/HillarPythonREST2/Flask01
```

In Windows, in the Command Prompt, execute the following command to create a virtual environment:

```
python -m venv %USERPROFILE%\HillarPythonREST2\Flask01
```

In case you want to work with Windows PowerShell, execute the following command to create a virtual environment:

```
python -m venv $env:userprofile\HillarPythonREST2\Flask01
```

The previous commands don't produce any output. Any of the previous scripts created the specified target folder and installed `pip` by invoking `ensurepip` because we didn't specify the `--without-pip` option.

Now, we will analyze the directory structure for a virtual environment. The specified target folder has a new directory tree that contains Python executable files and other files that indicate it is a PEP 405 virtual environment.

In the root directory for the virtual environment, the `pyenv.cfg` configuration file specifies different options for the virtual environment and its existence is an indicator that we are in the root folder for a virtual environment. In Linux and macOS, the folder will have the following main subfolders:

- `bin`
- `include`
- `lib`
- `lib/python3.7`
- `lib/python3.7/site-packages`

The following diagram shows the folders and files in the directory trees generated for the `Flask01` virtual environment in macOS:

In Windows, the folder will have the following main subfolders:

- `Include`
- `Lib`
- `Lib\site-packages`
- `Scripts`

The directory trees for the virtual environment in each platform are the same as the layout of the Python installation in these platforms.

The following diagram shows the main folders in the directory trees generated for the virtual environment in Windows:

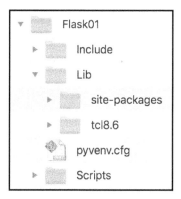

After we activate the virtual environment, we will install third-party packages in the virtual environment and the modules will be located within the `lib/python3.7/site-packages` or `Lib\site-packages` folder, depending on the platform. The executables will be copied in the `bin` or `Scripts` folder, based on the platform. The packages we install won't make changes to other virtual environments or our base Python environment.

Now that we have created a virtual environment, we will run a platform-specific script to activate it. After we activate the virtual environment, we will install packages that will only be available in this virtual environment. This way, we will work with an isolated environment in which all the packages we install won't affect our main Python environment.

Run the following command in the Terminal in Linux or macOS. Notice that the results of this command will be accurate if you don't start a shell different to than the default shell in the Terminal session. In case you have doubts, check your Terminal configuration and preferences:

```
echo $SHELL
```

The command will display the name of the shell you are using in the Terminal. In macOS, the default is /bin/bash, and this means you are working with the bash shell. Depending on the shell, you must run a different command to activate the virtual environment in Linux or macOS.

If your Terminal is configured to use the bash shell in Linux or macOS, run the following command to activate the virtual environment. The command also works for the zsh shell:

```
source ~/HillarPythonREST2/Flask01/bin/activate
```

If your Terminal is configured to use either the csh or tcsh shell, run the following command to activate the virtual environment:

```
source ~/HillarPythonREST2/Flask01/bin/activate.csh
```

If your Terminal is configured to use the fish shell, run the following command to activate the virtual environment:

```
source ~/HillarPythonREST2/Flask01/bin/activate.fish
```

After you activate the virtual environment, the Command Prompt will display the virtual environment root folder name, enclosed in parentheses as a prefix of the default prompt, to remind us that we are working in the virtual environment. In this case, we will see (**Flask01**) as a prefix for the Command Prompt because the root folder for the activated virtual environment is Flask01.

The following screenshot shows the virtual environment activated in a macOS High Sierra Terminal with a bash shell, after executing the commands shown previously:

```
⬆ gaston — -bash — 114×35
Gastons-MacBook-Pro:~ gaston$ python3 -m venv ~/HillarPythonREST2/Flask01
Gastons-MacBook-Pro:~ gaston$ echo $SHELL
/bin/bash
Gastons-MacBook-Pro:~ gaston$ source ~/HillarPythonREST2/Flask01/bin/activate
(Flask01) Gastons-MacBook-Pro:~ gaston$ ▌
```

As we can see from the previous screenshot, the prompt changed from `Gastons-MacBook-Pro:~ gaston$` to `(Flask01) Gastons-MacBook-Pro:~ gaston$` following activation of the virtual environment.

In Windows, you can run either a batch file in the Command Prompt or a Windows PowerShell script to activate the virtual environment.

If you prefer the Command Prompt, run the following command in the Windows command line to activate the virtual environment:

`%USERPROFILE%\HillarPythonREST2\Flask01\Scripts\activate.bat`

The following screenshot shows the virtual environment activated in a Windows 10 Command Prompt, after executing the commands shown previously:

```
Command Prompt
Microsoft Windows [Version 10.0.17134.345]
(c) 2018 Microsoft Corporation. All rights reserved.

C:\Users\gaston>python -m venv %USERPROFILE%\HillarPythonREST2\Flask01

C:\Users\gaston>%USERPROFILE%\HillarPythonREST2\Flask01\Scripts\activate.bat
(Flask01) C:\Users\gaston>
```

As we can see from the previous screenshot, the prompt changed from `C:\Users\gaston\AppData\Local\Programs\Python\Python36` to `(Flask01) C:\Users\gaston\AppData\Local\Programs\Python\Python36` following activation of the virtual environment.

If you prefer Windows PowerShell, launch it and run the following commands to activate the virtual environment. Notice that you must have script execution enabled in Windows PowerShell to be able to run the script:

`cd $env:USERPROFILE`
`HillarPythonREST2\Flask01\Scripts\Activate.ps1`

The following screenshot shows the virtual environment activated in the Windows 10 PowerShell, after executing the commands shown previously:

```
Windows PowerShell
Windows PowerShell
Copyright (C) Microsoft Corporation. All rights reserved.

PS C:\Users\gaston> cd $env:USERPROFILE
PS C:\Users\gaston> HillarPythonREST2\Flask01\Scripts\Activate.ps1
(Flask01) PS C:\Users\gaston>
```

It is extremely easy to deactivate a virtual environment generated by means of the process explained previously. Deactivation will remove all the changes made in the environment variables and will change the prompt back to its default message.

Once you deactivate a virtual environment, you will go back to the default Python environment.

In macOS or Linux, just type `deactivate` and press *Enter*.

In the Windows Command Prompt, you have to run the `deactivate.bat` batch file included in the `Scripts` folder. In our example, the full path for this file is `%USERPROFILE%\HillarPythonREST2\Flask01\Scripts\deactivate.bat`.

In Windows PowerShell, you have to run the `Deactivate.ps1` script in the `Scripts` folder.

The instructions in the next sections assume that the virtual environment we have created is activated.

Setting up a virtual environment with Flask and Flask-RESTful

We have followed the necessary steps to create and activate a virtual environment. Now, we will create a `requirements.txt` file to specify the set of packages that our application requires to be installed in any supported platform. This way, it will be extremely easy to repeat the installation of the specified packages with their versions in any new virtual environment.

Use your favorite editor to create a new text file, named `requirements.txt`, within the root folder of the recently created virtual environment. The following lines show the content of the file that declares the packages and the versions that our API requires. The code file for the sample is included in the `restful_python_2_01_01` folder, in the `Flask01/requirements.txt` file:

```
Flask==1.0.2
flask-restful==0.3.6
httpie==1.0.0
```

Each line in the `requirements.txt` file indicates the package and the version that needs to be installed. In this case, we are working with exact versions by using the == operator because we want to make sure that the specified version is installed. The following table summarizes the packages and the version numbers that we specified as requirements:

Package name	Version to be installed
Flask	1.0.2
flask-restful	0.3.6
httpie	1.0.0

Now, we must run the following command on macOS, Linux, or Windows to install the packages and the versions explained in the previous table with `pip` by using the recently created `requirements.txt` file. Notice that Flask is a dependency for Flask-RESTful. Make sure you are located in the folder that has the `requirements.txt` file before running the following command:

```
pip install -r requirements.txt
```

The last lines for the output will indicate all the packages that have been successfully installed, including `Flask`, `flask-restful`, and `httpie`:

```
Installing collected packages: itsdangerous, click, MarkupSafe, Jinja2,
Werkzeug, Flask, aniso8601, six, pytz, flask-restful, chardet, certifi,
idna, urllib3, requests, Pygments, httpie
        Running setup.py install for itsdangerous ... done
        Running setup.py install for MarkupSafe ... done
Successfully installed Flask-1.0.2 Jinja2-2.10 MarkupSafe-1.0
Pygments-2.2.0 Werkzeug-0.14.1 aniso8601-3.0.2 certifi-2018.8.24
chardet-3.0.4 click-7.0 flask-restful-0.3.6 httpie-1.0.0 idna-2.7
itsdangerous-0.24 pytz-2018.5 requests-2.19.1 six-1.11.0 urllib3-1.23
```

Declaring status codes for the responses with an enumerable

Neither Flask nor Flask-RESTful includes the declaration of variables for the different HTTP status codes. We don't want to return numbers as status codes. We want our code to be easy to read and understand, and therefore, we will use descriptive HTTP status codes. Specifically, we will take advantage of the support for enumerations added in Python 3.4 to declare a class that defines unique sets of names and values that represent the different HTTP status codes.

First, create a `service` folder within the root folder for the recently created virtual environment. Create a new `http_status.py` file within the `service` folder. The following lines show the code that declares the `HttpStatus` class that inherits from the `enum.Enum` class. The code file for the sample is included in the `restful_python_2_01_01` folder, in the `Flask01/service/http_status.py` file:

```
from enum import Enum


class HttpStatus(Enum):
    continue_100 = 100
    switching_protocols_101 = 101
    ok_200 = 200
    created_201 = 201
    accepted_202 = 202
    non_authoritative_information_203 = 203
    no_content_204 = 204
    reset_content_205 = 205
    partial_content_206 = 206
    multiple_choices_300 = 300
    moved_permanently_301 = 301
    found_302 = 302
    see_other_303 = 303
    not_modified_304 = 304
    use_proxy_305 = 305
    reserved_306 = 306
    temporary_redirect_307 = 307
    bad_request_400 = 400
    unauthorized_401 = 401
    payment_required_402 = 402
    forbidden_403 = 403
    not_found_404 = 404
    method_not_allowed_405 = 405
    not_acceptable_406 = 406
    proxy_authentication_required_407 = 407
    request_timetout_408 = 408
    conflict_409 = 409
    gone_410 = 410
    length_required_411 = 411
    precondition_failed_412 = 412
    request_entity_too_large_413 = 413
    request_uri_too_long_414 = 414
    unsupported_media_type_415 = 415
    requested_range_not_satisfiable_416 = 416
    expectation_failed_417 = 417
    precondition_required_428 = 428
    too_many_requests_429 = 429
```

```
request_header_fields_too_large_431 = 431
unavailable_for_legal_reasons_451 = 451
internal_server_error_500 = 500
not_implemented_501 = 501
bad_gateway_502 = 502
service_unavailable_503 = 503
gateway_timeout_504 = 504
http_version_not_supported_505 = 505
network_authentication_required_511 = 511

@staticmethod
def is_informational(cls, status_code):
    return 100 <= status_code.value <= 199

@staticmethod
def is_success(status_code):
    return 200 <= status_code.value <= 299

@staticmethod
def is_redirect(status_code):
    return 300 <= status_code.value <= 399

@staticmethod
def is_client_error(status_code):
    return 400 <= status_code.value <= 499

@staticmethod
def is_server_error(status_code):
    return 500 <= status_code.value <= 599
```

The `HttpStatus` class defines unique sets of names and values that represent the different HTTP status codes. The names use the description as a prefix and the HTTP status code number as a suffix. For example, the 200 value of the HTTP 200 OK status code is defined in the `HttpStatus.ok_200` name, and the HTTP 404 Not Found status code is defined in the `HttpStatus.not_found_404` name.

> We will use the names defined in the enumerable to return a specific status code whenever necessary in our code. For example, in case we have to return an HTTP 404 Not Found status code, we will return `HttpStatus.not_found_404.value`, instead of just 404. This way, it will be easier to understand the code because we won't have to remember the meaning of each number.

In addition, the `HttpStatus` class declares five static methods that receive any of the HTTP status codes defined in the enumerable as an argument and determines which of the following categories the status code belongs to: informational, success, redirect, client error, or server error.

Creating the model

Now, we will create a simple `NotificationModel` class that we will use to represent notifications. Remember that we won't be persisting the model in any database or file, and therefore, in this case, our class will just provide the required attributes and no mapping information. Create a new `models.py` file in the `service` folder. The following lines show the code that creates a `NotificationModel` class in the `service/models.py` file. The code file for the sample is included in the `restful_python_2_01_01` folder, in the `Flask01/service/models.py` file:

```
class NotificationModel:
    def __init__(self, message, ttl, creation_date, notification_category):
        # We will automatically generate the new id
        self.id = 0
        self.message = message
        self.ttl = ttl
        self.creation_date = creation_date
        self.notification_category = notification_category
        self.displayed_times = 0
        self.displayed_once = False
```

The `NotificationModel` class just declares a constructor, that is, the `__init__` method. This method receives many arguments and uses them to initialize the attributes with the same names: `message`, `ttl`, `creation_date`, and `notification_category`. The `id` attribute is set to 0, `displayed_times` is set to 0, and `displayed_once` is set to `False`. We will automatically increment the identifier for each new notification generated with API calls.

Using a dictionary as a repository

Now, we will create a `NotificationManager` class that we will use to persist the `NotificationModel` instances in an in-memory dictionary. Our API methods will call methods for the `NotificationManager` class to retrieve, insert, update, and delete `NotificationModel` instances. Create a new `service.py` file in the `service` folder. The following lines show the code that creates a `NotificationManager` class in the `service/service.py` file. In addition, the following lines declare all the `imports` we will need for all the code we will write in this file. The code file for the sample is included in the `restful_python_2_01_01` folder, in the `Flask01/service/service.py` file:

```python
from flask import Flask
from flask_restful import abort, Api, fields, marshal_with, reqparse, Resource
from datetime import datetime
from models import NotificationModel
from http_status import HttpStatus
from pytz import utc


class NotificationManager():
    last_id = 0
    def __init__(self):
        self.notifications = {}

    def insert_notification(self, notification):
        self.__class__.last_id += 1
        notification.id = self.__class__.last_id
        self.notifications[self.__class__.last_id] = notification

    def get_notification(self, id):
        return self.notifications[id]

    def delete_notification(self, id):
        del self.notifications[id]
```

The `NotificationManager` class declares a `last_id` class attribute and initializes it to `0`. This class attribute stores the last ID that was generated and assigned to a `NotificationModel` instance stored in a dictionary. The constructor, that is, the `__init__` method, creates and initializes the `notifications` attribute as an empty dictionary.

The code declares the following three methods for the class:

- `insert_notification`: This method receives a recently created `NotificationModel` instance in the `notification` argument. The code increases the value for the `last_id` class attribute and then assigns the resulting value to the ID for the received notification. The code uses `self.__class__` to reference the type of the current instance. Finally, the code adds `notification` as a value to the key identified with the generated ID, `last_id`, in the `self.notifications` dictionary.

- `get_notification`: This method receives the `id` of the notification that has to be retrieved from the `self.notifications` dictionary. The code returns the value related to the key that matches the received `id` in the `self.notifications` dictionary that we are using as our data source.

- `delete_notification`: This method receives the `id` of the notification that has to be removed from the `self.notifications` dictionary. The code deletes the key-value pair whose key matches the ID received in the `self.notifications` dictionary that we are using as our data source.

We don't need a method to update a notification because we will just make changes to the attributes of the `NotificationModel` instance that is already stored in the `self.notifications` dictionary. The value stored in the dictionary is a reference to the `NotificationModel` instance that we are updating and, therefore, we don't need to call a specific method to update the instance in the dictionary. However, in case we were working with a database, we would need to call an update method for our ORM, data repository, or database service.

Configuring output fields

Now, we will create a `notification_fields` dictionary that we will use to control the data that we want Flask-RESTful to render in our responses when we return `NotificationModel` instances. Open the `service/service.py` file created previously and add the following lines to the existing code. The code file for the sample is included in the `restful_python_2_01_01` folder, in the `Flask01/service/service.py` file:

```
notification_fields = {
    'id': fields.Integer,
    'uri': fields.Url('notification_endpoint'),
    'message': fields.String,
    'ttl': fields.Integer,
    'creation_date': fields.DateTime,
```

```
        'notification_category': fields.String,
        'displayed_times': fields.Integer,
        'displayed_once': fields.Boolean
    }


    notification_manager = NotificationManager()
```

We declared the `notification_fields` dictionary (`dict`) with key-value pairs of strings and classes declared in the `flask_restful.fields` module. The keys are the names of the attributes we want to render from the `NotificationModel` class, and the values are the classes that format and return the value for the field. In the previous code, we worked with the following classes that format and return the value for the specified field in the key:

- `fields.Integer`: Outputs an integer value.
- `fields.Url`: Generates a string representation of a URL. By default, this class generates a relative URI for the resource that is being requested. The code specifies `'notification_endpoint'` for the `endpoint` argument. This way, the class will use the specified endpoint name. We will declare this endpoint later in the `service.py` file. We don't want to include the hostname in the generated URI and, therefore, we use the default value for the `absolute` Boolean attribute, which is `False`.
- `fields.DateTime`: Outputs a formatted date and time string in UTC, in the default RFC 822 format.
- `fields.Boolean`: Generates a string representation of a Boolean value.

The `'uri'` field uses `fields.Url` and is related to the specified endpoint instead of being associated with an attribute of the `NotificationModel` class. It is the only case in which the specified field name doesn't have an attribute in the `NotificationModel` class. The other strings specified as keys indicate all the attributes we want to be rendered in the output when we use the `notification_fields` dictionary to make up the final serialized response output.

After we declare the `notification_fields` dictionary, the next line of code creates an instance of the `NotificationManager` class created previously, named `notification_manager`. We will use this instance to create, retrieve, and delete `NotificationModel` instances.

Working with resourceful routing on top of Flask pluggable views

Flask-RESTful uses resources built on top of Flask pluggable views as the main building block for a RESTful API. We just need to create a subclass of the flask_restful.Resource class and declare the methods for each supported HTTP verb.

 A subclass of flask_restful.Resource represents a RESTful resource and, therefore, we will have to declare one class to represent the collection of notifications and another one to represent the notification resource.

First, we will create a Notification class that we will use to represent the notification resource. Open the service/service.py file created previously and add the following lines. The code file for the sample is included in the restful_python_2_01_01 folder, in the Flask01/service/service.py file:

```
class Notification(Resource):
    def abort_if_notification_not_found(self, id):
        if id not in notification_manager.notifications:
            abort(
                HttpStatus.not_found_404.value,
                message="Notification {0} doesn't exist".format(id))

    @marshal_with(notification_fields)
    def get(self, id):
        self.abort_if_notification_not_found(id)
        return notification_manager.get_notification(id)

    def delete(self, id):
        self.abort_if_notification_not_found(id)
        notification_manager.delete_notification(id)
        return '', HttpStatus.no_content_204.value

    @marshal_with(notification_fields)
    def patch(self, id):
        self.abort_if_notification_not_found(id)
        notification = notification_manager.get_notification(id)
        parser = reqparse.RequestParser()
        parser.add_argument('message', type=str)
        parser.add_argument('ttl', type=int)
        parser.add_argument('displayed_times', type=int)
        parser.add_argument('displayed_once', type=bool)
        args = parser.parse_args()
        print(args)
```

```
        if 'message' in args and args['message'] is not None:
            notification.message = args['message']
        if 'ttl' in args and args['ttl'] is not None:
            notification.ttl = args['ttl']
        if 'displayed_times' in args and args['displayed_times']
is not None:
            notification.displayed_times = args['displayed_times']
        if 'displayed_once' in args and args['displayed_once'] is
not None:
            notification.displayed_once = args['displayed_once']
        return notification
```

The `Notification` class is a subclass of the `flask_restful.Resource` superclass and declares the following three methods that will be called when the HTTP method with the same name arrives as a request on the represented resource:

- `get`: This method receives the ID of the notification that has to be retrieved in the `id` argument. The code calls the `self.abort_if_notification_not_found` method to abort in case there is no notification with the requested ID. In case the notification exists, the code returns the `NotificationModel` instance whose `id` matches the specified `id` returned by the `notification_manager.get_notification` method. The `get` method uses the `@marshal_with` decorator, with `notification_fields` as an argument. The decorator will take the `NotificationModel` instance and apply the field filtering and output formatting specified in the `notification_fields` dictionary.

- `delete`: This method receives the ID of the notification that has to be deleted in the `id` argument. The code calls the `self.abort_if_notification_not_found` method to abort in case there is no notification with the requested ID. In case the notification exists, the code calls the `notification_manager.delete_notification` method with the received ID as an argument to remove the `NotificationModel` instance from our data repository. Then, the code returns a tuple composed of an empty response body and a `204 No Content` status code. Notice that the returned status code in the tuple is specified with `HttpStatus.no_content_204.value` because we want to return the value of the enumerable, which is `204`. We used multiple return values in the tuple to set the response code.

- `patch`: This method receives the ID of the notification that has to be updated or patched in the `id` argument. The code calls the `self.abort_if_notification_not_found` method to abort in case there is no notification with the requested ID. In case the notification exists, the code saves the `NotificationModel` instance whose `id` matches the specified `id` returned by the `notification_manager.get_notification` method in the `notification` variable. The next line creates a `flask_restful.reqparse.RequestParser` instance named `parser`. The `RequestParser` instance allows us to add arguments with their names and types and then easily parse the arguments received with the request. The code makes four calls to the `parser.add_argument` method with the argument name and the type of the four arguments we want to parse. Then, the code calls the `parser.parse_args` method to parse all the arguments from the request and saves the returned dictionary (`dict`) in the `args` variable. The code updates all the attributes that have new values in the `args` dictionary in the `NotificationModel` instance, which is `notification`. In case the request didn't include values for certain fields, the code won't make changes to the related attributes because the code doesn't consider the values that are `None`. The request doesn't need to include the four fields that can be updated with values. The code returns the updated `notification`. The `patch` method uses the `@marshal_with` decorator, with `notification_fields` as an argument. The decorator will take the `NotificationModel` instance, `notification`, and apply the field filtering and output formatting specified in the `notification_fields` dictionary.

As previously explained, the three methods call the internal `abort_if_notification_not_found` method, which receives the ID for an existing `NotificationModel` instance in the `id` argument. If the received `id` is not in the keys of the `notification_manager.notifications` dictionary, the method calls the `flask_restful.abort` function with `HttpStatus.not_found_404.value` as the `http_status_code` argument and a message indicating that the notification with the specified ID doesn't exist. The `abort` function raises an `HTTPException` exception for the received `http_status_code` and attaches the additional keyword arguments to the exception for later processing. In this case, we generate an HTTP `404 Not Found` status code.

Both the `get` and `patch` methods use the `@marshal_with` decorator, which takes a single data object or a list of data objects, and applies the field filtering and output formatting specified as an argument. The marshalling can also work with dictionaries (`dict`). In both methods, we specified `notification_fields` as an argument and, therefore, the code renders the following fields: `id`, `uri`, `message`, `ttl`, `creation_date`, `notification_category`, `displayed_times`, and `displayed_once`.

> Whenever we use the `@marshal_with` decorator, we are automatically returning an HTTP `200 OK` status code.

The following `return` statement with the `@marshal_with(notification_fields)` decorator returns an `HTTP 200 OK` status code because we didn't specify any status code after the returned object (`notification`):

```
return notification
```

The next line is the code that is actually executed with the `@marshal_with(notification_fields)` decorator and we can use it instead of working with the decorator:

```
return marshal(notification, resource_fields), HttpStatus.
HttpStatus.ok_200.value
```

For example, we can call the `marshal` function as shown in the previous line, instead of using the `@marshal_with` decorator, and the code will produce the same result.

Now, we will create a `NotificationList` class that we will use to represent the collection of notifications. Open the `service/service.py` file created previously and add the following lines.

The code file for the sample is included in the `restful_python_2_01_01` folder, in the `Flask01/service/service.py` file:

```
class NotificationList(Resource):
    @marshal_with(notification_fields)
    def get(self):
        return [v for v in
notification_manager.notifications.values()]

    @marshal_with(notification_fields)
    def post(self):
        parser = reqparse.RequestParser()
        parser.add_argument('message', type=str, required=True,
help='Message cannot be blank!')
        parser.add_argument('ttl', type=int, required=True,
help='Time to live cannot be blank!')
        parser.add_argument('notification_category', type=str,
required=True, help='Notification category cannot be blank!')
        args = parser.parse_args()
        notification = NotificationModel(
            message=args['message'],
            ttl=args['ttl'],
            creation_date=datetime.now(utc),
            notification_category=args['notification_category']
            )
        notification_manager.insert_notification(notification)
        return notification, HttpStatus.created_201.value
```

The `NotificationList` class is a subclass of the `flask_restful.Resource` superclass and declares the following two methods that will be called when the HTTP method with the same name arrives as a request on the resource represented:

- `get`: This method returns a list with all the `NotificationModel` instances saved in the `notification_manager.notifications` dictionary. The `get` method uses the `@marshal_with` decorator, with `notification_fields` as an argument. The decorator will take each `NotificationModel` instance in the returned list and apply the field filtering and output formatting specified in `notification_fields`.

- post: This method creates a `flask_restful.reqparse.RequestParser` instance named `parser`. The `RequestParser` instance allows us to add arguments with their names and types and then easily parse the arguments received with the `POST` request to create a new `NotificationModel` instance. The code makes three calls to `parser.add_argument`, with the argument name and the type of the three arguments we want to parse. Then, the code calls the `parser.parse_args` method to parse all the arguments from the request and saves the returned dictionary (`dict`) in the `args` variable. The code uses the parsed arguments in the dictionary to specify the values for the `message`, `ttl`, and `notification_category` attributes to create a new `NotificationModel` instance and save it in the `notification` variable. The value for the `creation_date` argument is set to the current date and time with time zone information, and therefore, it isn't parsed from the request. Then, the code calls the `notification_manager.insert_notification` method with the new `NotificationModel` instance (`notification`) to add this new instance to the dictionary. The `post` method uses the `@marshal_with` decorator with `notification_fields` as an argument. The decorator will take the recently created and stored `NotificationModel` instance, `notification`, and apply the field filtering and output formatting specified in `notification_fields`. Then, the code returns a tuple composed of the inserted `NotificationModel` instance and a `201 Created` status code. Notice that the returned status code in the tuple is specified with `HttpStatus.created_201.value` because we want to return the value of the enumerable, which is `201`. We used multiple return values in the tuple to set the response code.

The following table shows the method of our classes created previously that we want to be executed for each combination of HTTP verb and scope:

HTTP verb	Scope	Class and method
GET	Collection of notifications	NotificationList.get
GET	Notification	Notification.get
POST	Collection of notifications	NotificationList.post
PATCH	Notification	Notification.patch
DELETE	Notification	Notification.delete

 If the request results in the invocation of a resource with an unsupported HTTP method, Flask-RESTful will return a response with the HTTP `405 Method Not Allowed` status code.

Configuring resource routing and endpoints

We must make the necessary resource routing configurations to call the appropriate methods and pass them all the necessary arguments by defining URL rules. The following lines create the main entry point for the application, initialize it with a Flask application, and configure the resource routing for the service. Open the previously created `service/service.py` file and add the following lines. The code file for the sample is included in the `restful_python_2_01_01` folder, in the `Flask01/service/service.py` file:

```
app = Flask(__name__)
service = Api(app)
service.add_resource(NotificationList, '/service/notifications/')
service.add_resource(Notification, '/service/notifications/<int:id>',
endpoint='notification_endpoint')


if __name__ == '__main__':
    app.run(debug=True)
```

The code creates an instance of the `flask_restful.Api` class and saves it in the `service` variable. Each call to the `service.add_resource` method routes a URL to a resource, specifically to one of the previously declared subclasses of the `flask_restful.Resource` superclass. When there is a request to the service and the URL matches one of the URLs specified in the `service.add_resource` method, Flask will call the method that matches the HTTP verb in the request for the specified class. The method follows standard Flask routing rules.

For example, the following line will make an HTTP GET request to `/service/notifications/` without any additional parameters to call the `NotificationList.get` method:

```
service.add_resource(NotificationList, '/service/notifications/')
```

Flask will pass the URL variables to the called method as arguments. For example, the following line will make an HTTP GET request to `/service/notifications/26` to call the `Notification.get` method, with `26` passed as the value for the `id` argument:

```
service.add_resource(Notification, '/service/notifications/<int:id>',
endpoint='notification_endpoint')
```

In addition, we can specify a string value for the endpoint argument to make it easy to reference the specified route in the `fields.Url` fields. We pass the same endpoint name, `'notification_endpoint'`, as an argument in the `uri` field declared as `fields.Url` in the `notification_fields` dictionary that we use to render each `NotificationModel` instance. This way, `fields.Url` will generate a URI that considers this route.

We just required a few lines of code to configure resource routing and endpoints. The last line just calls the `app.run` method to start the Flask application, with the `debug` argument set to `True` to enable debugging. In this case, we start the application by calling the `run` method to immediately launch a local server. We could also achieve the same goal by using the `flask` command-line script. However, this option would require us to configure environment variables and the instructions are different for the platforms that we are covering in this book: macOS, Windows, and Linux.

As with any other web framework, you should never enable debugging in a production environment.

Making HTTP requests to the Flask API

Now, we can run the `service/service.py` script that launches Flask's development server to compose and send HTTP requests to our unsecured and simple web API (we will definitely add security later). Execute the following command. Make sure you have the virtual environment activated:

```
python service/service.py
```

The following lines show the output after we execute the previous command. The development server is listening at port `5000`:

```
* Serving Flask app "service" (lazy loading)
* Environment: production
  WARNING: Do not use the development server in a production
environment.
  Use a production WSGI server instead.
* Debug mode: on
* Running on http://127.0.0.1:5000/ (Press CTRL+C to quit)
* Restarting with stat
* Debugger is active!
* Debugger PIN: 122-606-712
```

With the previous command, we will start the Flask development server and we will only be able to access it in our development computer. The previous command starts the development server in the default IP address, that is, 127.0.0.1 (localhost). It is not possible to access this IP address from other computers or devices connected to our LAN. Thus, if we want to make HTTP requests to our API from other computers or devices connected to our LAN, we should use the development computer IP address, 0.0.0.0 (for IPv4 configurations) or :: (for IPv6 configurations) as the desired IP address for our development server.

If we specify 0.0.0.0 as the desired IP address for IPv4 configurations, the development server will listen on every interface on port 5000. In addition, it is necessary to open the default port 5000 in our firewalls (software and/or hardware) and configure port forwarding to the computer that is running the development server. The same configuration applies whenever we want to run the application on any cloud provider.

We just need to specify '0.0.0.0' as the value for the host argument in the call to the app.run method, specifically, the last line in the service/service.py file. The following line shows the new call to app.run, which launches Flask's development server in an IPv4 configuration and allows requests to be made from other computers and devices connected to our LAN. The line generates an externally visible server. The code file for the sample is included in the restful_python_2_01_02 folder, in the Flask01/service/service.py file:

```
if __name__ == '__main__':
    app.run(host='0.0.0.0', debug=True)
```

If you decide to compose and send HTTP requests from other computers or devices connected to the LAN, remember that you have to use the development computer's assigned IP address instead of localhost. For example, if the computer's assigned IPv4 IP address is 192.168.1.127, instead of localhost:5000, you should use 192.168.1.127:5000. Of course, you can also use the hostname instead of the IP address. The configurations explained previously are very important because mobile devices might be the consumers of our RESTful APIs and future microservices. We will always want to test the apps that make use of our APIs in our development environments. In addition, we can work with useful tools, such as ngrok, that allow us to generate secure tunnels to localhost. You can read more about ngrok at http://www.ngrok.com.

The Flask development server is running on localhost (127.0.0.1), listening on port 5000, and waiting for our HTTP requests. Now, we will compose and send HTTP requests locally in our development computer or from other computers or devices connected to our LAN.

Throughout this book, we will use the following tools to compose and send HTTP requests:

- Command-line tools
- GUI tools
- Python code
- The web browser

 Notice that you can use any other application that allows you to compose and send HTTP requests. There are many apps that run on tablets and smartphones that allow you to accomplish this task. However, we will focus our attention on the most useful tools when building RESTful Web APIs and microservices.

Working with the curl and httpie command-line tools

We will start with command-line tools. One of the key advantages of command-line tools is that we can easily run again the HTTP requests after we build them for the first time, and we don't need to use the mouse or to tap the screen to run requests. We can also easily build a script with batch requests and run them. As happens with any command-line tool, it can take more time to perform the first requests compared with GUI tools, but it becomes easier once we've performed many requests and we can easily reuse the commands we have written in the past to compose new requests.

Curl, also known as **cURL**, is a very popular open source command-line tool and library that allows us to easily transfer data. We can use the `curl` command-line tool to easily compose and send HTTP requests and check their responses.

In macOS or Linux, you can open a Terminal and start using `curl` from the command line.

In Windows, you can work with `curl` in the Command Prompt or you can install `curl` as part of the Cygwin package installation option and execute it from the Cygwin terminal. In case you decide to use the `curl` command within the Command Prompt, download and unzip the latest version at `http://curl.haxx.se/download.html`. Then, make sure you include the folder in which the `curl.exe` file is included in your path to make it easy to run the command.

You can read more about the Cygwin terminal and its installation procedure at
`http://cygwin.com/install.html`. In case you decide to use the Cygwin terminal, use it
whenever you have to run the `curl` command instead of working with the Command
Prompt.

Notice that Windows PowerShell includes the `curl` alias that calls the
`Inovoke-WebRequest` command. Thus, in case you decide to work with
Windows PowerShell, you will have to remove the `curl` alias to use the
`curl` utility we use in this book.

We used the `requirements.txt` file to install the packages for our virtual environment. In
this file, we specified `httpie` as one of the required packages. This way, we installed
HTTPie, a command-line HTTP client written in Python that makes it easy to send HTTP
requests and uses a syntax that is easier than `curl`. One of the great advantages of HTTPie
is that it displays colorized output and uses multiple lines to display the response details.
Thus, HTTPie makes it easier to understand the responses than the `curl` utility. However,
it is very important to mention that HTTPie is slower than `curl`.

Whenever we compose HTTP requests with the command line, we will
use two versions of the same command: the first one with HTTPie, and
the second one with `curl`. This way, you will be able to use the one that is
most convenient for you.

Make sure you leave the Flask development server running. Don't close the Terminal or
Command Prompt that is running this development server. Open a new Terminal in
macOS or Linux, or a Command Prompt in Windows, and run the following command. It is
very important that you enter the ending slash (/) when specified because
`/service/notifications` won't match any of the configured URL routes. Thus, we must
enter `/service/notifications/`, including the ending slash (/). We will compose and
send an HTTP request to create a new notification. The code file for the sample is included
in the `restful_python_2_01_02` folder, in the `Flask01/cmd01.txt` file:

```
http POST ":5000/service/notifications/" message='eSports competition
starts in 2 minutes' ttl=20 notification_category='Information'
```

The following is the equivalent `curl` command. It is very important to use the `-H`
`"Content-Type: application/json"` option to tell `curl` to send the data specified after
the `-d` option as `application/json` instead of the default `application/x-www-form-`
`urlencoded` option.

The code file for the sample is included in the `restful_python_2_01_02` folder, in the `Flask01/cmd02.txt` file:

```
curl -iX POST -H "Content-Type: application/json" -d '{"message":"eSports
competition starts in 2 minutes", "ttl":20, "notification_category":
"Information"}' "localhost:5000/service/notifications/"
```

The previous commands will compose and send the `POST` `http://localhost:5000/service/notifications/` HTTP request with the following JSON key-value pairs:

```
{
    "message": "eSports competition starts in 2 minutes",
    "ttl": 20,
    "notification_category": "Information"
}
```

The request specifies `/service/notifications/` and, therefore, it will match `'/service/notifications/'` and run the `NotificationList.post` method. The method doesn't receive arguments because the URL route doesn't include any parameters. As the HTTP verb for the request is `POST`, Flask calls the `post` method. If the new `NotificationModel` was successfully persisted in the dictionary, the function returns an HTTP `201 Created` status code and the recently persisted `NotificationModel` serialized to JSON in the response body. The following lines show an example response for the HTTP request, with the new `NotificationModel` object in the JSON response:

```
HTTP/1.0 201 CREATED
Content-Length: 283
Content-Type: application/json
Date: Wed, 10 Oct 2018 01:01:44 GMT
Server: Werkzeug/0.14.1 Python/3.7.1
{
    "creation_date": "Wed, 10 Oct 2018 01:01:44 -0000",
    "displayed_once": false,
    "displayed_times": 0,
    "id": 1,
    "message": "eSports competition starts in 2 minutes",
    "notification_category": "Information",
    "ttl": 20,
    "uri": "/service/notifications/1"
}
```

We will compose and send an HTTP request to create another notification. Go back to the Command Prompt in Windows, or the Terminal in macOS or Linux, and run the following command. The code file for the sample is included in the `restful_python_2_01_02` folder, in the `Flask01/cmd03.txt` file:

```
http POST ":5000/service/notifications/" message='Ambient temperature is
above the valid range' ttl=15 notification_category='Warning'
```

The following is the equivalent `curl` command. The code file for the sample is included in the `restful_python_2_01_02` folder, in the `Flask01/cmd04.txt` file:

```
curl -iX POST -H "Content-Type: application/json" -d '{"message":"Ambient
temperature is above the valid range", "ttl":15, "notification_category":
"Warning"}' "localhost:5000/service/notifications/"
```

The previous commands will compose and send the POST `http://localhost:5000/service/notifications/` HTTP request with the following JSON key-value pairs:

```
{
    "message": "Ambient temperature is above the valid range",
    "ttl": 15,
    "notification_category": "Warning"
}
```

The following lines show an example response for the HTTP request, with the new `NotificationModel` object in the JSON response:

```
HTTP/1.0 201 CREATED
Content-Length: 280
Content-Type: application/json
Date: Wed, 10 Oct 2018 21:07:40 GMT
Server: Werkzeug/0.14.1 Python/3.7.1
{
    "creation_date": "Wed, 10 Oct 2018 21:07:40 -0000",
    "displayed_once": false,
    "displayed_times": 0,
    "id": 2,
    "message": "Ambient temperature is above valid range",
    "notification_category": "Warning",
    "ttl": 15,
    "uri": "/service/notifications/2"
}
```

We will compose and send an HTTP request to retrieve all the notifications. Go back to the Command Prompt in Windows, or the Terminal in macOS or Linux, and run the following command. The code file for the sample is included in the `restful_python_2_01_02` folder, in the `Flask01/cmd05.txt` file:

```
http ":5000/service/notifications/"
```

The following is the equivalent `curl` command. The code file for the sample is included in the `restful_python_2_01_02` folder, in the `Flask01/cmd06.txt` file:

```
curl -iX GET "localhost:5000/service/notifications/"
```

The previous commands will compose and send the `GET` `http://localhost:5000/service/notifications/` HTTP request. The request specifies `/service/notifications/` and, therefore, it will match `'/service/notifications/'` and run the `NotificationList.get` method. The method doesn't receive arguments because the URL route doesn't include any parameters. As the HTTP verb for the request is `GET`, Flask calls the `get` method. The method retrieves all the `NotificationModel` objects and generates a JSON response with all of these `NotificationModel` objects serialized.

The following lines show an example response for the HTTP request. The first lines show the HTTP response headers, including the status (`200 OK`) and the content type (`application/json`). After the HTTP response headers, we can see the details for the two `NotificationModel` objects in the JSON response:

```
HTTP/1.0 200 OK
Content-Length: 648
Content-Type: application/json
Date: Wed, 10 Oct 2018 21:09:43 GMT
Server: Werkzeug/0.14.1 Python/3.7.1
[
    {
        "creation_date": "Wed, 10 Oct 2018 21:07:31 -0000",
        "displayed_once": false,
        "displayed_times": 0,
        "id": 1,
        "message": "eSports competition starts in 2 minutes",
        "notification_category": "Information",
        "ttl": 20,
        "uri": "/service/notifications/1"
    },
    {
        "creation_date": "Wed, 10 Oct 2018 21:07:40 -0000",
        "displayed_once": false,
```

```
            "displayed_times": 0,
            "id": 2,
            "message": "Ambient temperature is above valid range",
            "notification_category": "Warning",
            "ttl": 15,
            "uri": "/service/notifications/2"
        }
    ]
```

After we run the three requests, we will see the following lines in the window that is running the Flask development server. The output indicates that the service received three HTTP requests, specifically two POST requests and one GET request with /service/notifications/ as the URI. The service processed the three HTTP requests, and returned the 201 status code for the first two requests and 200 for the last request:

```
127.0.0.1 - - [10/Oct/2018 18:07:31] "POST /service/notifications/
HTTP/1.1" 201 -
127.0.0.1 - - [10/Oct/2018 18:07:40] "POST /service/notifications/
HTTP/1.1" 201 -
127.0.0.1 - - [10/Oct/2018 18:09:43] "GET /service/notifications/ HTTP/1.1"
200 -
```

The following screenshot shows two Terminal windows side by side on macOS. The Terminal window on the left-hand side is running the Flask development server and displays the received and processed HTTP requests. The Terminal window on the right-hand side is running http commands to generate the HTTP requests. It is a good idea to use a similar configuration to check the output while we compose and send the HTTP requests:

Now, we will compose and send an HTTP request to retrieve a notification that doesn't exist. For example, in the previous list, there is no notification with an `id` value equal to 78. Run the following command to try to retrieve this notification. Make sure you use an `id` value that doesn't exist. We must make sure that the utilities display the headers as part of the response to see the returned status code. The code file for the sample is included in the `restful_python_2_01_02` folder, in the `Flask01/cmd07.txt` file:

```
http ":5000/service/notifications/78"
```

The following is the equivalent `curl` command. The code file for the sample is included in the `restful_python_2_01_02` folder, in the `Flask01/cmd08.txt` file:

```
curl -iX GET "localhost:5000/service/notifications/78"
```

The previous commands will compose and send the GET
http://localhost:5000/service/notifications/78 HTTP request. The request is
the same as the previous one we analyzed, with a different number for the id parameter.
The service will run the Notification.get method, with 78 as the value for the id
argument. The method will execute the code that retrieves the NotificationModel object
whose ID matches the id value received as an argument. However, the first line in the
NotificationList.get method calls the abort_if_notification_not_found
method, which won't find the ID in the dictionary keys, and it will call the
flask_restful.abort function because there is no notification with the specified id
value. Thus, the code will return an HTTP 404 Not Found status code. The following lines
show an example header response for the HTTP request and the message included in the
body. In this case, we just leave the default message. Of course, we can customize it based
on our specific needs:

```
HTTP/1.0 404 NOT FOUND
Content-Length: 155
Content-Type: application/json
Date: Wed, 10 Oct 2018 21:24:32 GMT
Server: Werkzeug/0.14.1 Python/3.7.1
{
    "message": "Notification 78 not found. You have requested this
URI [/service/notifications/78] but did you mean
/service/notifications/<int:id> ?"
}
```

We provide an implementation for the PATCH method to make it possible for our API to
update a single field for an existing resource. For example, we can use the PATCH method to
update two fields for an existing notification and set the value for its displayed_once
field to true and displayed_times to 1. We don't want to use the PUT method because
this method is meant to replace an entire notification.

> The PATCH method is meant to apply a delta to an existing notification
> and, therefore, it is the appropriate method to just change the value of the
> displayed_once and displayed_times fields.

Now, we will compose and send an HTTP request to update an existing notification,
specifically, to update the value of two fields. Make sure you replace 2 with the ID of an
existing notification in your configuration. The code file for the sample is included in the
restful_python_2_01_02 folder, in the Flask01/cmd09.txt file:

```
http PATCH ":5000/service/notifications/2" displayed_once=true
displayed_times=1
```

The following is the equivalent `curl` command. The code file for the sample is included in the `restful_python_2_01_02` folder, in the `Flask01/cmd10.txt` file:

```
curl -iX PATCH -H "Content-Type: application/json" -d
'{"displayed_once":"true", "displayed_times":1}'
"localhost:5000/service/notifications/2"
```

The previous command will compose and send a `PATCH` HTTP request with the specified JSON key-value pairs. The request has a number after `/service/notifications/` and, therefore, it will match `'/service/notifications/<int:id>'` and run the `Notification.patch` method, that is, the `patch` method for the `Notification` class. If a `NotificationModel` instance with the specified ID exists and was successfully updated, the call to the method will return an HTTP `200 OK` status code and the recently updated `NotificationModel` instance serialized to JSON in the response body. The following lines show a sample response:

```
HTTP/1.0 200 OK
Content-Length: 279
Content-Type: application/json
Date: Thu, 11 Oct 2018 02:15:13 GMT
Server: Werkzeug/0.14.1 Python/3.7.1

{
    "creation_date": "Thu, 11 Oct 2018 02:15:05 -0000",
    "displayed_once": true,
    "displayed_times": 1,
    "id": 2,
    "message": "Ambient temperature is above valid range",
    "notification_category": "Warning",
    "ttl": 15,
    "uri": "/service/notifications/2"
}
```

 The IoT device will execute the previously explained HTTP request when it displays the notification for the first time. Then, it will make additional `PATCH` requests to update the value for the `displayed_times` field.

Now, we will compose and send an HTTP request to delete an existing notification, specifically, the last one we added. As happened in our last HTTP requests, we have to check the value assigned to `id` in the previous response and replace 2 in the command with the returned value. The code file for the sample is included in the `restful_python_2_01_02` folder, in the `Flask01/cmd11.txt` file:

```
http DELETE ":5000/service/notifications/2"
```

The following is the equivalent `curl` command. The code file for the sample is included in the `restful_python_2_01_02` folder, in the `Flask01/cmd12.txt` file:

```
curl -iX DELETE "localhost:5000/service/notifications/2"
```

The previous commands will compose and send the DELETE `http://localhost:5000/service/notifications/2` HTTP request. The request has a number after `/service/notifications/` and, therefore, it will match `'/service/notifications/<int:id>'` and run the `Notification.delete` method, that is, the `delete` method for the `Notification` class. If a `NotificationModel` instance with the specified ID exists and was successfully deleted, the call to the method will return an HTTP `204 No Content` status code. The following lines show a sample response:

```
HTTP/1.0 204 NO CONTENT
Content-Length: 3
Content-Type: application/json
Date: Thu, 11 Oct 2018 02:22:09 GMT
Server: Werkzeug/0.14.1 Python/3.7.1
```

Working with GUI tools – Postman and others

So far, we have been working with two terminal-based, or command-line, tools to compose and send HTTP requests to our Flask development server: cURL and HTTPie. Now, we will work with a **GUI** (short for **Graphical User Interface**) tool.

Postman is a very popular API testing suite GUI tool that allows us to easily compose and send HTTP requests, among other features. Postman is available as a Chrome App and as a Macintosh App. We can execute it in Windows, Linux, and macOS as a native app. You can download the versions of the Postman app at `https://www.getpostman.com/apps`.

You can download and install Postman for free to compose and send HTTP requests to our RESTful APIs. You just need to sign up to Postman; we won't be using any of the paid features provided by Postman in our examples. All the instructions work with Postman 6.4.2 or higher.

Now, we will compose and send HTTP requests to `localhost:5000` and test the RESTful API with this GUI tool. Postman doesn't support shorthand for localhost and, therefore, we cannot use the same shorthand we have been using when composing requests with HTTPie.

Once you launch Postman, make sure you close the modal that provides shortcuts to common tasks. Select **GET** request in the + new drop-down menu in the upper-left corner of the Postman main window.

Select **GET** in the drop-down menu on the left-hand side of the **Enter request URL** textbox, and then enter `localhost:5000/service/notifications/` in this textbox on the right-hand side of the dropdown.

Then, click **Send** and Postman will display the following information:

- **Status**: 200 OK.
- **Time**: The time it took for the request to be processed.
- **Size**: The response size calculated by adding the body size to the header's size.
- **Body**: The response body with all the notifications formatted as JSON with syntax highlighting. The default view for the response body is the Pretty view, and it activates syntax highlighting that makes it easy to read JSON code.

The following screenshot shows the JSON response body in Postman for the HTTP GET request to `localhost:5000/service/notifications/`:

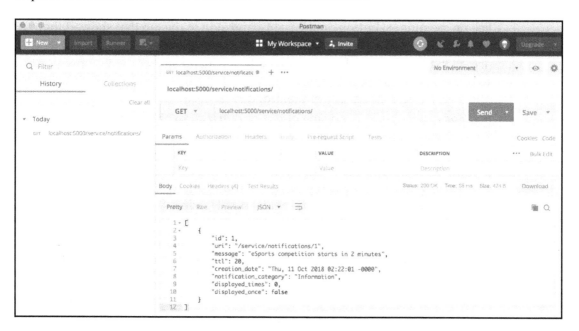

Click on the **Headers** tab on the right-hand side of the **Body** and **Cookies** tabs to read the response headers. The following screenshot shows the layout for the response headers that Postman displays for the previous response. Notice that Postman displays the **Status** in the right-hand side of the response and doesn't include it as the first line of the headers, as happened when we worked with both the `curl` and `http` command-line utilities:

Body Cookies Headers (4) Test Results	Status: 200 OK Time: 58 ms Size: 474 B	Download
Content-Type → application/json		
Content-Length → 327		
Server → Werkzeug/0.14.1 Python/3.6.6		
Date → Thu, 11 Oct 2018 18:49:39 GMT		

Now, we will compose and send an HTTP request to create a new notification, specifically, a `POST` request. Follow these steps:

1. Click on the plus (**+**) button on the right-hand side of the tab that showed the previous request. This is to create a new tab.
2. Select **POST** in the drop-down menu on the left-hand side of the **Enter request URL** textbox, and enter `localhost:5000/service/notifications/` in the textbox in the right-hand side of the dropdown.
3. Click **Body** in the right-hand side of the **Authorization** and **Headers** tabs, within the panel that composes the request.
4. Activate the raw radio button and select **JSON (application/json)** in the dropdown on the right-hand side of the binary radio button. Postman will automatically add a **Content-type = application/json** header and, therefore, you will notice the **Headers** tab will be renamed to **Headers (1)**, indicating that there is one key-value pair specified for the request headers.
5. Enter the following lines in the textbox under the radio buttons, within the **Body** tab. The code file for the sample is included in the `restful_python_2_01_02` folder, in the `Flask01/cmd13.txt` file:

```
{
    "message": "Calculating the most appropriate ambient
temperature",
    "ttl": 20,
    "notification_category": "Warning"
}
```

The following screenshot shows the request body in Postman:

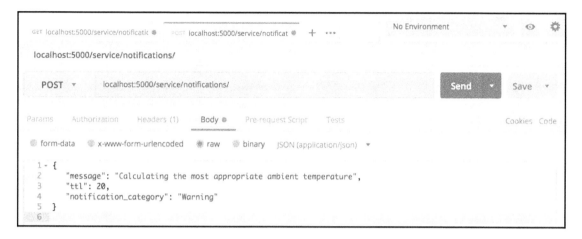

We followed the necessary steps to create an HTTP POST request with a JSON body that specifies the necessary key-value pairs to create a new notification. Click **Send** and Postman will display the following information:

- **Status**: **201 Created.**
- **Time**: The time it took for the request to be processed.
- **Size**: The response size calculated by adding the body size to the header's size.
- **Body**: The response body, with the recently added notification formatted as JSON with syntax highlighting (Pretty view).

The following screenshot shows the JSON response body in Postman for the HTTP POST request:

If we want to compose and send an HTTP PATCH request for our API with Postman, it is necessary to follow the steps explained previously to provide JSON data within the request body.

Click or tap on the value for the `uri` field in the JSON response body: `/service/notifications/3`. You will notice that the value will be underlined when you hover the mouse over it. Postman will automatically generate a GET request to `localhost:5000/service/notifications/3`, as shown in the following screenshot:

Click **Send** to run it and retrieve the recently added notification. Notice that the `uri` field is useful for browsing the API with a tool such as Postman.

One of the nice features included in Postman is that we can easily review and re-run the HTTP requests we have made by browsing the saved **History** shown on the left-hand side of the Postman window. The **History** panel displays a list with the HTTP verb, followed by the URL for each HTTP request we have composed and sent. We just need to click on the desired HTTP request and click **Send** to run it again. The following screenshot shows the many HTTP requests in the **History** panel with the first one selected to send it again:

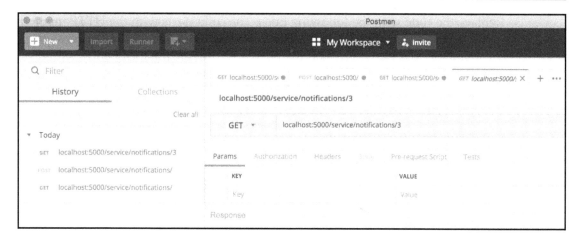

JetBrains PyCharm is a very popular multiplatform Python **IDE** (short for **Integrated Development Environment**) available on macOS, Linux, and Windows. Its paid professional version includes a REST Client that allows us to easily test RESTful Web Services and microservices. In case we work with this version of the IDE, we can compose and send HTTP requests without leaving the IDE. You don't need a JetBrains PyCharm Professional version license to run the examples included in this book. You can take advantage of the free 30-day trial. However, in case you don't want to install this IDE, you can skip the steps and use the provided `http` or `curl` commands, which perform the same task. Because the IDE is very popular, we will learn the necessary steps to compose and send an HTTP request for our API by using the HTTP client included in the editor that replaced the deprecated REST Client.

Now, we will use the HTTP client included in PyCharm Professional to compose and send an HTTP request to create a new game, specifically, a `POST` request. Follow these steps:

1. Select **File** | **New** | **HTTP Request** in the main menu.
2. Enter `notifications_post_pycharm` in the **Name** textbox and click **OK**. The IDE will create a new file with the `http` extension and with instructions on how to build HTTP requests.

3. Replace the code with the following lines. The code starts with the HTTP method name, POST, followed by the URL. The following line specifies the header with the value for Content-Type and the next lines provide the JSON body within curly brackets. The code file for the sample is included in the restful_python_2_01_02 folder, in the Flask01/notifications_post_pycharm.http file:

```
POST http://localhost:5000/service/notifications/
Content-Type: application/json

{
    "message": "Working with PyCharm Professional",
    "ttl": 12,
    "notification_category": "Information"
}
```

The following screenshot shows the request incorporated in PyCharm Professional's editor:

We followed the necessary steps to create an HTTP POST request with a JSON body that specifies the necessary key-value pairs to create a new notification.

Click the run HTTP request button, that is, the first button with the play icon in the upper-left corner of the editor, under the tab's name (notifications_post_1.http). Select **Run** localhost:5000 in the context menu that is displayed.

PyCharm will compose and send the HTTP POST request, which will activate the **Run** tab and display the request we made, the response headers, the response body, the response code 201 (Created), the time it took for the request to be processed, and the content length at the bottom of the output. By default, PyCharm will automatically apply JSON syntax highlighting to the response. The following screenshot shows the output in the **Run** tab for the HTTP POST request:

In case you don't want to work with PyCharm Professional, run any of the following commands to compose and send the HTTP POST request to create the new notification. The code file for the sample is included in the `restful_python_2_01_02` folder, in the `Flask01/cmd14.txt` file:

```
http POST ":5000/service/notifications/" message='Working with
PyCharm Professional' ttl=12 notification_category='Information'
```

The following is the equivalent `curl` command. The code file for the sample is included in the `restful_python_2_01_02` folder, in the `Flask01/cmd15.txt` file:

```
curl -iX POST -H "Content-Type: application/json" -d '{"message":"Working
with PyCharm Professional", "ttl":12, "notification_category":
"Information"}' "localhost:5000/service/notifications/"
```

Because we made the necessary changes to generate an externally visible Flask development server, we can also use apps that can compose and send HTTP requests from mobile devices to work with the RESTful API.

For example, we can work with the iCurlHTTP App on iOS devices such as iPad Pro, iPad, and iPhone: `https://itunes.apple.com/us/app/icurlhttp/id611943891?mt=8`. In Android devices, we can work with the HTTP Request App: `https://play.google.com/store/apps/details?id=air.http.request&hl=en`.

The next screenshot shows the results of composing and sending the following HTTP request with the `GET http://192.168.1.106:8000/service/notitications/` iCurlHTTP app. Remember that you have to perform the configurations explained previously in your LAN and router to be able to access the Flask development server from other devices connected to your LAN. In this case, the IP assigned to the computer running the Flask development server is `192.168.1.106` and, therefore, you must replace this IP with the IP assigned to your development computer. At the time this book was published, the mobile apps that allow you to compose and send HTTP requests do not provide all the features you can find in Postman or command-line utilities:

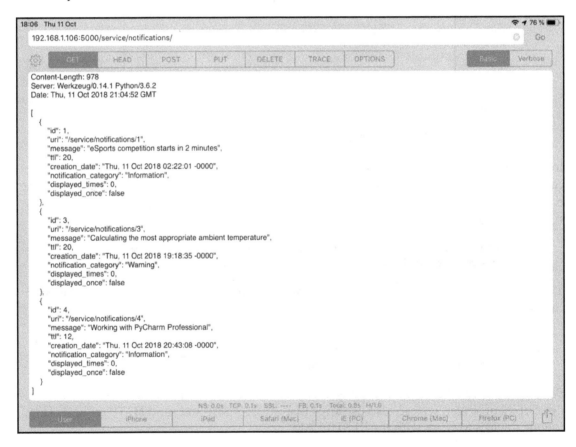

Consuming the API with other programming languages

We've built our first RESTful Web Service that is capable of running as a microservice with Flask and Python. We can consume the API with any modern programming language that can compose and send HTTP requests to the resources and verbs supported by the API and work easily with JSON content.

It is extremely important to make sure that we set the content type for the HTTP request as we did when working with the `curl` and `http` command-line utilities. We just need to check which is the most convenient way of doing so in the programming language that we have to use as a client.

The fact that we can easily run a Flask development server and check its console output whenever a new request is processed makes it easy to check which requests arrive at the server. In this case, we are working with a basic and unsecured API. However, we will work with secure and more advanced APIs in the forthcoming chapters.

Test your knowledge

Let's see whether you can answer the following questions correctly:

1. HTTPie is a:
    1. Command-line HTTP server written in Python that makes it easy to create a RESTful Web Server
    2. Command-line utility that allows us to run queries against a SQLite database
    3. Command-line HTTP client written in Python that makes it easy to compose and send HTTP requests

2. Flask-RESTful uses which of the following as the main building block for a RESTful API:
    1. Resources built on top of Flask pluggable views
    2. Statuses built on top of Flask resource views
    3. Resources built on top of Flask pluggable controllers

3. To process an HTTP PATCH request on a resource, which method should we declare in a subclass of `flask_restful.Resource`?
    1. `patch_restful`
    2. `patch_method`
    3. `patch`

4. To process an HTTP PUT request on a resource, which method should we declare in a subclass of `flask_restful.Resource`?
    1. `put_restful`
    2. `put_method`
    3. `put`

5. To process an HTTP POST request on a resource, which method should we declare in a subclass of `flask_restful.Resource`?
    1. `post_restful`
    2. `post_method`
    3. `post`

6. To process an HTTP GET request on a resource, which method should we declare in a subclass of `flask_restful.Resource`?
    1. `get_restful`
    2. `get_method`
    3. `get`

7. A subclass of `flask_restful.Resource` represents:
    1. A controller resource
    2. A RESTful resource
    3. A single RESTful HTTP verb

8. If we use the `@marshal_with` decorator with `notification_fields` as an argument, the decorator will:
    1. Apply the field filtering and output formatting specified in `notification_fields` to the appropriate instance
    2. Apply the field filtering specified in `notification_fields` to the appropriate instance, without considering output formatting
    3. Apply the output formatting specified in `notification_fields` to the appropriate instance, without considering field filtering

Summary

In this chapter, we designed a RESTful API to interact with a simple dictionary that acted as a data repository and performed CRUD operations with notifications, to be used as a baseline for a microservice. We defined the requirements for our API and understood the tasks performed by each HTTP method. We set up a virtual environment with Flask and Flask-RESTful. We followed best practices to generate a reproducible virtual environment.

We created a model to represent and persist notifications. We learned how to configure the serialization of notifications into JSON representations with the features included in Flask-RESTful. We wrote classes that represent resources and process the different HTTP requests, and we configured the URL patterns to route URLs to classes.

Finally, we started the Flask development server and we used command-line tools to compose and send HTTP requests to our RESTful API and analyzed how each HTTP requests was processed in our code. We also worked with many useful GUI tools to compose and send HTTP requests.

Now that we understand the basics of the combination of Flask and Flask-RESTful to create RESTful APIs that we can encapsulate in microservices, in the next chapter, we will expand the capabilities of the RESTful Web API by taking advantage of the advanced features included in Flask-RESTful and related ORMs.

2
Working with Models, SQLAlchemy, and Hyperlinked APIs in Flask

In this chapter, we will expand the capabilities of the RESTful API that we started in the previous chapter. We will use SQLAlchemy as our ORM to work with a PostgreSQL database, and we will take advantage of advanced features included in Flask and Flask-RESTful that will allow us to easily organize code for complex APIs, such as models and blueprints.

We will go through the following topics in this chapter:

- Design a RESTful API to interact with a PostgreSQL 10.5 database
- Understand the tasks performed by each HTTP method
- Install packages with the `requirements.txt` file to simplify our common tasks
- Create the database
- Configure the database
- Write code for the models with their relationships
- Use schemas to validate, serialize, and deserialize models
- Combine blueprints with resourceful routing
- Understand and configure resourceful routing
- Register the blueprint and run migrations
- Verify the contents of the PostgreSQL database
- Create and retrieve related resources

Designing a RESTful API to interact with a PostgreSQL 10.5 database

So far, our RESTful API has performed CRUD operations on a simple in-memory dictionary that acted as a data repository. The dictionary is never persisted and, therefore, the data is lost whenever we restart our Flask development server.

Now, we want to create a more complex RESTful API with Flask RESTful to interact with a database model that allows us to work with notifications that are grouped into notification categories. In our previous RESTful API, we used a string attribute to specify the notification category for a notification. In this case, we want to be able to easily retrieve all the notifications that belong to a specific notification category and, therefore, we will have a relationship between a notification and a notification category.

We must be able to perform CRUD operations on different related resources and resource collections. The following table enumerates the resources and the class name that we will create to represent the model:

Resources	Class name that represents the model
Notification categories	`NotificationCategory`
Notifications	`Notification`

The notification category (`NotificationCategory`) just requires the following data:

- An integer identifier
- A string name

We need the following data for a notification (`Notification`):

- An integer identifier
- A foreign key to a notification category (`NotificationCategory`)
- A string message
- A **TTL** (short for **Time to Live**), that is, a duration in seconds that will indicate the amount of time the notification message has to be displayed on the OLED display
- A creation date and time. The timestamp will be added automatically when adding a new notification to the collection

- An integer counter that indicates the times when the notification message has been displayed on the OLED display
- A bool value indicating whether the notification message was displayed at least once on the OLED display

 We will take advantage of many packages related to Flask RESTful and SQLAlchemy that make it easier to serialize and deserialize data, perform validations, and integrate SQLAlchemy with Flask and Flask RESTful. This way, we will reduce the boilerplate code.

Understanding the tasks performed by each HTTP method

The following table shows the HTTP verbs, the scope, and the semantics for the methods that our new API must support. Each method is composed by an HTTP verb and a scope, and all the methods have well-defined meanings for all the resources and collections:

HTTP verb	Scope	Semantics
GET	Collection of notification categories	Retrieve all the stored notification categories in the collection, sorted by their name in ascending order. Each notification category must include the full URL for the resource. In addition, each notification category must include a list containing all the details of the notifications that belong to the category. The notifications don't have to include the notification category in order to avoid repeating data.
GET	Notification category	Retrieve a single notification category. The notification category must include the same information explained for each category when we retrieve a collection of notification categories.
POST	Collection of notification categories	Create a new notification category in the collection.
PATCH	Notification category	Update the name of an existing notification category.
DELETE	Notification category	Delete an existing notification category.

GET	Collection of notifications	Retrieve all the stored notifications in the collection, sorted by their message in ascending order. Each notification must include its notification category details, including the full URL to access the related resource. The notification category details don't have to include the notifications that belong to the category. The notification must include the full URL to access the resource.
GET	Notification	Retrieve a single notification. The notification must include the same information explained for each notification when we retrieve a collection of notifications.
POST	Collection of notifications	Create a new notification in the collection.
PATCH	Notification	Update any of the following fields of an existing notification: `message`, `ttl`, `displayed_times`, and `displayed_once`.
DELETE	Notification	Delete an existing notification.

In addition, our RESTful API must support the OPTIONS method for all the resources and collections of resources. We will use SQLAlchemy as our ORM and we will work with a PostgreSQL database. However, if you don't want to spend time installing PostgreSQL 10.5, you can use any other database supported by SQLAlchemy, such as MySQL. If you want the simplest database, you can work with SQLite.

In the previous table, we have many methods and scopes. The following list enumerates the URIs for each scope mentioned in the previous table, where {id} has to be replaced with the numeric id or primary key of the resource. As happened in the previous example, we want our API to differentiate collections from a single resource of the collection in the URLs. When we refer a collection, we will use a slash (/) as the last character for the URL and, when we refer a single resource of the collection, we won't use a slash (/) as the last character for the URL:

- Collection of notification categories: /notification-categories/
- Notification category: /notification-category/{id}
- Collection of notifications: /notifications/
- Notification: /notification/{id}

Let's imagine that `http://localhost:5000/service/` is the URL for the API running on the Flask development server. We have to compose and send an HTTP request with the following HTTP verb (`GET`) and request URL (`http://localhost:5000/service/notification-categories/`) to retrieve all the stored notification categories in the collection. Each category will include a list with all the messages that belong to the category:

```
GET http://localhost:5000/service/notification-categories/
```

Installing packages with the requirements.txt file to simplify our common tasks

Make sure you quit Flask's development server. You just need to press *Ctrl + C* in the Terminal or Command Prompt window in which it is running.

Now, we will install a number of additional packages. Make sure you have activated the virtual environment we created in the previous chapter and named `Flask01`. After you activate the virtual environment, it is time to run numerous commands, which will be the same for either macOS, Linux, or Windows.

Now, we will edit the existing `requirements.txt` file to specify the additional set of packages that our application requires to be installed in any supported platform. This way, it will be extremely easy to repeat the installation of the specified packages with their versions in any new virtual environment.

Use your favorite editor to edit the existing text file named `requirements.txt` within the root folder for the virtual environment. Add the following lines after the last line to declare the additional packages and the versions that our new version of the API requires. The code file for the sample is included in the `restful_python_2_02_01` folder, in the `Flask01/requirements.txt` file:

```
Flask-SQLAlchemy==2.3.2
Flask-Migrate==2.2.1
marshmallow==2.16.0
marshmallow-sqlalchemy==0.14.1
flask-marshmallow==0.9.0
psycopg2==2.7.5
```

Each additional line added to the requirements.txt file indicates the package and the version that needs to be installed. The following table summarizes the packages and the version numbers that we specified as additional requirements to the previously included packages:

Package name	Version to be installed
Flask-SQLAlchemy	2.3.2
Flask-Migrate	2.2.1
marshmallow	2.16.0
marshmallow-sqlalchemy	0.14.1
flask-marshmallow	0.9.0
psycopg2	2.7.5

Flask-SQLAlchemy adds support for the SQLAlchemy ORM to Flask applications. This extension simplifies executing common SQLAlchemy tasks within a Flask application. SQLAlchemy is a dependency for Flask-SQLAlchemy.

Flask-Migrate uses the Alembic package to handle SQLAlchemy database migrations for Flask applications. We will use Flask-Migrate to set up our PostgreSQL database.

 If you've worked with previous versions of Flask-Migrate, it is very important to notice that Flask-Script is no longer a dependency for Flask-Migrate . Flask-Script was a popular package that added support for writing external scripts in Flask, including scripts to set up a database. The newest Flask versions install the flask script and a command-line interface based on the Click package in the virtual environment. Hence, it is no longer necessary to combine Flask-Migrate with Flask-Script.

Marshmallow is a lightweight library for converting complex datatypes to and from native Python datatypes. Marshmallow provides schemas that we can use to validate input data, deserialize input data to app-level objects, and serialize app-level objects to Python primitive types.

marshmallow-sqlalchemy provides SQLAlchemy integration with the previously installed marshmallow validation, serialization, and deserialization lightweight library.

Flask-Marshmallow integrates the previously installed marshmallow library with Flask applications and makes it easy to generate URL and hyperlink fields.

Psycopg 2 (`psycopg2`) is a Python-PostgreSQL database adapter and SQLAlchemy will use it to interact with our recently created PostgreSQL database. Again, it is very important to make sure that the PostgreSQL `bin` folder is included in the `PATH` environmental variable before we run the installation for this package.

Now, we must run the following command on macOS, Linux, or Windows to install the additional packages and the versions explained in the previous table with `pip` by using the recently edited `requirements` file. Make sure you are located in the folder that has the `requirements.txt` file before running the command:

```
pip install -r requirements.txt
```

The last lines for the output will indicate that all the new packages and their dependencies have been successfully installed. If you downloaded the source code for the example and you didn't work with the previous version of the API, `pip` will also install the other packages included in the `requirements.txt` file:

```
Installing collected packages: SQLAlchemy, Flask-SQLAlchemy, Mako, python-
editor, python-dateutil, alembic, Flask-Migrate, marshmallow, marshmallow-
sqlalchemy, flask-marshmallow, psycopg2
    Running setup.py install for SQLAlchemy ... done
    Running setup.py install for Mako ... done
    Running setup.py install for python-editor ... done
Successfully installed Flask-Migrate-2.2.1 Flask-SQLAlchemy-2.3.2
Mako-1.0.7 SQLAlchemy-1.2.12 alembic-1.0.0 flask-marshmallow-0.9.0
marshmallow-2.16.0 marshmallow-sqlalchemy-0.14.1 psycopg2-2.7.5
python-dateutil-2.7.3 python-editor-1.0.3
```

Creating the database

Now, we will create the PostgreSQL 10.5 database that we will use as a repository for our API. You will have to download and install a PostgreSQL database server if you aren't already running it in your computer or on a development server. You can download and install this database management system from its web page (`http://www.postgresql.org`). If you are working with macOS, `Postgres.app` provides a really easy way to install and use PostgreSQL on this operating system. You can refer to it from `http://postgresapp.com`. If you are working with Windows, EnterpriseDB and BigSQL provide graphics installers that simplify the configuration process on modern Windows server or desktop versions (visit `https://www.postgresql.org/download/windows` for more information).

Notice that the examples have been tested with PostgreSQL 10.5 on macOS, Linux, and Windows.

You have to make sure that the PostgreSQL bin folder is included in the PATH environmental variable. You should be able to execute the psql command-line utility from your current Terminal or Command Prompt. If the folder isn't included in the PATH variable, you will receive an error indicating that the pg_config file cannot be found when trying to install the psycopg2 package. In addition, you will have to use the full path to each of the PostgreSQL command-line tools we will use in the next steps.

We will use the PostgreSQL command-line tools to create a new database named notifications. If you already have a PostgreSQL database with this name, make sure that you use another name in all the commands and configurations. You can perform the same task as any PostgreSQL GUI tool. If you are developing on Linux, it is necessary to run the commands as the postgres user.

Run the following command in macOS or Windows to create a new database named notifications. Notice that the command won't produce any output:

```
createdb flask_notifications
```

In Linux, run the following command to use the postgres user:

```
sudo -u postgres createdb flask_notifications
```

Now, we will use the psql command-line tool to run some SQL statements to create a specific user that we will use in Flask and assign the necessary roles for it. In macOS or Windows, run the following command to launch psql:

```
psql
```

In Linux, run the following command to use the postgres user:

```
sudo -u psql
```

Then, run the following SQL statements and finally enter \q to exit the psql command-line tool. Replace your_user_name with your desired username to use in the new database and your_password with your chosen password. We will use the username and password in the Flask configuration.

You don't need to run the steps if you are already working with a specific user in PostgreSQL and you have already granted privileges to the database for the user. You will see the output indicating that the permission was granted. The code file for the sample is included in the `restful_python_2_02_01` folder, in the `Flask01/configure_database.sql` file:

```
CREATE ROLE your_user_name WITH LOGIN PASSWORD 'your_password';

GRANT ALL PRIVILEGES ON DATABASE "flask_notifications" TO
your_user_name;
ALTER USER your_user_name CREATEDB;
\q
```

Configuring the database

If you are using the same virtual environment we have created for the previous example, or you downloaded the code sample, the `service` folder already exists. If you created a new virtual environment, create a folder named `service` within the root folder for the virtual environment created.

Create a new `config.py` file within the `service` folder. The following lines show the code that declares variables that determine the configuration for Flask and SQLAlchemy. The `SQL_ALCHEMY_DATABASE_URI` variable generates an SQLAlchemy URI for the PostgreSQL database. Make sure you specify the desired database name in the value for `DB_NAME` and that you configure the user, password, host, and port based on your PostgreSQL configuration. If you followed the previous steps, use the settings specified in these steps. The code file for the sample is included in the `restful_python_2_02_01` folder, in the `Flask01/service/config.py` file:

```
import os

basedir = os.path.abspath(os.path.dirname(__file__))
SQLALCHEMY_ECHO = False
SQLALCHEMY_TRACK_MODIFICATIONS = True
# Replace your_user_name with the user name you configured for the database
# Replace your_password with the password you specified for the database
user
SQLALCHEMY_DATABASE_URI =
"postgresql://{DB_USER}:{DB_PASS}@{DB_ADDR}/{DB_NAME}".format(DB_USER="your
_user_name", DB_PASS="your_password", DB_ADDR="127.0.0.1",
DB_NAME="flask_notifications")
SQLALCHEMY_MIGRATE_REPO = os.path.join(basedir, 'db_repository')
```

We will specify the previously created module (`config`) as an argument to a function that will create a Flask app. This way, we have one module that specifies all the values for the different configuration variables related to SQLAlchemy, and another module that creates a Flask app. We will create the Flask app factory as our final step toward our new API.

Creating models with their relationships

Now, we will create the models that we will use to represent and persist the notification categories, notifications, and their relationships in the PostgreSQL database.

Open the `service/models.py` file and replace its contents with the following code. The lines that declare fields related to other models are highlighted in the code listing. If you created a new virtual environment, create a new `models.py` file within the `service` folder. The code file for the sample is included in the `restful_python_2_02_01` folder, in the `Flask01/service/models.py` file:

```
from marshmallow import Schema, fields, pre_load
from marshmallow import validate
from flask_sqlalchemy import SQLAlchemy
from flask_marshmallow import Marshmallow


orm = SQLAlchemy()
ma = Marshmallow()


class ResourceAddUpdateDelete():
    def add(self, resource):
        orm.session.add(resource)
        return orm.session.commit()

    def update(self):
        return orm.session.commit()

    def delete(self, resource):
        orm.session.delete(resource)
        return orm.session.commit()


class Notification(orm.Model, ResourceAddUpdateDelete):
    id = orm.Column(orm.Integer, primary_key=True)
    message = orm.Column(orm.String(250), unique=True, nullable=False)
    ttl = orm.Column(orm.Integer, nullable=False)
    creation_date = orm.Column(orm.TIMESTAMP,
```

```
    server_default=orm.func.current_timestamp(), nullable=False)
    notification_category_id = orm.Column(orm.Integer,
orm.ForeignKey('notification_category.id', ondelete='CASCADE'),
nullable=False)
    notification_category =
orm.relationship('NotificationCategory',
backref=orm.backref('notifications', lazy='dynamic' ,
order_by='Notification.message'))
    displayed_times = orm.Column(orm.Integer, nullable=False,
server_default='0')
    displayed_once = orm.Column(orm.Boolean, nullable=False,
server_default='false')

    def __init__(self, message, ttl, notification_category):
        self.message = message
        self.ttl = ttl
        self.notification_category = notification_category


class NotificationCategory(orm.Model, ResourceAddUpdateDelete):
    id = orm.Column(orm.Integer, primary_key=True)
    name = orm.Column(orm.String(150), unique=True, nullable=False)

    def __init__(self, name):
        self.name = name
```

First, the code creates an instance of the `flask_sqlalchemy.SQLAlchemy` class named
`orm`. This instance will allow us to control the SQLAlchemy integration for our Flask web
service. SQLAlchemy is our **Object-Relational Mapping** (**ORM**). In addition, this instance
will provide access to all the SQLAlchemy functions and classes.

Then, the code creates an instance of the `flask_marshmallow.Marshmallow` class named
`ma`. It is very important to create the `flask_sqlalchemy.SQLAlchemy` instance before the
`Marshmallow` instance and, therefore, the order of the lines matters in this case.
`Marshmallow` is a wrapper class that integrates `Mashmallow` with a Flask application. The
instance named `ma` will provide access to the `Schema` class, and to the fields defined in
`marshmallow.fields` and the Flask-specific fields declared in
`flask_marshmallow.fields`. We will use them later when we declare the schemas
related to our models.

The code creates the `ResourceAddUpdateDelete` class that declares the following three methods to add, update, and delete a resource through SQLAlchemy sessions:

- `add`: This method receives the object to be added to the `resource` argument and calls the `orm.session.add` method with the resource received as an argument to create the object in the underlying database. Finally, the code commits the session by calling the `orm.session.commit` method.
- `update`: This method just commits the session to persist the changes made to the objects in the underlying database by calling the `orm.session.commit` method.
- `delete`: This method receives the object to be deleted in the `resource` argument and calls the `db.session.delete` method with the resource received as an argument to remove the object in the underlying database. Finally, the code commits the session by calling the `orm.session.commit` method.

The code declares the following two models; specifically, two classes as subclasses of both the `db.Model` and the recently introduced `ResourceAddUpdateDelete` classes:

- `Notification`
- `NotificationCategory`

We specified the field types, maximum lengths, and defaults for many attributes. The attributes that represent fields without any relationship are instances of the `orm.Column` class. Both models declare an `id` attribute and specify the `True` value for the `primary_key` argument to indicate it is the primary key. SQLAlchemy will use the data to generate the necessary tables in the PostgreSQL database.

The `Notification` model declares the `category` field with the following line:

```
notification_category = orm.relationship('NotificationCategory',
backref=orm.backref('notifications', lazy='dynamic' ,
order_by='Notification.message'))
```

The previous line uses the `orm.relationship` function to provide a many-to-one relationship to the `NotificationCategory` model. The `backref` argument specifies a call to the `orm.backref` function with `'notifications'` as the first value that indicates the name to use for the relation from the related `NotificationCategory` object back to a `Notification` instance. The `order_by` argument specifies `'Notification.message'` because we want the notifications for each category to be sorted by the value of the message field in ascending order.

Both models declare a constructor, that is, the __init__ method. The constructor for the Notification model receives many arguments and uses them to initialize the attributes with the same names: message, ttl, and notification_category. The constructor for the NotificationCategory model receives a name argument and uses it to initialize the attribute with the same name.

Creating schemas to validate, serialize, and deserialize models

Now, we will create the Flask-Marshmallow schemas that we will use to validate, serialize, and deserialize the previously declared NotificationCategory and Notification models, and their relationships.

Open the models.py file within the service folder and add the following code after the last line. The lines that declare fields related to other schemas are highlighted in the code listing. The code file for the sample is included in the restful_python_2_02_01 folder, in the Flask01/service/models.py file:

```python
class NotificationCategorySchema(ma.Schema):
    id = fields.Integer(dump_only=True)
    # Minimum length = 3 characters
    name = fields.String(required=True,
        validate=validate.Length(3))
    url = ma.URLFor('service.notificationcategoryresource',
        id='<id>',
        _external=True)
    notifications = fields.Nested('NotificationSchema',
      many=True,
      exclude=('notification_category',))


class NotificationSchema(ma.Schema):
    id = fields.Integer(dump_only=True)
    # Minimum length = 5 characters
    message = fields.String(required=True,
        validate=validate.Length(5))
    ttl = fields.Integer()
    creation_date = fields.DateTime()
    notification_category =
fields.Nested(NotificationCategorySchema,
        only=['id', 'url', 'name'],
        required=True)
    displayed_times = fields.Integer()
    displayed_once = fields.Boolean()
```

```
    url = ma.URLFor('service.notificationresource',
        id='<id>',
        _external=True)

    @pre_load
    def process_notification_category(self, data):
        notification_category = data.get('notification_category')
        if notification_category:
            if isinstance(notification_category, dict):
                notification_category_name =
notification_category.get('name')
            else:
                notification_category_name = notification_category
            notification_category_dict =
dict(name=notification_category_name)
        else:
            notification_category_dict = {}
        data['notification_category'] = notification_category_dict
        return data
```

The code declares the following two schemas, that is, two subclasses of the `ma.Schema` class:

- `NotificationCategorySchema`
- `NotificationSchema`

We don't use the Flask-Marshmallow features that allow us to automatically determine the appropriate type for each attribute based on the fields declared in a model because we want to use specific options for each field.

We declare the attributes that represent fields as instances of the appropriate classes declared in the `marshmallow.fields` module. Whenever we specify the `True` value for the `dump_only` argument, it means that we want the field to be read-only. For example, we won't be able to provide a value for the `id` field in any of the schemas. The value for this field will be automatically generated by the auto-increment primary key in the PostgreSQL database.

The `NotificationCategorySchema` class declares the `name` attribute as an instance of `fields.String`. The `required` argument is set to `True` to specify that the field cannot be an empty string. The `validate` argument is set to `validate.Length(3)` to specify that the field must have a minimum length of three characters.

The class declares the `url` field with the following lines:

```
url = ma.URLFor('service.notificacion_categoryresource',
    id='<id>',
    _external=True)
```

The `url` attribute is an instance of the `ma.URLFor` class and this field will output the full URL of the resource, that is, the URL for the notification category. The first argument is the Flask endpoint's name: `'service.notificationcategoryresource'`. We will create a `NotificationCategoryResource` class later and the `URLFor` class will use it to generate the URL. The `id` argument specifies `'<id>'` because we want the `id` to be pulled from the object to be serialized. The `id` string enclosed within less than (<) and greater than (>) symbols specifies that we want the field to be pulled from the object that has to be serialized. The `_external` attribute is set to `True` because we want to generate the full URL for the resource. This way, every time we serialize a `NotificationCategory`, it will include the full URL for the resource in the `url` key or property.

In this case, we are using our insecure API behind HTTP. If our API is configured with HTTPS, we should set the `_scheme` argument to `'https'` when we create the `ma.URLFor` instance.

The class declares the `notifications` field with the following lines:

```
notifications = fields.Nested('NotificationSchema',
    many=True,
    exclude=('notification_category',))
```

The `notifications` attribute is an instance of the `marshmallow.fields.Nested` class, and this field will nest a collection of `Schema`, so, therefore, we specify `True` for the `many` argument. The first argument specifies the name for the nested `Schema` class as a string. We declare the `NotificationSchema` class after we defined the `NotificationCategorySchema` class. Thus, we specify the `Schema` class name as a string instead of using the type that we haven't defined yet.

In fact, we will end up with two objects that nest to each other; that is, we will create a two-way nesting between notification categories and notifications. We use the `exclude` parameter with a tuple of string to indicate that we want the `notification_category` field to be excluded from the fields that are serialized for each notification. This way, we avoid infinite recursion because the inclusion of the `notification_category` field would serialize all the notifications related to the category.

When we declared the `Notification` model, we used the `orm.relationship` function to provide a many-to-one relationship to the `NotificationCategory` model. The `backref` argument specified a call to the `orm.backref` function with `'notifications'` as the first value that indicates the name to use for the relation from the related `NotificationCategory` object back to a `Notification` object. With the previously explained line, we created the `notifications` fields that use the same name we indicated for the `db.backref` function.

The `NotificationSchema` class declares the `notification` attribute as an instance of `fields.String`. The `required` argument is set to `True` to specify that the field cannot be an empty string. The `validate` argument is set to `validate.Length(5)` to specify that the field must have a minimum length of five characters. The class declares the `ttl`, `creation_date`, `displayed_times`, and `displayed_once` fields with the corresponding classes based on the types we used in the `Message` model.

The class declares the `notification_category` field with the following lines:

```
notification_category = fields.Nested(CategorySchema,
    only=['id', 'url', 'name'],
    required=True)
```

The `notification_category` attribute is an instance of the `marshmallow.fields.Nested` class, and this field will nest a single `NotificationCategorySchema`. We specify `True` for the `required` argument because a notification must belong to a category. The first argument specifies the name for the nested `Schema` class. We already declared the `NotificationCategorySchema` class and, therefore, we specify `NotificationCategorySchema` as the value for the first argument. We use the `only` parameter with a list of strings to indicate the field names that we want to be included when the nested `NotificationCategorySchema` is serialized. We want the `id`, `url`, and `name` fields to be included. We don't specify the `notifications` field because we don't want the notification category to serialize the list of notifications that belong to it.

The class declares the `url` field with the following lines:

```
url = ma.URLFor('service.notificationresource',
    id='<id>',
    _external=True)
```

The url attribute is an instance of the ma.URLFor class and this field will output the full URL of the resource, that is, of the notification resource. The first argument is the Flask endpoint name: 'service.notificationresource'. We will create a NotificationResource class later and the URLFor class will use it to generate the URL. The id argument specifies '<id>' because we want id to be pulled from the object to be serialized. The _external attribute is set to True because we want to generate the full URL for the resource. This way, each time we serialize a Notification, it will include the full URL for the resource in the url key.

The NotificationSchema class declares a process_notification_category method that uses the @pre_load decorator, specifically, marshmallow.pre_load. This decorator registers a method to invoke before deserializing an object. This way, before Marshmallow deserializes a notification, the process_category method will be executed.

The method receives the data to be deserialized in the data argument and it returns the processed data. When we receive a request to POST a new notification, the notification category name can be specified in a key named 'notification_category'. If a category with the specified name exists, we will use the existing category as the one that is related to the new notification. If a category with the specified name doesn't exist, we will create a new notification category and then we will use this new category as the one that is related to the new notification. This way, we make it easy and straightforward for the user to create new notifications related to categories.

The data argument might have a notification category name specified as a string for the 'notification_category' key. However, in other cases, the 'notification_category' key will include the key-value pairs with the field name and field values for an existing notification category.

The code in the process_notification_category method checks the value of the 'notification_category' key and returns a dictionary with the appropriate data to make sure that we are able to deserialize a notification category with the appropriate key-value pairs, irrespective of the differences between the incoming data. Finally, the method returns the processed dictionary. We will dive deep on the work done by the process_notification_category method later when we start composing and sending HTTP requests to the new API.

Combining blueprints with resourceful routing

Now, we will create the resources that compose our main building blocks for the RESTful API. First, we will create a few instances that we will use in the different resources. Create a new `views.py` file within the `services` folder and add the following lines. Notice that the code imports the `HttpStatus` enum declared in the `http_status.py` module that we created in the previous chapter. The code file for the sample is included in the `restful_python_2_02_01` folder, in the `Flask01/service/views.py` file:

```
from flask import Blueprint, request, jsonify, make_response
from flask_restful import Api, Resource
from http_status import HttpStatus
from models import orm, NotificationCategory, NotificationCategorySchema,
Notification, NotificationSchema
from sqlalchemy.exc import SQLAlchemyError


service_blueprint = Blueprint('service', __name__)
notification_category_schema = NotificationCategorySchema()
notification_schema = NotificationSchema()
service = Api(service_blueprint)
```

The first lines declare the imports and create the following instances that we will use in the different classes:

- `service_blueprint`: This is an instance of the `flask.Blueprint` class that will allow us to factor the Flask application into this blueprint. The first argument specifies the URL prefix in which we want to register the blueprint: `'service'`.
- `notification_category_schema`: This is an instance of the `NotificationCategorySchema` class we declared in the `models.py` module. We will use this instance to validate, serialize, and deserialize notification categories.
- `notification_schema`: This is an instance of the `NotificationSchema` class we declared in the `models.py` module. We will use this instance to validate, serialize, and deserialize notifications.

- service: This is an instance of the `flask_restful.Api` class that represents the main entry point for the service. We pass the previously created `flask.Blueprint` instance named `service_blueprint` as an argument to link the `Api` to the `Blueprint`.

Now, we will create a `NotificationResource` class that we will use to represent the notification resource. Open the previously created `views.py` file within the `service` folder and add the following code after the last line. The code file for the sample is included in the `restful_python_2_02_01` folder, in the `Flask01/service/views.py` file:

```
class NotificationResource(Resource):
    def get(self, id):
        notification = Notification.query.get_or_404(id)
        dumped_notification = notification_schema.dump(notification).data
        return dumped_notification

    def patch(self, id):
        notification = Notification.query.get_or_404(id)
        notification_dict = request.get_json(force=True)
        if 'message' in notification_dict and
notification_dict['message'] is not None:
            notification.message = notification_dict['message']
        if 'ttl' in notification_dict and notification_dict['ttl']
is not None:
            notification.duration = notification_dict['duration']
        if 'displayed_times' in notification_dict and
notification_dict['displayed_times'] is not None:
            notification.displayed_times =
notification_dict['displayed_times']
        if 'displayed_once' in notification_dict and
notification_dict['displayed_once'] is not None:
            notification.displayed_once =
notification_dict['displayed_once']
        dumped_notification, dump_errors =
notification_schema.dump(message)
        if dump_errors:
            return dump_errors, HttpStatus.bad_request_400.value
        validate_errors = notification_schema.validate(dumped_notification)
        if validate_errors:
            return validate_errors, HttpStatus.bad_request_400.value
        try:
            notification.update()
            return self.get(id)
        except SQLAlchemyError as e:
                orm.session.rollback()
                response = {"error": str(e)}
                return response, HttpStatus.bad_request_400.value
```

```
def delete(self, id):
    notification = Notification.query.get_or_404(id)
    try:
        delete = notification.delete(notification)
        response = make_response()
        return response, HttpStatus.no_content_204.value
    except SQLAlchemyError as e:
            orm.session.rollback()
            response = {"error": str(e)}
            return response, HttpStatus.unauthorized_401.value
```

The `NotificationResource` class is a subclass of the `flask_restful.Resource` superclass and declares the following three methods that will be called when the HTTP method with the same name arrives as a request on the represented resource:

- `get`: This method receives the ID of the notification that has to be retrieved in the `id` argument. The code calls the `Notification.query.get_or_404` method to return an HTTP `404 Not Found` status in case there is no notification with the requested `id` in the underlying database. If the notification exists, the code calls the `notification_schema.dump` method with the retrieved message as an argument to use the `NotificationSchema` instance to serialize the `Notification` instance whose `id` matches the specified `id`. The `dump` method takes the `Notification` instance and applies the field filtering and output formatting specified in the `NotificationSchema` class. The code returns the `data` attribute of the result returned by the `dump` method, that is, the serialized message in JSON format as the body, with the default HTTP `200 OK` status code.

- `delete`: This method receives the ID of the notification that has to be deleted in the `id` argument. The code calls the `Notification.query.get_or_404` method to return an HTTP `404 Not Found` status in case there is no notification with the requested `id` in the underlying database. If the notification exists, the code calls the `notification.delete` method with the retrieved notification as an argument to use the `Notification` instance to erase itself from the database. Then, the code returns a tuple composed of an empty response body and a `204 No Content` status code. The returned status code in the tuple is specified with `HttpStatus.no_content_204.value`.

- `patch`: This method receives the ID of the notification that has to be updated or patched in the `id` argument. The code calls the `Notification.query.get_or_404` method to return an HTTP `404 Not Found` status if there is no notification with the requested `id` in the underlying database. If the notification exists, the code calls the `request.get_json` method to retrieve the key-value pairs received as arguments with the request. The code updates specific attributes if they have new values in the `notification_dict` dictionary in the `Notification` instance: `notification`. Then, the code calls the `notification_schema.dump` method to retrieve any errors generated when serializing the updated notification. If there were errors, the code returns a tuple composed of the errors and an HTTP `400 Bad Request` status. If the serialization didn't generate errors, the code calls the `notification_schema.validate` method to retrieve any errors generated when validating the updated notification. If there were validation errors, the code returns a tuple composed of the validation errors and an HTTP `400 Bad Request` status. If the validation is successful, the code calls the `update` method for the `Notification` instance to persist the changes in the database and returns the results of calling the previously explained `self.get` method with the ID of the updated notification as an argument. This way, the method returns the serialized updated notification in JSON format as the body, with the default HTTP `200 OK` status code.

Now, we will create a `NotificationListResource` class that we will use to represent the collection of notifications. Open the previously created `views.py` file within the `service` folder and add the following code after the last line. The code file for the sample is included in the `restful_python_2_02_01` folder, in the `Flask01/service/views.py` file:

```
class NotificationListResource(Resource):
    def get(self):
        notifications = Notification.query.all()
        dump_result = notification_schema.dump(notifications,
many=True).data
        return dump_result

    def post(self):
        notification_category_dict = request.get_json()
        if not notification_category_dict:
            response = {'message': 'No input data provided'}
            return response, HttpStatus.bad_request_400.value
        errors = notification_schema.validate(notification_category_dict)
        if errors:
            return errors, HttpStatus.bad_request_400.value
        try:
```

```
            notification_category_name =
notification_category_dict['notification_category']['name']
            notification_category =
NotificationCategory.query.filter_by(name=notification_category_name).first
()
            if notification_category is None:
                # Create a new NotificationCategory
                notification_category =
NotificationCategory(name=notification_category_name)
                orm.session.add(notification_category)
            # Now that we are sure we have a notification category,
            # we can create a new Notification
            notification = Notification(
                message=notification_category_dict['message'],
                ttl=notification_category_dict['ttl'],
                notification_category=notification_category)
            notification.add(notification)
            query = Notification.query.get(notification.id)
            dump_result = notification_schema.dump(query).data
            return dump_result, HttpStatus.created_201.value
        except SQLAlchemyError as e:
            orm.session.rollback()
            response = {"error": str(e)}
            return response, HttpStatus.bad_request_400.value
```

The `MessageListResource` class is a subclass of the `flask_restful.Resource` superclass and declares the following two methods that will be called when the HTTP method with the same name arrives as a request on the represented resource:

- `get`: This method returns a list with all the `Notification` instances saved in the database. First, the code calls the `Notification.query.all` method to retrieve all the `Notification` instances persisted in the database. Then, the code calls the `notification_schema.dump` method with the retrieved messages and the `many` argument set to `True` to serialize the iterable collection of objects. The `dump` method will take each `Notification` instance retrieved from the database and apply the field filtering and output formatting specified by the `NotificationSchema` class. The code returns the `data` attribute of the result returned by the `dump` method, that is, the serialized messages in JSON format as the body, with the default HTTP `200 OK` status code.

- `post`: This method retrieves the key-value pairs received in the JSON body, creates a new `Notification` instance, and persists it in the database. If the specified notification category name exists, it uses the existing category. Otherwise, the method creates a new `NotificationCategory` instance and associates the new `Notification` with this new notification category. First, the code calls the `request.get_json` method to retrieve the key-value pairs received as arguments with the request. Then, the code calls the `notification_schema.validate` method to validate the new notification built with the retrieved key-value pairs. Remember that the `NotificationSchema` class will execute the previously explained `process_notification_category` method before we call the `validate` method and, therefore, the data will be processed before the validation takes place. If there are validation errors, the code returns a tuple composed of the validation errors and an HTTP `400 Bad Request` status code. If the validation is successful, the code retrieves the notification category name received in the JSON body, specifically in the value for the `'name'` key of the `'notification_category'` key. Then, the code calls the `NotificationCategory.query.filter_by` method to retrieve a notification category that matches the retrieved notification category name. If no match is found, the code creates a new `NotificationCategory` with the retrieved name and persists it in the database. Then, the code creates a new notification with the `message`, `ttl`, and the appropriate `NotificationCategory` instance, and persists it in the database. Finally, the code returns the serialized saved notification in JSON format as the body, with the default HTTP `201 Created` status code.

Now, we will create a `NotificationCategoryResource` class that we will use to represent a notification category resource. Open the previously created `views.py` file within the `service` folder and add the following code after the last line. The code file for the sample is included in the `restful_python_2_02_01` folder, in the `Flask01/service/views.py` file:

```
class NotificationCategoryResource(Resource):
    def get(self, id):
        notification_category = NotificationCategory.query.get_or_404(id)
        dump_result =
notification_category_schema.dump(notification_category).data
        return dump_result

    def patch(self, id):
        notification_category = NotificationCategory.query.get_or_404(id)
        notification_category_dict = request.get_json()
        if not notification_category_dict:
```

```
            response = {'message': 'No input data provided'}
            return response, HttpStatus.bad_request_400.value
        errors =
notification_category_schema.validate(notification_category_dict)
        if errors:
            return errors, HttpStatus.bad_request_400.value
        try:
            if 'name' in notification_category_dict and
notification_category_dic['name'] is not None:
                notification_category.name =
notification_category_dict['name']
            notification_category.update()
            return self.get(id)
        except SQLAlchemyError as e:
            orm.session.rollback()
            response = {"error": str(e)}
            return response, HttpStatus.bad_request_400.value
    def delete(self, id):
        notification_category = NotificationCategory.query.get_or_404(id)
        try:
            notification_category.delete(notification_category)
            response = make_response()
            return response, HttpStatus.no_content_204.value
        except SQLAlchemyError as e:
            orm.session.rollback()
            response = {"error": str(e)}
            return response, HttpStatus.unauthorized_401.value
```

The NotificationCategoryResource class is a subclass of the flask_restful.Resource superclass and declares the following three methods that will be called when the HTTP method with the same name arrives as a request on the represented resource:

- get: This method receives the ID of the notification category that has to be retrieved in the id argument. The code calls the NotificationCategory.query.get_or_404 method to return an HTTP 404 Not Found status if there is no category with the requested id in the underlying database. If the notification category exists, the code calls the notification_category_schema.dump method with the retrieved notification category as an argument to use the NotificationCategorySchema instance to serialize the NotificationCategory instance whose id matches the specified id. The dump method takes the NotificationCategory instance and applies the field filtering and output formatting specified in the NotificationCategorySchema class. The code returns the data attribute of the result returned by the dump method, that is, the serialized message in JSON format as the body, with the default HTTP 200 OK status code.

- patch: This method receives the ID of the notification category that has to be updated or patched in the id argument. The code calls the Category.query.get_or_404 method to return an HTTP 404 Not Found status if there is no notification category with the requested id in the underlying database. If the notification category exists, the code calls the request.get_json method to retrieve the key-value pairs received as arguments with the request. The code updates just the name attribute in case it has a new value in the notification_category_dict dictionary in the NotificationCategory instance: notification_category. Then, the code calls the notification_category_schema.validate method to retrieve any errors generated when validating the updated notification category. If there are validation errors, the code returns a tuple composed of the validation errors and an HTTP 400 Bad Request status code. If the validation is successful, the code calls the update method for the NotificationCategory instance to persist the changes in the database and returns the results of calling the previously explained self.get method with the ID of the updated notification category as an argument. This way, the method returns the serialized updated notification category in JSON format as the body, with the default HTTP 200 OK status code.

- `delete`: This method receives the ID of the notification category that has to be deleted in the `id` argument. The code calls the `NotificationCategory.query.get_or_404` method to return an HTTP `404 Not Found` status if there is no notification category with the requested `id` in the underlying database. If the notification category exists, the code calls the `notification_category.delete` method with the retrieved notification category as an argument to use the `NotificationCategory` instance to erase itself from the database. Then, the code returns a tuple composed of an empty response body and a `204 No Content` status code.

Now, we will create a `NotificationCategoryListResource` class that we will use to represent the collection of notification categories. Open the previously created `views.py` file within the `service` folder and add the following code after the last line. The code file for the sample is included in the `restful_python_2_02_01` folder, in the `Flask01/service/views.py` file:

```
class NotificationCategoryListResource(Resource):
    def get(self):
        notification_categories = NotificationCategory.query.all()
        dump_results =
notification_category_schema.dump(notification_categories, many=True).data
        return dump_results

    def post(self):
        notification_category_dict = request.get_json()
        if not notification_category_dict:
            response = {'message': 'No input data provided'}
            return response, HttpStatus.bad_request_400.value
        errors =
notification_category_schema.validate(notification_category_dict)
        if errors:
            return errors, HttpStatus.bad_request_400.value
        try:
            notification_category =
NotificationCategory(notification_category_dict['name'])
            notification_category.add(notification_category)
            query =
NotificationCategory.query.get(notification_category.id)
            dump_result =
notification_category_schema.dump(query).data
            return dump_result, HttpStatus.created_201.value
        except SQLAlchemyError as e:
            orm.session.rollback()
            response = {"error": str(e)}
            return response, HttpStatus.bad_request_400.value
```

The CategoryListResource class is a subclass of the flask_restful.Resource superclass and declares the following two methods that will be called when the HTTP method with the same name arrives as a request on the represented resource:

- get: This method returns a list with all the NotificationCategory instances saved in the database. First, the code calls the NotificationCategory.query.all method to retrieve all the NotificationCategory instances persisted in the database. Then, the code calls the notification_category_schema.dump method with the retrieved notifications and the many argument set to True to serialize the iterable collection of objects. The dump method will take each NotificationCategory instance retrieved from the database and apply the field filtering and output formatting specified by the NotificationCategorySchema class. The code returns the data attribute of the result returned by the dump method, that is, the serialized notification categories in JSON format as the body, with the default HTTP 200 OK status code.

- post: This method retrieves the key-value pairs received in the JSON body, creates a new NotificationCategory instance, and persists it in the database. First, the code calls the request.get_json method to retrieve the key-value pairs received as arguments with the request. Then, the code calls the notification_category_schema.validate method to validate the new notification category built with the retrieved key-value pairs. If there are validation errors, the code returns a tuple composed of the validation errors and an HTTP 400 Bad Request status code. If the validation is successful, the code creates a new notification category with the specified name, and persists it in the database. Finally, the code returns the serialized saved category in JSON format as the body, with the HTTP 201 Created status code.

Understanding and configuring resourceful routing

The following table shows the method of our previously created classes that we want to be executed for each combination of HTTP verb and scope:

HTTP verb	Scope	Class and method
GET	Collection of notifications	NotificationListResource.get
GET	Notification	NotificationResource.get
POST	Collection of notifications	NotificationListResource.post
PATCH	Notification	NotificationResource.patch
DELETE	Notification	NotificationResource.delete
GET	Collection of notification categories	NotificationCategoryListResource.get
GET	Notification category	NotificationCategoryResource.get
POST	Collection of notification categories	NotificationCategoryListResource.post
PATCH	Notification category	NotificationCategoryResource.patch
DELETE	Notification category	NotificationCategoryResource.delete

If the request results in the invocation of a resource with an unsupported HTTP method, Flask-RESTful will return a response with the HTTP 405 Method Not Allowed status code.

We must make the necessary resource routing configurations to call the appropriate methods and pass them all the necessary arguments by defining URL rules. The following lines configure the resource routing for the service. Open the previously created views.py file within the service folder and add the following code after the last line. The code file for the sample is included in the restful_python_2_02_01 folder, in the Flask01/service/views.py file:

```
service.add_resource(NotificationCategoryListResource,
    '/notification_categories/')
service.add_resource(NotificationCategoryResource,
    '/notification_categories/<int:id>')
service.add_resource(NotificationListResource,
    '/notifications/')
service.add_resource(NotificationResource,
    '/notifications/<int:id>')
```

Each call to the `service.add_resource` method routes a URL to a resource; specifically, to one of the previously declared subclasses of the `flask_restful.Resource` superclass. Whenever there is a request to the API, and the URL matches one of the URLs specified in the `service.add_resource` method, Flask will call the method that matches the HTTP verb in the request for the specified class.

Registering the blueprint and running migrations

Create a new `app.py` file within the `service` folder. The following lines show the code that creates a Flask application. The code file for the sample is included in the `restful_python_2_02_01` folder, in the `Flask01/service/app.py` file:

```
from flask import Flask
from flask_sqlalchemy import SQLAlchemy
from flask_migrate import Migrate
from models import orm
from views import service_blueprint


def create_app(config_filename):
    app = Flask(__name__)
    app.config.from_object(config_filename)
    orm.init_app(app)
    app.register_blueprint(service_blueprint, url_prefix='/service')
    migrate = Migrate(app, orm)
    return app


app = create_app('config')
```

The code in the `service/app.py` file declares a `create_app` function that receives the configuration filename in the `config_filename` argument, customizes the SQLAlchemy database settings for the Flask app with this configuration file, and returns the `app` object. First, the function creates the main entry point for the Flask application named `app`. Then, the code calls the `app.config.from_object` method with the `config_filename` received as an argument. This way, the Flask app uses the values specified in the variables defined in the Python module received as an argument to set up the SQLAlchemy settings for the Flask app.

The next line calls the `init_app` method for the `flask_sqlalchemy.SQLAlchemy` instance created in the `models` module named `orm`. The code passes `app` as an argument to link the created Flask app with the SQLAlchemy instance.

The next line calls the `app.register_blueprint` method to register the blueprint created in the `views` module, named `service_blueprint`. The `url_prefix` argument is set to `'/service'` because we want the resources to be available with `/service` as a prefix. This way, `http://localhost:5000/service/` is going to be the URL for the API running on the Flask development server.

The next line creates an instance of `flask_migrate.Migrate` with the created Flask app, `app`, and the `flask_sqlalchemy.SQLAlchemy` instance created in the `models` module, `orm`. Finally, the `create_app` function returns the `app` object.

Then, the code calls the `create_app` function with `'config'` as an argument. The function will set up a Flask app with this module as the configuration file and the object is saved in the `app` variable. Notice that there is no code to start the Flask application with the host, port and debug values because we will use the `flask` **CLI** (short for **command-line script**) for this goal.

Now, we will use the `flask` CLI to run migrations and generate the necessary tables in the PostgreSQL 10.5 database. Make sure you run the scripts in the Terminal or Command Prompt window in which you have activated the virtual environment, and that you are located within the `service` folder.

In this case, we don't need to set the module name that creates the `flask` app in the `FLASK_APP` environment variable because the module is named `app`. The `flask` application discovery procedure will automatically use this module.

Run the first command that initializes migration support for the application:

```
flask db init
```

The following lines show the sample output generated after running the previous script. Notice that your output will be different according to the base folder in which you have created the virtual environment:

```
Creating directory
/Users/gaston/HillarPythonREST2/Flask01/service/migrations ... done
Creating directory
/Users/gaston/HillarPythonREST2/Flask01/service/migrations/versions ...
done
Generating
/Users/gaston/HillarPythonREST2/Flask01/service/migrations/script.py.mako
```

```
... done
Generating
/Users/gaston/HillarPythonREST2/Flask01/service/migrations/env.py ... done
Generating
/Users/gaston/HillarPythonREST2/Flask01/service/migrations/README ... done
Generating
/Users/gaston/HillarPythonREST2/Flask01/service/migrations/alembic.ini ...
done
        Please edit configuration/connection/logging settings in

'/Users/gaston/HillarPythonREST2/Flask01/service/migrations/alembic.ini'
before proceeding.
```

The script generated a new `migrations` subfolder within the `service` folder, with a `versions` subfolder and many other files.

Whenever you work with a version control system, you must add the new migrations sub-folder to version control.

Now, we will execute the second command that populates the migration script with the detected changes in the models. In this case, it is the first time we populate the migration script and, therefore, the migration script will generate the tables that will persist our two models: `NotificationCategory` and `Notification`:

```
flask db migrate
```

The following lines show the sample output generated after running the previous command. Your output will be different according to the base folder in which you have created the virtual environment:

```
INFO  [alembic.runtime.migration] Context impl PostgresqlImpl.
INFO  [alembic.runtime.migration] Will assume transactional DDL.
INFO  [alembic.autogenerate.compare] Detected added table
'notification_category'
INFO  [alembic.autogenerate.compare] Detected added table
'notification'
  Generating
/Users/gaston/HillarPythonREST2/Flask01/service/migrations
/versions/03f5d0f0642a_.py ... done
```

The output indicates that the `service/migrations/versions/03f5d0f0642a_.py` file includes the code to create the `notification_category` and `notification` tables. The following lines show the code for this file that was automatically generated based on the code for the `NotificationCategory` and `Notification` models. Notice that the filename will be different in your configuration. The code file for the sample is included in the `restful_python_2_02_01` folder, in the `Flask01/service/migrations/versions/03f5d0f0642a_.py` file:

```
"""empty message

Revision ID: 03f5d0f0642a
Revises:
Create Date: 2018-10-16 15:25:44.407608

"""
from alembic import op
import sqlalchemy as sa


# revision identifiers, used by Alembic.
revision = '03f5d0f0642a'
down_revision = None
branch_labels = None
depends_on = None


def upgrade():
    # ### commands auto generated by Alembic - please adjust! ###
    op.create_table('notification_category',
    sa.Column('id', sa.Integer(), nullable=False),
    sa.Column('name', sa.String(length=150), nullable=False),
    sa.PrimaryKeyConstraint('id'),
    sa.UniqueConstraint('name')
    )
    op.create_table('notification',
    sa.Column('id', sa.Integer(), nullable=False),
    sa.Column('message', sa.String(length=250), nullable=False),
    sa.Column('ttl', sa.Integer(), nullable=False),
    sa.Column('creation_date', sa.TIMESTAMP(),
server_default=sa.text('CURRENT_TIMESTAMP'), nullable=False),
    sa.Column('notification_category_id', sa.Integer(), nullable=False),
    sa.Column('displayed_times', sa.Integer(), server_default='0',
nullable=False),
    sa.Column('displayed_once', sa.Boolean(), server_default='false',
nullable=False),
    sa.ForeignKeyConstraint(['notification_category_id'],
['notification_category.id'], ondelete='CASCADE'),
```

```
        sa.PrimaryKeyConstraint('id'),
        sa.UniqueConstraint('message')
        )
        # ### end Alembic commands ###


    def downgrade():
        # ### commands auto generated by Alembic - please adjust! ###
        op.drop_table('notification')
        op.drop_table('notification_category')
        # ### end Alembic commands ###
```

The automatically generated code defines the following two functions:

- upgrade: This function runs the necessary code to create the
  notification_category and notification tables by making calls to
  the alembic.op.create_table method.
- downgrade: This function runs the necessary code to go back to the previous
  version.

Run the third command to upgrade the database:

flask db upgrade

The following lines show the sample output generated after running the previous script:

```
INFO   [alembic.runtime.migration] Context impl PostgresqlImpl.
INFO   [alembic.runtime.migration] Will assume transactional DDL.
INFO   [alembic.runtime.migration] Running upgrade  -> 03f5d0f0642a,
empty message
```

The previous script called the upgrade function defined in the automatically generated
api/migrations/versions/03f5d0f0642a_.py script. Don't forget that the filename
will be different in your configuration.

Verifying the contents of the PostgreSQL database

After we run the previous scripts, we can use the PostgreSQL command line or any other
application that allows us to easily verify the contents of the PostgreSQL 10.5 database to
check the tables that the migration generated.

Run the following command to list the generated tables. If the database name you are using is not named `flask_notifications`, make sure you use the appropriate database name. The code file for the sample is included in the `restful_python_2_02_01` folder, in the `Flask01/list_database_tables.sql` file:

```
psql --username=your_user_name --dbname=flask_notifications --command="\dt"
```

The following lines show the output with all the generated table names:

```
                    List of relations

 Schema |          Name          | Type  |     Owner
--------+------------------------+-------+----------------
 public | alembic_version        | table | your_user_name
 public | notification           | table | your_user_name
 public | notification_category  | table | your_user_name
(3 rows)
```

SQLAlchemy generated the following two tables with the unique constraints and the foreign keys based on the information included in our models:

- `notification_category`: This table persists the `NotificationCategory` model.
- `notification`: This table persists the `Notification` model.

The following command will allow you to check the contents of the two tables after we compose and send HTTP requests to the RESTful API and execute CRUD operations on the two tables. The commands assume that you are running PostgreSQL 10.5 on the same computer in which you are running the command. The code file for the sample is included in the `restful_python_2_02_01` folder, in the `Flask01/check_tables_contents.sql` file:

```
psql --username=your_user_name --dbname=flask_notifications --command="SELECT * FROM notification_category;"
psql --username=your_user_name --dbname=flask_notifications --command="SELECT * FROM notification;"
```

Instead of working with the PostgreSQL command-line utility, you can use your favorite GUI tool to check the contents of the PostgreSQL database.

Alembic generated an additional table named `alembic_version` that saves the version number for the database in the `version_num` column. This table makes it possible for the migration commands to retrieve the current version for the database and upgrade or downgrade it based on our needs.

Creating and retrieving related resources

Now, we will use the flask script to launch Flask's development server and our RESTful API. We want to enable the debug mode and, therefore, we will set the value for the `FLASK_ENV` environment variable to `development`.

Run the following command in the Terminal in Linux or macOS with a bash shell:

```
export FLASK_ENV=development
```

In Windows, if you are using the Command Prompt, run the following command:

```
set FLASK_ENV=development
```

In Windows, if you are using Windows PowerShell, run the following command:

```
$env:FLASK_ENV = "development"
```

Now, run the `flask` script that launches Flask's development server and the application.

Now that the `FLASK_ENV` environment variable is configured to work in development mode with the debug mode enabled, we can run the `service/run.py` script that launches Flask's development server and the application. Execute the following command within the `service` folder:

```
flask run
```

The following lines show the output after we execute the previous command. The development server is listening at port `5000`:

```
* Environment: development
* Debug mode: on
* Running on http://127.0.0.1:5000/ (Press CTRL+C to quit)
* Restarting with stat
* Debugger is active!
* Debugger PIN: 173-629-578
```

We can use the following settings with the `flask run` script to configure the interface and the port to which we want to bind the Flask development server:

- `-p`: This setting must be followed by the port to which we want to bind the Flask development server.
- `-h`: This setting must be followed by the interface to which we want to bind the Flask development server.

For example, if we want the development server to listen on every interface on port `5000`, we must run the following command:

```
flask run -h 0.0.0.0
```

The default port is `5000`. If we want to specify another port, we must use the `-p` option, followed by the desired port number.

Now, we will use the `http` command or its `curl` equivalents to compose and send HTTP requests to the API. We will use JSON for the requests that require additional data. Remember that you can perform the same tasks with your favorite GUI-based tool.

First, we will compose and send HTTP requests to create two notification categories. The code file for the sample is included in the `restful_python_2_02_01` folder, in the `Flask01/cmd201.txt` file:

```
http POST ":5000/service/notification_categories/"name='Information'
http POST ":5000/service/notification_categories/" name='Warning'
```

The following are the equivalent `curl` commands. The code file for the sample is included in the `restful_python_2_02_01` folder, in the `Flask01/cmd202.txt` file.

```
curl -iX POST -H "Content-Type: application/json" -d
'{"name":"Information"}' "localhost:5000/service/notification_categories/"
curl -iX POST -H "Content-Type: application/json" -d '{"name":"Warning"}'
"localhost:5000/service/notification_categories/"
```

The previous commands will compose and send two POST HTTP requests with the specified JSON key-value pair. The requests specify `/service/notification_categories/` and, therefore, they will match the `'/service'`url_prefix for the `service_blueprint` blueprint. Then, the request will match the `'/notification_categories/'` URL route for the `NotificationCategoryList` resource and run the `NotificationCategoryList.post` method. The method doesn't receive arguments because the URL route doesn't include any parameters.

As the HTTP verb for the request is POST, Flask calls the post method. If the two new
NotificationCategory instances were successfully persisted in the database, the two
calls will return an HTTP 201 Created status code and the recently persisted
NotificationCategory serialized to JSON in the response body. The following lines
show an example response for the two HTTP requests, with the new
NotificationCategory objects in the JSON responses. Notice that the responses include
the URL for each created notification category as the value for the url key. The
notifications array is empty in both cases because there aren't any messages related to
each new category yet:

```
HTTP/1.0 201 CREATED
Content-Length: 138
Content-Type: application/json
Date: Tue, 16 Oct 2018 23:33:59 GMT
Server: Werkzeug/0.14.1 Python/3.6.6

{
    "id": 1,
    "name": "Information",
    "notifications": [],
    "url": "http://localhost:5000/service/notification_categories/1"
}

HTTP/1.0 201 CREATED
Content-Length: 134
Content-Type: application/json
Date: Tue, 16 Oct 2018 23:34:24 GMT
Server: Werkzeug/0.14.1 Python/3.6.6

{
    "id": 2,
    "name": "Warning",
    "notifications": [],
    "url": "http://localhost:5000/service/notification_categories/2"
}
```

Now, we will compose and send HTTP requests to create two notifications that belong to
the first notification category we recently created: Information. We will specify the
notification_category key with the name of the desired notification category.

The database table that persists the `Notification` model, that is, the `notification` table, will save the value of the primary key of the related `NotificationCategory` whose `name` value matches the one we provide. The code file for the sample is included in the `restful_python_2_02_01` folder, in the `Flask01/cmd203.txt` file:

```
http POST ":5000/service/notifications/" message='eSports competition
finishes in 10 minutes' ttl=30 notification_category="Information"
http POST ":5000/service/notifications/" message='No winners yet' ttl=15
notification_category="Warning"
```

The following are the equivalent `curl` commands. The code file for the sample is included in the `restful_python_2_02_01` folder, in the `Flask01/cmd204.txt` file:

```
curl -iX POST -H "Content-Type: application/json" -d '{"message":"eSports
competition finishes in 10 minutes", "ttl":30,
"notification_category":"Information"}'
"localhost:5000/service/notifications/"
curl -iX POST -H "Content-Type: application/json" -d '{"message":"No
winners yet", "ttl": 15, "notification_category":"Warning"}'
"localhost:5000/service/notifications/"
```

The first command will compose and send the following HTTP request—POST `http://localhost:5000/service/notifications/` with the following JSON key-value pairs:

```
{
    "message": "Checking temperature sensor",
    "notification_category": "Information",
    "ttl": 30
}
```

The second command will compose and send the same HTTP request with the following JSON key-value pairs:

```
{
    "message": "Checking light sensor",
    "category": "Information",
    "ttl": 15
}
```

The requests specify `/service/notifications/` and, therefore, they will match the `'/service'url_prefix` for the `service_blueprint` blueprint. Then, the request will match the `'/notifications/'` URL route for the `NotificationList` resource and run the `NotificationList.post` method. The method doesn't receive arguments because the URL route doesn't include any parameters. As the HTTP verb for the request is `POST`, Flask calls the `post` method. The `NotificationSchema.process_notification_category` method will process the data for the notification category and the `NotificationListResource.post` method will retrieve the `NotificationCategory` instance that matches the specified category name from the database, to use it as the related category for the new notification.

If the two new `Notification` instances were successfully persisted in the database, the two calls will return an HTTP `201 Created` status code and the recently persisted `Notification` serialized to JSON in the response body. The following lines show an example response for the two HTTP requests, with the new `Notification` objects in the JSON responses. Notice that the responses include the URL for each created notification as the value for the `url` key. In addition, the response includes the `id`, `name`, and `url` for the related notification category:

```
HTTP/1.0 201 CREATED
Content-Length: 423
Content-Type: application/json
Date: Wed, 17 Oct 2018 00:57:15 GMT
Server: Werkzeug/0.14.1 Python/3.6.6
{
    "creation_date": "2018-10-16T21:57:15.867853+00:00",
    "displayed_once": false,
    "displayed_times": 0,
    "id": 1,
    "message": "eSports competition finishes in 10 minutes",
    "notification_category": {
        "id": 1,
        "name": "Information",
        "url":
"http://localhost:5000/service/notification_categories/1"
    },
    "ttl": 30,
    "url": "http://localhost:5000/service/notifications/1"
}
HTTP/1.0 201 CREATED
Content-Length: 391
Content-Type: application/json
Date: Wed, 17 Oct 2018 00:58:43 GMT
Server: Werkzeug/0.14.1 Python/3.6.6
{
```

```
            "creation_date": "2018-10-16T21:58:43.737812+00:00",
            "displayed_once": false,
            "displayed_times": 0,
            "id": 2,
            "message": "No winners yet",
            "notification_category": {
                "id": 2,
                "name": "Warning",
                "url":
    "http://localhost:5000/service/notification_categories/2"
            },
            "ttl": 15,
            "url": "http://localhost:5000/service/notifications/2"
        }
```

We can run the previously explained commands to check the contents of the tables that the migrations command created in the PostgreSQL database. We will notice that the `notification_category_id` column for the `notification` table saves the value of the primary key of the related row in the `notification_category` table. The `NotificationSchema` class uses a `fields.Nested` instance to render the `id`, `url`, and `name` fields for the related `NotificationCategory`. The following screenshot shows the contents for the `notification_category` and the `notification` table in a PostgreSQL 10.5 database after running the HTTP requests:

Now, we will compose and send an HTTP request to retrieve the notification category that contains two messages; that is, the notification category resource whose `id` or primary key is equal to `1`. Don't forget to replace `1` with the primary key value of the notification category whose name is equal to `'Information'` in your configuration. The code file for the sample is included in the `restful_python_2_02_01` folder, in the `Flask01/cmd205.txt` file:

```
http ":5000/service/notification_categories/1"
```

The following is the equivalent `curl` command. The code file for the sample is included in the `restful_python_2_02_01` folder, in the `Flask01/cmd206.txt` file:

```
curl -iX GET "localhost:5000/service/categories/1"
```

The previous command will compose and send a GET HTTP request. The request has a number after `/service/notification_ategories/` and, therefore, it will match `'/notification_categories/<int:id>'` and run the `NotificationCategoryResource.get` method, that is, the `get` method for the `NotificationCategoryResource` class. If a `NotificationCategory` instance with the specified `id` exists in the database, the call to the method will return an HTTP 200 OK status code and the `NotificationCategory` instance serialized to JSON in the response body. The `NotificationCategorySchema` class uses a `fields.Nested` instance to render all the fields for all the notifications related to the category with the exception of the notification category field. The following lines show a sample response:

```
HTTP/1.0 200 OK
Content-Length: 479
Content-Type: application/json
Date: Wed, 17 Oct 2018 01:55:18 GMT
Server: Werkzeug/0.14.1 Python/3.6.6
{
    "id": 1,
    "name": "Information",
    "notifications": [
        {
            "creation_date": "2018-10-16T21:57:15.867853+00:00",
            "displayed_once": false,
            "displayed_times": 0,
            "id": 1,
            "message": "eSports competition finishes in 10
            minutes",
            "ttl": 30,
            "url": "http://localhost:5000/service/notifications/1"
        }
    ],
    "url":"http://localhost:5000/service/notification_categories/1"
}
```

Now, we will compose and send a POST HTTP request to create a notification related to a notification category name that doesn't exist: `'Error'`. The code file for the sample is included in the `restful_python_2_02_01` folder, in the `Flask01/cmd207.txt` file:

```
http POST ":5000/service/notifications/" message='Score calculation error'
ttl=30 notification_category="Error"
```

The following is the equivalent `curl` command. The code file for the sample is included in the `restful_python_2_02_01` folder, in the `Flask01/cmd208.txt` file:

```
curl -iX POST -H "Content-Type: application/json" -d '{"message":"Score
calculation error", "ttl":30, "notification_category":"Error"}'
":5000/service/notifications/"
```

The `NotificationCategoryListResource.post` method won't be able to retrieve a `NotificationCategory` instance whose `name` is equal to the specified value and, therefore, the method will create a new `NotificationCategory`, save it, and use it as the related notification category for the new notification.

The following lines show an example response for the HTTP request, with the new `Notification` object in the JSON responses and the details of the new `NotificationCategory` object related to the notification:

```
HTTP/1.0 201 CREATED
Content-Length: 398
Content-Type: application/json
Date: Wed, 17 Oct 2018 02:07:27 GMT
Server: Werkzeug/0.14.1 Python/3.6.6
{
    "creation_date": "2018-10-16T23:07:27.372778+00:00",
    "displayed_once": false,
    "displayed_times": 0,
    "id": 3,
    "message": "Score calculation error",
    "notification_category": {
        "id": 3,
        "name": "Error",
        "url":
"http://localhost:5000/service/notification_categories/3"
    },
    "ttl": 30,
    "url": "http://localhost:5000/service/notifications/3"
}
```

We can run the previously explained commands to check the contents of the tables that the migrations command created in the PostgreSQL 10.5 database. We will notice that we have a new row in the `notification_category` table with the recently added notification category when we created a new notification. The following screenshot shows the contents for the `notification_category` and `notification` tables in the PostgreSQL database after running the HTTP requests:

Test your knowledge

Let's see whether you can answer the following questions correctly:

1. Which of the following commands start the Flask development server and the Flask application, and makes it listen on every interface on port `5000`?:
    1. `flask run -h 0.0.0.0`
    2. `flask run -p 0.0.0.0 -h 5000`
    3. `flask run -p 0.0.0.0`

2. `Flask-Migrate` is:
    1. A lightweight library for converting complex datatypes to and from native Python datatypes.
    2. A library that uses the Alembic package to handle SQLAlchemy database migrations for Flask applications.
    3. A library that replaces SQLAlchemy to run queries on PostgreSQL.

3. Marshmallow is:
    1. A lightweight library for converting complex datatypes to and from native Python datatypes.
    2. An ORM.
    3. A lightweight web framework that replaces Flask.

4. SQLAlchemy is:
   1. A lightweight library for converting complex datatypes to and from native Python datatypes.
   2. An ORM.
   3. A lightweight web framework that replaces Flask.

5. The `marshmallow.pre_load` decorator:
   1. Registers a method to run after any instance of the `Resource` class is created.
   2. Registers a method to invoke after serializing an object.
   3. Registers a method to invoke before deserializing an object.

6. The `dump` method for any instance of a `Schema` subclass:
   1. Routes URLs to Python primitives.
   2. Persists the instance or collection of instances passed as an argument to the database.
   3. Takes the instance or collection of instances passed as an argument and applies the field filtering and output formatting specified in the `Schema` subclass to the instance or collection of instances.

7. When we declare an attribute as an instance of the `marshmallow.fields.Nested` class:
   1. The field will nest a single `Schema` or a collection of `Schema` based on the value for the `many` argument.
   2. The field will nest a single `Schema`. If we want to nest a collection of `Schema`, we have to use an instance of the `marshmallow.fields.NestedCollection` class.
   3. The field will nest a collection of `Schema`. If we want to nest a single `Schema`, we have to use an instance of the `marshmallow.fields.NestedSingle` class.

Summary

In this chapter, we expanded the capabilities of the previous version of the RESTful API we created in the preceding chapter. We used SQLAlchemy as our ORM to work with a PostgreSQL 10.5 database. We added many packages to simplify many common tasks, we wrote code for the models and their relationships, and we worked with schemas to validate, serialize, and deserialize these models.

We combined blueprints with resourceful routing, and we were able to generate the database from the models. We composed and sent many HTTP requests to our RESTful API and analyzed how each HTTP request was processed in our code and how the models persisted in the database tables.

Now that we have built a complex API with Flask, Flask-RESTful, and SQLAlchemy, we will utilize additional features; we will add security and authentication, which are the topics of the next chapter.

3
Improving Our API and Adding Authentication to it with Flask

In this chapter, we will improve the capabilities of the RESTful API that we started in the previous chapter and we will add authentication-related security to it. We will do the following:

- Improve unique constraints in the models
- Understand the differences between the PUT and the PATCH methods
- Update fields for a resource with the PATCH method
- Code a generic pagination class
- Add pagination features to the API
- Understand the steps to add authentication and permissions
- Add a user model
- Create a schema to validate, serialize, and deserialize users
- Add authentication to resources
- Create resource classes to handle users
- Run migrations to generate the user table
- Compose requests with the necessary authentication

Improving unique constraints in the models

When we coded the NotificationCategory model in the previous chapter, we specified the True value for the unique argument in the creation of the orm.Column instance named name. As a result, the migrations process generated the necessary unique constraint to make sure that the name field has unique values in the notification_category table. This way, the PostgreSQL database won't allow us to insert duplicate values for the notification_category.name column. However, the error message generated when we try to do so is not clear. The message includes details about the database structure that shouldn't be mentioned in the error message.

Run the following command to create a category with a duplicate name. There is already an existing category with the name equal to 'Warning'. The code file for the sample is included in the restful_python_2_03_01 folder, in the Flask01/cmd301.txt file:

```
http POST ":5000/service/notification_categories/" name='Warning'
```

The following is the equivalent curl command. The code file for the sample is included in the restful_python_2_03_01 folder, in the Flask01/cmd302.txt file:

```
curl -iX POST -H "Content-Type: application/json" -d '
{"name":"Warning"}'
"localhost:5000/service/notification_categories/"
```

The previous command will compose and send a POST HTTP request with the specified JSON key-value pair. The unique constraint in the notification_category.name field won't allow the PostgreSQL database table to persist the new notification category. Thus, the request will return an HTTP 400 Bad Request status code with an integrity error message. The following lines show a sample response:

```
HTTP/1.0 400 BAD REQUEST
Content-Length: 370
Content-Type: application/json
Date: Thu, 18 Oct 2018 01:08:24 GMT
Server: Werkzeug/0.14.1 Python/3.7.1
{
    "error": "(psycopg2.IntegrityError) duplicate key value
violates unique constraint
\"notification_category_name_key\"\nDETAIL:  Key (name)=(Warning)
already exists.\n [SQL: 'INSERT INTO notification_category (name)
VALUES (%(name)s) RETURNING notification_category.id'] [parameters:
{'name': 'Warning'}] (Background on this error at:
http://sqlalche.me/e/gkpj)"
}
```

Obviously, the error message is extremely technical and provides too many details about the database and the query that failed. It is definitely not an appropriate error message for an API that will run as a microservice.

We might parse the error message to automatically generate a more user-friendly error message. However, instead of doing so, we want to avoid trying to insert a row that we know will fail. We will add code to make sure that a notification category is unique before we try to persist it. Of course, there is still a chance to receive the previously shown error if somebody inserts a notification category with the same name between the time we run our code that indicates a notification category name is unique, and we persist the changes in the database. However, the chances are lower.

In a production-ready REST API that runs as a microservice, we should never return the error messages returned by SQLAlchemy or any other database-related data, as it might include sensitive information that we don't want the users of our microservice to be able to retrieve. In this case, we are returning all the errors for debugging purposes and to be able to improve our API.

Now we will add a new class method to our existing `NotificationCategory` class to allow us to determine whether a name is unique or not. Open the `models.py` file within the `service` folder and add the following lines within the declaration of the `NotificationCategory` class. The code file for the sample is included in the `restful_python_2_03_01` folder, in the `Flask01/service/models.py` file:

```
    @classmethod
    def is_name_unique(cls, id, name):
        existing_notification_category =
cls.query.filter_by(name=name).first()
        if existing_notification_category is None:
            return True
        else:
            if existing_notification_category.id == id:
                return True
            else:
                return False
```

The new `NotificationCategory.is_name_unique` class method receives the `id` and the `name` arguments for the notification category that we want, to make sure that it has a unique name. If the notification category is a new one that hasn't been saved yet, we will receive a `0` for the `id` value because the database sequence didn't generate the value for `id`. Otherwise, we will receive the notification category ID in the `id` argument.

The method calls the `query.filter_by` method for the current class, `cls`, to retrieve a notification category whose `name` matches another notification category name. If there is a notification category that matches the criteria, the method will return `True` only if the `id` is the same one than the one received in the `id` argument. If no notification category matches the criteria, the method will return `True`.

Now we will use the previously created class method to check whether a category is unique or not before creating and persisting it in the `NotificationCategoryListResource.post` method. Open the `views.py` file within the `service` folder and replace the existing `post` method declared in the `NotificationCategoryListResource` class with the following lines. The lines that have been added or edited are highlighted. The code file for the sample is included in the `restful_python_2_03_01` folder, in the `Flask01/service/views.py` file:

```python
def post(self):
    print("Processing")
    notification_category_dict = request.get_json()
    if not notification_category_dict:
        response = {'message': 'No input data provided'}
        return response, HttpStatus.bad_request_400.value
    errors =
notification_category_schema.validate(notification_category_dict)
    if errors:
        return errors, HttpStatus.bad_request_400.value
    notification_category_name =
notification_category_dict['name']
    if not NotificationCategory.is_name_unique(id=0,
name=notification_category_name):
        response = {'error': 'A notification category with
the name {} already exists'.format(notification_category_name)}
        return response, HttpStatus.bad_request_400.value
    try:
        notification_category =
NotificationCategory(notification_category_name)
        notification_category.add(notification_category)
        query =
NotificationCategory.query.get(notification_category.id)
        dump_result = notification_category_schema.dump(query).data
        return dump_result, HttpStatus.created_201.value
    except SQLAlchemyError as e:
        print("Error")
        print(e)
        orm.session.rollback()
        response = {"error": str(e)}
        return response, HttpStatus.bad_request_400.value
```

Now we will perform the same validation in the
NotificationCategoryResource.patch method. Open the views.py file within the
service folder and replace the existing patch method declared in the
NotificationCategoryResource class with the following lines. The lines that have been
added or edited are highlighted. The code file for the sample is included in the
restful_python_2_03_01 folder, in the Flask01/service/views.py file:

```python
def patch(self, id):
    notification_category = NotificationCategory.query.get_or_404(id)
    notification_category_dict = request.get_json()
    if not notification_category_dict:
        response = {'message': 'No input data provided'}
        return response, HttpStatus.bad_request_400.value
    errors =
notification_category_schema.validate(notification_category_dict)
    if errors:
        return errors, HttpStatus.bad_request_400.value
    try:
        if 'name' in notification_category_dict and
notification_category_dict['name'] is not None:
            notification_category_name =
notification_category_dict['name']
            if NotificationCategory.is_name_unique(id=id,
name=notification_category_name):
                notification_category.name =
notification_category_name
            else:
                response = {'error': 'A category with the
name {} already exists'.format(notification_category_name)}
                return response,
HttpStatus.bad_request_400.value
        notification_category.update()
        return self.get(id)
    except SQLAlchemyError as e:
        orm.session.rollback()
        response = {"error": str(e)}
        return response, HttpStatus.bad_request_400.value
```

Run the following command to create a notification category with a duplicate name again.
The code file for the sample is included in the restful_python_2_03_01 folder, in the
Flask01/cmd303.txt file:

```
http POST ":5000/service/notification_categories/" name='Error'
```

The following is the equivalent `curl` command. The code file for the sample is included in the `restful_python_2_03_01` folder, in the `Flask01/cmd304.txt` file:

```
curl -iX POST -H "Content-Type: application/json" -d
'{"name":"Error"}' "localhost:5000/service/notification_categories/"
```

The previous command will compose and send a POST HTTP request with the specified JSON key-value pair that specifies a name for a notification category that already exists: `"Error"`. The changes we made will generate a response with a user-friendly error message and will avoid trying to persist the changes. The request will return an HTTP 400 Bad Request status code with the error message in the JSON body. The following lines show a sample response:

```
HTTP/1.0 400 BAD REQUEST
Content-Length: 78
Content-Type: application/json
Date: Thu, 18 Oct 2018 15:19:23 GMT
Server: Werkzeug/0.14.1 Python/3.7.1
{
    "error": "A notification category with the name Error already
exists"
}
```

Now we will add a new class method to the `Notification` class to allow us to determine whether a notification is unique or not. Open the `models.py` file within the `service` folder and add the following lines within the declaration of the `Notification` class. The code file for the sample is included in the `restful_python_2_03_01` folder, in the `Flask01/service/models.py` file:

```
@classmethod
def is_message_unique(cls, id, message):
    existing_notification =
cls.query.filter_by(message=message).first()
    if existing_notification is None:
        return True
    else:
        if existing_notification.id == id:
            return True
        else:
            return False
```

The new `Notification.is_message_unique` class method receives the `id` and the `message` for the notification that we want, to make sure that has a unique value for the `message` field. If the notification is a new one that hasn't been saved yet, we will receive a 0 for the `id` value. Otherwise, we will receive the notification ID in the `id` argument.

The method calls the `query.filter_by` method for the current class to retrieve a notification whose `message` field matches the other notification's message. If there is a notification that matches the criteria, the method will return `True`, only if the `id` is the same one as the one received in the argument. If no message matches the criteria, the method will return `True`.

We will use the previously created class method to check whether a notification is unique or not before creating and persisting it in the `NotificationListResource.post` method. Open the `views.py` file within the `service` folder and replace the existing `post` method declared in the `NotificationListResource` class with the following lines. The lines that have been added or edited are highlighted. The code file for the sample is included in the `restful_python_2_03_01` folder, in the `Flask01/service/views.py` file:

```python
def post(self):
    notification_category_dict = request.get_json()
    if not notification_category_dict:
        response = {'message': 'No input data provided'}
        return response, HttpStatus.bad_request_400.value
    errors = notification_schema.validate(notification_category_dict)
    if errors:
        return errors, HttpStatus.bad_request_400.value
    notification_message =
notification_category_dict['message']
    if not Notification.is_message_unique(id=0,
message=notification_message):
        response = {'error': 'A notification with the message {}
already exists'.format(notification_message)}
        return response, HttpStatus.bad_request_400.value
    try:
        notification_category_name =
notification_category_dict['notification_category']['name']
        notification_category =
NotificationCategory.query.filter_by(name=notification_category_name).first
()
        if notification_category is None:
            # Create a new NotificationCategory
            notification_category =
NotificationCategory(name=notification_category_name)
            orm.session.add(notification_category)
        # Now that we are sure we have a notification category,
        # we can create a new Notification
        notification = Notification(
            message=notification_message,
            ttl=notification_category_dict['ttl'],
            notification_category=notification_category)
        notification.add(notification)
```

```
        query = Notification.query.get(notification.id)
        dump_result = notification_schema.dump(query).data
        return dump_result, HttpStatus.created_201.value
    except SQLAlchemyError as e:
        orm.session.rollback()
        response = {"error": str(e)}
        return response, HttpStatus.bad_request_400.value
```

Now we will perform the same validation in the `NotificationResource.patch` method.
Open the `views.py` file within the `service` folder and replace the existing `patch` method
declared in the `NotificationResource` class with the following lines. The lines that have
been added or edited are highlighted. The code file for the sample is included in the
`restful_python_2_03_01` folder, in the `Flask01/service/views.py` file:

```
    def patch(self, id):
        notification = Notification.query.get_or_404(id)
        notification_dict = request.get_json(force=True)
        if 'message' in notification_dict and notification_dict['message']
is not None:
            notification_message = notification_dict['message']
            if not Notification.is_message_unique(id=0,
message=notification_message):
                response = {'error': 'A notification with the message {}
already exists'.format(notification_message)}
                return response, HttpStatus.bad_request_400.value
            notification.message = notification_message
        if 'ttl' in notification_dict and notification_dict['ttl'] is not
None:
            notification.duration = notification_dict['duration']
        if 'displayed_times' in notification_dict and
notification_dict['displayed_times'] is not None:
            notification.displayed_times =
notification_dict['displayed_times']
        if 'displayed_once' in notification_dict and
notification_dict['displayed_once'] is not None:
            notification.displayed_once =
notification_dict['displayed_once'] == 'true'
        dumped_notification, dump_errors =
notification_schema.dump(notification)
        if dump_errors:
            return dump_errors, HttpStatus.bad_request_400.value
        validate_errors = notification_schema.validate(dumped_notification)
        if validate_errors:
            return validate_errors, HttpStatus.bad_request_400.value
        try:
            notification.update()
            return self.get(id)
```

```
except SQLAlchemyError as e:
    orm.session.rollback()
    response = {"error": str(e)}
    return response, HttpStatus.bad_request_400.value
```

Run the following command to create a notification with a duplicate value for the message field. The code file for the sample is included in the restful_python_2_03_01 folder, in the Flask01/cmd305.txt file:

```
http POST ":5000/service/notifications/" message='eSports competition
finishes in 10 minutes' ttl=30 notification_category="Information"
```

The following is the equivalent curl command. The code file for the sample is included in the restful_python_2_03_01 folder, in the Flask01/cmd306.txt file:

```
curl -iX POST -H "Content-Type: application/json" -d '{"message":"eSports
competition finishes in 10 minutes", "ttl":30, "notification_category":
"Information"}' "localhost:5000/service/notifications/"
```

The previous command will compose and send a POST HTTP request with the specified JSON key-value pair that specifies a message for a notification that already exists: "eSports competition finishes in 10 minutes". The changes we made will generate a response with a user-friendly error message and will avoid trying to persist the notification. The request will return an HTTP 400 Bad Request status code with the error message in the JSON body. The following lines show a sample response:

```
HTTP/1.0 400 BAD REQUEST
Content-Length: 109
Content-Type: application/json
Date: Fri, 19 Oct 2018 03:15:21 GMT
Server: Werkzeug/0.14.1 Python/3.7.1
{
    "error": "A notification with the message eSports competition
finishes in 10 minutes already exists"
}
```

Understanding the differences between the PUT and the PATCH methods

The HTTP PUT and PATCH methods have different purposes. The HTTP PUT method is meant to replace an entire resource. The HTTP PATCH method is meant to apply a delta to an existing resource.

Our API is able to update a single field for an existing resource, and therefore, we provide an implementation for the PATCH method. For example, we can use the PATCH method to update an existing notification and set the value for its displayed_once and displayed_times fields to true and 1.

We don't want to use the PUT method to update two fields because this method is meant to replace an entire notification. The PATCH method is meant to apply a delta to an existing notification, and therefore, it is the appropriate method to just change the value of those two fields.

Updating fields for a resource with the PATCH method

Now we will compose and send an HTTP request to update an existing notification, specifically, to update the value of the displayed_once and displayed_times fields. Because we just want to update two fields, we will use the PATCH method instead of PUT. Make sure you replace 2 with the ID or primary key of an existing notification in your configuration. The code file for the sample is included in the restful_python_2_03_01 folder, in the Flask01/cmd307.txt file:

```
http PATCH ":5000/service/notifications/2" displayed_once=true
displayed_times=1
```

The following is the equivalent curl command. The code file for the sample is included in the restful_python_2_03_01 folder, in the Flask01/cmd308.txt file:

```
curl -iX PATCH -H "Content-Type: application/json" -d
'{"displayed_once":"true", "displayed_times":1}'
"localhost:5000/service/notifications/2"
```

The previous command will compose and send a PATCH HTTP request with the following JSON key-value pairs:

```
{
    "displayed_once": true,
    "displayed_times": 1
}
```

The request has a number after `/service/notifications/`, and therefore, it will match `'/notifications/<int:id>'` and run the `NotificationResource.patch` method, that is, the `patch` method for the `NotificationResource` class. If a `Notification` instance with the specified ID exists, the code will retrieve the values for the `displayed_times` and `displayed_once` keys from the request dictionary, and will update and validate the `Notification` instance. If the updated `Notification` instance is valid, the code will persist the changes in the database and the call to the method will return an HTTP `200 OK` status code and the recently updated `Notification` instance serialized to JSON in the response body. The following lines show a sample response:

```
HTTP/1.0 200 OK
Content-Length: 390
Content-Type: application/json
Date: Fri, 19 Oct 2018 04:02:04 GMT
Server: Werkzeug/0.14.1 Python/3.7.1
{
    "creation_date": "2018-10-16T21:58:43.737812+00:00",
    "displayed_once": true,
    "displayed_times": 1,
    "id": 2,
    "message": "No winners yet",
    "notification_category": {
        "id": 2,
        "name": "Warning",
        "url":
"http://localhost:5000/service/notification_categories/2"
    },
    "ttl": 15,
    "url": "http://localhost:5000/service/notifications/2"
}
```

We can run the commands explained in `Chapter 2`, *Working with Models, SQLAlchemy, and Hyperlinked APIs in Flask,* to check the contents of the tables that the migrations process created in the PostgreSQL 10.5 database. We will notice that the `displayed_times` and `displayed_once` values have been updated for the row in the `notification` table.

The following command will allow you to check the contents for the updated row of the `notification` table in a PostgreSQL database after running the HTTP request. The next command runs the following SQL query: `SELECT * FROM notification WHERE id = 2`. The code file for the sample is included in the `restful_python_2_02_01` folder, in the `Flask01/check_patched_notification.sql` file:

```
psql --username=your_user_name --dbname=flask_notifications --
command="SELECT * FROM notification WHERE id = 2;"
```

The following screenshot shows the contents for the updated row of the `notification` table in a PostgreSQL database after running the HTTP request:

```
● ● ●                                    service — -bash — 139×41
(Flask01) Gastons-MacBook-Pro:service gaston$ psql --username=your_user_name --dbname=flask_notifications --command="SELECT * FROM notifica
tion WHERE id = 2;"
 id |    message    | ttl |      creation_date       | notification_category_id | displayed_times | displayed_once
----+---------------+-----+--------------------------+--------------------------+-----------------+----------------
  2 | No winners yet |  15 | 2018-10-16 21:58:43.737812 |                        2 |               1 | t
(1 row)

(Flask01) Gastons-MacBook-Pro:service gaston$
```

Coding a generic pagination class

Right now, the table that persists the notifications in the database has just a few rows. However, after we start working with our API encapsulated in a microservice in a real-life production environment, we will have hundreds of notifications, and therefore, we will have to deal with large result sets. We don't want an HTTP GET request to retrieve 1,000 notifications in a single call. Thus, we will create a generic pagination class and we will use it to easily specify how we want large results sets to be split into individual pages of data.

First, we will compose and send HTTP POST requests to create nine notifications that belong to one of the notification categories we have created: Information. This way, we will have a total of 12 messages persisted in the database. We had three messages and we add nine more. The code file for the sample is included in the restful_python_2_03_01 folder, in the Flask01/cmd309.txt file:

```
http POST ":5000/service/notifications/" message='Clash Royale has a new
winner' ttl=25 notification_category='Information'
http POST ":5000/service/notifications/" message='Uncharted 4 has a new 2nd
position score' ttl=20 notification_category='Information'
http POST ":5000/service/notifications/" message='Fortnite has a new 4th
position score' ttl=18 notification_category='Information'
http POST ":5000/service/notifications/" message='Injustice 2 has a new
winner' ttl=14 notification_category='Information'
http POST ":5000/service/notifications/" message='PvZ Garden Warfare 2 has
a new winner' ttl=22 notification_category='Information'
http POST ":5000/service/notifications/" message='Madden NFL 19 has a new
3rd position score' ttl=15 notification_category='Information'
http POST ":5000/service/notifications/" message='Madden NFL 19 has a new
winner' ttl=18 notification_category='Information'
http POST ":5000/service/notifications/" message='FIFA 19 has a new 3rd
position score' ttl=16 notification_category='Information'
http POST ":5000/service/notifications/" message='NBA Live 19 has a new
winner' ttl=5 notification_category='Information'
```

The following are the equivalent `curl` commands. The code file for the sample is included in the `restful_python_2_03_01` folder, in the `Flask01/cmd310.txt` file.

```
curl -iX POST -H "Content-Type: application/json" -d '{"message":"Clash
Royale has a new winner", "ttl":25, "notification_category":
"Information"}'
"localhost:5000/service/notifications/"

curl -iX POST -H "Content-Type: application/json" -d '{"message":"Uncharted
4 has a new 2nd position score", "ttl":20, "notification_category":
"Information"}' "localhost:5000/service/notifications/"

curl -iX POST -H "Content-Type: application/json" -d '{"message":"Fortnite
has a new 4th position score", "ttl":18, "notification_category":
"Information"}' "localhost:5000/service/notifications/"

curl -iX POST -H "Content-Type: application/json" -d '{"message":"Injustice
2 has a new winner", "ttl":14, "notification_category": "Information"}'
"localhost:5000/service/notifications/"

curl -iX POST -H "Content-Type: application/json" -d '{"message":"PvZ
Garden Warfare 2 has a new winner", "ttl":22, "notification_category":
"Information"}'
"localhost:5000/service/notifications/"

curl -iX POST -H "Content-Type: application/json" -d '{"message":"Madden
NFL 19 has a new 3rd position score", "ttl":15, "notification_category":
"Information"}' "localhost:5000/service/notifications/"

curl -iX POST -H "Content-Type: application/json" -d '{"message":"Madden
NFL 19 has a new winner", "ttl":18, "notification_category":
"Information"}' "localhost:5000/service/notifications/"

curl -iX POST -H "Content-Type: application/json" -d '{"message":"FIFA 19
has a new 3rd position score", "ttl":16, "notification_category":
"Information"}' "localhost:5000/service/notifications/"

curl -iX POST -H "Content-Type: application/json" -d '{"message":"NBA Live
19 has a new winner", "ttl":5, "notification_category": "Information"}'
"localhost:5000/service/notifications/"
```

The previous commands will compose and send nine HTTP POST requests with the specified JSON key-value pairs. The requests specify `/service/notifications/`, and therefore, they will match `'/notifications/'` and run the `NotificationListResource.post` method, that is, the `post` method for the `NotificationListResource` class.

After running the previous commands, we will have 12 notifications persisted in our PostgreSQL database. However, we don't want to retrieve the 12 messages when we compose and send an HTTP GET request to /service/notifications/. We will create a customizable generic pagination class to include a maximum of four resources in each individual page of data.

Open the config.py file within the service folder and add the following lines that declare two variables that configure the global pagination settings.

Open the service/config.py file and add the following lines that declare two variables that configure the global pagination settings. The code file for the sample is included in the restful_python_2_03_01 folder, in the Flask01/service/config.py file:

```
PAGINATION_PAGE_SIZE = 4
PAGINATION_PAGE_ARGUMENT_NAME = 'page'
```

The value for the PAGINATION_PAGE_SIZE variable specifies a global setting with the default value for the page size, also known as limit. The value for PAGINATION_PAGE_ARGUMENT_NAME specifies a global setting with the default value for the argument name that we will use in our requests to specify the page number we want to retrieve.

Create a new helpers.py file within the service folder. The following lines show the code that creates a new PaginationHelper class. The code file for the sample is included in the restful_python_2_03_01 folder, in the Flask01/service/helpers.py file:

```
from flask import url_for
from flask import current_app


class PaginationHelper():
    def __init__(self, request, query, resource_for_url, key_name, schema):
        self.request = request
        self.query = query
        self.resource_for_url = resource_for_url
        self.key_name = key_name
        self.schema = schema
        self.page_size =
current_app.config['PAGINATION_PAGE_SIZE']
        self.page_argument_name =
current_app.config['PAGINATION_PAGE_ARGUMENT_NAME']

    def paginate_query(self):
        # If no page number is specified, we assume the request requires
page #1
```

```
        page_number = self.request.args.get(self.page_argument_name, 1,
type=int)
        paginated_objects = self.query.paginate(
            page_number,
            per_page=self.page_size,
            error_out=False)
        objects = paginated_objects.items
        if paginated_objects.has_prev:
            previous_page_url = url_for(
                self.resource_for_url,
                page=page_number-1,
                _external=True)
        else:
            previous_page_url = None
        if paginated_objects.has_next:
            next_page_url = url_for(
                self.resource_for_url,
                page=page_number+1,
                _external=True)
        else:
            next_page_url = None
        dumped_objects = self.schema.dump(objects, many=True).data
        return ({
            self.key_name: dumped_objects,
            'previous': previous_page_url,
            'next': next_page_url,
            'count': paginated_objects.total
        })
```

The `PaginationHelper` class declares a constructor, that is, the __init__ method, which receives the following arguments and uses them to initialize the attributes with the same names:

- `request`: The Flask request object that will allow the `paginate_query` method to retrieve the page number value specified with the HTTP request
- `query`: The SQLAlchemy query that the `paginate_query` method has to paginate
- `resource_for_url`: A string with the resource name that the `paginate_query` method will use to generate the full URLs for the previous page and the next page
- `key_name`: A string with the key name that the `paginate_query` method will use to return the serialized objects
- `schema`: The Flask-Marshmallow `Schema` subclass that the `paginate_query` method must use to serialize the objects

In addition, the constructor reads and saves the values for the configuration variables we added to the `config.py` file in the `page_size` and `page_argument_name` attributes.

The class declares the `paginate_query` method. First, the code retrieves the page number specified in the request and saves it in the `page_number` variable. If no page number is specified, the code assumes that the request requires the first page. Then, the code calls the `self.query.paginate` method to retrieve the page number specified by `page_number` of the paginated result of objects from the database, with a number of results per page indicated by the value of the `self.page_size` attribute. The next line saves the paginated items from the `paginated_object.items` attribute in the `objects` variable.

If the value for the `paginated_objects.has_prev` attribute is `True`, it means that there is a previous page available. In this case, the code calls the `flask.url_for` function to generate the full URL for the previous page with the value of the `self.resource_for_url` attribute. The `_external` argument is set to `True` because we want to provide the full URL.

If the value for the `paginated_objects.has_next` attribute is `True`, it means that there is a next page available. In this case, the code calls the `flask.url_for` function to generate the full URL for the next page with the value of the `self.resource_for_url` attribute.

Then, the code calls the `self.schema.dump` method to serialize the partial results previously saved in the `objects` variable, with the `many` argument set to `True`. The `dumped_objects` variable saves the reference to the `data` attribute of the results returned by the call to the `dump` method.

Finally, the method returns a dictionary with the following key-value pairs:

Key	Value
`self.key_name`	The serialized partial results saved in the `dumped_objects` variable.
`'previous'`	The full URL for the previous page saved in the `previous_page_url` variable.
`'next'`	The full URL for the next page saved in the `next_page_url` variable.
`'count'`	The total number of objects available in the complete result set retrieved from the `paginated_objects.total` attribute.

Adding pagination features

Open the `views.py` file within the `service` folder and replace the code for the `NotificationListResource.get` method with the highlighted lines in the next listing. In addition, make sure that you add the highlighted import statement. The code file for the sample is included in the `restful_python_2_03_01` folder, in the `Flask01/service/views.py` file:

```python
from helpers import PaginationHelper


class NotificationListResource(Resource):
    def get(self):
        pagination_helper = PaginationHelper(
            request,
            query=Notification.query,
            resource_for_url='service.notificationlistresource',
            key_name='results',
            schema=notification_schema)
        pagination_result = pagination_helper.paginate_query()
        return pagination_result
```

The new code for the `get` method creates an instance of the previously explained `PaginationHelper` class named `pagination_helper` with the `request` object as the first argument. The named arguments specify `query`, `resource_for_url`, `key_name`, and `schema` that the `PaginationHelper` instance has to use to provide a paginated query result.

The next line calls the `pagination_helper.paginate_query` method that will return the results of the paginated query with the page number specified in the request. Finally, the method returns the results of the call to this method that include the previously explained dictionary. In this case, the paginated result set with the messages will be rendered as a value of the `'results'` key, specified in the `key_name` argument.

Now we will compose and send an HTTP request to retrieve all the notifications, specifically, an HTTP GET method to `/service/notifications/`. Notice that we don't specify any desired page number. The code file for the sample is included in the `restful_python_2_03_01` folder, in the `Flask01/cmd311.txt` file:

```
http ":5000/service/notifications/"
```

The following is the equivalent `curl` command. The code file for the sample is included in the `restful_python_2_03_01` folder, in the `Flask01/cmd312.txt` file:

```
curl -iX GET "localhost:5000/service/notifications/"
```

The new code for the `NotificationListResource.get` method will work with pagination and the result will provide us with the first four notifications in the `results` key, the total number of messages for the query in the `count` key and a link to the next and previous pages in the `next` and `previous` keys. In this case, the result set is the first page, and therefore, the link to the previous page in the previous `key` is `null`. We will receive a `200 OK` status code in the response header and the four notifications in the `results` array. The next lines show the result of the previous command:

```
HTTP/1.0 200 OK
Content-Length: 2205
Content-Type: application/json
Date: Fri, 19 Oct 2018 16:11:58 GMT
Server: Werkzeug/0.14.1 Python/3.7.1
{
    "count": 12,
    "next": "http://localhost:5000/service/notifications/?page=2",
    "previous": null,
    "results": [
        {
            "creation_date": "2018-10-16T21:57:15.867853+00:00",
            "displayed_once": false,
            "displayed_times": 0,
            "id": 1,
            "message": "eSports competition finishes in 10
            minutes",
            "notification_category": {
                "id": 1,
                "name": "Information",
                "url":
"http://localhost:5000/service/notification_categories/1"
            },
            "ttl": 30,
            "url": "http://localhost:5000/service/notifications/1"
        },
        {
            "creation_date": "2018-10-16T23:07:27.372778+00:00",
            "displayed_once": false,
            "displayed_times": 0,
            "id": 3,
            "message": "Score calculation error",
            "notification_category": {
                "id": 3,
```

```
                    "name": "Error",
                    "url":
"http://localhost:5000/service/notification_categories/3"
                },
                "ttl": 30,
                "url": "http://localhost:5000/service/notifications/3"
            },
            {
                "creation_date": "2018-10-16T21:58:43.737812+00:00",
                "displayed_once": true,
                "displayed_times": 1,
                "id": 2,
                "message": "No winners yet",
                "notification_category": {
                    "id": 2,
                    "name": "Warning",
                    "url":
"http://localhost:5000/service/notification_categories/2"
                },
                "ttl": 15,
                "url": "http://localhost:5000/service/notifications/2"
            },
            {
                "creation_date": "2018-10-19T12:40:09.726102+00:00",
                "displayed_once": false,
                "displayed_times": 0,
                "id": 5,
                "message": "Clash Royale has a new winner",
                "notification_category": {
                    "id": 1,
                    "name": "Information",
                    "url": "http://localhost:5000/service
                    /notification_categories/1"
                },
                "ttl": 25,
                "url": "http://localhost:5000/service/notifications/5"
            }
        ]
    }
```

In the previous HTTP request, we didn't specify any value for the `page` parameter, and therefore, the `paginate_query` method in the `PaginationHelper` class requests the first page to the paginated query. If we compose and send the following HTTP request to retrieve the first page of all the messages by specifying 1 for the `page` value, the API will provide the same results shown before. The code file for the sample is included in the `restful_python_2_03_01` folder, in the `Flask01/cmd313.txt` file:

```
http ":5000/service/notifications/?page=1"
```

The following is the equivalent `curl` command. The code file for the sample is included in the `restful_python_2_03_01` folder, in the `Flask01/cmd314.txt` file:

```
curl -iX GET "localhost:5000/service/notifications/?page=1"
```

Notice that the code in the `PaginationHelper` class considers that the first page is page number 1. Thus, we don't work with zero-based numbering for pages.

Now we will compose and send an HTTP request to retrieve the next page, that is, the second page for the messages, specifically an HTTP `GET` method to `/service/notifications/` with the `page` value set to 2. Remember that the value for the `next` key returned in the JSON body of the previous result provides us with the full URL to the next page. The code file for the sample is included in the `restful_python_2_03_01` folder, in the `Flask01/cmd315.txt` file:

```
http ":5000/service/notifications/?page=2"
```

The following is the equivalent `curl` command. The code file for the sample is included in the `restful_python_2_03_01` folder, in the `Flask01/cmd316.txt` file:

```
curl -iX GET "localhost:5000/service/notifications/?page=2"
```

The result will provide us with the second set of four notification resources in the `results` key, the total number of messages for the query in the `count` key and a link to the next and previous pages in the `next` and `previous` keys. In this case, the result set is the second page, and therefore, the link to the previous page in the previous `key` is `http://localhost:5000/service/notifications/?page=1`. We will receive a 200 `OK` status code in the response header and the four messages in the `results` array:

```
HTTP/1.0 200 OK
Content-Length: 2299
Content-Type: application/json
Date: Fri, 19 Oct 2018 17:08:54 GMT
```

```
Server: Werkzeug/0.14.1 Python/3.7.1
{
    "count": 12,
    "next": "http://localhost:5000/service/notifications/?page=3",
    "previous":
 "http://localhost:5000/service/notifications/?page=1",
    "results": [
        {
            "creation_date": "2018-10-19T12:40:10.241868+00:00",
            "displayed_once": false,
            "displayed_times": 0,
            "id": 6,
            "message": "Uncharted 4 has a new 2nd position score",
            "notification_category": {
                "id": 1,
                "name": "Information",
                "url":
 "http://localhost:5000/service/notification_categories/1"
            },
            "ttl": 20,
            "url": "http://localhost:5000/service/notifications/6"
        },
        {
            "creation_date": "2018-10-19T12:40:10.738386+00:00",
            "displayed_once": false,
            "displayed_times": 0,
            "id": 7,
            "message": "Fortnite has a new 4th position score",
            "notification_category": {
                "id": 1,
                "name": "Information",
                "url":
 "http://localhost:5000/service/notification_categories/1"
            },
            "ttl": 18,
            "url": "http://localhost:5000/service/notifications/7"
        },
        {
            "creation_date": "2018-10-19T12:40:11.237577+00:00",
            "displayed_once": false,
            "displayed_times": 0,
            "id": 8,
            "message": "Injustice 2 has a new winner",
            "notification_category": {
                "id": 1,
                "name": "Information",
                "url":
   "http://localhost:5000/service/notification_categories/1"
```

```
        },
        "ttl": 14,
        "url": "http://localhost:5000/service/notifications/8"
    },
    {

        "creation_date": "2018-10-19T12:40:11.737706+00:00",
        "displayed_once": false,
        "displayed_times": 0,
        "id": 9,
        "message": "PvZ Garden Warfare 2 has a new winner",
        "notification_category": {
            "id": 1,
            "name": "Information",
            "url":
"http://localhost:5000/service/notification_categories/1"
        },
        "ttl": 22,
        "url": "http://localhost:5000/service/notifications/9"
    }
    ]
}
```

Finally, we will compose and send an HTTP request to retrieve the last page, that is, the third page for the notifications, specifically an HTTP GET method to /service/notifications/ with the page value set to 3. Remember that the value for the next key returned in the JSON body of the previous result provides us with the URL to the next page. The code file for the sample is included in the restful_python_2_03_01 folder, in the Flask01/cmd317.txt file:

```
http ":5000/service/notifications/?page=3"
```

The following is the equivalent curl command. The code file for the sample is included in the restful_python_2_03_01 folder, in the Flask01/cmd318.txt file.

```
curl -iX GET "localhost:5000/service/notifications/?page=3"
```

The result will provide us with the last set with four notification resources in the results key), the total number of messages for the query in the count key and a link to the next and previous pages in the next and previous keys. In this case, the result set is the last page, and therefore, the link to the next page (next key) is null. We will receive a 200 OK status code in the response header and the four notifications in the results array:

```
HTTP/1.0 200 OK
Content-Length: 2251
Content-Type: application/json
Date: Fri, 19 Oct 2018 17:19:32 GMT
```

```
Server: Werkzeug/0.14.1 Python/3.7.1
{
    "count": 12,
    "next": null,
    "previous":
"http://localhost:5000/service/notifications/?page=2",
    "results": [
        {
            "creation_date": "2018-10-19T12:40:12.246582+00:00",
            "displayed_once": false,
            "displayed_times": 0,
            "id": 10,
            "message": "Madden NFL 19 has a new 3rd position
score",
            "notification_category": {
                "id": 1,
                "name": "Information",
                "url":
"http://localhost:5000/service/notification_categories/1"
            },
            "ttl": 15,
            "url": "http://localhost:5000/service/notifications/10"
        },
        {
            "creation_date": "2018-10-19T12:40:12.748875+00:00",
            "displayed_once": false,
            "displayed_times": 0,
            "id": 11,
            "message": "Madden NFL 19 has a new winner",
            "notification_category": {
                "id": 1,
                "name": "Information",
                "url":
"http://localhost:5000/service/notification_categories/1"
            },
            "ttl": 18,
            "url": "http://localhost:5000/service/notifications/11"
        },
        {
            "creation_date": "2018-10-19T12:40:13.253900+00:00",
            "displayed_once": false,
            "displayed_times": 0,
            "id": 12,
            "message": "FIFA 19 has a new 3rd position score",
            "notification_category": {
                "id": 1,
                "name": "Information",
                "url":
```

```
    "http://localhost:5000/service/notification_categories/1"
            },
            "ttl": 16,
            "url": "http://localhost:5000/service/notifications/12"
        },
        {

            "creation_date": "2018-10-19T12:40:13.750718+00:00",
            "displayed_once": false,
            "displayed_times": 0,
            "id": 13,
            "message": "NBA Live 19 has a new winner",
            "notification_category": {
                "id": 1,
                "name": "Information",
                "url":
    "http://localhost:5000/service/notification_categories/1"
            },
            "ttl": 5,
            "url": "http://localhost:5000/service/notifications/13"
        }
    ]
}
```

Understanding the steps to add authentication and permissions

Our current version of the API processes all the incoming requests without requiring any kind of authentication. We will use a Flask extension and other packages to use an HTTP authentication scheme to identify the user that originated the request or the token that signed the request. Then, we will use these credentials to apply the permissions that will determine whether the request must be permitted or not. Unluckily, neither Flask nor Flask-RESTful provide an authentication framework that we can easily plug and configure. Thus, we will have to write code to perform many tasks related to authentication and permissions.

 We want to be able to create a new user without any authentication. However, all the other API calls are only going to be available for authenticated users.

First, we will install the `Flask-HTTPAuth` Flask extension to make it easier for us to work with HTTP authentication and the `passlib` package to allow us to hash a password and check whether a provided password is valid or not.

We will create a new `User` model that will represent a user. The model will provide methods to allow us to hash a password and verify whether a password provided for a user is valid or not. We will create a `UserSchema` class to specify how we want to serialize and deserialize a user.

Then, we will configure the Flask extension to work with our `User` model to verify passwords and set the authenticated user associated with a request. We will make changes to the existing resources to require authentication and we will add new resources to allow us to retrieve existing users and create a new one. Finally, we will configure the routes for the resources related to users.

Once we have completed the previously mentioned tasks, we will run the migrations process to generate the new table that persists the users in the database. Then, we will compose and send HTTP requests to understand how the authentication and permissions work with our new version of the API.

Make sure you quit Flask's development server. You just need to press Ctrl + C in the Terminal or Command Prompt window in which it is running.

Now, we will install many additional packages. Make sure you have activated the virtual environment we have created in Chapter 1, *Developing RESTful APIs and Microservices with Flask 1.0.2*, and we named `Flask01`. After you activate the virtual environment, it is time to run many commands that will be the same for either macOS, Linux, or Windows.

Now we will edit the existing `requirements.txt` file to specify the additional set of packages that our application requires to be installed in any supported platform. This way, it will be extremely easy to repeat the installation of the specified packages with their versions in any new virtual environment.

Use your favorite editor to edit the existing text file named `requirements.txt` within the root folder for the virtual environment. Add the following lines after the last line to declare the additional packages and the versions that our new version of the API requires. The code file for the sample is included in the `restful_python_2_03_02` folder, in the `Flask01/requirements.txt` file:

```
flask-HTTPAuth==3.2.4
passlib==1.7.1
```

Each additional line added to the `requirements.txt` file indicates the package and the version that needs to be installed. The following table summarizes the packages and the version numbers that we specified as additional requirements to the previously included packages:

Package name	Version to be installed
Flask-HTTPAuth	3.2.4
passlib	1.7.1

Now we must run the following command on macOS, Linux, or Windows to install the additional packages and the versions explained in the previous table with `pip` by using the recently edited `requirements.txt` file. Make sure you are in the folder that has the `requirements.txt` file before running the command:

```
pip install -r requirements.txt
```

The last lines for the output will indicate that all the new packages and their dependencies have been successfully installed. If you downloaded the source code for the example and you didn't work with the previous version of the API, `pip` will also install the other packages included in the `requirements.txt` file:

```
Installing collected packages: Flask-HTTPAuth, passlib
Successfully installed Flask-HTTPAuth-3.2.4 passlib-1.7.1
```

Adding a user model

Now we will create the model that we will use to represent and persist a user. Open the `models.py` file within the `service` folder and add the following lines after the declaration of the `ResourceAddUpdateDelete` class. Make sure that you add the highlighted import statements. The code file for the sample is included in the `restful_python_2_03_02` folder, in the `Flask01/service/models.py` file:

```python
from passlib.apps import custom_app_context as password_context
import re


class User(orm.Model, ResourceAddUpdateDelete):
    id = orm.Column(orm.Integer, primary_key=True)
    name = orm.Column(orm.String(50), unique=True, nullable=False)
    # I save the hash for the password (I don't persist the actual
password)
    password_hash = orm.Column(orm.String(120), nullable=False)
```

```
        creation_date = orm.Column(orm.TIMESTAMP,
server_default=orm.func.current_timestamp(), nullable=False)

    def verify_password(self, password):
        return password_context.verify(password, self.password_hash)

    def check_password_strength_and_hash_if_ok(self, password):
        if len(password) < 8:
            return 'The password is too short. Please, specify a password
with at least 8 characters.', False
        if len(password) > 32:
            return 'The password is too long. Please, specify a password
with no more than 32 characters.', False
        if re.search(r'[A-Z]', password) is None:
            return 'The password must include at least one
uppercase letter.', False
        if re.search(r'[a-z]', password) is None:
            return 'The password must include at least one
lowercase letter.', False
        if re.search(r'\d', password) is None:
            return 'The password must include at least one
number.', False
        if re.search(r"[ !#$%&'()*+,-./[\\\]^_`{|}~"+r'"]',
password) is None:
            return 'The password must include at least one
symbol.', False
        self.password_hash = password_context.hash(password)
        return '', True

    def __init__(self, name):
        self.name = name
```

The code declares the `User` model, specifically a subclass of both the `orm.Model` and the `ResourceAddUpdateDelete` classes. We specified the field types, maximum lengths, and defaults for the following four attributes: `id`, `name`, `password_hash`, and `creation_date`. These attributes represent fields without any relationship, and therefore, they are instances of the `orm.Column` class. The model declares an `id` attribute and specifies the `True` value for the `primary_key` argument to indicate it is the primary key. SQLAlchemy will use the data to generate the necessary table in the PostgreSQL database.

The `User` class declares the following two methods:

- `check_password_strength_and_hash_if_ok`: This method uses the `re` module, which provides regular expression matching operations to check whether the `password` received as an argument fulfills many qualitative requirements. The code requires the password to be longer than 8 characters with a maximum of 32 characters. The password must include at least one uppercase letter, one lowercase letter, one number, and one symbol. The code checks the results of many calls to the `re.search` method to determine whether the received password fulfills each requirement. If any of the requirements isn't fulfilled, the code returns a tuple with an error message and `False`. Otherwise, the code calls the `hash` method for the `passlib.apps.custom_app_context` instance imported as `password_context`, with the received `password` as an argument. The `hash` method chooses a reasonably strong scheme based on the platform, with the default settings for rounds selection, and the code saves the hash for the password in the `password_hash` attribute. Finally, the code returns a tuple with an empty string and `True`, indicating that the password fulfilled the qualitative requirements and its hash was generated.

> By default, the `passlib` library will use the SHA-512 scheme for 64-bit platforms and SHA-256 for 32-bit platforms. In addition, the minimum number of rounds will be set to 535,000. We will use the default configuration values for this example. However, you must take into account that these values might require too much processing time for each request that has to validate the password. You should definitely select the most appropriate algorithm and the number of rounds based on your security requirements.

- `verify_password`: This method calls the `verify` method for the `passlib.apps.custom_app_context` instance imported as `password_context`, with the received `password` and the stored hash for the password that the user has configured, `self.password_hash`, as the arguments. The `verify` method hashes the received password and returns `True` only if the hash for the received password matches the stored hash for the original password. We never restore the saved password in its original state. We just compare hashed values.

The model declares a constructor, that is, the `__init__` method. This constructor receives the username in the `name` argument and saves it in an attribute with the same name.

Creating schemas to validate, serialize, and deserialize users

Now we will create the Flask-Marshmallow schema that we will use to validate, serialize, and deserialize the previously declared `User` model. Open the `models.py` file within the `service` folder and add the following code after the existing lines. The code file for the sample is included in the `restful_python_2_03_02` folder, in the `Flask01/service/models.py` file:

```
class UserSchema(ma.Schema):
    id = fields.Integer(dump_only=True)
    name = fields.String(required=True,
        validate=validate.Length(3))
    url = ma.URLFor('service.userresource',
        id='<id>',
        _external=True)
```

The code declares the `UserSchema` schema, specifically a subclass of the `ma.Schema` class. Remember that the previous code we wrote for the `service/models.py` file created a `flask_marshmallow.Mashmallow` instance named `ma`.

We declare the attributes that represent fields as instances of the appropriate class declared in the `marshmallow.fields` module. The `UserSchema` class declares the `name` attribute as an instance of `fields.String`. The `required` argument is set to `True` to specify that the field cannot be an empty string. The `validate` argument is set to `validate.Length(5)` to specify that the field must have a minimum length of five characters.

The validation for the password isn't included in the schema. We will use the `check_password_strength_and_hash_if_ok` method defined in the `User` class to validate the password.

Adding authentication to resources

Now we will perform the following tasks:

1. Configure the `Flask-HTTPAuth` extension to work with our `User` model to verify passwords and set the authenticated user associated with a request.
2. Declare a custom function that the `Flask-HTTPAuth` extension will use as a callback to verify a password.
3. Create a new base class for our resources that will require authentication.

Open the `views.py` file within the `service` folder and add the following code after the last line that uses the `import` statement and before the lines that declare the `Blueprint` instance named `service_blueprint`. The code file for the sample is included in the `restful_python_2_03_02` folder, in the `Flask01/service/views.py` file:

```
from flask_httpauth import HTTPBasicAuth
from flask import g
from models import User, UserSchema


auth = HTTPBasicAuth()


@auth.verify_password
def verify_user_password(name, password):
    user = User.query.filter_by(name=name).first()
    if not user or not user.verify_password(password):
        return False
    g.user = user
    return True


class AuthenticationRequiredResource(Resource):
    method_decorators = [auth.login_required]

user_schema = UserSchema()
```

First, we create an instance of the `flask_httpauth.HTTPBasicAuth` class named `auth`. Then, we declare the `verify_user_password` function that receives two arguments: `name` and `password`. The function uses the `@auth.verify_password` decorator to make this function become the callback that `Flask-HTTPAuth` will use to verify the password for a specific user. The function retrieves the user whose name matches the name specified in the `name` argument and saves its reference in the `user` variable. If a user is found, the code checks the results of the `user.verify_password` method with the received password as an argument.

If either a user isn't found or the call to `user.verify_password` returns `False`, the function returns `False` and the authentication will fail. If the call to `user.verify_password` returns `True`, the function stores the authenticated `User` instance in the user attribute for the `flask.g` object.

The `flask.g` object is a proxy that allows us to store on this whatever we want to share for one request only. The `user` attribute we added to the `flask.g` object will be only valid for the active request and it will return different values for each different request. This way, it is possible to use `flask.g.user` in another function or method called during a request to access details about the authenticated user for the request.

Then, we declared the `AuthenticationRequiredResource` class as a subclass of `flask_restful.Resource`. We just specified `auth.login_required` as one of the members of the list that we assign to the `method_decorators` property inherited from the base class. This way, all the methods declared in a resource that uses the new `AuthenticationRequiredResource` class as its superclass will have the `auth.login_required` decorator applied to them, and therefore, any method that is called for the resource will require authentication.

Finally, the last line creates an instance of the `UserSchema` class and saves it in the `user_schema` variable.

Now we will replace the base class for the existing resource classes to make them inherit from `AuthenticationRequiredResource` instead of `Resource`. We want any of the requests that retrieve or modify categories and messages to be authenticated.

The following lines show the current declarations for the four resource classes:

```
class NotificationResource(Resource):
class NotificationListResource(Resource):
class NotificationCategoryResource(Resource):
class NotificationCategoryListResource(Resource):
```

Open the `views.py` file within the `service` folder and replace `Resource` with `AuthenticationRequiredResource` in the previously shown four lines that declare the resource classes. The following lines show the new code for each resource class declaration. The code file for the sample is included in the `restful_python_2_03_02` folder, in the `Flask01/service/views.py` file:

```
class NotificationResource(AuthenticationRequiredResource):
class NotificationListResource(AuthenticationRequiredResource):
class NotificationCategoryResource(AuthenticationRequiredResource):
class NotificationCategoryListResource(AuthenticationRequiredResource):
```

Creating resource classes to handle users

We just want to be able to create users and use them to authenticate requests. Thus, we will just focus on creating resource classes with just a few methods. We won't create a complete user management system.

We will create the resource classes that represent the user and the collection of users. First, we will create a `UserResource` class, which we will use to represent a user resource. Open the `views.py` file within the `service` folder and add the following lines after the line that creates the `Api` instance named `service` and before the declaration of the `NotificationResource` class. The code file for the sample is included in the `restful_python_2_03_02` folder, in the `Flask01/service/views.py` file:

```
class UserResource(AuthenticationRequiredResource):
    def get(self, id):
        user = User.query.get_or_404(id)
        result = user_schema.dump(user).data
        return result
```

The `UserResource` class is a subclass of the previously coded `AuthenticationRequiredResource` and declares a `get` method that will be called when the HTTP method with the same name arrives as a request on the represented resource.

The method receives the id of the user that has to be retrieved in the `id` argument. The code calls the `User.query.get_or_404` method to return an HTTP `404 Not Found` status if there is no user with the requested id in the underlying database. If the user exists, the code calls the `user_schema.dump` method with the retrieved user as an argument to use the `UserSchema` instance to serialize the `User` instance whose `id` matches the specified `id`. The `dump` method takes the `User` instance and applies the field filtering and output formatting specified in the `UserSchema` class. The field filtering specifies that we don't want the hash for the password to be serialized. The code returns the `data` attribute of the result returned by the `dump` method, that is, the serialized message in JSON format as the body, with the default HTTP `200 OK` status code.

Now we will create the `UserListResource` class that we will use to represent the collection of users. Open the `views.py` file within the `service` folder and add the following lines after the code that creates the `UserResource` class. The code file for the sample is included in the `restful_python_2_03_02` folder, in the `Flask01/service/views.py` file:

```
class UserListResource(Resource):
    @auth.login_required
    def get(self):
```

```
        pagination_helper = PaginationHelper(
            request,
            query=User.query,
            resource_for_url='service.userlistresource',
            key_name='results',
            schema=user_schema)
        result = pagination_helper.paginate_query()
        return result

    def post(self):
        user_dict = request.get_json()
        if not user_dict:
            response = {'user': 'No input data provided'}
            return response, HttpStatus.bad_request_400.value
        errors = user_schema.validate(user_dict)
        if errors:
            return errors, HttpStatus.bad_request_400.value
        user_name = user_dict['name']
        existing_user = User.query.filter_by(name=user_name).first()
        if existing_user is not None:
            response = {'user': 'An user with the name {} already
exists'.format(user_name)}
            return response, HttpStatus.bad_request_400.value
        try:
            user = User(name=user_name)
            error_message, password_ok = \
user.check_password_strength_and_hash_if_ok(user_dict['password'])
            if password_ok:
                user.add(user)
                query = User.query.get(user.id)
                dump_result = user_schema.dump(query).data
                return dump_result, HttpStatus.created_201.value
            else:
                return {"error": error_message},
HttpStatus.bad_request_400.value
        except SQLAlchemyError as e:
            orm.session.rollback()
            response = {"error": str(e)}
            return response, HttpStatus.bad_request_400.value
```

The UserListResource class is a subclass of the flask_restful.Resource superclass because we don't want all the methods to require authentication. We want to be able to create a new user without being authenticated, and therefore, we apply the @auth.login_required decorator only for the get method. The post method doesn't require authentication. The class declares the following two methods that will be called when the HTTP method with the same name arrives as a request on the represented resource:

- get: This method returns a list with all the User instances persisted in the database. First, the code calls the User.query.all method to retrieve all the User instances. Then, the code calls the user_schema.dump method with the retrieved users and the many argument set to True to serialize the iterable collection of objects. The dump method will take each User instance retrieved from the database and apply the field filtering and output formatting specified the UserSchema class. The code returns the data attribute of the result returned by the dump method, that is, the serialized messages in JSON format as the body, with the default HTTP 200 OK status code.

- post: This method retrieves the key-value pairs received in the JSON body, creates a new User instance and persists it in the database. First, the code calls the request.get_json method to retrieve the key-value pairs received as arguments with the request. Then, the code calls the user_schema.validate method to validate the new user built with the retrieved key-value pairs. In this case, the call to this method will just validate the name field for the user. If there were validation errors, the code returns a tuple composed of the validation errors and an HTTP 400 Bad Request status code. If the validation is successful, the code checks whether a user with the same name already exists in the database or not to return an appropriate error for the field that must be unique. If the username is unique, the code creates a new user with the specified name and calls its check_password_strength_and_hash_if_ok method. If the provided password fulfills all the quality requirements, the code persists the user with the hash for its password in the database. Finally, the code returns a tuple composed of the serialized saved user in JSON format as the body, with the HTTP 201 Created status code.

The following table shows the methods of our previously created classes related to users that we want to be executed for each combination of HTTP verb and scope:

HTTP verb	Scope	Class and method	Requires authentication
GET	Collection of users	UserListResource.get	Yes
GET	User	UserResource.get	Yes
POST	Collection of users	UserListResource.post	No

We must make the necessary resource routing configurations to call the appropriate methods and pass them all the necessary arguments by defining URL rules. The following lines configure the resource routing for the user-related resources to the `service` object. Open the `views.py` file within the `service` folder and add the following lines at the end of the code. The code file for the sample is included in the `restful_python_2_03_02` folder, in the `Flask01/service/views.py` file:

```
service.add_resource(UserListResource,
    '/users/')
service.add_resource(UserResource,
    '/users/<int:id>')
```

Each call to the `service.add_resource` method routes a URL to one of the previously coded user-related resources. When there is a request to the API, and the URL matches one of the URLs specified in the `service.add_resource` method, Flask will call the method that matches the HTTP verb in the request for the specified class.

Running migrations to generate the user table

Now we will run many scripts to run migrations and generate the necessary table to persist users in the PostgreSQL 10.5 database. Make sure you run the scripts in the Terminal or Command Prompt window in which you have activated the virtual environment and that you are located in the `service` folder.

Run the first command that populates the migration script with the detected changes in the models. In this case, it is the second time we populate the migration script, and therefore, the migration script will generate the new table that will persist our new `User` model: user:

```
flask db migrate
```

The following lines show the sample output generated after running the previous command. Your output will be different according to the base folder in which you have created the virtual environment:

```
INFO  [alembic.runtime.migration] Context impl PostgresqlImpl.
INFO  [alembic.runtime.migration] Will assume transactional DDL.
INFO  [alembic.autogenerate.compare] Detected added table 'user'
INFO  [alembic.ddl.postgresql] Detected sequence named
'notification_category_id_seq' as owned by integer column
'notification_category(id)', assuming SERIAL and omitting
INFO  [alembic.ddl.postgresql] Detected sequence named
'notification_id_seq' as owned by integer column'notification(id)',
assuming SERIAL and omitting
  Generating /Users/gaston/HillarPythonREST2/Flask01/service/migrat
  ions/versions/2029a0a9475f_.py ... done
```

The output indicates that the `service/migrations/versions/2029a0a9475f_.py` file includes the code to create the `user` table. The following lines show the code for this file that was automatically generated based on the `User` model. Notice that the filename will be different in your configuration. The code file for the sample is included in the `restful_python_2_03_02` folder, in the `Flask01/service/migrations/versions/2029a0a9475f_.py` file:

```
"""empty message

Revision ID: 2029a0a9475f
Revises: 03f5d0f0642a
Create Date: 2018-10-19 21:16:15.062238

"""
from alembic import op
import sqlalchemy as sa


# revision identifiers, used by Alembic.
revision = '2029a0a9475f'
down_revision = '03f5d0f0642a'
branch_labels = None
depends_on = None


def upgrade():
    # ### commands auto generated by Alembic - please adjust! ###
    op.create_table('user',
    sa.Column('id', sa.Integer(), nullable=False),
    sa.Column('name', sa.String(length=50), nullable=False),
    sa.Column('password_hash', sa.String(length=120), nullable=False),
```

```
        sa.Column('creation_date', sa.TIMESTAMP(),
server_default=sa.text('CURRENT_TIMESTAMP'), nullable=False),
        sa.PrimaryKeyConstraint('id'),
        sa.UniqueConstraint('name')
        )
        # ### end Alembic commands ###


def downgrade():
        # ### commands auto generated by Alembic - please adjust! ###
        op.drop_table('user')
        # ### end Alembic commands ###
```

The code defines two functions: `upgrade` and `downgrade`. The `upgrade` function runs the necessary code to create the `user` table by making calls to the `alembic.op.create_table` method. The `downgrade` function runs the necessary code to go back to the previous version.

Run the second command to upgrade the database:

```
flask db upgrade
```

The following lines show the sample output generated after running the previous script:

```
INFO    [alembic.runtime.migration] Context impl PostgresqlImpl.
INFO    [alembic.runtime.migration] Will assume transactional DDL.
INFO    [alembic.runtime.migration] Running upgrade 03f5d0f0642a ->
2029a0a9475f, empty message
```

The previous script called the `upgrade` function defined in the automatically generated `service/migrations/versions/2029a0a9475f_.py` script. Don't forget that the filename will be different in your configuration.

After we run the previous scripts, we can use the PostgreSQL command line or any other application that allows us to easily verify the contents of the PostgreSQL 10.5 database to check the new table that the migrations process generated. Run the following command to list the generated tables. If the database name you are using is not named `flask_notifications`, make sure you use the appropriate database name. The code file for the sample is included in the `restful_python_2_03_02` folder, in the `Flask01/list_database_tables.sql` file:

```
psql --username=your_user_name --dbname=flask_notifications --
command="\dt"
```

The following lines show the output with all the generated table names. The migration process generated a new table named `user`:

```
                        List of relations
     Schema |           Name          |  Type  |     Owner
    --------+-------------------------+--------+----------------
     public | alembic_version         | table  | your_user_name
     public | notification            | table  | your_user_name
     public | notification_category   | table  | your_user_name
     public | user                    | table  | your_user_name
    (4 rows)
```

SQLAlchemy generated the `User` table with its primary key, its unique constraint on the `name` field, and the `password_hash` field based on the information included in our `User` model.

The following command will allow you to check the contents of the `user` table after we compose and send HTTP requests to the RESTful API and create new users. The commands assume that you are running PostgreSQL on the same computer in which you are running the command:

```
psql --username=your_user_name --dbname=flask_notifications --
command="SELECT * FROM public.user;"
```

Now run the `flask` script that launches Flask's development server and the application. Make sure you have configured the `FLASK_ENV` environment variable as explained in `Chapter 2`, *Working with Models, SQLAlchemy, and Hyperlinked APIs in Flask*, in the *Creating and retrieving related resources* section:

```
flask run
```

After we execute the previous command, the development server will start listening at port `5000`.

Composing requests with the necessary authentication

Now we will compose and send an HTTP request to retrieve the first page of the notifications without authentication credentials. The code file for the sample is included in the `restful_python_2_03_01` folder, in the `Flask01/cmd317.txt` file:

```
http GET ":5000/service/notifications/?page=1"
```

The following is the equivalent `curl` command. The code file for the sample is included in the `restful_python_2_03_01` folder, in the `Flask01/cmd318.txt` file:

```
curl -iX GET "localhost:5000/service/notifications/?page=1"
```

We will receive a `401 Unauthorized` status code in the response header. The following lines show a sample response:

```
HTTP/1.0 401 UNAUTHORIZED
Content-Length: 19
Content-Type: text/html; charset=utf-8
Date: Sat, 20 Oct 2018 00:30:56 GMT
Server: Werkzeug/0.14.1 Python/3.7.1
WWW-Authenticate: Basic realm="Authentication Required"
Unauthorized Access
```

If we want to retrieve notification, that is, to make a `GET` request to `/service/notifications/`, we need to provide authentication credentials by using HTTP authentication. However, before we can do this, it is necessary to create a new user. We will use the new user to test our new resource classes related to users and our changes in the permissions policies. Run the following command to create a new user. The code file for the sample is included in the `restful_python_2_03_01` folder, in the `Flask01/cmd319.txt` file:

```
http POST ":5000/service/users/" name='gaston-hillar'
password='wrongpassword'
```

The following is the equivalent `curl` command. The code file for the sample is included in the `restful_python_2_03_01` folder, in the `Flask01/cmd320.txt` file:

```
curl -iX POST -H "Content-Type: application/json" -d '{"name":
"gaston-hillar", "password": "wrongpassword"}'
"localhost:5000/service/users/"
```

Of course, the creation of a user and the execution of the methods that require authentication should only be possible under HTTPS. This way, the username and the password would be encrypted. The microservice that encapsulates the API in production must work under HTTPS.

The previous command will compose and send an HTTP `POST` request with the specified JSON key-value pairs. The request specifies `/service/users/`, and therefore, it will match the `'/users/'` URL route for the `UserList` resource and run the `UserList.post` method that doesn't require authentication. The method doesn't receive arguments because the URL route doesn't include any parameters. As the HTTP verb for the request is `POST`, Flask calls the `post` method.

The previously specified password only includes lowercase letters, and therefore, it doesn't fulfill all the qualitative requirements we have specified for the passwords in the `User.check_password_strength_and_hash_if_ok` method. Thus, we will receive a `400 Bad Request` status code in the response header and the error message indicating the requirement that the password didn't fulfill the quality requirements in the JSON body. The following lines show a sample response:

```
HTTP/1.0 400 BAD REQUEST
Content-Length: 76
Content-Type: application/json
Date: Sat, 20 Oct 2018 04:19:45 GMT
Server: Werkzeug/0.14.1 Python/3.7.1
{
    "error": "The password must include at least one uppercase
letter."
}
```

The following command will create a user with a valid password. The code file for the sample is included in the `restful_python_2_03_01` folder, in the `Flask01/cmd321.txt` file:

```
http POST ":5000/service/users/" name='gaston-hillar'
password='TT1#ID16^eplG'
```

The following is the equivalent `curl` command. The code file for the sample is included in the `restful_python_2_03_01` folder, in the `Flask01/cmd322.txt` file:

```
curl -iX POST -H "Content-Type: application/json" -d '{"name": "gaston-
hillar", "password": "TT1#ID16^eplG"}' "localhost:5000/service/users/"
```

If the new `User` instance is successfully persisted in the database, the call will return an HTTP `201 Created` status code and the recently persisted `User` serialized to JSON in the response body. The following lines show an example response for the HTTP request, with the new `User` object in the JSON responses. Notice that the response includes the URL, `url`, for the created user and doesn't include any information related to the password:

```
HTTP/1.0 201 CREATED
Content-Length: 97
Content-Type: application/json
Date: Sat, 20 Oct 2018 15:58:15 GMT
Server: Werkzeug/0.14.1 Python/3.7.1
{
    "id": 1,
    "name": "gaston-hillar",
    "url": "http://localhost:5000/service/users/1"
}
```

We can run the previously explained command to check the contents of the `user` table that the migrations created in the PostgreSQL database. We will notice that the `password_hash` field contents are hashed for the new row in the `user` table. The following screenshot shows the contents for the new row of the `user` table in a PostgreSQL database after running the HTTP request:

If we want to retrieve the first page of notifications, that is, to make an HTTP GET request to `/service/notifications/`, we need to provide authentication credentials using HTTP authentication.

Now we will compose and send an HTTP request to retrieve the first page of messages with authentication credentials, that is, with the username we have recently created and his password. The code file for the sample is included in the `restful_python_2_03_01` folder, in the `Flask01/cmd323.txt` file:

```
http -a 'gaston-hillar':'TT1#ID16^ep1G'
":5000/service/notifications/?page=1"
```

The following is the equivalent `curl` command. The code file for the sample is included in the `restful_python_2_03_01` folder, in the `Flask01/cmd324.txt` file:

```
curl --user 'gaston-hillar':'TT1#ID16^ep1G' -iX GET
"localhost:5000/service/notifications/?page=1"
```

The user will be successfully authenticated and we will be able to process the request to retrieve the first page of the notifications persisted in the database. With all the changes we have made to our API, unauthenticated requests can only create a new user.

Test your knowledge

Let's see whether you can answer the following questions correctly:

1. Which HTTP verb is meant to replace an entire resource:
    1. `PATCH`
    2. `POST`
    3. `PUT`

2. Which HTTP verb is meant to apply a delta to an existing resource:
    1. `PATCH`
    2. `POST`
    3. `PUT`

3. By default, the `passlib` library will use the SHA-512 scheme for 64-bit platforms with the minimum number of rounds set to:
    1. 135,000
    2. 335,000
    3. 535,000

4. The `flask.g` object is:
    1. A proxy that provides access to the current request
    2. An instance of the `flask_httpauth.HTTPBasicAuth` class
    3. A proxy that allows us to store on this whatever we want to share for one request only

5. The `passlib` package provides:
    1. A password hashing framework that supports more than 30 schemes
    2. An authentication framework that automatically adds models for users and permissions to a Flask application
    3. A lightweight web framework that replaces Flask

6. The `auth.verify_password` decorator applied to a function:
    1. Makes this function become the callback that `Flask-HTTPAuth` will use to hash the password for a specific user
    2. Makes this function become the callback that SQLAlchmey will use to verify the password for a specific user
    3. Makes this function become the callback that `Flask-HTTPAuth` will use to verify the password for a specific user

7. When you assign a list that includes `auth.login_required` to the `method_decorators` property of any subclass of `flask_restful.Resource`, considering that auth is an instance of the `flask_httpauth.HTTPBasicAuth()`:
    1. All the methods declared in the resource will have the `auth.login_required` decorator applied to them
    2. The `post` method declared in the resource will have `auth.login_required` decorator applied to it
    3. Any of the following methods declared in the resource will have `auth.login_required` decorator applied to them: `delete`, `patch`, `post`, and `put`

8. Which of the following lines retrieve the integer value for the `'page'` argument from the `request` object, considering that the code would be running within a method defined in a subclass of `flask_restful.Resource` class?:
    1. `page_number = request.get_argument('page', 1, type=int)`
    2. `page_number = request.args.get('page', 1, type=int)`
    3. `page_number = request.arguments.get('page', 1, type=int)`

Summary

In this chapter, we improved the RESTful API in many ways. We added user-friendly error messages for when resources aren't unique. We tested how to update single or multiple fields with the `PATCH` method and we created our own generic pagination class to enable us to paginate result sets.

Then, we started working with authentication and permissions. We added a user model and we updated the underlying PostgreSQL database. We made many changes in the different pieces of code to achieve a specific security goal and we took advantage of `Flask-HTTPAuth` and `passlib` to use HTTP authentication in our API.

Now that we have built an improved a complex API that uses pagination and authentication, we will use additional abstractions included in the framework and we will code, execute and improve unit tests to get ready to encapsulate our API in a microservice, which are the topics of the next chapter.

4
Testing and Deploying an API in a Microservice with Flask

In this chapter, we will configure, write, and execute unit tests and learn a few things related to deployment. We will do the following:

- Set up unit tests with `pytest`
- Create a database for testing
- Create fixtures to perform setup and teardown tasks for running clean tests
- Write the first round of unit tests
- Run unit tests with `pytest` and check testing coverage
- Improve testing coverage
- Understand strategies for deployments and scalability

Setting up unit tests with pytest

So far, we have been writing code to add features to our RESTful API. We used command-line and GUI tools to understand how all the pieces worked together and to check the results of diverse HTTP requests made to the RESTful API with Flask's development server. Now we will write unit tests that will allow us to make sure that the RESTful API works as expected. Before we can start writing unit tests, it is necessary to install many additional packages in our virtual environment, create a new PostgreSQL database that we will use for testing, and build a configuration file for the testing environment.

Make sure you quit Flask's development server. You just need to press *Ctrl + C* in the Terminal or Command Prompt window in which it is running.

Now we will install many additional packages. Make sure you have activated the virtual environment named `Flask01`, which we created in Chapter 1, *Developing RESTful APIs and Microservices with Flask 1.0.2*. After you activate the virtual environment, it is time to run many commands, which will be the same for macOS, Linux, or Windows.

Now we will edit the existing `requirements.txt` file to specify the additional set of packages that our application requires to be installed in any supported platform. This way, it will be extremely easy to repeat the installation of the specified packages with their versions in any new virtual environment.

Use your favorite editor to edit the existing text file named `requirements.txt` within the root folder for the virtual environment. Add the following lines after the last line to declare the additional packages and the versions that our new version of the API requires. The code file for the sample is included in the `restful_python_2_04_01` folder, in the `Flask01/requirements.txt` file:

```
pytest==4.0.1
coverage==4.5.2
pytest-cov==2.6.0
```

Each additional line added to the `requirements.txt` file indicates the package and the version that needs to be installed. The following table summarizes the packages and the version numbers that we specified as additional requirements to the previously included packages:

Package name	Version to be installed
pytest	4.0.1
coverage	4.5.2
pytest-cov	2.6.0

We will install the following Python packages in our virtual environment:

- `pytest`: This is a very popular Python unit testing framework that makes testing easy and reduces boilerplate code.
- `coverage`: This tool measures code coverage of Python programs and we will use it to determine which parts of the code are being executed by unit tests and which parts aren't.
- `pytest-cov`: This plugin for `pytest` makes it easy to produce coverage reports that use the `coverage` tool under the hood, and provides some additional features.

Now we must run the following command on macOS, Linux, or Windows to install the additional packages and the versions outlined in the previous table with `pip` using the recently edited `requirements.txt` file. Make sure you are in the folder that has the `requirements.txt` file before running the command:

```
pip install -r requirements.txt
```

The last lines for the output will indicate all the new packages and their dependencies have been successfully installed. If you downloaded the source code for the example and you didn't work with the previous version of the API, `pip` will also install the other packages included in the `requirements.txt` file:

```
Installing collected packages: atomicwrites, six, more-itertools, pluggy,
py, attrs, pytest, coverage, pytest-cov
Successfully installed atomicwrites-1.2.1 attrs-18.2.0 coverage-4.5.2 more-
itertools-4.3.0 pluggy-0.8.0 py-1.7.0 pytest-4.0.1 pytest-cov-2.6.0
six-1.12.0
```

Creating a database for testing

Now we will create the PostgreSQL database that we will use as a repository for our testing environment. Notice that the testing computer or server must have PostgreSQL 10.5 installed on it, as explained in the previous chapters for the development environment. I assume that you are running the tests on the same computer in which you worked with the previous examples.

 Remember to make sure that the PostgreSQL bin folder is included in the `PATH` environmental variable. You should be able to execute the `psql` command-line utility from your current Terminal, Command Prompt, or Windows PowerShell.

We will use the PostgreSQL command-line tools to create a new database named `test_flask_notifications`. If you already have a PostgreSQL database with this name, make sure that you use another name in all the commands and configurations. You can perform the same task with any PostgreSQL GUI tool. If you are developing on Linux, it is necessary to run the commands as the `postgres` user. Run the following command in macOS or Windows to create a new database named `test_flask_notifications`. Notice that the command won't produce any output:

```
createdb test_flask_notifications
```

In Linux, run the following command to use the `postgres` user:

```
sudo -u postgres createdb test_flask_notifications
```

Now we will use the `psql` command-line tool to run some SQL statements to grant privileges on the database to a user. If you are using a different server than the development server, you will have to create the user before granting privileges. On macOS or Windows, run the following command to launch `psql`:

```
psql
```

On Linux, run the following command to use the `postgres` user:

```
sudo -u psql
```

Then, run the following SQL statements and finally enter `\q` to exit the `psql` command-line tool. Replace `your_user_name` with your desired username to use in the new database and `your_password` with your chosen password. We will use the username and password in the Flask testing configuration. You don't need to run the steps if you are already working with a specific user in PostgreSQL and you have already granted privileges to the database for the user. You will see the output indicating that the permission was granted. The code file for the sample is included in the `restful_python_2_04_01` folder, in the `Flask01/configure_test_database.sql` file:

```
GRANT ALL PRIVILEGES ON DATABASE "test_flask_notifications" TO
your_user_name;
\q
```

Create a new `test_config.py` file within the `service` folder. The following lines show the code that declares variables that determine the configuration for Flask and SQLAlchemy for our testing environment. The `SQL_ALCHEMY_DATABASE_URI` variable generates an SQLAlchemy URI for the PostgreSQL database. Make sure you specify the desired database name in the value for `DB_NAME` and that you configure the user, password, host, and port based on your PostgreSQL configuration. If you followed the previous steps, use the settings specified in these steps. The code file for the sample is included in the `restful_python_2_04_01` folder, in the `Flask01/service/test_config.py` file:

```
import os


basedir = os.path.abspath(os.path.dirname(__file__))
SQLALCHEMY_ECHO = False
SQLALCHEMY_TRACK_MODIFICATIONS = True
# Replace your_user_name with the user name you configured for the test
database
```

```
# Replace your_password with the password you specified for the test
database user
SQLALCHEMY_DATABASE_URI =
"postgresql://{DB_USER}:{DB_PASS}@{DB_ADDR}/{DB_NAME}".format(DB_USER="your
_user_name", DB_PASS="your_password", DB_ADDR="127.0.0.1",
DB_NAME="test_flask_notifications")
SQLALCHEMY_MIGRATE_REPO = os.path.join(basedir, 'db_repository')
# Pagination configuration
PAGINATION_PAGE_SIZE = 4
PAGINATION_PAGE_ARGUMENT_NAME = 'page'
# Enable the TESTING flag
TESTING = True
# Disable CSRF protection in the testing configuration
WTF_CSRF_ENABLED = False
# Necessary for flask.url_for to build the URLs
SERVER_NAME="127.0.0.1"
```

As we did with the similar `config.py` file we created for our development environment, we will specify the previously created module, `test_config`, as an argument to a function that will create a Flask app that we will use for testing. This way, we have one module that specifies all the values for the different configuration variables for our development environment and another module that creates a Flask app for our testing environment.

 It is also possible to create a class hierarchy with one class for each environment we want to use. However, in our sample case, it is easier to create a new configuration file for our testing environment.

The TESTING variable set to True enables a flag that indicates to Flask that we are running tests. This way, Flask extensions will also enable the test mode and the exceptions will propagate to the test client. The WTF_CSRF_ENABLED variable set to False disables the **CSRF** (short for **Cross-Site Request Forgery**) protection during test's execution. The SERVER_NAME variable specifies the host that is running the Flask server during tests. It is necessary to specify an appropriate value for this variable to make the flask.url_for method work OK when building the URLs for the different resources in our API.

Creating fixtures to perform setup and teardown tasks for running clean tests

Test fixtures provide a fixed baseline to enable us to reliably and repeatedly execute tests. Pytest makes it easy to declare a test fixture function by marking a function with the `@pytest.fixture` decorator. Then, whenever we use the fixture function name as an argument in a test function declaration, `pytest` will make the fixture function provide the fixture object. Now we will create the following two `pytest` fixture functions, which we will use in future test functions:

- `application`: This test fixture function will perform the necessary setup tasks to create the Flask test app with the appropriate testing configuration and create all the necessary tables in the test database. The fixture will launch the test execution and when the test finishes, the fixture will perform the necessary teardown tasks to leave the database as it was before running the test.

- `client`: This test fixture function receives `application` as an argument, and therefore, it receives the Flask app created in the previously explained application test fixture function in this argument. Hence, the `client` test fixture function configures the application for testing, initializes the database, creates a test client for this application and returns it. We will use the test client in our test methods to easily compose and send requests to our API.

Create a new `conftest.py` file within the `service` folder. Add the following lines that declare many `import` statements and the previously explained `pytest` test fixture functions. The code file for the sample is included in the `restful_python_2_04_01` folder, in the `Flask01/service/conftest.py` file:

```
import pytest
from app import create_app
from models import orm
from flask_sqlalchemy import SQLAlchemy
from flask import Flask
from views import service_blueprint


@pytest.fixture
def application():
    # Beginning of Setup code
    app = create_app('test_config')
    with app.app_context():
        orm.create_all()
        # End of Setup code
```

```
    # The test will start running here
    yield app
    # The test finished running here
    # Beginning of Teardown code
    orm.session.remove()
    orm.drop_all()
    # End of Teardown code


@pytest.fixture
def client(application):
    return application.test_client()
```

The `application` fixture function will be executed each time a test that uses either `application` or `client` as arguments. The function calls the `create_app` function, declared in the `app` module, with `'test_config'` as an argument. The function will set up a Flask app with this module as the configuration file, and therefore, the app will use the previously created configuration file that specifies the desired values for our testing database and environment.

The next line calls the `orm.create_all` method to create all the necessary tables in our test database configured in the `test_config.py` file. All the code after the `yield app` line works as the teardown code that is executed after `app` is used and the test is executed. The code removes the SQLAlchemy session and drops all the tables that we created in the test database before starting the execution of the test. This way, after each test finishes its execution, the test database will be empty again.

Writing the first round of unit tests

Now, we will write the first round of unit tests. Specifically, we will write unit tests related to the user and notification category resources: `UserResource`, `UserListResource`, `NotificationCategoryResource`, and `NotificationCategoryListResource`.

Create a new `tests` subfolder within the `service` folder. Then, create a new `test_views.py` file within the new `service/tests` subfolder. Add the following lines that declare many `import` statements and the first functions that we will use in many test functions. The code file for the sample is included in the `restful_python_2_04_01` folder, in the `Flask01/service/tests/test_views.py` file:

```
import pytest
from base64 import b64encode
from flask import current_app, json, url_for
from http_status import HttpStatus
```

```
from models import orm, NotificationCategory, Notification, User


TEST_USER_NAME = 'testuser'
TEST_USER_PASSWORD = 'T3s!p4s5w0RDd12#'


def get_accept_content_type_headers():
    return {
        'Accept': 'application/json',
        'Content-Type': 'application/json'
    }


def get_authentication_headers(username, password):
    authentication_headers = get_accept_content_type_headers()
    authentication_headers['Authorization'] = \
        'Basic ' + b64encode((username + ':' +
password).encode('utf-8')).decode('utf-8')
    return authentication_headers
```

The `get_accept_content_type_headers` function builds and returns a dictionary (`dict`) with the values of the `Accept` and `Content-Type` header keys set to `'application/json'`. We will call this function in our test functions whenever we have to build a header to compose our requests without authentication.

The `get_authentication_headers` function calls the previously explained `get_accept_content_type_headers` function to generate the header key-value pairs without authentication. Then, the code adds the necessary value to the `Authorization` key with the appropriate encoding to provide the username and password received in the `username` and `password` arguments. The last line returns the generated dictionary that includes authentication information. We will call this function in our test functions whenever we have to build a header to compose our requests with authentication. Most of the time, we will use the username and password we stored in the `TEST_USER_NAME` and `TEST_USER_PASSWORD` variables.

Open the previously created `test_views.py` file within the new `service/tests` subfolder. Add the following lines that declare three functions; two of them are test functions because they start with the `test_` prefix. The code file for the sample is included in the `restful_python_2_04_01` folder, in the `Flask01/service/tests/test_views.py` file:

```
def test_request_without_authentication(client):
    """
    Ensure we cannot access a resource that requires authentication without
```

```
an appropriate authentication header
    """
    response = client.get(
        url_for('service.notificationlistresource', _external=True),
        headers=get_accept_content_type_headers())
    assert response.status_code == HttpStatus.unauthorized_401.value


def create_user(client, name, password):
    url = url_for('service.userlistresource',
        _external=True)
    data = {'name': name, 'password': password}
    response = client.post(
        url,
        headers=get_accept_content_type_headers(),
        data=json.dumps(data))
    return response


def create_notification_category(client, name):
    url = url_for('service.notificationcategorylistresource',
        _external=True)
    data = {'name': name}
    response = client.post(
        url,
        headers=get_authentication_headers(TEST_USER_NAME,
TEST_USER_PASSWORD),
        data=json.dumps(data))
    return response


def test_create_and_retrieve_notification_category(client):
    """
    Ensure we can create a new Notification Category and then retrieve it
    """
    create_user_response = create_user(client, TEST_USER_NAME,
TEST_USER_PASSWORD)
    assert create_user_response.status_code == HttpStatus.created_201.value
    new_notification_category_name = 'New Information'
    post_response = create_notification_category(client,
new_notification_category_name)
    assert post_response.status_code ==
HttpStatus.created_201.value
    assert NotificationCategory.query.count() == 1
    post_response_data = json.loads(post_response.get_data(as_text=True))
    assert post_response_data['name'] ==
new_notification_category_name
    new_notification_category_url = post_response_data['url']
```

```
    get_response = client.get(
        new_notification_category_url,
        headers=get_authentication_headers(TEST_USER_NAME,
TEST_USER_PASSWORD))
    assert get_response.status_code == HttpStatus.ok_200.value
    get_response_data =
json.loads(get_response.get_data(as_text=True))
    assert get_response_data['name'] ==
new_notification_category_name
```

The `test_request_without_authentication` method tests whether we are rejected access to a resource that requires authentication when we don't provide an appropriate authentication header with the request. The method uses the test client received in the `client` argument to compose and send an HTTP `GET` request to the URL generated for the `'service.notificationlistresource'` resource to retrieve the list of notifications. We need an authenticated request to retrieve the list of notifications. However, the code calls the `get_authentication_headers` method to set the value for the headers argument in the call to the `client.get` method, and therefore, the code generates a request without authentication. Finally, the method uses `assert` to check that the `status_code` for the response is HTTP `401 Unauthorized` (`HttpStatus.unauthorized_401.value`).

The `create_user` method uses the test client received as an argument in the `client` parameter to compose and send an HTTP `POST` request to the URL generated for the `'service.userlistresource'` resource to create a new user with the `name` and `password` received as arguments. We don't need an authenticated request to create a new user, and therefore, the code calls the previously explained `get_accept_content_type_headers` function to set the value for the headers argument in the call to the `client.post` method. Finally, the code returns the response from the HTTP `POST` request. Whenever we have to create an authenticated request, we will call the `create_user` method to create a new user before performing this request.

The `create_notification_category` function uses the test client received as an argument in the `client` parameter to compose and send an HTTP `POST` request to the URL generated for the `'service.notificationcategorylistresource'` resource to create a new notification category with the name received as an argument. We need an authenticated request to create a new `NotificationCategory`, and therefore, the code calls the previously explained `get_authentication_headers` function to set the value for the headers argument in the call to the `client.post` method. The username and password are set to `TEST_USER_NAME` and `TEST_USER_PASSWORD`. Finally, the code returns the response from the HTTP `POST` request. Whenever we have to create a notification category, we will call the `create_notification_category` function after the appropriate user that authenticates the request has been created.

The `test_create_and_retrieve_notification_category` function tests whether we can create a new `NotificationCategory` and then retrieve it. The function calls the previously explained `create_user` function to create a new user and then use it to authenticate the HTTP `POST` request generated in the `create_notification_category` function. Then, the code composes and sends an HTTP `GET` method to retrieve the recently created `NotificationCategory` with the URL received in the response of the previous HTTP `POST` request. The method uses `assert` to check for the following expected results:

- The `status_code` for the HTTP `POST` response is HTTP `201 Created` (`HttpStatus.created_201.value`)
- The total number of `NotificationCategory` objects retrieved from the database is `1`
- The `status_code` for the HTTP `GET` response is HTTP `200 OK` (`HttpStatus.ok_200.value`)
- The value for the `name` key in the HTTP `GET` response is equal to the name specified for the new notification category

Open the previously created `test_views.py` file within the `service/tests` subfolder. Add the following lines, which declare three new test functions that start with the `test_` prefix. The code file for the sample is included in the `restful_python_2_04_01` folder, in the `Flask01/service/tests/test_views.py` file:

```
def test_create_duplicated_notification_category(client):
    """
    Ensure we cannot create a duplicated Notification Category
    """
    create_user_response = create_user(client, TEST_USER_NAME,
TEST_USER_PASSWORD)
    assert create_user_response.status_code == HttpStatus.created_201.value
    new_notification_category_name = 'New Information'
    post_response = create_notification_category(client,
new_notification_category_name)
    assert post_response.status_code ==
HttpStatus.created_201.value
    assert NotificationCategory.query.count() == 1
    post_response_data = json.loads(post_response.get_data(as_text=True))
    assert post_response_data['name'] ==
new_notification_category_name
    second_post_response = create_notification_category(client,
new_notification_category_name)
    assert second_post_response.status_code ==
HttpStatus.bad_request_400.value
    assert NotificationCategory.query.count() == 1
```

```python
def test_retrieve_notification_categories_list(client):
    """
    Ensure we can retrieve the notification categories list
    """
    create_user_response = create_user(client, TEST_USER_NAME,
TEST_USER_PASSWORD)
    assert create_user_response.status_code == HttpStatus.created_201.value
    new_notification_category_name_1 = 'Error'
    post_response_1 = create_notification_category(client,
new_notification_category_name_1)
    assert post_response_1.status_code,
HttpStatus.created_201.value
    new_notification_category_name_2 = 'Warning'
    post_response_2 = create_notification_category(client,
new_notification_category_name_2)
    assert post_response_2.status_code,
HttpStatus.created_201.value
    url = url_for('service.notificationcategorylistresource',
_external=True)
    get_response = client.get(
        url,
        headers=get_authentication_headers(TEST_USER_NAME,
TEST_USER_PASSWORD))
    assert get_response.status_code == HttpStatus.ok_200.value
    get_response_data =
json.loads(get_response.get_data(as_text=True))
    assert len(get_response_data) == 2
    assert get_response_data[0]['name'] == new_notification_category_name_1
    assert get_response_data[1]['name'] == new_notification_category_name_2


def test_update_notification_category(client):
    """
    Ensure we can update the name for an existing notification category
    """
    create_user_response = create_user(client, TEST_USER_NAME,
TEST_USER_PASSWORD)
    assert create_user_response.status_code == HttpStatus.created_201.value
    new_notification_category_name_1 = 'Error 1'
    post_response_1 = create_notification_category(client,
new_notification_category_name_1)
    assert post_response_1.status_code ==
HttpStatus.created_201.value
    post_response_data_1 =
json.loads(post_response_1.get_data(as_text=True))
    new_notification_category_url = post_response_data_1['url']
    new_notification_category_name_2 = 'Error 2'
    data = {'name': new_notification_category_name_2}
```

```
    patch_response = client.patch(
        new_notification_category_url,
        headers=get_authentication_headers(TEST_USER_NAME,
TEST_USER_PASSWORD),
        data=json.dumps(data))
    assert patch_response.status_code == HttpStatus.ok_200.value
    get_response = client.get(
        new_notification_category_url,
        headers=get_authentication_headers(TEST_USER_NAME,
TEST_USER_PASSWORD))
    assert get_response.status_code == HttpStatus.ok_200.value
    get_response_data =
json.loads(get_response.get_data(as_text=True))
    assert get_response_data['name'] == new_notification_category_name_2
```

The class declares the following test functions whose name start with the `test_` prefix and receive the test client as an argument in the `client` parameter:

- `test_create_duplicated_notification_category`: This function tests whether the unique constraints make it possible for us to create two notification categories with the same name. The second time we compose and send an HTTP `POST` request with a duplicate notification category name, we must receive an HTTP `400 Bad Request` status code (`HttpStatus.bad_request_400`) and the total number of `NotificationCategory` objects retrieved from the database must be `1`.

- `test_retrieve_notification_categories_list`: This function tests whether we can retrieve the notification categories list. First, the function creates two notification categories and then it makes sure that the retrieved list includes the two created notification categories.

- `test_update_notification_category`: This function tests whether we can update a single field for a notification category, specifically, its `name` field. The code makes sure that the name has been updated in the underlying database.

Notice that each test that requires a specific condition in the database must execute all the necessary code for the database to be in this specific condition. For example, in order to update an existing notification category, first, we must create a new notification category and then we can update it. As previously explained, each test method will be executed without data from the previously executed test methods in the database, that is, each test will run with a database cleaned of data from previous tests. It is possible to work with fixtures to reduce boilerplate code in the previously coded functions. However, we are focused on making the functions easy to understand. Then, you can use the code as a baseline and improve it by taking full advantage of additional features provided by pytest fixtures.

Running unit tests with pytest and checking testing coverage

Create a new setup.cfg file within the service folder. The following lines show the code that specifies the desired configuration for pytest and the coverage tools. The code file for the sample is included in the restful_python_2_04_01 folder, in the Flask01/service/setup.cfg file:

```
[tool:pytest]
testpaths = tests

[coverage:run]
branch = True
source =
    models
    views
```

The tool:pytest section specifies the configuration for pytest. The testpaths setting assigns the tests value to indicate that the tests are located within the tests subfolder.

The `coverage:run` section specifies the configuration for the `coverage` tool. The `branch` setting is set to `True` to enable branch coverage measurement, in addition to the default statement coverage. The `source` setting specifies the modules that we want to be considered for the coverage measurement. We just want to include the `models` and `views` modules.

Now we will use the `pytest` command to run tests and measure their code coverage. Make sure you run the command in the Terminal or Command Prompt window in which you have activated the virtual environment and that you are located within the `service` folder. Run the following command:

```
pytest --cov -s
```

The test runner will execute all the functions defined in the `test_views.py` that start with the `test_` prefix and will display the results. We will use the `-v` option to instruct `pytest` to print the test function names and statuses in verbose mode. The `--cov` option turns on test-coverage-reporting generation with the usage of the `pytest-cov` plugin.

 The tests won't make changes to the database we have been using when working on the API. Remember that we configured the `test_flask_notifications` database as our test database.

The following lines show the sample output:

```
==================================== test session starts
====================================
 latform darwin -- Python 3.7.1, pytest-4.0.1, py-1.7.0, pluggy-0.8.0 -
- /Users/gaston/HillarPythonREST2/Flask01/bin/python3
cachedir: .pytest_cache
rootdir: /Users/gaston/HillarPythonREST2/Flask01/service, inifile:
setup.cfg
plugins: cov-2.6.0
collected 5 items
   tests/test_views.py::test_request_without_authentication PASSED
   [ 20%]
   tests/test_views.py::test_create_and_retrieve_notification_category
   PASSED           [ 40%]
   tests/test_views.py::test_create_duplicated_notification_category
   PASSED            [ 60%]
   tests/test_views.py::test_retrieve_notification_categories_list
   PASSED             [ 80%]
   tests/test_views.py::test_update_notification_category PASSED
   [100%]
   ---------- coverage: platform darwin, python 3.7.1-final-0 --------
```

```
---
Name          Stmts   Miss Branch BrPart  Cover
----------------------------------------------
models.py      101     27     24      7    66%
views.py       208    112     46     10    43%
----------------------------------------------
TOTAL          309    139     70     17    51%
========================= 5 passed, 1 warnings in 18.15 seconds
=========================
```

Pytest uses the configuration specified in the previously created `setup.cfg` file to determine which path includes the modules whose names start with the `test` prefix. In this case, the only module that matches the criteria is the `test_views` module. In the modules that match the criteria, `pytest` loads tests from all the functions whose names start with the `test` prefix.

The output provided details that the test runner discovered and executed five tests and all of them passed. The output displays the module and function names for each method in the `test_views` module that started with the `test_` prefix and represented a test to be executed.

The test code coverage measurement report provided by the `coverage` package in combination with the `pytest-cov` plugin uses the code analysis tools and the tracing hooks included in the Python standard library to determine which lines of code are executable and which of these lines have been executed. The report provides a table with the following columns:

- `Name`: The Python module name
- `Stmts`: The count of executable statements for the Python module
- `Miss`: The number of executable statements missed, that is, the ones that weren't executed
- `Branch`: The count of possible branches for the Python module
- `BrPart`: The number of branches that were executed during tests
- `Cover`: The coverage of executable statements and branches, expressed as a percentage

We definitely have incomplete coverage for the `views.py` and `models.py` modules based on the measurements shown in the report. In fact, we just wrote a few tests related to the notification categories and users, and therefore, it makes sense that the coverage is lower than 50% for the `views.py` module. We didn't create tests related to notifications.

We can run the `coverage` command with the `-m` command-line option to display the line numbers of the missing statements in a new `Missing` column:

```
coverage report -m
```

The command will use the information from the last execution and will display the missing statements and the missing branches. The next lines show a sample output that corresponds to the previous execution of the unit tests. A dash (–) is used to indicate a range of lines that were missed. For example, `22-23` means that lines `22` and `23` were missing statements. A dash followed by a greater than sign (–>) indicates that the branch from the line before –> to the line after it was missed. For example, `41->42` means that the branch from line `41` to line `42` was missed:

```
Name           Stmts   Miss Branch BrPart   Cover   Missing
-----------------------------------------------------------
models.py        101     27     24      7     66%    22-23, 38, 40, 42,
44, 46, 48, 68-75, 78-80, 94, 133-143, 37->38, 39->40, 41>42, 43-
>44, 45->46, 47->48, 93->94
views.py         208    112     46     10     43%    37-39, 45-52, 57-
58, 61, 65-66, 77-81, 86-88, 91-118, 121-129, 134-141, 144-175,
188-189, 192, 199-200, 203-206, 209-217, 230-231, 234, 245-250, 56-
>57, 60->61, 64->65, 71->77, 187->188, 191->192, 194->201, 196-
>199, 229->230, 233->234
-----------------------------------------------------------
TOTAL            309    139     70     17     51%
```

Now run the following command to get annotated HTML listings detailing missed lines. The command won't produce any output:

```
coverage html
```

Open the `index.html` HTML file generated in the `htmlcov` folder with your web browser. The following screenshot shows an example report that coverage generated in HTML format:

Module ↓	statements	missing	excluded	branches	partial	coverage
Coverage report: 51%			filter…			
models.py	101	27	0	24	7	66%
views.py	208	112	0	46	10	43%
Total	**309**	**139**	**0**	**70**	**17**	**51%**

coverage.py v4.5.1, created at 2018-10-22 19:13

Click or tap `views.py` and the web browser will render a web page that displays the statements that were run, including the missing ones, the excluded ones, and the partially executed ones, with different colors. We can click or tap on the **run**, **missing**, **excluded**, and **partial** buttons to show or hide the background color that represents the status for each line of code. By default, the missing lines of code will be displayed with a pink background and the partially executed will be displayed with a yellow background. Thus, we must write unit tests that target these lines of code to improve our tests coverage. The following screenshot shows the buttons with the summary:

Coverage for views.py : 43%

208 statements | 96 run | 112 missing | 0 excluded | 10 partial

```
1   from flask import Blueprint, request, jsonify, make_response
2   from flask_restful import Api, Resource
3   from http_status import HttpStatus
4   from models import orm, NotificationCategory, NotificationCategorySchema, Notification, NotificationSchema
5   from sqlalchemy.exc import SQLAlchemyError
6   from helpers import PaginationHelper
7   from flask_httpauth import HTTPBasicAuth
8   from flask import g
9   from models import User, UserSchema
10
11
12  auth = HTTPBasicAuth()
13
14
```

The next screenshot shows the highlighted missing lines and the partially evaluated branches for some lines of code in the `views.py` module:

```
35   class UserResource(AuthenticationRequiredResource):
36       def get(self, id):
37           user = User.query.get_or_404(id)
38           result = user_schema.dump(user).data
39           return result
40
41
42   class UserListResource(Resource):
43       @auth.login_required
44       def get(self):
45           pagination_helper = PaginationHelper(
46               request,
47               query=User.query,
48               resource_for_url='service.userlistresource',
49               key_name='results',
50               schema=user_schema)
51           result = pagination_helper.paginate_query()
52           return result
53
54       def post(self):
55           user_dict = request.get_json()
56           if not user_dict:
57               response = {'user': 'No input data provided'}
58               return response, HttpStatus.bad_request_400.value
59           errors = user_schema.validate(user_dict)
60           if errors:
61               return errors, HttpStatus.bad_request_400.value
62           user_name = user_dict['name']
63           existing_user = User.query.filter_by(name=user_name).first()
```

Improving testing coverage

Now we will write additional tests functions to improve the testing coverage. Specifically, we will write unit tests related to notifications and users.

Open the existing `service/tests/test_views.py` file and insert the following lines after the last line. The code file for the sample is included in the `restful_python_2_04_02` folder, in the `Flask01/service/tests/test_views.py` file:

```python
def create_notification(client, message, ttl,
notification_category):
    url = url_for('service.notificationlistresource',
        _external=True)
    data = {'message': message, 'ttl': ttl, 'notification_category':
notification_category}
    response = client.post(
        url,
        headers=get_authentication_headers(TEST_USER_NAME,
TEST_USER_PASSWORD),
        data=json.dumps(data))
    return response


def test_create_and_retrieve_notification(client):
    """
    Ensure we can create a new notification and then retrieve it
    """
    create_user_response = create_user(client, TEST_USER_NAME,
TEST_USER_PASSWORD)
    assert create_user_response.status_code == HttpStatus.created_201.value
    new_notification_message = 'Welcome to the eSports Competition'
    new_notification_category = 'Information'
    post_response = create_notification(client, new_notification_message,
15, new_notification_category)
    assert post_response.status_code ==
HttpStatus.created_201.value
    assert Notification.query.count() == 1
    # The notification should have created a new notification
catagory
    assert NotificationCategory.query.count() == 1
    post_response_data = json.loads(post_response.get_data(as_text=True))
    assert post_response_data['message'] == new_notification_message
    new_notification_url = post_response_data['url']
    get_response = client.get(
        new_notification_url,
        headers=get_authentication_headers(TEST_USER_NAME,
TEST_USER_PASSWORD))
    assert get_response.status_code == HttpStatus.ok_200.value
    get_response_data =
json.loads(get_response.get_data(as_text=True))
    assert get_response_data['message'] ==
new_notification_message
    assert get_response_data['notification_category']['name'] ==
```

```
    new_notification_category

def test_create_duplicated_notification(client):
    """
    Ensure we cannot create a duplicated Notification
    """
    create_user_response = create_user(client, TEST_USER_NAME,
TEST_USER_PASSWORD)
    assert create_user_response.status_code == HttpStatus.created_201.value
    new_notification_message = 'Welcome to the 4th eSports Competition'
    new_notification_category = 'Information'
    post_response = create_notification(client, new_notification_message,
25, new_notification_category)
    assert post_response.status_code == HttpStatus.created_201.value
    assert Notification.query.count() == 1
    post_response_data = json.loads(post_response.get_data(as_text=True))
    assert post_response_data['message'] == new_notification_message
    new_notification_url = post_response_data['url']
    get_response = client.get(
        new_notification_url,
        headers=get_authentication_headers(TEST_USER_NAME,
TEST_USER_PASSWORD))
    assert get_response.status_code == HttpStatus.ok_200.value
    get_response_data = json.loads(get_response.get_data(as_text=True))
    assert get_response_data['message'] == new_notification_message
    assert get_response_data['notification_category']['name'] ==
new_notification_category
    second_post_response = create_notification(client,
new_notification_message, 15, new_notification_category)
    assert second_post_response.status_code ==
HttpStatus.bad_request_400.value
    assert Notification.query.count() == 1
```

The previous code added many functions to the `test_views` module. The `create_notification` function receives the test client, the desired `message`, `ttl`, and `notification_category` (notification category name) for the new notification as arguments. The method builds the URL and the data dictionary, composes and sends an HTTP POST method to create a new notification, and returns the response generated by this request. Many test functions will call the `create_notification` method to create a notification and then compose and send other HTTP requests to the test client.

The previous code declares the following test functions whose name start with the `test_` prefix:

- `test_create_and_retrieve_notification`: This function tests whether we can create a new `Notification` and then retrieve it.
- `test_create_duplicated_notification`: This function tests whether the unique constraints make it possible for us to create two notifications with the same message. The second time we compose and send an HTTP `POST` request with a duplicate notification, we must receive an HTTP `400 Bad Request` status code (`HttpStatus.bad_request_400.value`) and the total number of `Notification` objects retrieved from the database must be equal to `1`.

Open the existing `service/tests/test_views.py` file and insert the following lines after the last line. The code file for the sample is included in the `restful_python_2_04_02` folder, in the `Flask01/service/tests/test_views.py` file:

```
def test_retrieve_notifications_list(client):
    """
    Ensure we can retrieve the notifications paginated list
    """
    create_user_response = create_user(client, TEST_USER_NAME,
TEST_USER_PASSWORD)
    assert create_user_response.status_code == HttpStatus.created_201.value
    new_notification_message_1 = 'The winners will be announced in 1
minute'
    new_notification_category_1 = 'Information'
    post_response = create_notification(client, new_notification_message_1,
15, new_notification_category_1)
    assert post_response.status_code == HttpStatus.created_201.value
    assert Notification.query.count() == 1
    new_notification_message_2 = 'There is a problem with one score'
    new_notification_category_2 = 'Error'
    post_response = create_notification(client, new_notification_message_2,
10, new_notification_category_2)
    assert post_response.status_code == HttpStatus.created_201.value
    assert Notification.query.count() == 2
    get_first_page_url = url_for('service.notificationlistresource',
_external=True)
    get_first_page_response = client.get(
        get_first_page_url,
        headers=get_authentication_headers(TEST_USER_NAME,
TEST_USER_PASSWORD))
    assert get_first_page_response.status_code == HttpStatus.ok_200.value
    get_first_page_response_data =
json.loads(get_first_page_response.get_data(as_text=True))
```

```
    assert get_first_page_response_data['count'] == 2
    assert get_first_page_response_data['previous'] is None
    assert get_first_page_response_data['next'] is None
    assert get_first_page_response_data['results'] is not None
    assert len(get_first_page_response_data['results']) == 2
    assert get_first_page_response_data['results'][0]['message'] ==
new_notification_message_1
    assert get_first_page_response_data['results'][1]['message'] ==
new_notification_message_2
    get_second_page_url = url_for('service.notificationlistresource',
page=2)
    get_second_page_response = client.get(
        get_second_page_url,
        headers=get_authentication_headers(TEST_USER_NAME,
TEST_USER_PASSWORD))
    assert get_second_page_response.status_code == HttpStatus.ok_200.value
    get_second_page_response_data =
json.loads(get_second_page_response.get_data(as_text=True))
    assert get_second_page_response_data['previous'] is not None
    assert get_second_page_response_data['previous'] ==
url_for('service.notificationlistresource', page=1)
    assert get_second_page_response_data['next'] is None
    assert get_second_page_response_data['results'] is not None
    assert len(get_second_page_response_data['results']) == 0
```

The previous code declared the `test_retrieve_notifications_list` test function. This function tests whether we can retrieve the paginated notifications list. First, the function creates two notifications and then it makes sure that the retrieved list includes the two created notifications on the first page. In addition, the method makes sure that the second page doesn't include any message and that the value for the previous page includes the URL for the first page.

Open the existing `service/tests/test_views.py` file and insert the following lines after the last line. The code file for the sample is included in the `restful_python_2_04_02` folder, in the `Flask01/service/tests/test_views.py` file:

```
def test_update_notification(client):
    """
    Ensure we can update a single field for an existing notification
    """
    create_user_response = create_user(client, TEST_USER_NAME,
TEST_USER_PASSWORD)
    assert create_user_response.status_code == HttpStatus.created_201.value
    new_notification_message_1 = 'Fortnite has a new winner'
    new_notification_category_1 = 'Information'
    post_response = create_notification(client, new_notification_message_1,
30, new_notification_category_1)
```

```
    assert post_response.status_code == HttpStatus.created_201.value
    assert Notification.query.count() == 1
    post_response_data = json.loads(post_response.get_data(as_text=True))
    new_notification_url = post_response_data['url']
    new_displayed_times = 1
    new_displayed_once = True
    data = {'displayed_times': new_displayed_times, 'displayed_once':
str.lower(str(new_displayed_once))}
    patch_response = client.patch(
        new_notification_url,
        headers=get_authentication_headers(TEST_USER_NAME,
TEST_USER_PASSWORD),
        data=json.dumps(data))
    assert patch_response.status_code == HttpStatus.ok_200.value
    get_response = client.get(
        new_notification_url,
        headers=get_authentication_headers(TEST_USER_NAME,
TEST_USER_PASSWORD))
    assert get_response.status_code == HttpStatus.ok_200.value
    get_response_data = json.loads(get_response.get_data(as_text=True))
    assert get_response_data['displayed_times'] == new_displayed_times
    assert get_response_data['displayed_once'] == new_displayed_once


def test_create_and_retrieve_user(client):
    """
    Ensure we can create a new User and then retrieve it
    """
    new_user_name = TEST_USER_NAME
    new_user_password = TEST_USER_PASSWORD
    post_response = create_user(client, new_user_name, new_user_password)
    assert post_response.status_code == HttpStatus.created_201.value
    assert User.query.count() == 1
    post_response_data = json.loads(post_response.get_data(as_text=True))
    assert post_response_data['name'] == new_user_name
    new_user_url = post_response_data['url']
    get_response = client.get(
        new_user_url,
        headers=get_authentication_headers(new_user_name,
new_user_password))
    assert get_response.status_code == HttpStatus.ok_200.value
    get_response_data = json.loads(get_response.get_data(as_text=True))
    assert get_response_data['name'] == new_user_name
```

The previous code added the following two test functions:

- `test_update_notification`: This function tests whether we can update many fields for a notification, specifically, the values for the `displayed_times` and `displayed_once` fields. The code makes sure that both fields have been updated.
- `test_create_and_retrieve_user`: This function tests whether we can create a new `User` and then retrieve it.

We just coded a few tests related to notifications and one test related to users in order to improve test coverage and notice the impact on the test coverage report.

Now we will use the `pytest` command to run tests and measure their code coverage. Make sure you run the command in the Terminal or Command Prompt window in which you have activated the virtual environment and that you are located within the `service` folder. Run the following command:

```
pytest --cov -s
```

The following lines show the sample output:

```
==================================== test session starts
====================================
platform darwin -- Python 3.7.1, pytest-4.0.1, py-1.7.0, pluggy-
0.8.0 -     - /Users/gaston/HillarPythonREST2/Flask01/bin/python3
cachedir: .pytest_cache
rootdir: /Users/gaston/HillarPythonREST2/Flask01/service, inifile:
setup.cfg
plugins: cov-2.6.0
collected 10 items
tests/test_views.py::test_request_without_authentication PASSED
[ 10%]
tests/test_views.py::test_create_and_retrieve_notification_category
PASSED          [ 20%]
tests/test_views.py::test_create_duplicated_notification_category
PASSED              [ 30%]
tests/test_views.py::test_retrieve_notification_categories_list
PASSED                  [ 40%]
tests/test_views.py::test_update_notification_category PASSED
[ 50%]
tests/test_views.py::test_create_and_retrieve_notification PASSED
[ 60%]
tests/test_views.py::test_create_duplicated_notification PASSED
[ 70%]
tests/test_views.py::test_retrieve_notifications_list PASSED
[ 80%]
```

```
tests/test_views.py::test_update_notification PASSED
[ 90%]
tests/test_views.py::test_create_and_retrieve_user PASSED
[100%]
---------- coverage: platform darwin, python 3.7.1-final-0 --------
---
Name          Stmts   Miss Branch BrPart  Cover
-------------------------------------------------
models.py      101     11     24      9    84%
views.py       208     68     46     19    65%
-------------------------------------------------
TOTAL          309     79     70     28    71%
========================= 10 passed, 1 warnings in 39.45 seconds
===========================
```

The output provided details indicating that the test runner executed 10 tests and all of them passed. The test code coverage measurement report provided by the `coverage` package increased the `Cover` percentage of the `models.py` module from 66% to 84%. In addition, the `Cover` percentage of the `views.py` module increased from 43% in the previous run to 65%. The new additional tests we wrote executed additional code in different modules, and therefore, there was a significant impact upon the coverage report. The total coverage increased from 51% to 71%.

We just created a few unit tests to understand how we can code them. However, of course, it would be necessary to write more tests to provide an appropriate coverage of all the features and execution scenarios included in the API.

Understanding strategies for deployments and scalability

Flask is a lightweight microframework for the web, and therefore, it is an ideal choice whenever we have to provide a RESTful API encapsulated in a microservice. So far, we have been working with the built-in development server provided by Werkzeug and with plain HTTP.

It is very important to understand that Flask's built-in development server is not suitable for production.

There are dozens of deployment options for Flask, and the different stacks and procedures are out of the scope of this book, which is focused on development tasks for RESTful APIs with the most popular Python frameworks. The most prominent cloud providers include instructions on how to deploy Flask applications with diverse possible configurations. In addition, there are many options to use **WSGI** (short for **Web Server Gateway Interface**) servers, which implement the web server side of the WSGI interface, allowing us to run Python web applications, such as Flask applications, in production.

Of course, in a production environment, we will also want to work with HTTPS instead of HTTP. We will have to configure the appropriate TLS certificates, also known as SSL certificates.

We used Flask to develop a RESTful web service. The key advantage of these kinds of web services is that they are stateless, that is, they shouldn't keep a client state on any server. Our API is a good example of a stateless RESTful web service with Flask. Flask-RESTful and PostgreSQL 10.5 can be containerized in a Docker container. For example, we can produce an image with our application configured to run with NGINX, uWSGI, Redis, and Flask. Thus, we can make the API run as a microservice.

We always have to make sure that we profile the API and the database before we deploy our first version of our API. It is very important to make sure that the generated queries run properly on the underlying database and that the most popular queries do not end up in sequential scans. It is usually necessary to add the appropriate indexes to the tables in the database.

We have been using basic HTTP authentication. We can improve it with a token-based authentication. We must make sure that the API runs under HTTPS in production environments.

It is convenient to use a different configuration file for production. However, another approach that is becoming extremely popular, especially for cloud-native applications, is storing configuration in the environment. If we want to deploy cloud-native RESTful web services and follow the guidelines established in the Twelve-Factor App, we should store config in the environment.

Each platform includes detailed instructions to deploy our application. All of them will require us to generate the `requirements.txt` file, which lists the application dependencies together with their versions. This way, the platforms will be able to install all the necessary dependencies listed in the file. We have been updating this file each time we needed to install a new package in our virtual environment. However, it is a good idea to run the following `pip freeze` within the root folder of our virtual environment, `Flask01`, to generate the final `requirements.txt` file:

```
pip freeze > requirements.txt
```

The following lines show the contents of a sample generated `requirements.txt` file. Notice that the generated file also includes all the dependencies that were installed by the packages we specified in the original `requirements.txt` file:

```
alembic==1.0.0
aniso8601==3.0.2
atomicwrites==1.2.1
attrs==18.2.0
certifi==2018.8.24
chardet==3.0.4
Click==7.0
coverage==4.5.1
Flask==1.0.2
Flask-HTTPAuth==3.2.4
flask-marshmallow==0.9.0
Flask-Migrate==2.3.0
Flask-RESTful==0.3.6
Flask-SQLAlchemy==2.3.2
httpie==1.0.0
idna==2.7
itsdangerous==0.24
Jinja2==2.10
Mako==1.0.7
MarkupSafe==1.0
marshmallow==2.16.3
marshmallow-sqlalchemy==0.15.0
more-itertools==4.3.0
passlib==1.7.1
pluggy==0.8.0
psycopg2==2.7.6.1
py==1.7.0
Pygments==2.2.0
pytest==4.0.1
pytest-cov==2.6.0
python-dateutil==2.7.3
python-editor==1.0.3
pytz==2018.5
```

```
requests==2.19.1
six==1.11.0
SQLAlchemy==1.2.12
urllib3==1.23
Werkzeug==0.14.1
```

Test your knowledge

Let's see whether you can answer the following questions correctly:

1. Pytest makes it easy to declare a test fixture function by marking a function with which of the following decorators?:
    1. `@pytest.fixture_function`
    2. `@pytest.test_fixture`
    3. `@pytest.fixture`

2. By default, pytest discovers and executes functions as text functions when they start with which of the following prefixes?:
    1. `test`
    2. `test_`
    3. `test-`

3. Which of the following commands displays the line numbers of the missing statements in the `Missing` column for a coverage report?:
    1. `coverage report -m`
    2. `coverage report missing`
    3. `coverage -missing`

4. Pytest is a very popular Python:
    1. Unit test framework that makes testing easy and reduces boilerplate code
    2. WSGI server that we can use to run Flask applications in production
    3. Load balancing solution that is suitable for Flask applications

5. The `coverage` tool:
    1. Load balances requests to a Flask-RESTful API built with Flask-RESTful
    2. Measures code coverage of Python programs
    3. Replaces the Flask development server with one that has better features and a GUI monitoring tool

Summary

In this chapter, we set up a testing environment. We installed `pytest` to make it easy to discover and execute unit tests and we created a new database to be used for testing. We wrote a first round of unit tests, measured test coverage with the `pytest-cov` plugin combined with the `coverage` tool, and then we wrote additional unit tests to improve test coverage. Finally, we understood many considerations for deployment and scalability.

We built a complex API with Flask combined with Flask-RESTful and a PostgreSQL 10.5 database that we can run as a microservice, and we tested it. Now we will move to another popular Python web framework, Django, which is the topic for the next chapter.

Developing RESTful APIs with Django 2.1

In this chapter, we will start working with Django and Django REST framework, and we will create a RESTful web API that performs CRUD operations on a simple SQLite database. We will do the following:

- Design a RESTful API to interact with a simple SQLite database
- Understand the tasks performed by each HTTP method
- Set up a virtual environment with Django REST framework
- Create models
- Manage serialization and deserialization
- Understand status codes for responses
- Write API views
- Make HTTP requests to the API with command-line tools
- Make HTTP requests to the API with GUI tools

Designing a RESTful API to interact with a simple SQLite database

Imagine that we have to start working on a mobile app that has to interact with a RESTful API to perform CRUD operations with games. We don't want to spend time choosing and configuring the most appropriate **ORM** (short for **Object-Relational Mapping**); we just want to finish the RESTful API as soon as possible to start interacting with it in our mobile app. We really want the games to persist in a database but we don't need it to be production-ready, and therefore, we can use the simplest possible relational database, as long as we don't have to spend time making complex installations or configurations.

We need the shortest possible development time. **Django Rest Framework** (**DRF**) will allow us to easily accomplish this task and start making HTTP requests to our first version of our RESTful web service. In this case, we will work with a very simple SQLite database, the default database for a new Django Rest Framework project.

First, we must specify the requirements for our main resource: a game. We need the following attributes or fields for a game:

- An integer identifier
- A name or title
- A release date
- An **ESRB** (short for **Entertainment Software Rating Board**) rating description, such as *T* (*Teen*) and *EC* (*Early Childhood*). You can read more about the ESRB at http://www.esrb.org
- A `bool` value indicating whether the game was played at least once by a player or not
- An integer indicating the number of times the game was played

In addition, we want our database to save a timestamp with the date and time in which the game was inserted in the database.

The following table shows the HTTP verbs, the scope, and the semantics for the methods that our first version of the API must support. Each method is composed by an HTTP verb and a scope and all the methods have a well-defined meaning for the games and the collection of games:

HTTP verb	Scope	Semantics
GET	Collection of games	Retrieve all the stored games in the collection, sorted by their name in ascending order
GET	Game	Retrieve a single game
POST	Collection of games	Create a new game in the collection
PUT	Game	Update an existing game
DELETE	Game	Delete an existing game

In a RESTful API, each resource has its own unique URL. In our API, each game has its own unique URL.

Understanding the tasks performed by each HTTP method

In the previous table, the GET HTTP verb appears twice but with two different scopes. The first row shows a GET HTTP verb applied to a collection of games (collection of resources) and the second row shows a GET HTTP verb applied to a game (a single resource).

Let's assume that http://localhost:8000/games/ is the URL for the collection of games. If we add a number and a slash (/) to the previous URL, we identify a specific game whose ID is equal to the specified numeric value. For example, http://localhost:8000/games/25/ identifies the game whose ID is equal to 25.

We have to compose and send an HTTP request with the following HTTP verb (POST) and request URL (http://localhost:8000/games/) to create a new game. In addition, we have to provide the **JSON** (short for **JavaScript Object Notation**) key-value pairs with the field names and the values to create the new game. As a result of the request, the server will validate the provided values for the fields, make sure that it is a valid game, and persist it in the database. The server will insert a new row with the new game in the appropriate table and it will return a 201 Created status code and a JSON body with the recently added game serialized to JSON, including the assigned ID that was automatically generated by the database and assigned to the game object:

```
POST http://localhost:8000/games/
```

We have to compose and send an HTTP request with the following HTTP verb (GET) and request URL (http://localhost:8000/games/{id}/) to retrieve the game whose ID matches the specified numeric value in the place where {id} is written. For example, if we use the request URL http://localhost:8000/games/21/, the server will retrieve the game whose id matches 21. As a result of the request, the server will retrieve a game with the specified id from the database and create the appropriate game object in Python. If a game is found, the server will serialize the game object into JSON and return a 200 OK status code and a JSON body with the serialized game object. If no game matches the specified id, the server will return just a 404 Not Found status code:

```
GET http://localhost:8000/games/{id}/
```

We have to compose and send an HTTP request with the following HTTP verb (GET) and request URL (`http://localhost:8000/games/{id}/`) to retrieve the game whose id matches the specified numeric value in the place where `{id}` is written and replace it with a game created with the provided data. In addition, we have to provide the JSON key-value pairs with the field names and the values to create the new game, which will replace the existing one. As a result of the request, the server will validate the provided values for the fields, make sure that it is a valid game, and replace the one that matches the specified id with the new one in the database. The ID for the game will be the same after the update operation. The server will update the existing row in the appropriate table and it will return a `200 OK` status code and a JSON body with the recently updated game serialized to JSON. If we don't provide all the necessary data for the new game, the server will return a `400 Bad Request` status code. If the server doesn't find a game with the specified id, the server will return just a `404 Not Found` status code:

```
PUT http://localhost:8000/games/{id}/
```

We have to compose and send an HTTP request with the following HTTP verb (DELETE) and request URL (`http://localhost:8000/games/{id}/`) to remove the game whose id matches the specified numeric value in the place where `{id}` is written. For example, if we use the request URL `http://localhost:8000/games/51/`, the server will delete the game whose id matches `51`. As a result of the request, the server will retrieve a game with the specified id from the database and create the appropriate game object in Python. If a game is found, the server will request the ORM to delete the game row associated with this game object and the server will return a `204 No Content` status code. If no game matches the specified id, the server will return just a `404 Not Found` status code:

```
DELETE http://localhost:8000/games/{id}/
```

Setting up the virtual environment with Django REST framework

In `Chapter 1`, *Developing RESTful APIs and Microservices with Flask 1.0.2*, we learned that, throughout this book, we are going to work with the lightweight virtual environments introduced and improved in Python 3.4. Now we will follow many steps to create a new lightweight virtual environment to work with Flask and Flask-RESTful.

It is highly recommended that you read the section named *Working with lightweight virtual environments* in `Chapter 1`, *Developing RESTful APIs and Microservices with Flask 1.0.2*, if you don't have experience with lightweight virtual environments in modern Python. The chapter includes all the detailed explanations about the effects of the steps we are going to follow.

The following commands assume that you have Python 3.7.1 or greater installed on Linux, macOS, or Windows.

First, we have to select the target folder or directory for our lightweight virtual environment. The following is the path we will use in the example for Linux and macOS:

```
~/HillarPythonREST2/Django01
```

The target folder for the virtual environment will be the `HillarPythonREST2/Django01` folder within our home directory. For example, if our home directory in macOS or Linux is `/Users/gaston`, the virtual environment will be created within `/Users/gaston/HillarPythonREST2/Django01`. You can replace the specified path with your desired path in each command.

The following is the path we will use in the example for Windows:

```
%USERPROFILE%\HillarPythonREST2\Django01
```

The target folder for the virtual environment will be the `HillarPythonREST2\Django01` folder within our user profile folder. For example, if our user profile folder is `C:\Users\gaston`, the virtual environment will be created within `C:\Users\gaston\HillarPythonREST2\Django01`. Of course, you can replace the specified path with your desired path in each command.

In Windows PowerShell, the previous path would be as follows:

```
$env:userprofile\HillarPythonREST2\Django01
```

Now we have to use the `-m` option followed by the `venv` module name and the desired path to make Python run this module as a script and create a virtual environment in the specified path. The instructions are different depending on the platform in which we are creating the virtual environment. Thus, make sure you follow the instructions for your operating system.

Open a Terminal in Linux or macOS and execute the following command to create a virtual environment:

```
python3 -m venv ~/HillarPythonREST2/Django01
```

In Windows, in the Command Prompt, execute the following command to create a virtual environment:

```
python -m venv %USERPROFILE%\HillarPythonREST2\Django01
```

If you want to work with Windows PowerShell, execute the following command to create a virtual environment:

```
python -m venv $env:userprofile\HillarPythonREST2\Django01
```

The previous commands don't produce any output. Now that we have created a virtual environment, we will run a platform-specific script to activate it. After we activate the virtual environment, we will install packages that will only be available in this virtual environment.

If your Terminal is configured to use the bash shell in macOS or Linux, run the following command to activate the virtual environment. The command also works for the zsh shell:

```
source ~/PythonREST/Django01/bin/activate
```

If your Terminal is configured to use either the csh or tcsh shell, run the following command to activate the virtual environment:

```
source ~/PythonREST/Django01/bin/activate.csh
```

If your Terminal is configured to use the fish shell, run the following command to activate the virtual environment:

```
source ~/PythonREST/Django01/bin/activate.fish
```

In Windows, you can run either a batch file in the Command Prompt or a Windows PowerShell script to activate the virtual environment. If you prefer the Command Prompt, run the following command in the Windows command line to activate the virtual environment:

```
%USERPROFILE%\PythonREST\Django01\Scripts\activate.bat
```

If you prefer the Windows PowerShell, launch it and run the following commands to activate the virtual environment. However, notice that you should have script execution enabled in Windows PowerShell to be able to run the script:

```
cd $env:USERPROFILE
PythonREST\Django01\Scripts\Activate.ps1
```

After you activate the virtual environment, the Command Prompt will display the virtual environment root folder name enclosed in parenthesis as a prefix of the default prompt to remind us that we are working in the virtual environment. In this case, we will see (Django01) as a prefix for the Command Prompt because the root folder for the activated virtual environment is Django01.

We have followed the necessary steps to create and activate a virtual environment. Now we will create a requirements.txt file to specify the set of packages that our application requires to be installed in any supported platform. This way, it will be extremely easy to repeat the installation of the specified packages with their versions in any new virtual environment.

Use your favorite editor to create a new text file named requirements.txt within the root folder for the recently created virtual environment. The following lines show the contents for the file that declares the packages and the versions that our API requires. The code file for the sample is included in the restful_python_2_05_01 folder, in the Django01/requirements.txt file:

```
Django==2.1.4
djangorestframework==3.9.0
httpie==0.9.9
```

Each line in the requirements.txt file indicates the package and the version that needs to be installed. In this case, we are working with exact versions by using the == operator because we want to make sure that the specified version is installed. The following table summarizes the packages and the version numbers that we specified as requirements:

Package name	Version to be installed
Django	2.1.4
djangorestframework	3.9.0
httpie	1.0.2

Go to the root folder for the virtual environment: Django01. In macOS or Linux, enter the following command:

```
cd ~/PythonREST/Django01
```

In Windows Command Prompt, enter the following command:

```
cd /d %USERPROFILE%\PythonREST\Django01
```

In Windows PowerShell, enter the following command:

```
cd $env:USERPROFILE
cd PythonREST\Django01
```

Now we must run the following command on macOS, Linux, or Windows to install the packages and the versions explained in the previous table with `pip` by using the recently created `requirements` file. Notice that `Django` is a dependency for `djangorestframework`. Make sure you are in the folder that has the `requirements.txt` file before running the command (`Django01`):

```
pip install -r requirements.txt
```

The final lines for the output will indicate all the packages that have been successfully installed, including `Django`, `djangorestframework`, and `httpie`:

```
Installing collected packages: pytz, Django, djangorestframework, Pygments,
certifi, chardet, idna, urllib3, requests, httpie
Successfully installed Django-2.1.4 Pygments-2.2.0 certifi-2018.10.15
chardet-3.0.4 djangorestframework-3.9.0 httpie-1.0.2 idna-2.7 pytz-2018.6
requests-2.20.0 urllib3-1.24
```

Now run the following command to create a new Django project named `games_service`. The command won't produce any output:

```
django-admin.py startproject games_service
```

The previous command created a `games_service` folder with other subfolders and Python files. Now go to the recently created `games_service` folder. Just execute the following command:

```
cd games_service
```

Then, run the following command to create a new Django app named `games` within the `games_service` Django project. The command won't produce any output:

```
python manage.py startapp games
```

The previous command created a new `games_service/games` subfolder, with the following files:

- __init__.py
- admin.py
- apps.py
- models.py

- `tests.py`
- `views.py`

In addition, the `games_service/games` folder will have a `migrations` subfolder with a `__init__.py` Python script. The following screenshot shows the folders and files in the directory trees starting at the `games_service` folder:

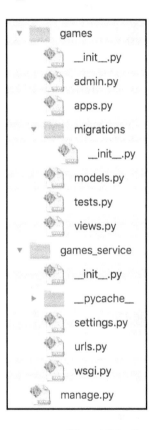

Let's check the Python code in the `apps.py` file within the `games_service/games` folder. The following lines show the code for this file:

```
from django.apps import AppConfig


class GamesConfig(AppConfig):
    name = 'games'
```

The code declares the `GamesConfig` class as a subclass of the `django.apps.AppConfig` superclass, which represents a Django application and its configuration. The `GamesConfig` class just defines the `name` class attribute and sets its value to `'games'`.

We have to add `games.apps.GamesConfig` as one of the installed apps in the `games_service/game_service/settings.py` file, which configures settings for the `games_service` Django project. We built the previous string as follows: app name + `.apps.` + class name, which is `games` + `.apps.` + `GamesConfig`. In addition, we have to add the `rest_framework` app to make it possible for us to use Django REST Framework.

The `games_service/games_service/settings.py` file is a Python module with module-level variables that define the configuration of Django for the `games_service` project. We will make some changes to this Django settings file. Open the `games_service/games_service/settings.py` file and locate the following lines, which specify the strings list that declares the installed apps and save it in the `INSTALLED_APPS` variable:

```
INSTALLED_APPS = [
    'django.contrib.admin',
    'django.contrib.auth',
    'django.contrib.contenttypes',
    'django.contrib.sessions',
    'django.contrib.messages',
    'django.contrib.staticfiles',
]
```

Add the following two strings to the `INSTALLED_APPS` strings list and save the changes to the `games_service/games_service/settings.py` file:

- `'rest_framework'`
- `'games.apps.GamesConfig'`

The following lines show the new code that declares the `INSTALLED_APPS` strings list with the added lines highlighted. The code file for the sample is included in the `restful_python_2_05_01` folder, in the `Django01/games_service/games-service/settings.py` file:

```
INSTALLED_APPS = [
    'django.contrib.admin',
    'django.contrib.auth',
    'django.contrib.contenttypes',
    'django.contrib.sessions',
    'django.contrib.messages',
    'django.contrib.staticfiles',
```

```
    # Django REST Framework
    'rest_framework',
    # Our Games application
    'games.apps.GamesConfig',
]
```

This way, we have added Django REST Framework and the `games` application to our initial Django project named `games_service`.

Creating the models

Now we will create a simple `Game` model that we will use to represent and persist games. Open the `games_service/games/models.py` file. The following lines show the initial code for this file, with just one import statement and a comment that indicates we should create the models:

```
from django.db import models

# Create your models here.
```

Replace the code for the `games_service/games/models.py` file with the following lines. The new code creates a `Game` class, specifically, a `Game` model in the `games/models.py` file. The code file for the sample is included in the `restful_python_2_05_01` folder, in the `Django01/games_service/games/apps.py` file:

```
from django.db import models


class Game(models.Model):
    created_timestamp = models.DateTimeField(auto_now_add=True)
    name = models.CharField(max_length=200, default='')
    release_date = models.DateTimeField()
    esrb_rating = models.CharField(max_length=150, default='')
    played_once = models.BooleanField(default=False)
    played_times = models.IntegerField(default=0)

    class Meta:
        ordering = ('name',)
```

The `Game` class is a subclass of the `django.db.models.Model` superclass. Each attribute declared within the `Game` class represents a database column or field. Django automatically adds an auto-increment integer primary key column named `id` when it creates the database table related to the model. We specified the field types, maximum lengths, and defaults for many attributes.

The Game class declares an inner class named Meta that declares an ordering attribute and sets its value to a tuple of a string whose first value is the 'name' string, indicating that, by default, we want the results ordered by the name attribute in ascending order.

 By default, Django has its ORM configured to use an SQLite database. In this example, we will be working with this default configuration.

Then, it is necessary to create the initial migration for the new Game model we recently coded. Run the following Python script:

```
python manage.py makemigrations games
```

The following lines show the output generated after running the previous command:

```
Migrations for 'games':
  games/migrations/0001_initial.py
    - Create model Game
```

The output indicates that the games_service/games/migrations/0001_initial.py file includes the code to create the Game model. The following lines show the code for this file that was automatically generated by Django. The code file for the sample is included in the restful_python_2_05_01 folder, in the Django01/games_service/games/migrations/0001_initial.py file:

```
# Generated by Django 2.1.4 on 2018-10-24 15:45

from django.db import migrations, models


class Migration(migrations.Migration):

    initial = True

    dependencies = [
    ]

    operations = [
        migrations.CreateModel(
            name='Game',
            fields=[
                ('id', models.AutoField(auto_created=True,
primary_key=True, serialize=False, verbose_name='ID')),
                ('created_timestamp',
models.DateTimeField(auto_now_add=True)),
```

```
            ('name', models.CharField(max_length=200)),
            ('release_date', models.DateTimeField()),
            ('esrb_rating', models.CharField(max_length=150)),
            ('played_once', models.BooleanField(default=False)),
            ('played_times', models.IntegerField(default=0)),
        ],
        options={
            'ordering': ('name',),
        },
    ),
]
```

The code defines a subclass of the django.db.migrations.Migration superclass named
Migration that defines an operation that creates the Game model's table. Now, run the
following Python script to apply all the generated migrations:

```
python manage.py migrate
```

The following lines show the output generated after running the previous command:

```
Operations to perform:
  Apply all migrations: admin, auth, contenttypes, games, sessions
Running migrations:
  Applying contenttypes.0001_initial... OK
  Applying auth.0001_initial... OK
  Applying admin.0001_initial... OK
  Applying admin.0002_logentry_remove_auto_add... OK
  Applying admin.0003_logentry_add_action_flag_choices... OK
  Applying contenttypes.0002_remove_content_type_name... OK
  Applying auth.0002_alter_permission_name_max_length... OK
  Applying auth.0003_alter_user_email_max_length... OK
  Applying auth.0004_alter_user_username_opts... OK
  Applying auth.0005_alter_user_last_login_null... OK
  Applying auth.0006_require_contenttypes_0002... OK
  Applying auth.0007_alter_validators_add_error_messages... OK
  Applying auth.0008_alter_user_username_max_length... OK
  Applying auth.0009_alter_user_last_name_max_length... OK
  Applying games.0001_initial... OK
  Applying sessions.0001_initial... OK
```

After we run the previous command, we will notice that the root folder for our
games_service project now has a db.sqlite3 file. We can use the SQLite command line
or any other application that allows us to easily check the contents of the SQLite database to
check the tables that Django generated.

In macOS and most modern Linux distributions, SQLite is already installed, and therefore, you can run the `sqlite3` command-line utility. However, in Windows, if you want to work with the `sqlite3.exe` command-line utility, you will have to download and install SQLite from its web page `http://www.sqlite.org` and add the path in which the executable file is located to the `PATH` environment variable.

Run the following command to list the generated tables. The code file for the sample is included in the `restful_python_2_05_01` folder, in the `Django01/cmd/list_sqlite3_tables.txt` file:

```
sqlite3 db.sqlite3 ".tables"
```

The following lines show the output for the previous command:

```
auth_group                      django_admin_log
auth_group_permissions          django_content_type
auth_permission                 django_migrations
auth_user                       django_session
auth_user_groups                games_game
auth_user_user_permissions
```

Run the following command to retrieve the SQL used to create the `games_game` table. The code file for the sample is included in the `restful_python_2_05_01` folder, in the `Django01/cmd/retrieve_sql_sqlite3_games_game_table.txt` file:

```
sqlite3 db.sqlite3 ".schema games_game"
```

The following command will allow you to check the contents of the `games_game` table after we compose and send HTTP requests to the RESTful API and make CRUD operations to the `games_game` table. The code file for the sample is included in the `restful_python_2_05_01` folder, in the `Django01/cmd/check_contents_sqlite3_games_game_table.txt` file:

```
sqlite3 db.sqlite3 "SELECT * FROM games_game ORDER BY name;"
```

Instead of working with the SQLite command-line utility, you can use a GUI tool to check the contents of the SQLite database. DB Browser for SQLite is a useful multiplatform and free GUI tool that allows us to easily check the database contents of an SQLite database in macOS, Linux, and Windows. You can read more information about this tool and download its different versions from `http://sqlitebrowser.org`. Once you have installed the tool, you just need to open the `db.sqlite3` file and you can check the database structure and browse the data for the different tables. You can use also the database tools included in your favorite IDE to check the contents for the SQLite database.

The SQLite database engine and the database file name are specified in the `games_service/games_service/settings.py` Python file. The following lines show the declaration of the `DATABASES` dictionary that contains the settings for all the databases that Django uses. The nested dictionary maps the database named `default` with the `django.db.backends.sqlite3` database engine and the `db.sqlite3` database file located in the `BASE_DIR` folder (`games_service`):

```
DATABASES = {
    'default': {
        'ENGINE': 'django.db.backends.sqlite3',
        'NAME': os.path.join(BASE_DIR, 'db.sqlite3'),
    }
}
```

After we have executed the migrations, the SQLite database will have the following tables:

- `auth_group`
- `auth_group_permissions`
- `auth_permission`
- `auth_user`
- `auth_user_groups`
- `auth_user_user_permissions`
- `django_admin_log`
- `django_content_type`
- `django_migrations`
- `django_session`
- `games_game`

The `games_game` table persists the `Game` class, specifically, the `Game` model, in the database. Django's integrated ORM generated the `games_game` table based on our `Game` model. The `games_game` table has the following rows (also known as **fields**) with their SQLite types, all of them not nullable:

- `id`: The integer primary key, an `autoincrement` row
- `created_timestamp`: `datetime`
- `name`: `varchar(200)`

- release_date: datetime
- Esrb_rating: varchar(150)
- played_once: bool
- played_times: integer

The following lines show the SQL creation script that Django generated when we executed the migrations:

```
CREATE TABLE IF NOT EXISTS "games_game" (
    "id" integer NOT NULL PRIMARY KEY AUTOINCREMENT,
    "created_timestamp" datetime NOT NULL,
    "name" varchar(200) NOT NULL,
    "release_date" datetime NOT NULL,
    "esrb_rating" varchar(150) NOT NULL,
    "played_once" bool NOT NULL,
    "played_times" integer NOT NULL);
```

Django generated the additional tables that it requires to support the web framework and the authentication features that we will use later.

Managing serialization and deserialization

Our RESTful web API has to be able to serialize the game instances into JSON representations and also deserialize the JSON representations to build game instances. With Django REST Framework, we just need to create a serializer class for the game instances to manage serialization to JSON and deserialization from JSON.

 Django REST Framework uses a two-phase process for serialization. The serializers are mediators between the model instances and Python primitives. Parsers and renderers act as mediators between Python primitives and HTTP requests and responses.

We will configure our mediator between the Game model instances and Python primitives by creating a subclass of the rest_framework.serializers.Serializer class to declare the fields and the necessary methods to manage serialization and deserialization. We will repeat some of the information about the fields that we have included in the Game model so that we understand all the things that we can configure in a subclass of the Serializer class. However, we will work with shortcuts that will reduce boilerplate code later in the next examples. We will write less code in the next examples by using the ModelSerializer class.

Now go to the `games_service/games` folder and create a new Python code file named
`serializers.py`. The following lines show the code that declares the new
`GameSerializer` class. The code file for the sample is included in the
`restful_python_2_05_01` folder, in the
`Django01/games_service/games/serializers.py` file:

```python
from rest_framework import serializers
from games.models import Game


class GameSerializer(serializers.Serializer):
    id = serializers.IntegerField(read_only=True)
    name = serializers.CharField(max_length=200)
    release_date = serializers.DateTimeField()
    esrb_rating = serializers.CharField(max_length=150)
    played_once = serializers.BooleanField(required=False)
    played_times = serializers.IntegerField(required=False)

    def create(self, validated_data):
        return Game.objects.create(**validated_data)

    def update(self, instance, validated_data):
        instance.name = validated_data.get('name',
            instance.name)
        instance.release_date = validated_data.get('release_date',
            instance.release_date)
        instance.esrb_rating = validated_data.get('esrb_rating',
            instance.esrb_rating)
        instance.played_once = validated_data.get('played_once',
            instance.played_once)
        instance.played_times = validated_data.get('played_times',
            instance.played_times)
        instance.save()
        return instance
```

The `GameSerializer` class declares the attributes that represent the fields that we want to
be serialized. Notice that we have omitted the `created_timestamp` attribute that was
present in the `Game` model. When there is a call to the inherited `save` method for this class,
the overridden `create` and `update` methods define how to create or modify an instance. In
fact, these methods must be implemented in our class because they just raise a
`NotImplementedError` exception in their base declaration in the `Serializer` superclass.

The `create` method receives the validated data in the `validated_data` argument. The code creates and returns a new `Game` instance based on the received validated data.

The `update` method receives an existing `Game` instance that is being updated and the new validated data in the `instance` and `validated_data` arguments. The code updates the values for the attributes of the instance with the updated attribute values retrieved from the validated data, calls the save method for the updated `Game` instance, and returns the updated and saved instance.

We can launch our default Python interactive shell and make all the Django project modules available before it starts. This way, we can check that the serializer works as expected. In addition, it will help us understand how serialization works in Django.

Run the following command to launch the interactive shell. Make sure you are within the `games_service` folder in the Terminal or Command Prompt:

```
python manage.py shell
```

You will notice that a line that says (`InteractiveConsole`) is displayed after the usual lines that introduce your default Python interactive shell. Enter the following code in the Python interactive shell to import all the things we will need to test the `Game` model and its serializer. The code file for the sample is included in the `restful_python_2_05_01` folder, in the `Django01/cmd/serializers_test_01.py` file:

```
from datetime import datetime
from django.utils import timezone
from django.utils.six import BytesIO
from rest_framework.renderers import JSONRenderer
from rest_framework.parsers import JSONParser
from games.models import Game
from games.serializers import GameSerializer
```

Now enter the following code to create two instances of the `Game` model and save them. The code file for the sample is included in the `restful_python_2_05_01` folder, in the `Django01/cmd/serializers_test_01.py` file:

```
gamedatetime = timezone.make_aware(datetime.now(),
timezone.get_current_timezone())
game1 = Game(name='PAW Patrol: On A Roll!', release_date=gamedatetime,
esrb_rating='E (Everyone)')
game1.save()
game2 = Game(name='Spider-Man', release_date=gamedatetime, esrb_rating='T
(Teen)')
game2.save()
```

After we execute the previous code, we can check the SQLite database with the previously introduced command-line command or GUI tool to check the contents of the games_game table. We will notice the table has two rows and the columns have the values we have provided to the different attributes of the Game instances. However, make sure you run the commands in another Terminal or Command Prompt to avoid leaving the interactive shell that we will continue to use. The following screenshot shows the contents of the games_game table:

Enter the following commands in the interactive shell to check the values for the identifiers for the saved Game instances and the value of the created_timestamp attribute that includes the date and time in which we saved the instance to the database. The code file for the sample is included in the restful_python_2_05_01 folder, in the Django01/cmd/serializers_test_01.py file:

```
print(game1.id)
print(game1.name)
print(game1.created_timestamp)
print(game2.id)
print(game2.name)
print(game2.created_timestamp)
```

Now let's write the following code to serialize the first game instance (game1). The code file for the sample is included in the restful_python_2_05_01 folder, in the Django01/cmd/serializers_test_01.py file:

```
game_serializer1 = GameSerializer(game1)
print(game_serializer1.data)
```

The following line shows the generated dictionary, specifically, a rest_framework.utils.serializer_helpers.ReturnDict instance:

```
{'id': 1, 'name': 'PAW Patrol: On A Roll!', 'release_date':
'2018-10-24T17:47:30.177610Z', 'esrb_rating': 'E (Everyone)',
'played_once': False, 'played_times': 0}
```

Now let's serialize the second game instance (game2). The code file for the sample is included in the restful_python_2_05_01 folder, in the Django01/cmd/serializers_test_01.py file:

```
game_serializer2 = GameSerializer(game2)
print(game_serializer2.data)
```

The following line shows the generated dictionary:

```
{'id': 2, 'name': 'Spider-Man', 'release_date':
'2018-10-24T17:47:30.177610Z', 'esrb_rating': 'T (Teen)', 'played_once':
False, 'played_times': 0}
```

We can easily render the dictionaries held in the data attribute into JSON with the help of the rest_framework.renderers.JSONRenderer class. The following lines create an instance of this class and then call the render method to render the dictionaries held in the data attribute into their JSON representation. The code file for the sample is included in the restful_python_2_05_01 folder, in the Django01/cmd/serializers_test_01.py file:

```
renderer = JSONRenderer()
rendered_game1 = renderer.render(game_serializer1.data)
rendered_game2 = renderer.render(game_serializer2.data)
print(rendered_game1)
print(rendered_game2)
```

The following lines show the output generated from the two calls to the render method:

```
b'{"id":1,"name":"PAW Patrol: On A
Roll!","release_date":"2018-10-24T17:47:30.177610Z","esrb_rating":"E
(Everyone)","played_once":false,"played_times":0}'
    b'{"id":2,"name":"Spider-
Man","release_date":"2018-10-24T17:47:30.177610Z","esrb_rating":"T
(Teen)","played_once":false,"played_times":0}'
```

Now we will work in the opposite direction, from serialized data to the population of a Game instance. The following lines generate a new Game instance from a JSON string (serialized data); that is, we will write code that deserializes. The code file for the sample is included in the restful_python_2_05_01 folder, in the Django01/cmd/serializers_test_01.py file:

```
json_string_for_new_game = '{"name":"Tomb Raider Extreme
Edition","release_date":"2016-05-18T03:02:00.776594Z","game_category":"3D
RPG","played":false}'
json_bytes_for_new_game = bytes(json_string_for_new_game ,
encoding="UTF-8")
```

```
stream_for_new_game = BytesIO(json_bytes_for_new_game)
parser = JSONParser()
parsed_new_game = parser.parse(stream_for_new_game)
print(parsed_new_game)
```

The first line creates a new string with the JSON that defines a new game (`json_string_for_new_game`). Then, the code converts the string to `bytes` and saves the results of the conversion in the `json_bytes_for_new_game` variable. The `django.utils.six.BytesIO` class provides a buffered I/O implementation using an in-memory bytes buffer. The code uses this class to create a stream from the previously generated JSON bytes with the serialized data, `json_bytes_for_new_game`, and saves the generated instance in the `stream_for_new_game` variable.

We can easily deserialize and parse a stream into the Python models with the help of the `rest_framework.parsers.JSONParser` class. The next line creates an instance of this class and then calls the `parse` method with `stream_for_new_game` as an argument, parses the stream into Python native datatypes, and saves the results in the `parsed_new_game` variable.

After executing the previous lines, `parsed_new_game` holds a Python dictionary, parsed from the stream. The following lines show the output generated after executing the previous code snippet:

```
{'name': 'Red Dead Redemption 2', 'release_date':
'2018-10-26T01:01:00.776594Z', 'esrb_rating': 'M (Mature)'}
```

The following lines use the `GameSerializer` class to generate a fully populated `Game` instance named `new_game` from the Python dictionary, parsed from the stream. The code file for the sample is included in the `restful_python_2_05_01` folder, in the `Django01/cmd/serializers_test_01.py` file:

```
new_game_serializer = GameSerializer(data=parsed_new_game)
if new_game_serializer.is_valid():
    new_game = new_game_serializer.save()
    print(new_game.name)
```

First, the code creates an instance of the `GameSerializer` class with the Python dictionary that we previously parsed from the stream (`parsed_new_game`) passed as the `data` keyword argument. Then, the code calls the `is_valid` method to determine whether the data is valid or not.

Notice that we must always call `is_valid` before we attempt to access the serialized data representation when we pass a `data` keyword argument in the creation of a serializer.

If the method returns `true`, we can access the serialized representation in the `data` attribute, and therefore, the code calls the `save` method that inserts the corresponding row in the database and returns a fully populated `Game` instance, saved in the `new_game` local variable. Then, the code prints one of the attributes from the fully populated `Game` instance named `new_game`.

As we can see from the previous code, Django REST Framework makes it easy to serialize from objects to JSON and deserialize from JSON to objects, which are core requirements for our RESTful web API, which has to perform CRUD operations.

Enter the following command to leave the shell with the Django project modules that we started to test serialization and deserialization:

```
quit()
```

Understanding status codes for the responses

Django REST Framework declares a set of named constants for the different HTTP status codes in the `status` module. We will always use these named constants to return HTTP status codes.

It is bad practice to return numbers as status codes. We want our code to be easy to read and understand, and therefore, we will use descriptive HTTP status codes.

For example, in case we have to return a `404 Not Found` status code, we will return `status.HTTP_404_NOT_FOUND`, instead of just `404`. If we have to return a `201 Created` status code, we will return `status.HTTP_201_CREATED`, instead of just `201`.

Writing API views

Now we will create Django views that will use the previously created `GameSerializer` class to return JSON representations for each HTTP request that our API will handle. Open the `views.py` file located within the `games_service/games` folder. The following lines show the initial code for this file, with just one import statement and a comment that indicates we should create the views:

```
from django.shortcuts import render

# Create your views here.
```

Replace the existing code with the following lines. The new code creates a `JSONResponse` class and declares two functions: `game_collection` and `game_detail`. We are creating our first version of the API, and we use functions to keep the code as simple as possible. We will work with classes and more complex code in the next examples. The highlighted lines show the expressions that evaluate the value of the `request.method` attribute to determine the actions to be performed based on the HTTP verb. The code file for the sample is included in the `restful_python_2_05_01` folder, in the `Django01/games-service/games/views.py` file:

```
from django.http import HttpResponse
from django.views.decorators.csrf import csrf_exempt
from rest_framework.renderers import JSONRenderer
from rest_framework.parsers import JSONParser
from rest_framework import status
from games.models import Game
from games.serializers import GameSerializer


class JSONResponse(HttpResponse):
    def __init__(self, data, **kwargs):
        content = JSONRenderer().render(data)
        kwargs['content_type'] = 'application/json'
        super(JSONResponse, self).__init__(content, **kwargs)


@csrf_exempt
def game_collection(request):
    if request.method == 'GET':
        games = Game.objects.all()
        games_serializer = GameSerializer(games, many=True)
        return JSONResponse(games_serializer.data)
    elif request.method == 'POST':
        game_data = JSONParser().parse(request)
```

```
            game_serializer = GameSerializer(data=game_data)
            if game_serializer.is_valid():
                game_serializer.save()
                return JSONResponse(game_serializer.data,
                    status=status.HTTP_201_CREATED)
            return JSONResponse(game_serializer.errors,
                status=status.HTTP_400_BAD_REQUEST)


    @csrf_exempt
    def game_detail(request, id):
        try:
            game = Game.objects.get(id=id)
        except Game.DoesNotExist:
            return HttpResponse(status=status.HTTP_404_NOT_FOUND)
        if request.method == 'GET':
            game_serializer = GameSerializer(game)
            return JSONResponse(game_serializer.data)
        elif request.method == 'PUT':
            game_data = JSONParser().parse(request)
            game_serializer = GameSerializer(game,
                data=game_data)
            if game_serializer.is_valid():
                game_serializer.save()
                return JSONResponse(game_serializer.data)
            return JSONResponse(game_serializer.errors,
                status=status.HTTP_400_BAD_REQUEST)
        elif request.method == 'DELETE':
            game.delete()
            return HttpResponse(status=status.HTTP_204_NO_CONTENT)
```

The JSONResponse class is a subclass of the django.http.HttpResponse class. The superclass represents an HTTP response with a string as content. The JSONResponse class renders its content into JSON. The class defines just declare the __init__ method that created a rest_framework.renderers.JSONRenderer instance and calls its render method to render the received data into JSON and save the returned bytestring in the content local variable. Then, the code adds the 'content_type' key to the response header with 'application/json' as its value. Finally, the code calls the initializer for the base class with the JSON bytestring and the key-value pair added to the header. This way, the class represents a JSON response that we use in the two functions to easily return a JSON response.

The code uses the @csrf_exempt decorator in the two functions to ensure that the view sets a **CSRF** (short for **Cross-Site Request Forgery**) cookie. We do this to make it simple to test this example that doesn't represent a production-ready web service. We will add security features to our RESTful API later.

When the Django server receives an HTTP request, Django creates an HttpRequest instance, specifically a django.http.HttpRequest object. This instance contains metadata about the request, including the HTTP verb. The method attribute provides a string representing the HTTP verb or method used in the request.

When Django loads the appropriate view that will process the requests, it passes the HttpRequest instance as the first argument to the view function. The view function has to return an HttpResponse instance, specifically, a django.http.HttpResponse instance.

The game_collection function lists all the games or creates a new game. The function receives an HttpRequest instance in the request argument. The function is capable of processing two HTTP verbs: GET and POST. The code checks the value of the request.method attribute to determine the code to be executed based on the HTTP verb. If the HTTP verb is GET, the request.method == 'GET' expression will evaluate to True and the code has to list all the games. The code will retrieve all the Game objects from the database, use the GameSerializer to serialize all of them and return a JSONResponse instance built with the data generated by GameSerializer. The code creates the GameSerializer instance with the many=True argument to specify that multiple instances have to be serialized and not just one. Under the hood, Django uses a ListSerializer when the many argument value is set to True.

If the HTTP verb is POST, the code has to create a new game based on the JSON data that is included in the HTTP request. First, the code uses a JSONParser instance and calls its parse method with request as an argument to parse the game data provided as JSON data in the request and saves the results in the game_data local variable. Then, the code creates a GameSerializer instance with the previously retrieved data and calls the is_valid method to determine whether the Game instance is valid or not. If the instance is valid, the code calls the save method to persist the instance in the database and returns a JSONResponse with the saved data in its body and a status equal to status.HTTP_201_CREATED, that is, 201 Created.

The `game_detail` function retrieves, updates, or deletes an existing game. The function receives an `HttpRequest` instance in the `request` argument and the ID for the game to be retrieved, updated, or deleted in the `id` argument. The function is capable of processing three HTTP verbs: `GET`, `PUT`, and `DELETE`. The code checks the value of the `request.method` attribute to determine the code to be executed based on the HTTP verb. Irrespective of the HTTP verb, the function calls the `Game.objects.get` method with the received `id` as the `id` argument to retrieve a `Game` instance from the database based on the specified id, and saves it in the `game` local variable. If a game with the specified id doesn't exist in the database, the code returns an `HttpResponse` with its status equal to `status.HTTP_404_NOT_FOUND`, that is, `404 Not Found`.

If the HTTP verb is `GET`, the code creates a `GameSerializer` instance with `game` as an argument and returns the data for the serialized game in a `JSONResponse` that will include the default `200 OK` status. The code returns the retrieved game serialized as JSON.

If the HTTP verb is `PUT`, the code has to create a new game based on the JSON data that is included in the HTTP request, and use it to replace an existing game. First, the code uses a `JSONParser` instance and calls its parse method with `request` as an argument to parse the game data provided as `JSON` data in the request and saves the results in the `game_data` local variable. Then, the code creates a `GameSerializer` instance with the `Game` instance previously retrieved from the database, `game`, and the retrieved data that will replace the existing data, `game_data`. Then, the code calls the `is_valid` method to determine whether the `Game` instance is valid or not. If the instance is valid, the code calls the `save` method to persist the instance with the replaced values in the database and returns a `JSONResponse` with the saved data in its body and the default `200 OK` status. If the parsed data doesn't generate a valid `Game` instance, the code returns a `JSONResponse` with a status equal to `status.HTTP_400_BAD_REQUEST`, that is, `400 Bad Request`.

If the HTTP verb is `DELETE`, the code calls the `delete` method for the `Game` instance previously retrieved from the database (`game`). The call to the `delete` method erases the underlying row in the `games_game` table, and therefore, the game won't be available anymore. Then, the code returns a `JSONResponse` with a status equal to `status.HTTP_204_NO_CONTENT` that is, `204 No Content`.

Now we have to create a new Python file named `urls.py` in the `games_service/games` folder, specifically, the `games_service/games/urls.py` file. The following lines show the code for this file that defines the URL patterns that specifies the regular expressions that have to be matched in the request to run a specific function defined in the `views.py` file. The code file for the sample is included in the `restful_python_2_05_01` folder, in the `Django01/games-service/games/urls.py` file:

```
from django.conf.urls import url
from games import views

urlpatterns = [
    url(r'^games/$', views.game_collection),
    url(r'^games/(?P<id>[0-9]+)/$', views.game_detail),
]
```

The `urlpatterns` list makes it possible to route URLs to views. The code calls the `django.conf.urls.url` function with the regular expression that has to be matched, and the view function defined in the views module as arguments to create a `RegexURLPattern` instance for each entry in the `urlpatterns` list.

Now we have to replace the code in the `urls.py` that Django built automatically in the `games_service` folder, specifically, the `games_service/urls.py` file. Don't confuse this file with the previously created `urls.py` file that is saved in another folder. The `games_service/urls.py` file defines the root URL configurations, and therefore, we must include the URL patterns declared in the previously coded `games_service/games/urls.py` file. The following lines show the new code for the `games_service/urls.py` file. The code file for the sample is included in the `restful_python_2_05_01` folder, in the `Django01/games-service/urls.py` file:

```
from django.conf.urls import url, include

urlpatterns = [
    url(r'^', include('games.urls')),
]
```

Making HTTP requests to the Django API

Now we can launch Django's development server to compose and send HTTP requests to our unsecure web API (we will definitely add security later). Execute the following command:

```
python manage.py runserver
```

The following lines show the output after we execute the previous command. The development server is listening at port 8000.

```
Performing system checks...
System check identified no issues (0 silenced).
October 24, 2018 - 19:58:03
Django version 2.1.2, using settings 'games_service.settings'
Starting development server at http://127.0.0.1:8000/
Quit the server with CONTROL-C.
```

With the previous command, we will start Django development server and we will only be able to access it in our development computer. The previous command starts the development server in the default IP address, that is, 127.0.0.1 (localhost). It is not possible to access this IP address from other computers or devices connected to our LAN. Thus, if we want to make HTTP requests to our API from other computers or devices connected to our LAN, we should use the development computer IP address, 0.0.0.0 (for IPv4 configurations) or :: (for IPv6 configurations) as the desired IP address for our development server.

If we specify 0.0.0.0 as the desired IP address for IPv4 configurations, the development server will listen on every interface on port 8000. When we specify :: for IPv6 configurations, it will have the same effect. In addition, it is necessary to open the default port 8000 in our firewalls (software and/or hardware) and configure port-forwarding to the computer that is running the development server. The following command launches Django's development server in an IPv4 configuration and allows requests to be made from other computers and devices connected to our LAN:

```
python manage.py runserver 0.0.0.0:8000
```

If you decide to compose and send HTTP requests from other computers or devices connected to the LAN, remember that you have to use the development computer's assigned IP address instead of localhost. For example, if the computer's assigned IPv4 IP address is 192.168.1.103, instead of localhost:8000, you should use 192.168.1.103:8000. Of course, you can also use the hostname instead of the IP address. The previously explained configurations are very important because mobile devices might be the consumers of our RESTful APIs that can be encapsulated in microservices and we will always want to test the apps that make use of our APIs in our development environments.

Working with command-line tools - curl and httpie

We will start composing and sending HTTP requests with the `curl` and HTTPie command-line tools we introduced in `Chapter 1`, *Developing RESTful APIs and Microservice with Flask 1.0.2*, in the section named *Working with command-line tools - curl and httpie*. Make sure you read this section before executing the next examples.

Whenever we compose HTTP requests with the command line, we will use two versions of the same command: the first one with HTTPie and the second one with `curl`. This way, you will be able to use the most convenient for you.

Make sure you leave the Django development server running. Don't close the Terminal or Command Prompt that is running this development server. Open a new Terminal in macOS or Linux, or a Command Prompt in Windows, and run the following command. We will compose and send an HTTP request to create a new notification. The code file for the sample is included in the `restful_python_2_05_01` folder, in the `Django01/cmd/cmd01.txt` file:

```
http ":8000/games/"
```

The following is the equivalent `curl` command. The code file for the sample is included in the `restful_python_2_05_01` folder, in the `Django01/cmd/cmd02.txt` file:

```
curl -iX GET "localhost:8000/games/"
```

It is very important that you enter the ending slash (/) when specified because `/service/notifications` won't match any of the configured URL routes. Thus, we must enter `/service/notifications/`, including the ending slash (/).

The previous command will compose and send the following HTTP request: GET `http://localhost:8000/games/`. The request is the simplest case in our RESTful API because it will match and run the `views.game_collection` function, that is, the `game_collection` function declared within the `game_service/games/views.py` file. The function only receives `request` as a parameter because the URL pattern doesn't include any parameters. As the HTTP verb for the request is GET, the `request.method` property is equal to `'GET'`, and therefore, the function will execute the code that retrieves all the Game objects and generate a JSON response with all of these Game objects serialized.

The following lines show an example response for the HTTP request, with three `Game` objects in the JSON response:

```
HTTP/1.1 200 OK
Content-Length: 438
Content-Type: application/json
Date: Wed, 24 Oct 2018 20:25:45 GMT
Server: WSGIServer/0.2 CPython/3.7.1
X-Frame-Options: SAMEORIGIN
[
    {
        "esrb_rating": "E (Everyone)",
        "id": 1,
        "name": "PAW Patrol: On A Roll!",
        "played_once": false,
        "played_times": 0,
        "release_date": "2018-10-24T17:47:30.177610Z"
    },
    {
        "esrb_rating": "M (Mature)",
        "id": 3,
        "name": "Red Dead Redemption 2",
        "played_once": false,
        "played_times": 0,
        "release_date": "2018-10-26T01:01:00.776594Z"
    },
    {
        "esrb_rating": "T (Teen)",
        "id": 2,
        "name": "Spider-Man",
        "played_once": false,
        "played_times": 0,
        "release_date": "2018-10-24T17:47:30.177610Z"
    }
]
```

After we run a request, we will see the following line in the window that is running the Django development server. The output indicates that the server received an HTTP request with the `GET` verb and `/games/` as the URI. The server processed the HTTP requests, the returned status code `200` and the response length was equal to `438` characters. The response length can be different because the value for `id` assigned to each game will have an incidence in the response length. The first number after `HTTP/1.1."` indicates the returned status code (`200`) and the second number the response length (`438`):

```
[24/Oct/2018 20:25:45] "GET /games/ HTTP/1.1" 200 438
```

The following screenshot shows two Terminal windows side by side on macOS. The Terminal window at the left-hand side is running the Django development server and displays the received and processed HTTP requests. The Terminal window at the right-hand side is running `http` commands to generate the HTTP requests. It is a good idea to use a similar configuration to check the output while we compose and send the HTTP requests:

Now we will select one of the games from the previous list and we will compose an HTTP request to retrieve just the chosen game. For example, in the previous list, the first game has an `id` value equal to 3. Run the following command to retrieve this game. Use the `id` value you have retrieved in the previous command for the first game, as the `id` number might be different. The code file for the sample is included in the `restful_python_2_05_01` folder, in the `Django01/cmd/cmd03.txt` file:

```
http ":8000/games/3/"
```

The following is the equivalent `curl` command. The code file for the sample is included in the `restful_python_2_05_01` folder, in the `Django01/cmd/cmd04.txt` file:

```
curl -iX GET "localhost:8000/games/3/"
```

The previous commands will compose and send the following HTTP request: GET
http://localhost:8000/games/3/. The request has a number after /games/, and
therefore, it will match '^games/(?P<id>[0-9]+)/$' and run the views.game_detail
function, that is, the game_detail function declared within the
games_service/games/views.py file. The function receives request and id as
parameters because the URL pattern passes the number specified after /games/ in the id
parameter. As the HTTP verb for the request is GET, the request.method property is equal
to 'GET', and therefore, the function will execute the code that retrieves the Game object
whose primary key matches the id value received as an argument and, if found, generates
a JSON response with this Game object serialized. The following lines show an example
response for the HTTP request, with the Game object that matches the id value in the JSON
response:

```
HTTP/1.1 200 OK
Content-Length: 148
Content-Type: application/json
Date: Wed, 24 Oct 2018 22:04:50 GMT
Server: WSGIServer/0.2 CPython/3.7.1
X-Frame-Options: SAMEORIGIN
{
    "esrb_rating": "M (Mature)",
    "id": 3,
    "name": "Red Dead Redemption 2",
    "played_once": false,
    "played_times": 0,
    "release_date": "2018-10-26T01:01:00.776594Z"
}
```

Now we will compose and send an HTTP request to retrieve a game that doesn't exist. For
example, in the previous list, there is no game with an id value equal to 888. Run the
following command to try to retrieve this game. Make sure you use an id value that doesn't
exist. We must make sure that the utilities display the headers as part of the response
because the response won't have a body. The code file for the sample is included in the
restful_python_2_05_01 folder, in the Django01/cmd/cmd05.txt file:

```
http ":8000/games/888/"
```

The following is the equivalent curl command. The code file for the sample is included in
the restful_python_2_05_01 folder, in the Django01/cmd/cmd06.txt file:

```
curl -iX GET "localhost:8000/games/888/"
```

The previous commands will compose and send the following HTTP request: GET
http://localhost:8000/games/888/. The request is the same as the previous one we
have analyzed, with a different number for the id parameter. The server will run the
views.game_detail function, that is, the game_detail function declared within the
games_service/games/views.py file. The function will execute the code that retrieves
the Game object whose primary key matches the id value received as an argument and a
Game.DoesNotExist exception will be thrown and captured because there is no game
with the specified id value. Thus, the code will return an HTTP 404 Not Found status
code. The following lines show an example header response for the HTTP request:

```
HTTP/1.1 404 Not Found
Content-Length: 0
Content-Type: text/html; charset=utf-8
Date: Wed, 24 Oct 2018 22:12:02 GMT
Server: WSGIServer/0.2 CPython/3.7.1
X-Frame-Options: SAMEORIGIN
```

Now run the following command to compose and send an HTTP POST request to create a
new game. The code file for the sample is included in the restful_python_2_05_01
folder, in the Django01/cmd/cmd07.txt file:

```
http POST ":8000/games/" name='Fortnite' esrb_rating='T (Teen)'
release_date='2017-05-18T03:02:00.776594Z'
```

The following is the equivalent curl command. It is very important to use the -H
"Content-Type: application/json" option to indicate curl to send the data specified
after the -d option as application/json instead of the default application/x-www-
form-urlencoded. The code file for the sample is included in the
restful_python_2_05_01 folder, in the Django01/cmd/cmd08.txt file:

```
curl -iX POST -H "Content-Type: application/json" -d '{"name":"Fortnite",
"esrb_rating":"T (Teen)", "release_date": "2017-05-18T03:02:00.776594Z"}'
"localhost:8000/games/"
```

The previous commands will compose and send the following HTTP request: POST
http://localhost:8000/games/ with the following JSON key-value pairs:

```
{
    "name": "Fortnite",
    "esrb_rating": "T (Teen)",
    "release_date": "2017-05-18T03:02:00.776594Z"
}
```

The request specifies /games/, and therefore, it will match '^games/$' and run the views.game_collection function, that is, the game_collection function declared within the games_service/ames/views.py file. The function just receives request as a parameter because the URL pattern doesn't include any parameters. As the HTTP verb for the request is POST, the request.method property is equal to 'POST', and therefore, the function executes the code that parses the JSON data received in the request, creates a new Game and, if the data is valid, it saves the new Game instance. If the new Game instance was successfully persisted in the database, the function returns an HTTP 201 Created status code and the recently persisted Game serialized to JSON in the response body. The following lines show an example response for the HTTP request, with the new Game object in the JSON response:

```
HTTP/1.1 201 Created
Content-Length: 133
Content-Type: application/json
Date: Wed, 24 Oct 2018 22:18:36 GMT
Server: WSGIServer/0.2 CPython/3.6.2
X-Frame-Options: SAMEORIGIN
{
    "esrb_rating": "T (Teen)",
    "id": 4,
    "name": "Fortnite",
    "played_once": false,
    "played_times": 0,
    "release_date": "2017-05-18T03:02:00.776594Z"
}
```

Now we run the following command to compose and send an HTTP PUT request to update an existing game, specifically, to replace the previously added game with a new one. We have to check the value assigned to id in the previous response and replace 4 in the command with the returned value. For example, if the value for id was 8, you should use games/8/ instead of games/4/. The code file for the sample is included in the restful_python_2_05_01 folder, in the Django01/cmd/cmd09.txt file:

```
http PUT ":8000/games/4/" name='Fortnite Battle Royale' esrb_rating='T (Teen)' played_once=true played_times=3 release_date='2017-05-20T03:02:00.776594Z'
```

The following is the equivalent `curl` command. As happened with the previous `curl` example, it is very important to use the `-H "Content-Type: application/json"` option to indicate `curl` to send the data specified after the `-d` option as `application/json` instead of the default `application/x-www-form-urlencoded`. The code file for the sample is included in the `restful_python_2_05_01` folder, in the `Django01/cmd/cmd10.txt` file:

```
curl -iX PUT -H "Content-Type: application/json" -d '{"name":"Fortnite
Battle Royale", "esrb_rating":"T (Teen)", "played_once": "true",
"played_times": 3, "release_date": "2017-05-20T03:02:00.776594Z"}'
"localhost:8000/games/4/"
```

The previous commands will compose and send the HTTP request `PUT` `http://localhost:8000/games/15/` with the following JSON key-value pairs:

```
{
    "name": "Fortnite Battle Royale",
    "esrb_rating": "T (Teen)",
    "played_once": true,
     "played_times": 3,
    "release_date": "2017-05-20T03:02:00.776594Z"
}
```

The request has a number after `/games/`, and therefore, it will match `'^games/(?P<id>[0-9]+)/$'` and run the `views.game_detail` function, that is, the `game_detail` function declared within the `games_service/games/views.py` file. The function receives `request` and `id` as parameters because the URL pattern passes the number specified after `/games/` in the `id` parameter. As the HTTP verb for the request is `PUT`, the `request.method` property is equal to `'PUT'`, and therefore, the function executes the code that parses the JSON data received in the request, creates a `Game` instance from this data and updates all the fields for the existing game in the database. If the game was successfully updated in the database, the function returns an HTTP `200 OK` status code and the recently updated `Game` serialized to JSON in the response body. The following lines show an example response for the HTTP request, with the updated `Game` object in the JSON response:

```
HTTP/1.1 200 OK
Content-Length: 146
Content-Type: application/json
Date: Wed, 24 Oct 2018 22:27:36 GMT
Server: WSGIServer/0.2 CPython/3.6.2
X-Frame-Options: SAMEORIGIN
{
    "esrb_rating": "T (Teen)",
```

```
        "id": 4,
        "name": "Fortnite Battle Royale",
        "played_once": true,
        "played_times": 3,
        "release_date": "2017-05-20T03:02:00.776594Z"
    }
```

In order to successfully process an HTTP PUT request that updates an existing game with a new one, we must provide values for all the required fields. We will compose and send an HTTP request to try to update an existing game, and we will fail to do so because we will just provide a value for the name. As happened in the previous request, we will use the value assigned to id in the last game we added. The code file for the sample is included in the restful_python_2_05_01 folder, in the Django01/cmd/cmd11.txt file:

```
http PUT ":8000/games/4/" name='Fortnite Forever'
```

The following is the equivalent curl command. The code file for the sample is included in the restful_python_2_05_01 folder, in the Django01/cmd/cmd12.txt file:

```
curl -iX PUT -H "Content-Type: application/json" -d '{"name":"Fortnite
Forever"}' "localhost:8000/games/4/"
```

The previous commands will compose and send the HTTP request PUT http://localhost:8000/games/15/ with the following JSON key-value pair:

```
{
    "name": "Fortnite Forever",
}
```

The request will execute the same code we explained for the previous request. Because we didn't provide all the required values for a Game instance, the game_serializer.is_valid() method will return False and the function will return an HTTP 400 Bad Request status code and the details generated in the game_serializer.errors attribute are serialized to JSON in the response body. The following lines show an example response for the HTTP request, with the required fields that didn't include values in our request listed in the JSON response. The list uses the field name as a key and the error message as a value:

```
HTTP/1.1 400 Bad Request
Content-Length: 86
Content-Type: application/json
Date: Wed, 24 Oct 2018 22:33:37 GMT
Server: WSGIServer/0.2 CPython/3.6.2
X-Frame-Options: SAMEORIGIN
{
    "esrb_rating": [
```

```
            "This field is required."
        ],
        "release_date": [
            "This field is required."
        ]
    }
```

When we want our API to be able to update a single field for an existing resource, in this case, an existing game, we should provide an implementation for the PATCH method. The PUT method is meant to replace an entire resource and the PATCH method is meant to apply a delta to an existing resource. We can write code in the handler for the PUT method to apply a delta to an existing resource, but it is a better practice to use the PATCH method for this specific task. We will work with the PATCH method later when we code an improved version of our API.

Now run the following command to compose and send an HTTP request to delete an existing game, specifically, the last game we added and updated. As happened in our last HTTP requests, we have to check the value assigned to id in the previous response and replace 4 in the command with the returned value. The code file for the sample is included in the restful_python_2_05_01 folder, in the Django01/cmd/cmd13.txt file:

```
http DELETE ":8000/games/4/"
```

The following is the equivalent curl command. The code file for the sample is included in the restful_python_2_05_01 folder, in the Django01/cmd/cmd14.txt file:

```
curl -iX DELETE "localhost:8000/games/4/"
```

The previous commands will compose and send the following HTTP request: DELETE http://localhost:8000/games/4/. The request has a number after /games/, and therefore, it will match '^games/(?P<id>[0-9]+)/$' and run the views.game_detail function, that is, the game_detail function declared within the games_service/views.py file. The function receives request and id as parameters because the URL pattern passes the number specified after /games/ in the id parameter. As the HTTP verb for the request is DELETE, the request.method property is equal to 'DELETE', and therefore, the function will execute the code that parses the JSON data received in the request, creates a Game instance from this data and deletes the existing game in the database. If the game was successfully deleted in the database, the function returns an HTTP 204 No Content status code.

The following lines show an example response for the HTTP request after successfully deleting an existing game:

```
HTTP/1.1 204 No Content
Content-Length: 0
Content-Type: text/html; charset=utf-8
Date: Wed, 24 Oct 2018 22:39:15 GMT
Server: WSGIServer/0.2 CPython/3.6.2
X-Frame-Options: SAMEORIGIN
```

Working with GUI tools - Postman and others

So far, we have been working with two Terminal-based or command-line tools to compose and send HTTP requests to our Django development server: cURL and HTTPie. Now we will work with Postman, one of the GUI tools we used when composing and sending HTTP requests to the Flask development server on Chapter 1, *Developing RESTful APIs and Microservices with Flask 1.0.2*. If you skipped this chapter, make sure you check the installation instructions in the section named *Working with GUI tools - Postman and others* in that chapter.

Once you launch Postman, make sure you close the modal dialog box that provides shortcuts to common tasks. Select **GET Request** in the + new drop-down menu at the upper-left corner of the Postman main window.

Select **GET** in the drop-down menu on the left-hand side of the **Enter request URL** textbox, and enter localhost:8000/games/ in this textbox at the right-hand side of the drop-down.

Then, click **Send** and Postman will display the following information:

- **Status: 200 OK.**
- **Time**: The time it took for the request to be processed.
- **Size**: The response size calculated by adding the body size to the headers size.
- **Body**: The response body with all the notifications formatted as JSON with syntax highlighting. The default view for the response body is the Pretty view, and it activates syntax highlighting, which makes it easy to read JSON code.

The following screenshot shows the JSON response body in Postman for the HTTP GET request to `localhost:8000/games/`:

Click on the **Headers** tab at the right-hand side of the **Body** and **Cookies** tabs to read the response headers. The following screenshot shows the layout for the response headers that Postman displays for the previous response. Notice that Postman displays the **Status** at the right-hand side of the response and doesn't include it as the first line of the headers, as happened when we worked with both the `curl` and `http` command-line utilities:

Body Cookies **Headers (5)** Test Results	Status: 200 OK Time: 39 ms Size: 614 B	Download

Date → Wed, 24 Oct 2018 23:29:44 GMT

Server → WSGIServer/0.2 CPython/3.6.6

Content-Type → application/json

X-Frame-Options → SAMEORIGIN

Content-Length → 438

Now we will compose and send an HTTP request to create a new game, specifically, an HTTP `POST` request. Follow the next steps:

1. Click on the plus (+) button on the right-hand side of the tab that showed the previous request. This way, you will create a new tab.
2. Select **POST** in the drop-down menu at the left-hand side of the **Enter request URL** textbox, and enter `localhost:8000/games/` in this textbox at the right-hand side of the drop-down.
3. Click **Body** at the right-hand side of the **Authorization** and **Headers** tabs, within the panel that composes the request.
4. Activate the raw radio button and select **JSON (application/json)** in the drop-down at the right-hand side of the binary radio button. Postman will automatically add a **Content-type = application/json** header, and therefore, you will notice the **Headers** tab will be renamed to **Headers (1)**, indicating to us that there is one key-value pair specified for the request headers.
5. Enter the following lines in the following textbox the radio buttons, within the **Body** tab. The code file for the sample is included in the `restful_python_2_05_01` folder, in the `Django01/cmd15.txt` file:

```
{
    "name": "Crazy Kong 2019",
    "esrb_rating":"E (Everyone)",
    "release_date": "2019-02-01T03:02:00.776594Z"
}
```

The following screenshot shows the request body in Postman:

We followed the necessary steps to create an HTTP POST request with a JSON body that specifies the necessary key-value pairs to create a new game. Click **Send** and Postman will display the following information:

- **Status: 201 Created**
- **Time**: The time it took for the request to be processed
- **Size**: The response size calculated by adding the body size to the headers size
- **Body**: The response body with the recently added notification formatted as JSON with syntax highlighting (Pretty view)

The following screenshot shows the JSON response body in Postman for the HTTP POST request:

```
Body    Cookies    Headers (5)    Test Results              Status: 201 Created    Time: 35 ms    Size: 325 B       Download

Pretty    Raw    Preview    JSON  ▼    ⊡

1 ▾ {
2       "id": 5,
3       "name": "Crazy Kong 2019",
4       "release_date": "2019-02-01T03:02:00.776594Z",
5       "esrb_rating": "E (Everyone)",
6       "played_once": false,
7       "played_times": 0
8   }
```

Test your knowledge

Let's see whether you can answer the following questions correctly:

1. Which of the following commands run the script to create a new Django app named `recipes`:

    1. `python django.py startapp recipes`
    2. `python manage.py startapp recipes`
    3. `python starapp.py recipes`

2. Which of the following strings must be added to the `INSTALLED_APPS` variable to add Django REST Framework in the Django application:

    1. `'rest-framework'`
    2. `'django-rest-framework'`
    3. `'rest_framework'`

3. Django's ORM:

    1. Is integrated with Django
    2. Has to be configured as an optional component in Django
    3. Has to be installed after configuring SQLAlchemy

4. In Django REST Framework, serializers are:

    1. Mediators between the view functions and Python primitives
    2. Mediators between the URLs and view functions
    3. Mediators between the model instances and Python primitives

5. The `urlpatterns` list declared in the `urls.py` file makes it possible to:

    1. Route URLs to models
    2. Route URLs to Python primitives
    3. Route URLs to views

6. In Django REST Framework, parsers and renderers handle as mediators between:

    1. Model instances and Python primitives
    2. Python primitives and HTTP requests and responses
    3. URLs and view functions

7. If we want to create a simple `Game` model to represent and persist games in Django REST Framework, we can create:

   1. A `Game` class as a subclass of the `django.db.models.Model` superclass

   2. A `Game` class as a subclass of the `djangorestframework.models.Model` superclass

   3. A `Game` function in the `restframeworkmodels.py` file

Summary

In this chapter, we designed a RESTful API to interact with a simple SQLite database and perform CRUD operations with games. We defined the requirements for our API and we understood the tasks performed by each HTTP method. We set up a virtual environment with Django and Django REST Framework.

We created a model to represent and persist games and we executed migrations in Django. We learned to manage serialization and serialization of game instances into JSON representations with Django REST Framework. We wrote API views to process the different HTTP requests and we configured the URL patterns list to route URLs to views.

Finally, we started the Django development server and we used command-line tools to compose and send HTTP requests to our RESTful API and analyzed how each HTTP request was processed in our code. We also worked with GUI tools to compose and send HTTP requests.

Now that we understand the basics of Django REST Framework, we will expand the capabilities of the RESTful web API by taking advantage of advanced features included in Django REST Framework, which is the topic of the next chapter.

6
Working with Class-Based Views and Hyperlinked APIs in Django 2.1

In this chapter, we will expand the capabilities of the RESTful API that we started in the previous chapter. We will change the ORM settings to work with a more powerful PostgreSQL 10.5 database and we will take advantage of advanced features included in **Django REST Framework (DRF)** that allow us to reduce boilerplate code for complex APIs, such as class-based views. We will look at the following:

- Use model serializers to eliminate duplicate code
- Work with wrappers to write API views
- Use the default parsing and rendering options and move beyond JSON
- Browse the API
- Design a RESTful API to interact with a complex PostgreSQL 10.5 database
- Understand the tasks performed by each HTTP method
- Declare relationships with the models
- Install packages with the requirements file to work with PostgreSQL
- Configure the database
- Run migrations
- Verify the contents of the PostgreSQL database
- Manage serialization and deserialization with relationships and hyperlinks
- Create class-based views and use generic classes
- Take advantage of generic class-based views
- Work with endpoints for the API
- Browse an API with relationships
- Create and retrieve related resources

Using model serializers to eliminate duplicate code

The GameSerializer class we coded in Chapter 5, *Developing RESTful APIs with Django 2.1*, declares many attributes with the same names that we used in the Game model and repeats information such as the field types and the max_length values. The GameSerializer class is a subclass of the rest_framework.serializers.Serializer superclass and it declares attributes that we manually mapped to the appropriate types, and overrides the create and update methods.

Now we will create a new version of the GameSerializer class that will inherit from the rest_framework.serializers.ModelSerializer superclass. The ModelSerializer class automatically populates both a set of default fields and a set of default validators. In addition, the class provides default implementations for the create and update methods. Hence, this new version of the GameSerializer class will have less code than the previous version and will be easier to maintain.

 If you have any experience with Django Web Framework, you will notice that the Serializer and ModelSerializer classes are similar to the Form and ModelForm classes.

Open the serializers.py file in the games_service/games folder. Replace the code in this file with the following lines. The new code declares the new version of the GameSerializer class. The code file for the sample is included in the restful_python_2_06_01 folder, in the Django01/games-service/games/serializers.py file:

```
from rest_framework import serializers
from games.models import Game


class GameSerializer(serializers.ModelSerializer):
    class Meta:
        model = Game
        fields = ('id',
                  'name',
                  'release_date',
                  'esrb_rating',
                  'played_once',
                  'played_times',)
```

The new `GameSerializer` class declares a `Meta` inner class that declares two attributes:

- `model`: This attribute specifies the model related to the serializer, that is, the `Game` class
- `fields`: This attribute specifies a tuple of the string whose values indicate the field names that we want to include in the serialization from the related model

There is no need to override either the `create` or `update` methods because the generic behavior will be enough in this case. The `ModelSerializer` superclass provides implementations for both methods.

Now that we've understood how things work with Django REST Framework, we have reduced the boilerplate code that we didn't require in the `GameSerializer` class. We just needed to specify the desired set of fields in a tuple. Now, the types related to the game fields are included only in the `Game` class. This way, we are ready to write more serializer classes in a new version of the API that is more complex, without writing a huge amount of code.

Press *Ctrl + C* to quit Django's development server and execute the following command to start it again:

```
python manage.py runserver
```

Working with wrappers to write API views

Our code in the `games_service/games/views.py` file declared a `JSONResponse` class and two function-based views. These functions returned `JSONResponse` when it was necessary to return JSON data and a `django.Http.Response.HttpResponse` instance when the response was just an HTTP status code. Hence, no matter what the accepted content type that's specified in the HTTP request header, the view functions always provide the same content in the response body—JSON.

Run the following two commands to retrieve all the games with different values for the `Accept` request header: `text/html` and `application/json`. The code file for the sample is included in the `restful_python_2_06_01` folder, in the `Django01/cmd/cmd601.txt` file:

```
http -v ":8000/games/" "Accept:text/html"
http -v ":8000/games/" "Accept:application/json"
```

The following are the equivalent `curl` commands. The code file for the sample is included in the `restful_python_2_06_01` folder, in the `Django01/cmd/cmd602.txt` file:

```
curl -H "Accept: text/html" -viX GET "localhost:8000/games/"
curl -H "Accept: application/json" -viX GET "localhost:8000/games/"
```

The previous commands will compose and send the following HTTP request: `GET http://localhost:8000/games/`. We have requested both `http` and `curl` to enable the verbose mode with the `-v` option in which they specify more details about the operation and display the whole request, including the request header.

The first command defines the `text/html` value for the `Accept` request header. The second command defines the `application/json` value for the `Accept` request header. You will notice that both commands produce the same results, and therefore, the view functions don't take into account the value specified for the `Accept` request header in the HTTP requests. The header response for both commands will include the following line:

```
Content-Type: application/json
```

The second request specified that it will only accept `text/html`, but the response included a JSON body, that is, `application/json` content. Thus, our first version of the RESTful API is not prepared to render content other from JSON. We will make some changes to enable the API to render other contents.

Whenever we have doubts about the methods supported by a resource or resource collection in a RESTful API, we can compose and send an HTTP request with the `OPTIONS` HTTP verb and the URL for the resource or resource collection. If the RESTful API implements the `OPTIONS` HTTP verb for a resource or resource collection, it provides a comma-separated list of HTTP verbs or methods that it supports as a value for the `Allow` header in the response. In addition, the response header will include additional information about other supported options, such as the content type it is capable of parsing from the request and the content type it is capable of rendering on the response.

For example, if we want to know which HTTP verbs the games collection supports, we can run the following command. The code file for the sample is included in the `restful_python_2_06_01` folder, in the `Django01/cmd/cmd603.txt` file:

```
http OPTIONS ":8000/games/"
```

The following is the equivalent `curl` command. The code file for the sample is included in the `restful_python_2_06_01` folder, in the `Django01/cmd/cmd604.txt` file:

```
curl -iX OPTIONS "localhost:8000/games/"
```

The previous command will compose and send the following HTTP request: `OPTIONS http://localhost:8000/games/`. The request will match and run the `views.game_collection` function, that is, the `game_collection` function declared within the `game_service/games/views.py` file. This function only runs code when the `request.method` is equal to `'GET'` or `'POST'`. In this case, `request.method` is equal to `'OPTIONS'`, and therefore, the function won't run any code and won't return any response, specifically, it won't return an `HttpResponse` instance. As a result, we will see the `Internal Server Error` shown in the next screenshot listed in Django's development server console output:

The following lines show the header for the output that also includes a huge HTML document with detailed information about the error because the debug mode is activated for Django. We receive a `500 Internal Server Error` status code. Notice that you will have to scroll up in the Terminal or Command Prompt to find these lines:

```
HTTP/1.1 500 Internal Server Error
Content-Length: 51566
Content-Type: text/html
Date: Thu, 25 Oct 2018 04:14:09 GMT
Server: WSGIServer/0.2 CPython/3.7.1
Vary: Cookie
X-Frame-Options: SAMEORIGIN
```

Obviously, we want to provide a more consistent API and we want to provide an accurate response when we receive a request with the `OPTIONS` verbs for either a game resource or the games collection.

If we compose and send an HTTP request with the `OPTIONS` verb for a game resource, we will see the same error and we will have a similar response because the `views.game_detail` function only runs code when `request.method` is equal to `'GET'`, `'PUT'`, or `'DELETE'`.

The following commands will produce the explained error when we try to see the options offered for the game resource whose ID is equal to 2. Don't forget to replace 2 with a primary key value of an existing game in your configuration. The code file for the sample is included in the `restful_python_2_06_01` folder, in the `Django01/cmd/cmd605.txt` file:

```
http OPTIONS ":8000/games/3/"
```

The following is the equivalent `curl` command. The code file for the sample is included in the `restful_python_2_06_01` folder, in the `Django01/cmd/cmd606.txt` file:

```
curl -iX OPTIONS "localhost:8000/games/3/"
```

We just need to make a few small changes in the `games_service/games/views.py` file to solve the issues we have been analyzing for our RESTful API. We will use the useful `@api_view` decorator, declared in the `rest_framework.decorators` module, for our function-based views. This decorator allows us to specify which are the HTTP verbs that our function can process. If the request that has to be processed by the view function has an HTTP verb that isn't included in the string list specified as the `http_method_names` argument for the `@api_view` decorator, the default behavior returns a `405 Method Not Allowed` status code. This way, we make sure that whenever we receive an HTTP verb that isn't considered within our function view, we won't generate an unexpected error as the decorator handles the response for the unsupported HTTP verbs or methods.

Under the hood, the `@api_view` decorator is a wrapper that converts a function-based view into a subclass of the `rest_framework.views.APIView` class. This class is the base class for all view in Django REST Framework. As we might guess, if we want to work with class-based views, we can create classes that inherit from this class and we will have the same benefits we have analyzed for the function-based views that use the decorator. We will start working with class-based views in the forthcoming examples in this chapter.

In addition, as we specify a string list with the supported HTTP verbs, the decorator automatically builds the response for the `OPTIONS` HTTP verb with the supported methods, parser, and rendering capabilities. Our actual version of the API is just capable of rendering JSON as its output. The usage of the decorator makes sure that we always receive an instance of the `rest_framework.request.Request` class in the `request` argument when Django calls our view function. The decorator also handles the `ParserError` exceptions when our function views access the `request.data` attribute that might cause parsing problems.

Using the default parsing and rendering options and moving beyond JSON

The APIView class specifies default settings for each view that we can override by specifying appropriate values in the games_service/settings.py file or by overriding the class attributes in subclasses of the APIView superclass. As we learned, the usage of the APIView class under the hoods makes the decorator apply these default settings. Thus, whenever we use the decorator, the default parser classes and the default renderer classes will be associated with the function views.

By default, the value for the DEFAULT_PARSER_CLASSES configuration variable is the following tuple of strings with three parser class names:

```
(
    'rest_framework.parsers.JSONParser',
    'rest_framework.parsers.FormParser',
    'rest_framework.parsers.MultiPartParser'
)
```

When we use the @api_view decorator, the API will be able to handle any of the following content types through the appropriate parser classes when accessing the request.data attribute:

Content type	Parser class
application/json	rest_framework.parsers.JSONParser
application/x-www-form-urlencoded	rest_framework.parsers.FormParser
multipart/form-data	rest_framework.parsers.MultiPartParser

When we access the request.data attribute in the functions, Django REST Framework examines the value for the Content-Type header in the incoming request and determines the appropriate parser to parse the requested content. If we use the previously explained default values, Django REST Framework will be able to parse the previously listed content types. However, it is extremely important that the request specifies the appropriate value in the Content-Type header.

We have to remove the usage of the `rest_framework.parsers.JSONParser` class in the functions to make them work with all the configured parsers and stop working with a parser that only works with JSON. The `game_collection` function executes the following two lines when `request.method` is equal to `'POST'`:

```
game_data = JSONParser().parse(request)
game_serializer = GameSerializer(data=game_data)
```

We will remove the first line that uses the `JSONParser` and we will pass `request.data` as the data argument for the creation of a `GameSerializer` instance. The following line will replace the previous lines:

```
game_serializer = GameSerializer(data=request.data)
```

The `game_detail` function executes the following two lines when `request.method` is equal to `'PUT'`:

```
game_data = JSONParser().parse(request)
game_serializer = GameSerializer(game, data=game_data)
```

We will make the same edits done for the code in the `game_collection` function. We will remove the first line that uses the `JSONParser` and we will pass `request.data` as the data argument for the `GameSerializer`. The following line will replace the previous lines:

```
game_serializer = GameSerializer(game, data=request.data)
```

By default, the value for the `DEFAULT_RENDERER_CLASSES` configuration variable is the following tuple of classes:

```
(
    'rest_framework.renderers.JSONRenderer',
    'rest_framework.renderers.BrowsableAPIRenderer',
)
```

When we use the `@api_view` decorator, the API will be able to render any of the following content types in the response through the rendering classes when working with the `rest_framework.response.Response` object:

Response type	Rendering class
application/json	rest_framework.renderers.JSONRenderer
text/html	rest_framework.renderers.BrowsableAPIRenderer

By default, the value for the DEFAULT_CONTENT_NEGOTIATION_CLASS configuration variable defines the usage of the rest_framework.negotiation.DefaultContentNegotiation class. When we use the @api_view decorator, the API will use this content negotiation class to select the appropriate renderer for the response based on the incoming request. This way, when a request specifies that it will accept text/html, the content negotiation class selects the rest_framework.renderers.BrowsableAPIRenderer to render the response and generate a text/html response instead of an application/json response.

We have to replace the usages of both the JSONResponse and HttpResponse classes in the functions with the rest_framework.response.Response class. The Response class uses the previously explained content negotiation features, renders the received data into the appropriate content type, and returns it to the client.

Open the views.py file located within the games_service/games folder. Replace the code in this file with the following code, which removes the JSONResponse class and uses the @api_view decorator for the functions and the rest_framework.response.Response class. The added and edited lines are highlighted. The code file for the sample is included in the restful_python_2_06_01 folder, in the Django01/games-service/games/views.py file:

```python
from rest_framework.parsers import JSONParser
from rest_framework import status
from rest_framework.decorators import api_view
from rest_framework.response import Response
from games.models import Game
from games.serializers import GameSerializer


@api_view(['GET', 'POST'])
def game_collection(request):
    if request.method == 'GET':
        games = Game.objects.all()
        games_serializer = GameSerializer(games, many=True)
        return Response(games_serializer.data)
    elif request.method == 'POST':
        game_serializer = GameSerializer(data=request.data)
        if game_serializer.is_valid():
            game_serializer.save()
            return Response(game_serializer.data,
status=status.HTTP_201_CREATED)
        return Response(game_serializer.errors,
status=status.HTTP_400_BAD_REQUEST)
```

```
@api_view(['GET', 'PUT', 'POST'])
def game_detail(request, id):
    try:
        game = Game.objects.get(id=id)
    except Game.DoesNotExist:
        return Response(status=status.HTTP_404_NOT_FOUND)
    if request.method == 'GET':
        game_serializer = GameSerializer(game)
        return Response(game_serializer.data)
    elif request.method == 'PUT':
        game_serializer = GameSerializer(game, data=request.data)
        if game_serializer.is_valid():
            game_serializer.save()
            return Response(game_serializer.data)
        return Response(game_serializer.errors,
status=status.HTTP_400_BAD_REQUEST)
    elif request.method == 'DELETE':
        game.delete()
    return Response(status=status.HTTP_204_NO_CONTENT)
```

After you save the previous changes and make sure the Django development server is running again, run the following command. The code file for the sample is included in the `restful_python_2_06_01` folder, in the `Django01/cmd/cmd607.txt` file:

```
http OPTIONS ":8000/games/"
```

The following is the equivalent `curl` command. The code file for the sample is included in the `restful_python_2_06_01` folder, in the `Django01/cmd/cmd608.txt` file:

```
curl -iX OPTIONS "localhost:8000/games/"
```

The previous command will compose and send the following HTTP request: `OPTIONS http://localhost:8000/games/`. The request will match and run the `views.game_collection` function, that is, the `game_collection` function declared within the `games/views.py` file. We added the `@api_view` decorator to this function, and therefore, now it is capable of determining the supported HTTP verbs, parsing, and rendering capabilities. The following lines show the output:

```
HTTP/1.1 200 OK
Allow: GET, POST, OPTIONS
Content-Length: 174
Content-Type: application/json
Date: Thu, 25 Oct 2018 14:12:51 GMT
Server: WSGIServer/0.2 CPython/3.7.1
Vary: Accept, Cookie
X-Frame-Options: SAMEORIGIN
{
```

```
    "description": "",
    "name": "Game Collection",
    "parses": [
        "application/json",
        "application/x-www-form-urlencoded",
        "multipart/form-data"
    ],
    "renders": [
        "application/json",
        "text/html"
    ]
}
```

The response header includes an `Allow` key with a comma-separated list of the HTTP verbs supported by the resource collection as its value: `GET`, `POST`, `OPTIONS`. As our request didn't specify the allowed content type, the function rendered the response with the default `application/json` content type. The response body specifies the `Content-type` that the resource collection parses and the `Content-type` that it renders.

Now run the following command to compose and send an HTTP request with the `OPTIONS` verb for a game resource. Don't forget to replace `2` with a primary key value of an existing game in your configuration. The code file for the sample is included in the `restful_python_2_06_01` folder, in the `Django01/cmd/cmd609.txt` file:

```
http OPTIONS ":8000/games/2/"
```

The following is the equivalent `curl` command. The code file for the sample is included in the `restful_python_2_06_01` folder, in the `Django01/cmd/cmd610.txt` file:

```
curl -iX OPTIONS "localhost:8000/games/2/"
```

The previous command will compose and send the following HTTP request: `OPTIONS http://localhost:8000/games/2/`. The request will match and run the `views.game_detail` function, that is, the `game_detail` function declared within the `games/views.py` file. We also added the `@api_view` decorator to this function, and therefore, now it is capable of determining the supported HTTP verbs, parsing, and rendering capabilities. The following lines show the output:

```
HTTP/1.1 200 OK
Allow: GET, PUT, POST, OPTIONS
Content-Length: 170
Content-Type: application/json
Date: Thu, 25 Oct 2018 14:16:29 GMT
Server: WSGIServer/0.2 CPython/3.7.1
Vary: Accept, Cookie
X-Frame-Options: SAMEORIGIN
```

```
{
    "description": "",
    "name": "Game Detail",
    "parses": [
        "application/json",
        "application/x-www-form-urlencoded",
        "multipart/form-data"
    ],
    "renders": [
        "application/json",
        "text/html"
    ]
}
```

The response header includes an `Allow` key with a comma-separated list of HTTP verbs supported by the resource as its value: `GET`, `POST`, `OPTIONS`, `PUT`. The response body specifies the content-type that the resource parses and the content-type that it renders, with the same contents received in the previous `OPTIONS` request applied to a resource collection, that is, to a games collection.

In `Chapter 1`, *Developing RESTful APIs and Microservices with Flask 1.0.2*, when we composed and sent `POST` and `PUT` commands, we had to use the `-H "Content-Type: application/json"` option to indicate `curl` to send the data specified after the `-d` option as `application/json` instead of the default `application/x-www-form-urlencoded`. Now, in addition to `application/json`, our API is capable of parsing `application/x-www-form-urlencoded` and `multipart/form-data` data specified in the `POST` and `PUT` requests. Hence, we can compose and send a `POST` command that sends the data as `application/x-www-form-urlencoded` with the changes made to our API.

Now we will compose and send an HTTP request to create a new game. In this case, we will use the `-f` option for the `http` command that serializes data items from the command line as form fields and sets the `Content-Type` header key to the `application/x-www-form-urlencoded` value. The code file for the sample is included in the `restful_python_2_06_01` folder, in the `Django01/cmd/cmd611.txt` file:

```
http -vf POST ":8000/games/" name='Kingdom Hearts III' esrb_rating='E10+
(Everyone 10+)' release_date='2019-01-25T03:02:00.776594Z'
```

The following is the equivalent `curl` command. Notice that we don't use the `-H` option and `curl` will send the data in the default `application/x-www-form-urlencoded`. The code file for the sample is included in the `restful_python_2_06_01` folder, in the `Django01/cmd/cmd612.txt` file:

```
curl -viX POST -d '{"name":"Kingdom Hearts III", "esrb_rating":"E10+
(Everyone 10+)", "release_date": "2019-01-25T03:02:00.776594Z"}'
"localhost:8000/games/"
```

The previous commands will compose and send the following HTTP request: `POST` `http://localhost:8000/games/` with the `Content-Type` header key set to the `application/x-www-form-urlencoded` value and the following data:

```
name=Kingdom+Hearts+III&esrb_rating=E10%2B+%28Everyone+10%2B%29&release_dat
e=2019-01-25T03%3A02%3A00.776594Z
```

The request specifies `/games/`, and therefore, it will match `'^games/$'` and run the `views.game_collection` function, that is, the updated `game_collection` function declared within the `games_service/games/views.py` file. As the HTTP verb for the request is `POST`, the `request.method` property is equal to `'POST'`, and therefore, the function will execute the code that creates a `GameSerializer` instance and passes `request.data` as the data argument for its creation. The `rest_framework.parsers.FormParser` class will parse the data received in the request, the code creates a new `Game` and, if the data is valid, it saves the new `Game`. If the new `Game` was successfully persisted in the database, the function returns an `HTTP 201 Created` status code and the recently persisted `Game` serialized to JSON in the response body. The following lines show an example response for the HTTP request, with the new `Game` object in the JSON response:

```
HTTP/1.1 201 Created
Allow: GET, POST, OPTIONS
Content-Length: 154
Content-Type: application/json
Date: Thu, 25 Oct 2018 14:26:50 GMT
Server: WSGIServer/0.2 CPython/3.7.1
Vary: Accept, Cookie
X-Frame-Options: SAMEORIGIN
{
    "esrb_rating": "E10+ (Everyone 10+)",
    "id": 6,
    "name": "Kingdom Hearts III",
    "played_once": false,
    "played_times": 0,
    "release_date": "2019-01-25T03:02:00.776594Z"
}
```

After the changes we made in the code, we can run the following command to see what happens when we compose and send an HTTP request with an HTTP verb that is not supported. The code file for the sample is included in the `restful_python_2_06_01` folder, in the `Django01/cmd/cmd613.txt` file:

```
http PUT ":8000/games/"
```

The following is the equivalent `curl` command. The code file for the sample is included in the `restful_python_2_06_01` folder, in the `Django01/cmd/cmd614.txt` file:

```
curl -iX PUT "localhost:8000/games/"
```

The previous command will compose and send the following HTTP request: `PUT http://localhost:8000/games/`. The request will match and try to run the `views.game_collection` function, that is, the `game_collection` function declared within the `games_service/games/views.py` file. The `@api_view` decorator we added to this function doesn't include `'PUT'` in the string list with the allowed HTTP verbs, and therefore, the default behavior returns a `405 Method Not Allowed` status code. The following lines show the output with the response from the previous request. A JSON content provides a `detail` key with a string value that indicates the `PUT` method is not allowed:

```
HTTP/1.1 405 Method Not Allowed
Allow: GET, POST, OPTIONS
Content-Length: 40
Content-Type: application/json
Date: Thu, 25 Oct 2018 14:54:33 GMT
Server: WSGIServer/0.2 CPython/3.7.1
Vary: Accept, Cookie
X-Frame-Options: SAMEORIGIN
{
    "detail": "Method \"PUT\" not allowed."
}
```

Browsing the API

With the recent edits, we made it possible for our API to use the default content renderers configured in Django REST Framework, and therefore, our API is capable of rendering `text/html` content. We can take advantage of the browsable API, a feature included in Django REST Framework that generates human-friendly HTML output for each resource whenever the request specifies `text/html` as the value for the `Content-type` key in the request header.

Whenever we enter a URL for an API resource in a web browser, the browser will require an HTML response, and therefore, Django REST Framework will provide an HTML response built with the Bootstrap popular frontend component library. You can read more about Bootstrap here: `http://getbootstrap.com`. This response will include a section that displays the resource content in JSON, buttons to perform different requests, and forms to submit data to the resources. As with everything in Django REST Framework, we can customize the templates and themes used to generate the browsable API.

Open a web browser and enter `http://localhost:8000/games/`. The browsable API will compose and send an HTTP `GET` request to `/games/` and will display the results of its execution, that is, the headers and the JSON games list. The following screenshot shows the rendered web page after entering the URL in a web browser with the resource description of **Game List**

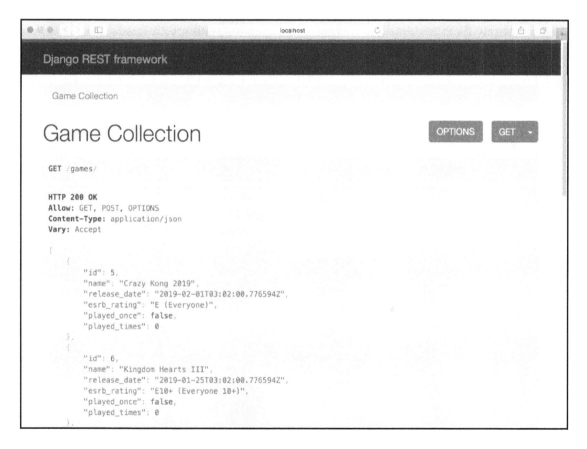

If you decide to browse the API in a web browser running on another computer or device connected to the LAN, remember that you have to use the development computer's assigned IP address, instead of localhost. For example, if the computer's assigned IPv4 IP address is `192.168.1.103`, instead of `http://localhost:8000/games/`, you should use `http://192.168.1.103:8000/games/`. Of course, you can also use the hostname instead of the IP address.

The browsable API uses information about the allowed methods for a resource to provide us with buttons to run these methods. At the right-hand side of the resource description, the browsable API shows an **OPTIONS** button and a **GET** drop-down button. The **OPTIONS** button allows us to make an `OPTIONS` request to `/games/`, that is, to the current resource. The **GET** drop-down button allows us to make a `GET` request to `/games/` again. If we click or tap the down arrow, we can select the **json** option and the browsable API will display the raw JSON results of a `GET` request to `/games/` without the headers.

At the bottom of the rendered web page, the browsable API provides us some controls to generate a `POST` request to `/games/`. The **Media type** drop-down allows us to select between the configured supported parsers for our API:

- `application/json`
- `application/x-www-form-urlencoded`
- `multipart/form-data`

The **Content** textbox allows us to specify the data to be sent to the `POST` request formatted as specified in the **Media type** drop-down. Select **application/json** in the **Media type** drop-down and enter the following JSON content in the **Content** textbox:

```
{
    "name": "Assassin's Creed Origins",
    "release_date": "2018-01-10T03:02:00.776594Z",
    "esrb_rating": "M (Mature)"
}
```

Click or tap **POST**. The browsable API will compose and send a POST request to /games/ with the previously specified data as JSON and we will see the results of the call in the web browser. The following screenshot shows a web browser displaying the HTTP status code 201 Created in the response and the previously explained drop-down and textbox with the **POST** button to allow us to continue composing and sending POST requests to /games/:

Now enter the URL for an existing game resource, such as
`http://localhost:8000/games/7/`. Make sure you replace 7 with the ID of an existing game in the previously rendered **Games List**. The browsable API will compose and send an HTTP GET request to /games/7/ and will display the results of its execution, that is, the headers and the JSON data for the game. The following screenshot shows the rendered web page after entering the URL in a web browser with the resource description of **Game Detail**:

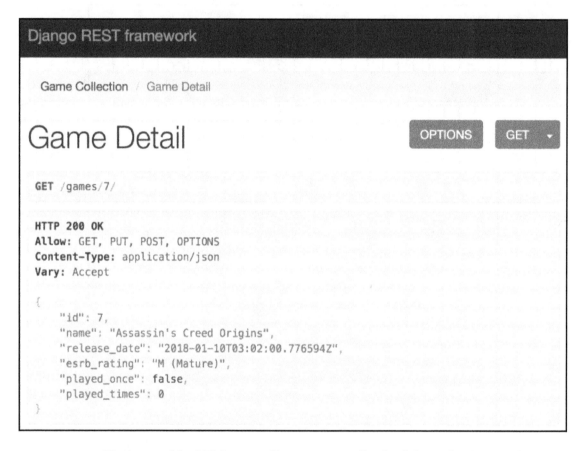

The browsable API feature allows us to easily check how the API works and to compose and send HTTP requests with different methods in any web browser that has access to our LAN. We will take advantage of additional features included in the browsable API, such as HTML forms that allow us to easily create new resources later after we build a new more complex RESTful API with Python and Django REST Framework.

Designing a RESTful API to interact with a complex PostgreSQL 10.5 database

So far, our Django-based RESTful API performed CRUD operations on a single database table in an SQLite database. Now, we want to create a more complex RESTful API with Django REST Framework to interact with a complex database model that has to allow us to register player scores for playing games that are grouped into ESRB ratings. In our previous RESTful API, we used a string field to specify the ESRB rating for a game. In this case, we want to be able to easily retrieve all the games that have a specific ESRB rating, and therefore, we will have a relationship between a game and an ESRB rating.

We must be able to perform CRUD operations on different related resources and resource collections. The following table enumerates the resources and the class name we will create to represent the model with Django REST Framework:

Resources	Class name that represents the model
ESRB ratings	`EsrbRating`
Games	`Game`
Players	`Player`
Player scores	`PlayerScore`

The ESRB rating (`EsrbRating`) just requires the following data:

- An integer identifier
- A string description

We need the following data for a game (`Game`):

- An integer identifier
- A foreign key to an ESRB rating (`EsrbRating`)
- A name or title
- A release date
- A `bool` value, indicating whether the game was played at least once by a player or not
- An integer indicating the number of times the game was played
- A timestamp with the date and time in which the game was inserted in the database

We need the following data for a player (`Player`):

- An integer identifier
- A gender value
- A name
- A timestamp with the date and time in which the player was inserted in the database

We need the following data for the score achieved by a player (`PlayerScore`):

- A foreign key to a player (`Player`)
- A foreign key to a game (`Game`)
- A score value
- A date in which the score value was achieved by the player

We will take advantage of all the resources and their relationships to analyze different options that Django REST Framework provides us when working with related resources. Instead of building an API that uses the same configuration to display related resources, we will use diverse configurations that will allow us to select the most appropriate options based on the particular requirements of the APIs that we are developing.

Understanding the tasks performed by each HTTP method

The following table shows the HTTP verbs, the scope, and the semantics for the methods that our API must support. Each method is composed by an HTTP verb and a scope and all the methods have well-defined meanings for all the resources and collections:

HTTP verb	Scope	Semantics
GET	Collection of ESRB ratings	Retrieve all the stored ESRB ratings in the collection, sorted by their description in ascending order. Each ESRB rating must include a list of URLs for each game resource that belongs to the rating.
GET	ESRB rating	Retrieve a single ESRB rating. The ESRB rating must include a list of URLs for each game resource that belongs to the rating.

POST	Collection of ESRB ratings	Create a new ESRB rating in the collection.
PUT	ESRB rating	Update an existing ESRB rating.
PATCH	ESRB rating	Update one or more fields of an existing ESRB rating.
DELETE	ESRB rating	Delete an existing ESRB rating.
GET	Collection of games	Retrieve all the stored games in the collection, sorted by their name in ascending order. Each game must include its ESRB rating description.
GET	Game	Retrieve a single game. The game must include its ESRB rating description.
POST	Collection of games	Create a new game in the collection.
PUT	ESRB rating	Update an existing game.
PATCH	ESRB rating	Update one or more fields of an existing game.
DELETE	ESRB rating	Delete an existing game.
GET	Collection of players	Retrieve all the stored players in the collection, sorted by their name in ascending order. Each player must include a list of the registered scores, sorted by score in descending order. The list must include all the details for the score achieved by the player and its related game.
GET	Player	Retrieve a single player. The player must include a list of the registered scores, sorted by score in descending order. The list must include all the details for the score achieved by the player and its related game.
POST	Collection of players	Create a new player in the collection.
PUT	Player	Update an existing player.
PATCH	Player	Update one or more fields of an existing player.
DELETE	Player	Delete an existing player.
GET	Collection of scores	Retrieve all the stored scores in the collection, sorted by score in descending order. Each score must include the player's name that achieved the score and the game's name.
GET	Score	Retrieve a single score. The score must include the player's name that achieved the score and the game's name.
POST	Collection of scores	Create a new score in the collection. The score must be related to an existing player and an existing game.
PUT	Score	Update an existing score.

PATCH	Score	Update one or more fields of an existing score.
DELETE	Score	Delete an existing score.

We want our API to be able to update a single field for an existing resource, and therefore, we will provide an implementation for the PATCH method. In addition, our RESTful API must support the OPTIONS method for all the resources and collection of resources.

We will use all the features and reusable elements included in Django REST Framework to make it easy to build our API. We will work with a PostgreSQL 10.5 database. In case you don't want to spend time installing PostgreSQL, you can skip the changes we make in the Django REST Framework ORM configuration and continue working with the default SQLite database. However, it is highly recommended to work with PostgreSQL as the database engine.

In the previous table, we have a huge number of methods and scopes. The following list enumerates the URIs for each scope mentioned in the previous table, where {id} has to be replaced with the numeric id of the resource:

- **Collection of ESRB ratings**: /esrb-ratings/
- **ESRB rating**: /esrb-rating/{id}/
- **Collection of games**: /games/
- **Game**: /game/{id}/
- **Collection of players**: /players/
- **Player**: /player/{id}/
- **Collection of scores**: /player-scores/
- **Score**: /player-score/{id}/

Let's consider that http://localhost:8000/ is the URL for the API running on the Django development server. We have to compose and send an HTTP request with the following HTTP verb (GET) and request URL (http://localhost:8000/esrb-ratings/) to retrieve all the stored ESRB ratings in the collection:

```
GET http://localhost:8000/esrb-ratings/
```

Declaring relationships with the models

Make sure you quit the Django's development server. Remember that you just need to press *Ctrl + C* in the Terminal or Command Prompt window in which it is running. Now we will create the models that we will use to represent and persist the ESRB ratings, games, players and scores, and their relationships.

Open the `models.py` file in the `games_service/games` folder. Replace the code in this file with the following lines. The lines that declare fields related to other models are highlighted in the code listing. The code file for the sample is included in the `restful_python_2_06_01` folder, in the `Django01/games-service/games/models.py` file:

```
from django.db import models


class EsrbRating(models.Model):
    description = models.CharField(max_length=200)

    class Meta:
        ordering = ('description',)

    def __str__(self):
        return self.description


class Game(models.Model):
    created = models.DateTimeField(auto_now_add=True)
    name = models.CharField(max_length=200)
    esrb_rating = models.ForeignKey(
        EsrbRating,
        related_name='games',
        on_delete=models.CASCADE)
    release_date = models.DateTimeField()
    played_once = models.BooleanField(default=False)
    played_times = models.IntegerField(default=0)

    class Meta:
        ordering = ('name',)

    def __str__(self):
        return self.name


class Player(models.Model):
    MALE = 'M'
```

```
        FEMALE = 'F'
        GENDER_CHOICES = (
            (MALE, 'Male'),
            (FEMALE, 'Female'),
        )
        created = models.DateTimeField(auto_now_add=True)
        name = models.CharField(max_length=50)
        gender = models.CharField(
            max_length=2,
            choices=GENDER_CHOICES,
            default=MALE,
        )

        class Meta:
            ordering = ('name',)

        def __str__(self):
            return self.name


    class PlayerScore(models.Model):
        player = models.ForeignKey(
            Player,
            related_name='scores',
            on_delete=models.CASCADE)
        game = models.ForeignKey(
            Game,
            on_delete=models.CASCADE)
        score = models.IntegerField()
        score_date = models.DateTimeField()

        class Meta:
            # Order by score (descending)
            ordering = ('-score',)
```

The code declares the following four models; specifically, four classes as subclasses of the `django.db.models.Model` superclass:

- EsrbRating
- Game
- Player
- PlayerScore

Django automatically adds an auto-increment integer primary key column, named id, when it creates the database table related to each model. We specified the field types, maximum lengths, and defaults for many attributes. Each class declares a Meta inner class that declares an ordering attribute.

> The Meta inner class declared within the PlayerScore class specifies '-score' as the value of the ordering tuple, with a dash as a prefix of the field name to order by score in descending order, instead of the default ascending order.

The EsrbRating, Game and Player classes declare a __str__ method that returns the contents of the attribute that provides the description, name or title for each of these models. This way, whenever Django has to provide a human-readable representation for the model, it will call this method.

The Game model declares the esrb_rating field with the following line:

```
esrb_rating = models.ForeignKey(
    EsrbRating,
    related_name='games',
    on_delete=models.CASCADE)
```

The previous line uses the django.db.models.ForeignKey class to provide a many-to-one relationship from the Game model to the EsrbRating model. The 'games' value specified for the related_name argument creates a backward relation from the EsrbRating model to the Game model. This value indicates the name to use for the relation from the related EsrbRating object back to a Game object. This way, we will be able to access all the games that belong to a specific ESRB rating. Whenever we delete an ESRB rating, we want all the games that belong to this rating to be deleted too, and therefore, we specified the models.CASCADE value for the on_delete argument.

The PlayerScore model declares the player field with the following line:

```
player = models.ForeignKey(
    Player,
    related_name='scores',
    on_delete=models.CASCADE)
```

The previous line uses the `django.db.models.ForeignKey` class to provide a many-to-one relationship to the `Player` model. The `'scores'` value specified for the `related_name` argument creates a backward relation from the `Player` model to the `PlayerScore` model. This value indicates the name to use for the relation from the related `Player` object back to a `PlayerScore` object. This way, we will be able to access all the scores achieves by a specific player. Whenever we delete a player, we want all the scores achieved by this player to be deleted too, and therefore, we specified the `models.CASCADE` value for the `on_delete` argument.

The `PlayerScore` model declares the `game` field with the following line:

```
game = models.ForeignKey(
    Game,
    on_delete=models.CASCADE)
```

The previous line uses the `django.db.models.ForeignKey` class to provide a many-to-one relationship to the `Game` model. In this case, we don't create a backward relation because we don't need it. Thus, we don't specify a value for the `related_name` argument. Whenever we delete a game, we want all the registered scores for this game to be deleted too, and therefore, we specified the `models.CASCADE` value for the `on_delete` argument.

If you created a new virtual environment to work with this example or you downloaded the sample code for the book, you don't need to delete any existing database. However, in case you are making changes to the code from our previous API example, you have to delete the `games_service/db.sqlite3` file and the `games_service/games/migrations` folder.

Then, it is necessary to create the initial migration for the new models we recently coded. We just need to run the following Python scripts and we will also synchronize the database for the first time. As we learned from our previous API example, by default, Django uses an SQLite database. In this example, we will be working with a PostgreSQL 10.5 database.

Now, we will create the PostgreSQL 10.5 database that we will use as a repository for our API. You will have to download and install a PostgreSQL database server if you aren't already running it in your computer or on a development server. If you worked with the example introduced in Chapter 2, *Working with Models, SQLAlchemy, and Hyperlinked APIs in Flask*, you already have a PostgreSQL 10.5 database server running.

You can download and install this database management system from its web page: `http://www.postgresql.org`. If you are working with macOS, `Postgres.app` provides a really easy way to install and use PostgreSQL on this operating system: `http://postgresapp.com`. If you are working with Windows, EnterpriseDB and BigSQL provide graphics installers that simplify the configuration process on modern Windows server or desktop versions: `https://www.postgresql.org/download/windows`.

Notice that the examples have been tested with PostgreSQL 10.5 on macOS, Linux, and Windows.

You have to make sure that the PostgreSQL `bin` folder is included in the `PATH` environmental variable. You should be able to execute the `psql` command-line utility from your current Terminal or Command Prompt. If the folder isn't included in `PATH`, you will receive an error indicating that the `pg_config` file cannot be found when trying to install the `psycopg2` package. In addition, you will have to use the full path to each of the PostgreSQL command-line tools we will use in the next steps.

We will use the PostgreSQL command-line tools to create a new database named `django_games`. If you already have a PostgreSQL database with this name, make sure that you use another name in all the commands and configurations. You can perform the same task with any PostgreSQL GUI tool. If you are developing on Linux, it is necessary to run the commands as the `postgres` user.

Run the following command in macOS or Windows to create a new database named `django_games`. Notice that the command won't produce any output:

```
createdb django_games
```

In Linux, run the following command to use the `postgres` user:

```
sudo -u postgres createdb django_games
```

Now we will use the `psql` command-line tool to run some SQL statements to create a specific user that we will use in Flask and assign the necessary roles for it. In macOS or Windows, run the following command to launch `psql`:

```
psql
```

In Linux, run the following command to use the `postgres` user:

```
sudo -u psql
```

Then, run the following SQL statements and finally enter `\q` to exit the `psql` command-line tool. Replace `your_games_user_name` with your desired username to use in the new database and `your_games_password` with your chosen password.

We will use the username and password in the Django configuration. You don't need to run the steps if you are already working with a specific user in PostgreSQL and you have already granted privileges to the database for the user. You will see the output indicating that the permission was granted. The code file for the sample is included in the `restful_python_2_06_01` folder, in the `Django01/cmd/configure_django_database.sql` file:

```
CREATE ROLE your_games_user_name WITH LOGIN PASSWORD
'your_games_password';


GRANT ALL PRIVILEGES ON DATABASE "django_games" TO
your_games_user_name;
ALTER USER your_games_user_name CREATEDB;
\q
```

Installing packages with the requirements.txt file to work with PostgreSQL

Make sure you quit Django development server. You just need to press *Ctrl* + *C* in the Terminal or Command Prompt window in which it is running.

Now we will install an additional package. Make sure you have activated the virtual environment we have created in the previous chapter and we named `Django01`. After you activate the virtual environment, it is time to run many commands, which will be the same for either macOS, Linux, or Windows.

Now we will edit the existing `requirements.txt` file to specify the additional package that our application requires to be installed on any supported platform. This way, it will be extremely easy to repeat the installation of the specified packages with their versions in any new virtual environment.

Use your favorite editor to edit the existing text file named `requirements.txt` within the root folder for the virtual environment. Add the following lines after the last line to declare the additional package and the version that our new version of the API requires: `psycopg2` version 2.7.5. The code file for the sample is included in the `restful_python_2_06_01` folder, in the `Django01/requirements.txt` file:

```
psycopg2==2.7.5
```

Psycopg 2 (`psycopg2`) is a Python-PostgreSQL database adapter and Django's integrated ORM will use it to interact with our recently created PostgreSQL database. Again, it is very important to make sure that the PostgreSQL `bin` folder is included in the `PATH` environmental variable before we run the installation for this package.

Now we must run the following command on macOS, Linux, or Windows to install the additional packages and the versions explained in the previous table with `pip` by using the recently edited `requirements.txt` file. Make sure you are in the folder that has the `requirements.txt` file (`Django01`) before running the command:

```
pip install -r requirements.txt
```

The last lines for the output will indicate the new package has been successfully installed. If you downloaded the source code for the example and you didn't work with the previous version of the API, `pip` will also install the other packages included in the `requirements.txt` file:

```
Installing collected packages: psycopg2
Successfully installed psycopg2-2.7.5
```

Configuring the database

The default SQLite database engine and the database file name are specified in the `games_service/games_service/settings.py` Python file. In order to work with PostgreSQL 10.5 instead of SQLite for this example, replace the declaration of the `DATABASES` dictionary in this file with the following lines. The nested dictionary maps the database named `default` with the `django.db.backends.postgresql` database engine, the desired database name, and its settings. In this case, we will create a database named games.

Make sure you specify the desired database name in the value for the `'NAME'` key and that you configure the user, password, host, and port based on the user you recently created and your PostgreSQL 10.5 configuration. If you followed the previous steps, use the settings specified in these steps:

```
DATABASES = {
    'default': {
        'ENGINE': 'django.db.backends.postgresql',
        # Replace django_games with your desired database name
        'NAME': 'django_games',
        # Replace username with your desired user name
        'USER': 'your_games_user_name',
        # Replace password with your desired password
        'PASSWORD': 'your_games_password',
        # Replace 127.0.0.1 with the PostgreSQL host
        'HOST': '127.0.0.1',
        # Replace 5432 with the PostgreSQL configured port
        # in case you aren't using the default port
        'PORT': '5432',
    }
}
```

Running migrations

Now run the following Python script to generate the migrations that will allow us to synchronize the database for the first time. Make sure you are in the `games_service` folder within the root folder for the virtual environment (`Django01`). Notice that we use the Django app name, `games`, and not the PostgreSQL database name, `django_games` in the next script:

```
python manage.py makemigrations games
```

The following lines show the output generated after running the previous command:

```
Migrations for 'games':
  games/migrations/0001_initial.py
    - Create model EsrbRating
    - Create model Game
    - Create model Player
    - Create model PlayerScore
```

The output indicates that the `games_service/games/migrations/0001_initial.py` file includes the code to create the `EsrbRating`, `Game`, `Player`, and `PlayerScore` models. The following lines show the code for this file that was automatically generated by Django and its integrated ORM. The code file for the sample is included in the `restful_python_2_06_01` folder, in the `Django01/games-service/games/migrations/0001_initial.py` file:

```
# Generated by Django 2.1.2 on 2018-10-25 20:15

from django.db import migrations, models
import django.db.models.deletion


class Migration(migrations.Migration):

    initial = True

    dependencies = [
    ]

    operations = [
        migrations.CreateModel(
            name='EsrbRating',
            fields=[
                ('id', models.AutoField(auto_created=True,
primary_key=True, serialize=False, verbose_name='ID')),
                ('description', models.CharField(max_length=200)),
            ],
            options={
                'ordering': ('description',),
            },
        ),
        migrations.CreateModel(
            name='Game',
            fields=[
                ('id', models.AutoField(auto_created=True,
primary_key=True, serialize=False, verbose_name='ID')),
                ('created', models.DateTimeField(auto_now_add=True)),
                ('name', models.CharField(max_length=200)),
                ('release_date', models.DateTimeField()),
                ('played_once', models.BooleanField(default=False)),
                ('played_times', models.IntegerField(default=0)),
                ('esrb_rating',
models.ForeignKey(on_delete=django.db.models.deletion.CASCADE,
related_name='games', to='games.EsrbRating')),
            ],
            options={
```

```
                    'ordering': ('name',),
                },
            ),
            migrations.CreateModel(
                name='Player',
                fields=[
                    ('id', models.AutoField(auto_created=True,
primary_key=True, serialize=False, verbose_name='ID')),
                    ('created', models.DateTimeField(auto_now_add=True)),
                    ('name', models.CharField(max_length=50)),
                    ('gender', models.CharField(choices=[('M', 'Male'), ('F',
'Female')], default='M', max_length=2)),
                ],
                options={
                    'ordering': ('name',),
                },
            ),
            migrations.CreateModel(
                name='PlayerScore',
                fields=[
                    ('id', models.AutoField(auto_created=True,
primary_key=True, serialize=False, verbose_name='ID')),
                    ('score', models.IntegerField()),
                    ('score_date', models.DateTimeField()),
                    ('game',
models.ForeignKey(on_delete=django.db.models.deletion.CASCADE,
to='games.Game')),
                    ('player',
models.ForeignKey(on_delete=django.db.models.deletion.CASCADE,
related_name='scores', to='games.Player')),
                ],
                options={
                    'ordering': ('-score',),
                },
            ),
        ]
```

The code defines a subclass of the `django.db.migrations.Migration` class named `Migration` that defines an `operations` list with many `migrations.CreateModel`. Each `migrations.CreateModel` method will create the table for each of the related models. Notice that Django has automatically added an `id` field for each of the models.

The `operations` are executed in the same order in which they appear in the list. The code creates `EsrbRating`, `Game`, `Player`, and `PlayerScore`. The code creates the foreign keys for `Game` and `PlayerScore` when it creates these models.

Now run the following Python script to apply all the generated migrations:

```
python manage.py migrate
```

The following lines show the output generated after running the previous command:

```
Operations to perform:
  Apply all migrations: admin, auth, contenttypes, games, sessions
Running migrations:
  Applying contenttypes.0001_initial... OK
  Applying auth.0001_initial... OK
  Applying admin.0001_initial... OK
  Applying admin.0002_logentry_remove_auto_add... OK
  Applying admin.0003_logentry_add_action_flag_choices... OK
  Applying contenttypes.0002_remove_content_type_name... OK
  Applying auth.0002_alter_permission_name_max_length... OK
  Applying auth.0003_alter_user_email_max_length... OK
  Applying auth.0004_alter_user_username_opts... OK
  Applying auth.0005_alter_user_last_login_null... OK
  Applying auth.0006_require_contenttypes_0002... OK
  Applying auth.0007_alter_validators_add_error_messages... OK
  Applying auth.0008_alter_user_username_max_length... OK
  Applying auth.0009_alter_user_last_name_max_length... OK
  Applying games.0001_initial... OK
  Applying sessions.0001_initial... OK
```

Verifying the contents of the PostgreSQL database

After we run the previous command, we can use the PostgreSQL command line or any other application that allows us to easily check the contents of the PostgreSQL 10.5 database to check the tables that Django generated.

Run the following command to list the generated tables. If the database name you are using is not named django_games, make sure you use the appropriate database name. The code file for the sample is included in the restful_python_2_06_01 folder, in the Django01/cmd/list_database_tables.sql file:

```
psql --username=your_games_user_name --dbname=django_games --
command="\dt"
```

The following lines show the output with all the generated table names:

```
                          List of relations
    Schema |              Name               |  Type  |        Owner
   --------+---------------------------------+--------+---------------------
    public | auth_group                      | table  | your_games_user_name
    public | auth_group_permissions          | table  | your_games_user_name
    public | auth_permission                 | table  | your_games_user_name
    public | auth_user                       | table  | your_games_user_name
    public | auth_user_groups                | table  | your_games_user_name
    public | auth_user_user_permissions      | table  | your_games_user_name
    public | django_admin_log                | table  | your_games_user_name
    public | django_content_type             | table  | your_games_user_name
    public | django_migrations               | table  | your_games_user_name
    public | django_session                  | table  | your_games_user_name
    public | games_esrbrating                | table  | your_games_user_name
    public | games_game                      | table  | your_games_user_name
    public | games_player                    | table  | your_games_user_name
    public | games_playerscore               | table  | your_games_user_name
   (14 rows)
```

As happened in our previous example, Django uses the `games_` prefix for the following four table names related to the `games` application. Django's integrated ORM generated these tables and the foreign keys based on the information included in our models:

- `games_esrbRating`: Persists the `EsrbRating` model
- `games_game`: Persists the `Game` model
- `games_player`: Persists the `Player` model
- `games_playerscore`: Persists the `PlayerScore` model

The following command will allow you to check the contents of the four tables after we compose and send HTTP requests to the RESTful API and make CRUD operations to the four tables. The commands assume that you are running PostgreSQL 10.5 on the same computer in which you are running the command. The code file for the sample is included in the `restful_python_2_06_01` folder, in the `Django01/cmd/check_tables_contents.sql` file:

```
    psql --username=your_games_user_name --dbname=django_games --
command="SELECT * FROM games_esrbrating;"
    psql --username=your_games_user_name --dbname=django_games --
command="SELECT * FROM games_game;"
    psql --username=your_games_user_name --dbname=django_games --
command="SELECT * FROM games_player;"
    psql --username=your_games_user_name --dbname=django_games --
command="SELECT * FROM games_playerscore;"
```

Instead of working with the PostgreSQL command-line utility, you can use your favorite GUI tool to check the contents of the PostgreSQL database.

Django generated additional tables that it requires to support the web framework and the authentication features that we will use later.

Managing serialization and deserialization with relationships and hyperlinks

Our new RESTful Web API has to be able to serialize and deserialize the `EsrbRating`, `Game`, `Player`, and `PlayerScore` instances into JSON representations. In this case, we also have to pay special attention to the relationships between the different models when we create the serializer classes to manage serialization to JSON and deserialization from JSON.

In our last version of the previous API, we created a subclass of the `rest_framework.serializers.ModelSerializer` class to make it easier to generate a serializer and reduce boilerplate code. In this case, we will also declare a class that inherits from `ModelSerializer` but three classes will inherit from the `rest_framework.serializers.HyperlinkedModelSerializer` class.

`HyperlinkedModelSerializer` is a type of `ModelSerializer` that uses hyperlinked relationships instead of primary key relationships, and therefore, it represents the relationships to other model instances with hyperlinks instead of primary key values. In addition, `HyperlinkedModelSerializer` generates a field named `url` with the URL for the resource as its value. As happens with `ModelSerializer`, the `HyperlinkedModelSerializer` class provides default implementations for the `create` and `update` methods.

Open the `serializers.py` file in the `games_service/games` folder. Replace the code in this file with the following lines. The new code declares the required imports and the `EsrbRatingSerializer` class. We will add more classes to this file later. The code file for the sample is included in the `restful_python_2_06_01` folder, in the `Django01/games-service/games/serializers.py` file:

```
from rest_framework import serializers
from games.models import EsrbRating
from games.models import Game
from games.models import Player
```

```
from games.models import PlayerScore
import games.views


class EsrbRatingSerializer(serializers.HyperlinkedModelSerializer):
    games = serializers.HyperlinkedRelatedField(
        many=True,
        read_only=True,
        view_name='game-detail')

    class Meta:
        model = EsrbRating
        fields = (
            'url',
            'id',
            'description',
            'games')
```

The EsrbRatingSerializer class is a subclass of the HyperlinkedModelSerializer superclass. The EsrbRatingSerializer class declares a games attribute as an instance of serializers.HyperlinkedRelatedField with many and read_only equal to True because it is a one-to-many relationship and it is read-only. We use the games name that we specified as the related_name string value when we created the esrb_rating field as a models.ForeignKey instance in the Game model. This way, the games field will provide us with an array of hyperlinks to each game that belongs to the ESRB rating. The view_name value is 'game-detail' because we want the browsable API feature to use the game detail view to render the hyperlink when the user clicks or taps on it.

The EsrbRatingSerializer class declares a Meta inner class that declares the following two attributes:

- model: This attribute specifies the model related to the serializer, that is, the EsrbRating class.
- fields: This attribute specifies a tuple of the string whose values indicate the field names that we want to include in the serialization from the related model. We want to include both the primary key and the URL, and therefore, the code specifies both 'id' and 'url' as members of the tuple.

There is no need to override either the create or update methods because the generic behavior will be enough in this case. The HyperlinkedModelSerializer superclass provides implementations for both methods.

Open the `serializers.py` file in the `games_service/games` folder and add the following lines after the last line to declare the `GameSerializer` class. The code file for the sample is included in the `restful_python_2_06_01` folder, in the `Django01/games-service/games/serializers.py` file:

```
class GameSerializer(serializers.HyperlinkedModelSerializer):
    # We want to display the game ESRB rating description instead of its id
    esrb_rating = serializers.SlugRelatedField(
        queryset=EsrbRating.objects.all(),
        slug_field='description')

    class Meta:
        model = Game
        fields = (
            'url',
            'esrb_rating',
            'name',
            'release_date',
            'played_once',
            'played_times')
```

The `GameSerializer` class is a subclass of the `HyperlinkedModelSerializer` superclass. The `GameSerializer` class declares an `esrb_rating` attribute as an instance of the `serializers.SlugRelatedField` class with its `queryset` argument set to `EsrbRating.objects.all()` and its `slug_field` argument set to `'description'`.

 `SlugRelatedField` is a read-write field that represents the target of the relationship by a unique slug attribute, that is, the description.

We created the `esrb_rating` field as a `models.ForeignKey` instance in the `Game` model and we want to display the ESRB rating's `description` value as the description (slug field) for the related `EsrbRating`. Hence, we specified `'description'` as the `slug_field`. If it is necessary to display the possible options for the related ESRB rating in a form in the browsable API, Django will use the expression specified in the `queryset` argument to retrieve all the possible instances and display their specified slug field.

The EsrbRatingSerializer class declares a Meta inner class that declares the following two attributes:

- model: This attribute specifies the model related to the serializer, that is, the Game class.
- fields: This attribute specifies a tuple of the string whose values indicate the field names that we want to include in the serialization from the related model. We just want to include the URL, and therefore, the code specifies 'url' as a member of the tuple but doesn't specify 'id'. The esrb_rating field will specify the description field for the related EsrbRating.

Open the serializers.py file in the games_service/games folder and add the following lines after the last line to declare the ScoreSerializer class. The code file for the sample is included in the restful_python_2_06_01 folder, in the Django01/games-service/games/serializers.py file:

```
class ScoreSerializer(serializers.HyperlinkedModelSerializer):
    # We want to display all the details for the related game
    game = GameSerializer()
    # We don't include the player because a score will be nested in the
player

    class Meta:
        model = PlayerScore
        fields = (
            'url',
            'id',
            'score',
            'score_date',
            'game')
```

The ScoreSerializer class is a subclass of the HyperlinkedModelSerializer superclass. We will use the ScoreSerializer class to serialize PlayerScore instances related to a Player, that is, to display all the scores for a specific player when we serialize a Player. We want to display all the details for the related Game but we don't include the related Player because Player will use this ScoreSerializer serializer.

The ScoreSerializer class declares a game attribute as an instance of the previously coded GameSerializer class. We created the game field as a models.ForeignKey instance in the PlayerScore model and we want to serialize the same data for the game that we coded in the GameSerializer class.

The ScoreSerializer class declares a Meta inner class that declares the following two attributes:

- model: This attribute specifies the model related to the serializer, that is, the PlayerScore class.
- fields: This attribute specifies a tuple of the string whose values indicate the field names that we want to include in the serialization from the related model. In this case, we include both the 'url' and the 'id'. As previously explained, we don't include the 'player' field name in this tuple of string to avoid serializing the player again.

We will use PlayerSerializer as a master and ScoreSerializer as the detail.

Open the serializers.py file in the games_service/games folder and add the following lines after the last line to declare the PlayerSerializer class. The code file for the sample is included in the restful_python_2_06_01 folder, in the Django01/games-service/games/serializers.py file:

```
class PlayerSerializer(serializers.HyperlinkedModelSerializer):
    scores = ScoreSerializer(many=True, read_only=True)
    gender = serializers.ChoiceField(
        choices=Player.GENDER_CHOICES)
    gender_description = serializers.CharField(
        source='get_gender_display',
        read_only=True)

    class Meta:
        model = Player
        fields = (
                'url',
                'name',
                'gender',
                'gender_description',
                'scores')
```

The PlayerSerializer class is a subclass of the HyperlinkedModelSerializer superclass. We will use the PlayerSerializer class to serialize Player instances and we will use the previously declared ScoreSerializer class to serialize all the PlayerScore instances related to Player.

The `PlayerSerializer` class declares a `scores` attribute as an instance of the previously coded `ScoreSerializer` class. The `many` argument is set to `True` because it is a one-to-many relationship. We use the `scores` name that we specified as the `related_name` string value when we created the `player` field as a `models.ForeignKey` instance in the `PlayerScore` model. This way, the `scores` field will render each `PlayerScore` that belongs to the `Player` by using the previously declared `ScoreSerializer`.

The `Player` model declared `gender` as an instance of `models.CharField` with the `choices` attribute set to the `Player.GENDER_CHOICES` string tuple. The `ScoreSerializer` class declares a `gender` attribute as an instance of `serializers.ChoiceField` with the `choices` argument set to the `Player.GENDER_CHOICES` string tuple. In addition, the class declares a `gender_description` attribute with `read_only` set to `True` and the `source` argument set to `'get_gender_display'`. The `source` string is built with `get_` followed by the field name, `gender`, and `_display`. This way, the read-only `gender_description` attribute will render the description for the gender choices instead of the single char stored values. The `ScoreSerializer` class declares a `Meta` inner class that declares the `model` and `fields` attributes. The `model` attribute specifies the `Player` class.

Open the `serializers.py` file in the `games_service/games` folder and add the following lines after the last line to declare the `PlayerScoreSerializer` class. The code file for the sample is included in the `restful_python_2_06_01` folder, in the `Django01/games-service/games/serializers.py` file:

```
class PlayerScoreSerializer(serializers.ModelSerializer):
    # We want to display the players's name instead of its id
    player = serializers.SlugRelatedField(queryset=Player.objects.all(),
slug_field='name')
    # We want to display the game's name instead of its id
    game = serializers.SlugRelatedField(queryset=Game.objects.all(),
slug_field='name')

    class Meta:
        model = PlayerScore
        fields = (
            'url',
            'id',
            'score',
            'score_date',
            'player',
            'game')
```

The `PlayerScoreSerializer` class is a subclass of the `HyperlinkedModelSerializer` superclass. We will use the `PlayerScoreSerializer` class to serialize `PlayerScore` instances. Previously, we created the `ScoreSerializer` class to serialize `PlayerScore` instances as the detail of a player. We will use the new `PlayerScoreSerializer` class when we want to display the related player's name and the related game's name. In the other serializer class, we didn't include any information related to the player and we included all the details for the game.

The `PlayerScoreSerializer` class declares a `player` attribute as an instance of `serializers.SlugRelatedField` with its `queryset` argument set to `Player.objects.all()` and its `slug_field` argument set to `'name'`. We created the `player` field as a `models.ForeignKey` instance in the `PlayerScore` model, and we want to display the player's name as the description (slug field) for the related `Player`. Thus, we specified `'name'` as the `slug_field` argument. If it is necessary to display the possible options for the related player in a form in the browsable API, Django will use the expression specified in the `queryset` argument to retrieve all the possible players and display their specified slug field.

The `PlayerScoreSerializer` class declares a `game` attribute as an instance of `serializers.SlugRelatedField` with its `queryset` argument set to `Game.objects.all()` and its `slug_field` argument set to `'name'`. We created the `game` field as a `models.ForeignKey` instance in the `PlayerScore` model and we want to display the game's name as the description (slug field) for the related `Game`.

Creating class-based views and using generic classes

This time, we will write our API views by declaring class-based views, instead of function-based views. We might code classes that inherit from the `rest_framework.views.APIView` class and declare methods with the same names than the HTTP verbs we want to process: `get`, `post`, `put`, `patch`, `delete`, and so on. These methods receive a `request` argument as happened with the functions that we created for the views. However, this approach would require us to write a lot of code. Instead, we can take advantage of a set of generic views that we can use as our base classes for our class-based views to reduce the required code to the minimum and take advantage of the behavior that has been generalized in Django REST Framework.

We will create subclasses of the two following generic class views declared in the
`rest_framework.generics` module:

- `ListCreateAPIView`: Implements the `get` method, which retrieves a listing of a
  `queryset`, and the `post` method, which creates a model instance
- `RetrieveUpdateDestroyAPIView`: Implements the `get`, `put`, `patch`, and
  `delete` methods to retrieve, completely update, partially update, or delete a
  model instance

Those two generic views are composed by combining reusable bits of behavior in Django
REST Framework implemented as mixin classes declared in the `rest_framework.mixins`
module. We can create a class that uses multiple inheritances and combines the features
provided by many of these mixin classes. The following line shows the declaration of the
`ListCreateAPIView` class as the composition of the `ListModelMixin`,
`CreateModelMixin` and `rest_framework.generics.GenericAPIView` classes:

```
class ListCreateAPIView(mixins.ListModelMixin,
                        mixins.CreateModelMixin,
                        GenericAPIView):
```

The following line shows the declaration of the `RetrieveUpdateDestroyAPIView` class as
the composition of the `RetrieveModelMixin`, `UpdateModelMixin`, `DestroyModelMixin`,
and `rest_framework.generics.GenericAPIView` classes:

```
class RetrieveUpdateDestroyAPIView(mixins.RetrieveModelMixin,
                                   mixins.UpdateModelMixin,
                                   mixins.DestroyModelMixin,
                                   GenericAPIView):
```

Now we will create Django class-based views that will use the previously explained generic
classes and the serializer classes to return JSON representations for each HTTP request that
our API will handle. We will just have to specify `queryset` that retrieves all the objects in
the `queryset` attribute and the serializer class in the `serializer_class` attribute for each
subclass that we declare. The generic classes will do the rest for us. In addition, we will
declare a `name` attribute with the string name we will use to identify the view.

Taking advantage of generic class-based views

Open the `views.py` file in the `games_service/games` folder. Replace the code in this file with the following lines. The new code declares the required imports and the class-based views. We will add more classes to this file later. The code file for the sample is included in the `restful_python_2_06_01` folder, in the `Django01/games-service/games/views.py` file:

```
from games.models import EsrbRating
from games.models import Game
from games.models import Player
from games.models import PlayerScore
from games.serializers import EsrbRatingSerializer
from games.serializers import GameSerializer
from games.serializers import PlayerSerializer
from games.serializers import PlayerScoreSerializer
from rest_framework import generics
from rest_framework.response import Response
from rest_framework.reverse import reverse


class EsrbRatingList(generics.ListCreateAPIView):
    queryset = EsrbRating.objects.all()
    serializer_class = EsrbRatingSerializer
    name = 'esrbrating-list'


class EsrbRatingDetail(generics.RetrieveUpdateDestroyAPIView):
    queryset = EsrbRating.objects.all()
    serializer_class = EsrbRatingSerializer
    name = 'esrbrating-detail'


class GameList(generics.ListCreateAPIView):
    queryset = Game.objects.all()
    serializer_class = GameSerializer
    name = 'game-list'


class GameDetail(generics.RetrieveUpdateDestroyAPIView):
    queryset = Game.objects.all()
    serializer_class = GameSerializer
    name = 'game-detail'
```

```
class PlayerList(generics.ListCreateAPIView):
    queryset = Player.objects.all()
    serializer_class = PlayerSerializer
    name = 'player-list'


class PlayerDetail(generics.RetrieveUpdateDestroyAPIView):
    queryset = Player.objects.all()
    serializer_class = PlayerSerializer
    name = 'player-detail'


class PlayerScoreList(generics.ListCreateAPIView):
    queryset = PlayerScore.objects.all()
    serializer_class = PlayerScoreSerializer
    name = 'playerscore-list'


class PlayerScoreDetail(generics.RetrieveUpdateDestroyAPIView):
    queryset = PlayerScore.objects.all()
    serializer_class = PlayerScoreSerializer
    name = 'playerscore-detail'
```

The following table summarizes the methods that each class-based view is going to process:

Scope	Class-based view name	HTTP verbs that it will process
Collection of ESRB ratings: `/esrb-ratings/`	`EsrbRatingList`	GET, POST, and OPTIONS
ESRB rating: `/esrb-rating/{id}/`	`EsrbRatingDetail`	GET, PUT, PATCH, DELETE, and OPTIONS
Collection of games: `/games/`	`GameList`	GET, POST, and OPTIONS
Game: `/game/{id}/`	`GameDetail`	GET, PUT, PATCH, DELETE, and OPTIONS
Collection of players: `/players/`	`PlayerList`	GET, POST, and OPTIONS
Player: `/player/{id}/`	`PlayerDetail`	GET, PUT, PATCH, DELETE, and OPTIONS
Collection of scores: `/player-scores/`	`PlayerScoreList`	GET, POST, and OPTIONS
Score: `/player-score/{id}/`	`PlayerScoreDetail`	GET, PUT, PATCH, DELETE, and OPTIONS

Working with endpoints for the API

We will create an endpoint for the root of our API to make it easier to browse the API with the browsable API feature and understand how everything works. Open the `views.py` file in the `games_service/games` folder and add the following code after the last line to declare the `ApiRoot` class. The code file for the sample is included in the `restful_python_2_06_01` folder, in the `Django01/games-service/games/serializers.py` file:

```
class ApiRoot(generics.GenericAPIView):
    name = 'api-root'
    def get(self, request, *args, **kwargs):
        return Response({
            'players': reverse(PlayerList.name, request=request),
            'esrb-ratings': reverse(EsrbRatingList.name, request=request),
            'games': reverse(GameList.name, request=request),
            'scores': reverse(PlayerScoreList.name, request=request)
            })
```

The `ApiRoot` class is a subclass of the `rest_framework.generics.GenericAPIView` class and declares the `get` method. The `GenericAPIView` class is the base class for all the other generic views. The `ApiRoot` class defines the `get` method that returns a `Response` object with a dictionary composed of key-value pairs of string that provide a descriptive name for the view and its URL, generated with the `rest_framework.reverse.reverse` function. This URL resolver function returns a fully qualified URL for the view.

Open the `urls.py` file in the `games_service/games` folder. Replace the code in this file with the following lines. The new code defines the URL patterns that specify the regular expressions that have to be matched in the request to run a specific method for a class-based view defined in the `views.py` file. Instead of specifying a function that represents a view, we call the `as_view` method for the class-based view. The code file for the sample is included in the `restful_python_2_06_01` folder, in the `Django01/games-service/games/urls.py` file:

```
from django.conf.urls import url
from games import views


urlpatterns = [
    url(r'^esrb-ratings/$',
        views.EsrbRatingList.as_view(),
        name=views.EsrbRatingList.name),
    url(r'^esrb-ratings/(?P<pk>[0-9]+)/$',
        views.EsrbRatingDetail.as_view(),
```

```
                name=views.EsrbRatingDetail.name),
    url(r'^games/$',
          views.GameList.as_view(),
          name=views.GameList.name),
    url(r'^games/(?P<pk>[0-9]+)/$',
          views.GameDetail.as_view(),
          name=views.GameDetail.name),
    url(r'^players/$',
          views.PlayerList.as_view(),
          name=views.PlayerList.name),
    url(r'^players/(?P<pk>[0-9]+)/$',
          views.PlayerDetail.as_view(),
          name=views.PlayerDetail.name),
    url(r'^player-scores/$',
          views.PlayerScoreList.as_view(),
          name=views.PlayerScoreList.name),
    url(r'^player-scores/(?P<pk>[0-9]+)/$',
          views.PlayerScoreDetail.as_view(),
          name=views.PlayerScoreDetail.name),
    url(r'^$',
          views.ApiRoot.as_view(),
          name=views.ApiRoot.name),
]
```

When we coded our previous version of the API, we replaced the code in the other `urls.py` file, which is located in the `games_service` folder, specifically, the `games_service/urls.py` file. We made the necessary changes to define the root URL configuration and include the URL patterns declared in the previously coded `games-service/games/urls.py` file.

Browsing an API with relationships

Now we can launch Django's development server to compose and send HTTP requests to our still unsecured, yet much more complex, web API (we will definitely add security later). Execute any of the following two commands based on your needs to access the API in other devices or computers connected to your LAN. Remember that we analyzed the difference between them in the previous chapter:

```
python manage.py runserver
python manage.py runserver 0.0.0.0:8000
```

After we run any of the previous commands, the development server will start listening at port `8000`.

Open a web browser and enter `http://localhost:8000/` or the appropriate URL if you are using another computer or device to access the browsable API. The browsable API will compose and send a `GET` request to `/` and will display the results of its execution, that is, the headers and the JSON response from the execution of the `get` method defined in the `ApiRoot` class within the `views.py` file. The following screenshot shows the rendered web page after entering the URL in a web browser with the resource description of **api-root**:

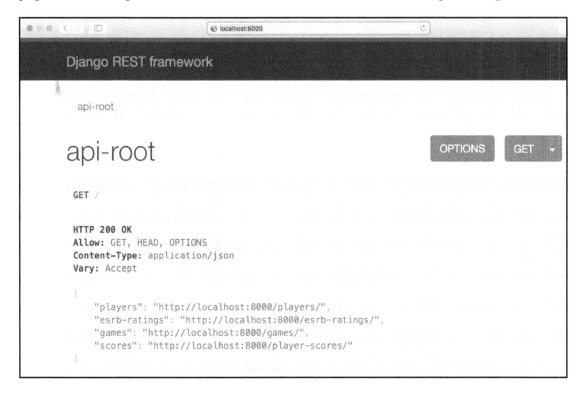

The **api-root** provides us with hyperlinks to see the list of ESRB ratings, games, players, and scores. This way, it becomes extremely easy to access the lists and perform operations on the different resources through the browsable API. In addition, when we visit the other URLs, the breadcrumb will allow us to go back to the **api-root**.

In this new version of the API, we worked with the generic views that provide many functions under the hood, and therefore, the browsable API will provide us additional features compared with the previous version. Click or tap on the URL at the right-hand side of **"esrb-ratings"**. If you are browsing in localhost, the URL will be `http://localhost:8000/esrb-ratings/`. The browsable API will render the web page for the ESRB rating List.

At the bottom of the rendered web page, the browsable API provides us some controls to generate a POST request to /esrb-ratings/. In this case, by default, the browsable API displays the HTML form tab with an automatically generated form that we can use to generate a POST request without having to deal with the raw data as we did in our previous version. The HTML forms make it easy to generate requests to test our API. The following screenshot shows the HTML form to create a new ESRB rating:

We just need to enter the desired name, AO (Adults Only), in the Name textbox and click or tap POST to create a new ESRB rating. The browsable API will compose and send a POST request to /esrb-ratings/ with the previously specified data and we will see the results of the call in the web browser. The following screenshot shows a web browser displaying the HTTP status code 201 Created in the response and the previously explained HTML form with the POST button to allow us to continue composing and sending POST requests to /esrb-ratings/:

Now click on the URL displayed as a value for the "url" key in the JSON data displayed for the ESRB rating, such as http://localhost:8000/esrb-ratings/1/. Make sure you replace 1 with the ID of an existing ESRB rating in the previously rendered esrbrating-list. The browsable API will compose and send a GET request to /esrb-ratings/1/ and will display the results of its execution, that is, the headers and the JSON data for the ESRB rating. The web page will display a **DELETE** button because we are working with the ESRB rating **Detail** view.

We can use the breadcrumb to go back to the API root and start creating games related to an ESRB rating, players, and finally, scores related to a game and a player. We can do all this with easy-to-use HTML forms and the browsable API feature. This feature is extremely useful for testing CRUD operations with a RESTful API.

Creating and retrieving related resources

Now we will use the HTTP command or its `curl` equivalents to compose and send HTTP requests to the API. We will use JSON for the requests that require additional data. Remember that you can perform the same tasks as your favorite GUI-based tool or with the browsable API.

First, we will run the following command to compose and send an HTTP `POST` request to create a new ESRB rating. Remember that we used the browsable API to create an ESRB rating with the following description: `'AO (Adults Only)'`. The code file for the sample is included in the `restful_python_2_06_01` folder, in the `Django01/cmd/cmd615.txt` file:

```
http POST ":8000/esrb-ratings/" description='T (Teen)'
```

The following is the equivalent `curl` command. The code file for the sample is included in the `restful_python_2_06_01` folder, in the `Django01/cmd/cmd616.txt` file:

```
curl -iX POST -H "Content-Type: application/json" -d '{"description":"T (Teen)"}' "localhost:8000/esrb-ratings/"
```

The previous command will compose and send an HTTP `POST` request with the specified JSON key-value pair. The request specifies `/esrb-ratings/`, and therefore, it will match `'^esrb-ratings/$'` and run the `post` method for the `views.EsrbRatingList` class-based view. Remember that the method is defined in the `ListCreateAPIView` superclass and it ends up calling the create method defined in `mixins.CreateModelMixin`.

If the new `EsrbRating` instance was successfully persisted in the database, the call to the method will return an HTTP `201 Created` status code and the recently persisted `EsrbRating` serialized to JSON in the response body. The following line shows a sample response for the HTTP request with the new `EsrbRating` object in the JSON response.

The response doesn't include the header. Notice that the response includes both the `id` and the `url`, for the created ESRB rating. The `games` array is empty because there aren't games related to each new ESRB rating yet:

```
{
    "description": "T (Teen)",
    "games": [],
    "id": 2,
    "url": "http://localhost:8000/esrb-ratings/2/"
}
```

Now we will compose and send HTTP requests to create two games that belong to the first ESRB rating we created with the browsable API: `AO (Adults Only)`. We will specify the `esrb_rating` value with the description of the desired `ESRB rating`. However, the database table that persists the `Game` model will save the value of the id of the related `EsrbRating` whose description value matches the one we provide. The code file for the sample is included in the `restful_python_2_06_01` folder, in the `Django01/cmd/cmd617.txt` file:

```
http POST ":8000/games/" name='Battlefield V' esrb_rating='AO (Adults
Only)' release_date='2017-05-01T01:02:00.776594Z'
    http POST ":8000/games/" name='Mutant Football League: Dynasty Edition'
esrb_rating='AO (Adults Only)' release_date='2018-10-20T03:02:00.776594Z'
```

The following are the equivalent `curl` commands. The code file for the sample is included in the `restful_python_2_06_01` folder, in the `Django01/cmd/cmd618.txt` file:

```
curl -iX POST -H "Content-Type: application/json" -d
'{"name":"Battlefield V", "esrb_rating":"AO (Adults Only)", "release_date":
"2017-05-01T01:02:00.776594Z"}' "localhost:8000/games/"
    curl -iX POST -H "Content-Type: application/json" -d '{"name":"Mutant
Football League: Dynasty Edition", "esrb_rating":"AO (Adults Only)",
"release_date": "2018-10-20T03:02:00.776594Z"}' "localhost:8000/games/"
```

The previous commands will compose and send two HTTP `POST` requests with the specified JSON key-value pairs. The requests specify `/games/`, and therefore, they will match `'^games/$'` and run the `post` method for the `views.GameList` class-based view. The following lines show sample responses for the two HTTP requests with the new `Game` objects in the JSON responses. The responses don't include the headers. Notice that the response includes only the `url` for the created games and doesn't include the ID. The value for `esrb_rating` is the `description` for the related `EsrbRating`:

```
{
    "esrb_rating": "AO (Adults Only)",
    "name": "Battlefield V",
```

```
            "played_once": false,
            "played_times": 0,
            "release_date": "2017-05-01T01:02:00.776594Z",
            "url": "http://localhost:8000/games/1/"
    }
    {
            "esrb_rating": "AO (Adults Only)",
            "name": "Mutant Football League: Dynasty Edition",
            "played_once": false,
            "played_times": 0,
            "release_date": "2018-10-20T03:02:00.776594Z",
            "url": "http://localhost:8000/games/2/"
    }
```

We can run the previously explained commands to check the contents of the tables that Django created after executing the migrations process in the PostgreSQL database. We will notice that the `esrb_rating_id` column for the `games_game` table saves the value of the id of the related row in the `games_esrb_rating` table. The `GameSerializer` class uses the `SlugRelatedField` to display the name value for the related `EsrbRating`. The following screenshot shows the contents for the `games_esrb_rating` and the `games_game` table in a PostgreSQL 10.5 database after running the HTTP requests:

Now we will compose and send an HTTP `GET` request to retrieve the ESRB rating that contains two games, that is, the ESRB rating resource whose id is equal to 1. Don't forget to replace 1 with the id value of the ESRB rating whose description is equal to `'AO (Adults Only)'` in your configuration. The code file for the sample is included in the `restful_python_2_06_01` folder, in the `Django01/cmd/cmd619.txt` file:

```
http ":8000/esrb-ratings/1/"
```

The following is the equivalent curl command. The code file for the sample is included in the `restful_python_2_06_01` folder, in the `Django01/cmd/cmd620.txt` file:

```
curl -iX GET "localhost:8000/esrb-ratings/1/"
```

The previous commands will compose and send the following HTTP request: GET
http://localhost:8000/esrb-ratings/1/. The request has a number after /esrb-
ratings/, and therefore, it will match '^esrb-ratings/(?P<pk>[0-9]+)/$' and run
the get method for the views.EsrbRatingDetail class-based view. Remember that the
method is defined in the RetrieveUpdateDestroyAPIView superclass and it ends up
calling the retrieve method defined in mixins.RetrieveModelMixin. The following
lines show a sample response for the HTTP request, with the EsrbRating object and the
hyperlinks of the related games in the JSON response:

```
HTTP/1.1 200 OK
Allow: GET, PUT, PATCH, DELETE, HEAD, OPTIONS
Content-Length: 163
Content-Type: application/json
Date: Fri, 26 Oct 2018 02:18:39 GMT
Server: WSGIServer/0.2 CPython/3.7.1
Vary: Accept, Cookie
X-Frame-Options: SAMEORIGIN
{
    "description": "AO (Adults Only)",
    "games": [
        "http://localhost:8000/games/1/",
        "http://localhost:8000/games/2/"
    ],
    "id": 1,
    "url": "http://localhost:8000/esrb-ratings/1/"
}
```

The EsrbRatingSerializer class defined the games attribute as a
HyperlinkedRelatedField, and therefore, the serializer renders the URL for each related
Game instance in the value for the games array. If we view the results in a web browser
through the browsable API, we will be able to click or tap on the hyperlink to see the details
for each game.

Now we will compose and send an HTTP POST request to create a game related to an ESRB
rating name that doesn't exist: 'Virtual reality'. The code file for the sample is
included in the restful_python_2_06_01 folder, in the Django01/cmd/cmd621.txt
file:

```
http POST ":8000/games/" name='LEGO DC Super-Villains' esrb_rating='EC
(Early Childhood)' release_date='2018-01-10T03:02:00.776594Z'
```

The following is the equivalent curl command. The code file for the sample is included in the `restful_python_2_06_01` folder, in the `Django01/cmd/cmd622.txt` file:

```
curl -iX POST -H "Content-Type: application/json" -d '{"name":"LEGO DC
Super-Villains", "esrb_rating":"EC (Early Childhood)", "release_date":
"2018-01-10T03:02:00.776594Z"}' "localhost:8000/games/"
```

Django won't be able to retrieve an `EsrbRating` instance whose `description` is equal to the specified value, and therefore, we will receive a `400 Bad Request` status code in the response header and a message related to the value specified in for `esrb_rating` in the JSON body. The following lines show a sample response:

```
HTTP/1.1 400 Bad Request
Allow: GET, POST, HEAD, OPTIONS
Content-Length: 80
Content-Type: application/json
Date: Fri, 26 Oct 2018 02:42:07 GMT
Server: WSGIServer/0.2 CPython/3.7.1
Vary: Accept, Cookie
X-Frame-Options: SAMEORIGIN
{
    "esrb_rating": [
        "Object with description=EC (Early Childhood) does not exist."
    ]
}
```

Now we will compose and send two HTTP `POST` requests to create two players. The code file for the sample is included in the `restful_python_2_06_01` folder, in the `Django01/cmd/cmd623.txt` file:

```
http POST ":8000/players/" name='Gaston Hillar' gender='M'
http POST ":8000/players/" name='Enzo Scocco' gender='M'
```

The following are the equivalent curl commands. The code file for the sample is included in the `restful_python_2_06_01` folder, in the `Django01/cmd/cmd624.txt` file:

```
curl -iX POST -H "Content-Type: application/json" -d '{"name":"Gaston
Hillar", "gender":"M"}' "localhost:8000/players/"
curl -iX POST -H "Content-Type: application/json" -d '{"name":"Enzo
Scocco", "gender":"M"}' "localhost:8000/players/"
```

The previous commands will compose and send two HTTP `POST` requests with the specified JSON key-value pairs. The request specifies `/players/`, and therefore, it will match `'^players/$'` and run the `post` method for the `views.PlayerList` class-based view. The following lines show sample responses for the two HTTP requests with the new `Player` objects in the JSON responses. The responses don't include the headers. Notice that each response includes only the `url` for the created players and doesn't include the id. The value for `gender_description` is the choice description for the `gender` char. The `scores` array is empty because there aren't scores related to each new player yet:

```
{
    "gender": "M",
    "gender_description": "Male",
    "name": "Gaston Hillar",
    "scores": [],
    "url": "http://localhost:8000/players/1/"
}
{
    "url":"http://localhost:8000/players/2/",
    "name":"Enzo Scocco",
    "gender":"M",
    "gender_description":"Male",
    "scores":[]
}
```

Now we will compose and send HTTP requests to create four scores. The code file for the sample is included in the `restful_python_2_06_01` folder, in the `Django01/cmd/cmd625.txt` file:

```
    http POST ":8000/player-scores/" score=17500
score_date='2019-01-01T03:02:00.776594Z' player='Gaston Hillar'
game='Battlefield V'
    http POST ":8000/player-scores/" score=3225
score_date='2019-01-01T01:02:00.776594Z' player='Gaston Hillar'
game='Mutant Football League: Dynasty Edition'
    http POST ":8000/player-scores/" score=43200
score_date='2019-01-01T03:02:00.776594Z' player='Enzo Scocco'
game='Battlefield V'
    http POST ":8000/player-scores/" score=17420
score_date='2019-01-01T05:02:00.776594Z' player='Enzo Scocco' game='Mutant
Football League: Dynasty Edition'
```

The following are the equivalent `curl` commands. The code file for the sample is included in the `restful_python_2_06_01` folder, in the `Django01/cmd/cmd626.txt` file:

```
    curl -iX POST -H "Content-Type: application/json" -d '{"score":"17500",
"score_date":"2019-01-01T03:02:00.776594Z", "player":"Gaston Hillar",
"game":"Battlefield V"}' "localhost:8000/player-scores/"
    curl -iX POST -H "Content-Type: application/json" -d '{"score":"3225",
"score_date":"2019-01-01T01:02:00.776594Z", "player":"Gaston Hillar",
"game":"Mutant Football League: Dynasty Edition"}' "localhost:8000/player-
scores/"
    curl -iX POST -H "Content-Type: application/json" -d '{"score":"43200",
"score_date":"2019-01-01T03:02:00.776594Z", "player":"Enzo Scocco",
"game":"Battlefield V"}' "localhost:8000/player-scores/"
    curl -iX POST -H "Content-Type: application/json" -d '{"score":"17420",
"score_date":"2019-01-01T05:02:00.776594Z", "player":"Enzo Scocco",
"game":"Mutant Football League: Dynasty Edition"}' "localhost:8000/player-
scores/"
```

The previous commands will compose and send four `POST` HTTP requests with the specified JSON key-value pairs. The request specifies `/player-scores/`, and therefore, it will match `'^player-scores/$'` and run the `post` method for the `views.PlayerScoreList` class-based view. The following lines show sample responses for the four HTTP requests with the new `Player` objects in the JSON responses. The responses don't include the headers. Django REST Framework uses the `PlayerScoreSerializer` class to generate the JSON response. Thus, the value for `game` is the name for the related `Game` instance and the value for `player` is the name for the related `Player` instance. The `PlayerScoreSerializer` class used `SlugRelatedField` for both fields:

```
{
    "game": "Battlefield V",
    "id": 1,
    "player": "Gaston Hillar",
    "score": 17500,
    "score_date": "2019-01-01T03:02:00.776594Z",
    "url": "http://localhost:8000/player-scores/1/"
}
{
    "game": "Mutant Football League: Dynasty Edition",
    "id": 2,
    "player": "Gaston Hillar",
    "score": 3225,
    "score_date": "2019-01-01T01:02:00.776594Z",
    "url": "http://localhost:8000/player-scores/2/"
}
{
```

```
        "game": "Battlefield V",
        "id": 3,
        "player": "Enzo Scocco",
        "score": 43200,
        "score_date": "2019-01-01T03:02:00.776594Z",
        "url": "http://localhost:8000/player-scores/3/"
    }
    {

        "game": "Mutant Football League: Dynasty Edition",
        "id": 4,
        "player": "Enzo Scocco",
        "score": 17420,
        "score_date": "2019-01-01T05:02:00.776594Z",
        "url": "http://localhost:8000/player-scores/4/"
    }
```

We can run the previously explained commands to check the contents of the tables that Django created after executing the migrations process in the PostgreSQL database. We will notice that the `game_id` column for the `games_playerscore` table saves the value of the id of the related row in the `games_game` table. In addition, the `player_id` column for the `games_playerscore` table saves the value of the id of the related row in the `games_player` table. The following screenshot shows the contents for the `games_esrb_rating`, `games_game`, `games_player`, and `games_playerscore` tables in a PostgreSQL 10.5 database after running the HTTP requests:

Now we will compose and send an HTTP request to retrieve a specific player that contains two scores, which is the player resource whose id is equal to 1. Don't forget to replace 1 with the id value of the player whose name is equal to 'Gaston Hillar' in your configuration. The code file for the sample is included in the restful_python_2_06_01 folder, in the Django01/cmd/cmd627.txt file:

```
http ":8000/players/1/"
```

The following is the equivalent curl command. The code file for the sample is included in the restful_python_2_06_01 folder, in the Django01/cmd/cmd628.txt file:

```
curl -iX GET "localhost:8000/players/1/"
```

The previous command will compose and send the following HTTP request: GET http://localhost:8000/players/1/. The request has a number after /players/, and therefore, it will match '^players/(?P<pk>[0-9]+)/$' and run the get method for the views.PlayerDetail class-based view. Remember that the method is defined in the RetrieveUpdateDestroyAPIView superclass and it ends up calling the retrieve method defined in mixins.RetrieveModelMixin. The following lines show a sample response for the HTTP request, with the Player object, the related PlayerScore objects, and the Game object related to each PlayerScore object in the JSON response:

```
HTTP/1.1 200 OK
Allow: GET, PUT, PATCH, DELETE, HEAD, OPTIONS
Content-Length: 740
Content-Type: application/json
Date: Fri, 26 Oct 2018 03:13:15 GMT
Server: WSGIServer/0.2 CPython/3.7.1
Vary: Accept, Cookie
X-Frame-Options: SAMEORIGIN
{
    "gender": "M",
    "gender_description": "Male",
    "name": "Gaston Hillar",
    "scores": [
        {
            "game": {
                "esrb_rating": "AO (Adults Only)",
                "name": "Battlefield V",
                "played_once": false,
                "played_times": 0,
                "release_date": "2017-05-01T01:02:00.776594Z",
                "url": "http://localhost:8000/games/1/"
            },
            "id": 1,
            "score": 17500,
```

```
            "score_date": "2019-01-01T03:02:00.776594Z",
            "url": "http://localhost:8000/player-scores/1/"
        },
        {
            "game": {
                "esrb_rating": "AO (Adults Only)",
                "name": "Mutant Football League: Dynasty Edition",
                "played_once": false,
                "played_times": 0,
                "release_date": "2018-10-20T03:02:00.776594Z",
                "url": "http://localhost:8000/games/2/"
            },
            "id": 2,
            "score": 3225,
            "score_date": "2019-01-01T01:02:00.776594Z",
            "url": "http://localhost:8000/player-scores/2/"
        }
    ],
    "url": "http://localhost:8000/players/1/"
}
```

The `PlayerSerializer` class defined the `scores` attribute as a `ScoreSerializer` with `many` equal to `True`, and therefore, this serializer renders each score related to the player. The `ScoreSerializer` class defined the `game` attribute as `GameSerializer`, and therefore, this serializer renders each game related to the score. If we view the results in a web browser through the browsable API, we will be able to click or tap on the hyperlink of each of the related resources. However, in this case, we also see all their details without having to follow the hyperlink.

Test your knowledge

Let's see whether you can answer the following questions correctly:

1. Under the hood, the `@api_view` decorator is:
    1. A wrapper that converts a function-based view into a subclass of the `rest_framework.views.APIView` class
    2. A wrapper that converts a function-based view into a serializer
    3. A wrapper that converts a function-based view into a subclass of the `rest_framework.views.api_view` class

2. The `Serializer` and `ModelSerializer` classes in Django REST Framework are similar to which of the following two classes in Django Web framework?
    1. `Form` and `ModelForm`
    2. `View` and `ModelView`
    3. `Controller` and `ModelController`

3. Which of the following classes is a read-write field that represents the target of the relationship by a unique slug attribute, that is, the description?
    1. `SlugLinkedField`
    2. `HyperlinkedRelatedField`
    3. `SlugRelatedField`

4. Which of the following classes renders the URL for a related object?
    1. `SlugLinkedField`
    2. `HyperlinkedRelatedField`
    3. `SlugRelatedField`

5. The browsable API is a feature included in Django REST Framework that:
    1. Generates human-friendly JSON output for each resource whenever the request specifies `application/json` as the value for the `Content-type` key in the request header
    2. Generates human-friendly HTML output for each resource whenever the request specifies `text/html` as the value for the `Content-type` key in the request header
    3. . Generates human-friendly HTML output for each resource whenever the request specifies `application/json` as the value for the `Content-type` key in the request header

Summary

In this chapter, we took advantage of many features included in Django REST Framework that allow us to eliminate duplicate code and build our API reusing generalized behaviors. We used model serializers, wrappers, default parsing and rendering options, class-based views, and generic classes.

We used the browsable API feature and we designed a RESTful API that interacted with a complex PostgreSQL 10.5 database. We declared relationships with the models, and we configured serialization and deserialization with hyperlinks. Finally, we created and retrieved related resources and understood how things work under the hood.

Now that we built a complex API with Django REST Framework that we can encapsulate in a microservice, we will use additional abstractions included in the framework to improve our API and will add security and authentication, which is the topic of the next chapter.

7
Improving Our API and Adding Authentication to it with Django

In this chapter, we will improve the Django RESTful API with a PostgreSQL 10.5 database that we started in the previous chapter. We will use many of the features included in Django REST framework to add new functions to the API and will add authentication-related security to it. We will do the following:

- Add unique constraints to the models
- Update a single field for a resource with the PATCH method
- Take advantage of pagination
- Customize pagination classes
- Understand authentication, permissions, and throttling
- Add security-related data to the models
- Create a customized permission class for object-level permissions
- Persist the user that makes a request and configure permission policies
- Set a default value for a new required field in migrations
- Compose requests with the necessary authentication
- Browse the API with authentication credentials

Adding unique constraints to the models

Our API has some important issues that we need to solve quickly. Right now, we can create many ESRB ratings with the same description. We shouldn't be able to do so, and therefore, we will make the necessary changes to the `EsrbRating` model to add a unique constraint on the `description` field. We will also add a unique constraint on the `name` field for the `Game` and `Player` models. This way, we will learn the necessary steps to make changes to the constraints for many models and reflect the changes in the underlying database schema through migrations.

Make sure you quit the Django development server. Remember that you just need to press *Ctrl + C* in the Terminal or Command Prompt window in which it is running.

Now we will make changes to introduce unique constraints to the description and name fields for the models that we use to represent and persist the ESRB ratings, games, and players. Open the `models.py` file in the `games_service/games` folder and replace the code that declares the `EsrbRating`, `Game`, and `Player` classes with the following code. The three lines that have been edited are highlighted. The code file for the sample is included in the `restful_python_2_07_01` folder, in the `Django01/games-service/games/models.py` file:

```python
from django.db import models


class EsrbRating(models.Model):
    description = models.CharField(max_length=200, unique=True)

    class Meta:
        ordering = ('description',)

    def __str__(self):
        return self.description


class Game(models.Model):
    created = models.DateTimeField(auto_now_add=True)
    name = models.CharField(max_length=200, unique=True)
    esrb_rating = models.ForeignKey(
        EsrbRating,
        related_name='games',
        on_delete=models.CASCADE)
    release_date = models.DateTimeField()
    played_once = models.BooleanField(default=False)
    played_times = models.IntegerField(default=0)
```

```
    class Meta:
        ordering = ('name',)

    def __str__(self):
        return self.name


class Player(models.Model):
    MALE = 'M'
    FEMALE = 'F'
    GENDER_CHOICES = (
        (MALE, 'Male'),
        (FEMALE, 'Female'),
    )
    created = models.DateTimeField(auto_now_add=True)
    name = models.CharField(max_length=50, unique=True)
    gender = models.CharField(
        max_length=2,
        choices=GENDER_CHOICES,
        default=MALE,
    )

    class Meta:
        ordering = ('name',)

    def __str__(self):
        return self.name
```

We just needed to add `unique=True` as one of the named arguments in the lines that created a `models.CharField` instance. This way, we indicate that the field must be unique and Django will create the necessary unique constraints for the fields in the underlying database tables.

Now run the following Python script to generate the migrations that will allow us to synchronize the database with the unique constraints we added for the fields in the models. Make sure you are located in the `games_service` folder within the root folder for the virtual environment (`Django01`). Notice that we use the Django app name, `games`, and not the PostgreSQL database name, `django_games`, in the next script:

```
python manage.py makemigrations games
```

The following lines show the output generated after running the previous command:

```
Migrations for 'games':
  games/migrations/0002_auto_20181026_0450.py
    - Alter field description on esrbrating
    - Alter field name on game
    - Alter field name on player
```

The output indicates that the
`games_service/games/migrations/0002_auto_20181026_0450.py` file includes the
code to alter the field named `description` on `esrbrating`, and the fields named name on
`game` and `player`. Notice that the generated filename will be different in your
configuration, because it includes an encoded date and time. The following lines show the
code for this file that was automatically generated by Django and its integrated ORM. The
code file for the sample is included in the `restful_python_2_07_01` folder, in the
`Django01/games-service/games/migrations/0002_auto_20181026_0450.py` file:

```python
# Generated by Django 2.1.2 on 2018-10-26 04:50

from django.db import migrations, models


class Migration(migrations.Migration):

    dependencies = [
        ('games', '0001_initial'),
    ]

    operations = [
        migrations.AlterField(
            model_name='esrbrating',
            name='description',
            field=models.CharField(max_length=200, unique=True),
        ),
        migrations.AlterField(
            model_name='game',
            name='name',
            field=models.CharField(max_length=200, unique=True),
        ),
        migrations.AlterField(
            model_name='player',
            name='name',
            field=models.CharField(max_length=50, unique=True),
        ),
    ]
```

The code defines a subclass of the `django.db.migrations.Migration` class named `Migration`, which defines an `operations` list with many `migrations.AlterField` instances. Each `migrations.AlterField` object will alter the field in the table for each of the related models.

Now run the following Python script to apply all the generated migrations and execute the changes in the PostgreSQL 10.5 database tables:

```
python manage.py migrate
```

The following lines show the output generated after running the previous command. Notice that the ordering for the migrations might be different in your configuration:

```
Operations to perform:
  Apply all migrations: admin, auth, contenttypes, games, sessions
Running migrations:
  Applying games.0002_auto_20181026_0450... OK
```

After we run the previous command, we will have unique indexes on the description field for the `games_esrbrating` table and unique indexes on the name field for the `games_game`, and `games_player` tables in the PostgreSQL database. We can use the PostgreSQL command line or any other application that allows us to easily check the contents of the PostgreSQL database to check the tables that Django updated.

Run the following commands to check the indexes for each of the tables. If the database name you are using is not named `django_games`, make sure you use the appropriate database name. The code file for the sample is included in the `restful_python_2_07_01` folder, in the `Django01/cmd/check_tables_indexes.sql` file:

```
psql --username=your_games_user_name --dbname=django_games --command="\d games_esrbrating"
psql --username=your_games_user_name --dbname=django_games --command="\d games_game"
psql --username=your_games_user_name --dbname=django_games --command="\d games_player"
```

The following screenshot shows the results of running the previous commands, in which we can see that Django's ORM generated unique constraints, whose names end with the "_uniq" suffix in each PostgreSQL 10.5 database table after running migrations:

```
● ● ●                                bin — -bash — 111×36
(Django01) Gastons-MacBook-Pro:bin gaston$ psql --username=your_games_user_name --dbname=django_games --command
="\d games_esrbrating"
                                Table "public.games_esrbrating"
    Column    |          Type          | Collation | Nullable |                   Default
--------------+------------------------+-----------+----------+-----------------------------------------------
 id           | integer                |           | not null | nextval('games_esrbrating_id_seq'::regclass)
 description  | character varying(200) |           | not null |
Indexes:
    "games_esrbrating_pkey" PRIMARY KEY, btree (id)
    "games_esrbrating_description_360ae479_uniq" UNIQUE CONSTRAINT, btree (description)
    "games_esrbrating_description_360ae479_like" btree (description varchar_pattern_ops)
Referenced by:
    TABLE "games_game" CONSTRAINT "games_game_esrb_rating_id_59e5b261_fk_games_esrbrating_id" FOREIGN KEY (esrb
_rating_id) REFERENCES games_esrbrating(id) DEFERRABLE INITIALLY DEFERRED


(Django01) Gastons-MacBook-Pro:bin gaston$ psql --username=your_games_user_name --dbname=django_games --command
="\d games_game"
                                Table "public.games_game"
    Column      |          Type           | Collation | Nullable |               Default
----------------+-------------------------+-----------+----------+-------------------------------------
 id             | integer                 |           | not null | nextval('games_game_id_seq'::regclass)
 created        | timestamp with time zone |          | not null |
 name           | character varying(200)  |           | not null |
 release_date   | timestamp with time zone |          | not null |
 played_once    | boolean                 |           | not null |
 played_times   | integer                 |           | not null |
 esrb_rating_id | integer                 |           | not null |
 owner_id       | integer                 |           | not null |
Indexes:
    "games_game_pkey" PRIMARY KEY, btree (id)
    "games_game_name_4e86b7e1_uniq" UNIQUE CONSTRAINT, btree (name)
    "games_game_esrb_rating_id_59e5b261" btree (esrb_rating_id)
    "games_game_name_4e86b7e1_like" btree (name varchar_pattern_ops)
    "games_game_owner_id_c554a59d" btree (owner_id)
Foreign-key constraints:
    "games_game_esrb_rating_id_59e5b261_fk_games_esrbrating_id" FOREIGN KEY (esrb_rating_id) REFERENCES games_e
srbrating(id) DEFERRABLE INITIALLY DEFERRED
    "games_game_owner_id_c554a59d_fk_auth_user_id" FOREIGN KEY (owner_id) REFERENCES auth_user(id) DEFERRABLE I
NITIALLY DEFERRED
Referenced by:
    TABLE "games_playerscore" CONSTRAINT "games_playerscore_game_id_9e96c1f4_fk_games_game_id" FOREIGN KEY (gam
e_id) REFERENCES games_game(id) DEFERRABLE INITIALLY DEFERRED

(Django01) Gastons-MacBook-Pro:bin gaston$ psql --username=your_games_user_name --dbname=django_games --command
="\d games_player"
                                Table "public.games_player"
   Column  |          Type           | Collation | Nullable |               Default
-----------+-------------------------+-----------+----------+-------------------------------------
 id        | integer                 |           | not null | nextval('games_player_id_seq'::regclass)
 created   | timestamp with time zone |          | not null |
 name      | character varying(50)   |           | not null |
 gender    | character varying(2)    |           | not null |
Indexes:
    "games_player_pkey" PRIMARY KEY, btree (id)
    "games_player_name_16dd04a0_uniq" UNIQUE CONSTRAINT, btree (name)
    "games_player_name_16dd04a0_like" btree (name varchar_pattern_ops)
Referenced by:
    TABLE "games_playerscore" CONSTRAINT "games_playerscore_player_id_fcaa094c_fk_games_player_id" FOREIGN KEY
(player_id) REFERENCES games_player(id) DEFERRABLE INITIALLY DEFERRED

(Django01) Gastons-MacBook-Pro:bin gaston$ ▌
```

Now we can launch Django's development server to compose and send HTTP requests. Execute any of the following two commands based on your needs to access the API on other devices or computers connected to your LAN. Remember that we analyzed the difference between them in `Chapter 5`, *Developing RESTful APIs with Django 2.1*:

```
python manage.py runserver
python manage.py runserver 0.0.0.0:8000
```

After we run any of the previous commands, the development server will start listening at port `8000`.

Now we will compose and send an HTTP request to create an ESRB rating with a description that already exists: `'T (Teen)'`. The code file for the sample is included in the `restful_python_2_07_01` folder, in the `Django01/cmd/cmd701.txt` file:

```
http POST ":8000/esrb-ratings/" description='T (Teen)'
```

The following is the equivalent `curl` command. The code file for the sample is included in the `restful_python_2_07_01` folder, in the `Django01/cmd/cmd702.txt` file:

```
curl -iX POST -H "Content-Type: application/json" -d '{"description":"T (Teen)"}' "localhost:8000/esrb-ratings/"
```

Django won't be able to persist an `EsrbRating` instance whose `description` is equal to the specified value because it would violate the unique constraint added to the `description` field. Hence, we will receive a `400 Bad Request` status code in the response header and a message related to the value specified for the `description` field in the JSON body. The following lines show a sample response:

```
HTTP/1.1 400 Bad Request
Allow: GET, POST, HEAD, OPTIONS
Content-Length: 69
Content-Type: application/json
Date: Fri, 26 Oct 2018 16:15:13 GMT
Server: WSGIServer/0.2 CPython/3.7.1
Vary: Accept, Cookie
X-Frame-Options: SAMEORIGIN
{
    "description": [
        "esrb rating with this description already exists."
    ]
}
```

After the changes we made, we won't be able to add duplicate values for the `description` field in ESRB ratings, games, or players.

This way, we are sure that whenever we specify the description or name for any of these resources, we are going to reference the same unique resource.

Updating a single field for a resource with the PATCH method

Due to the usage of generic class-based views, our API is able to update a single field for an existing resource, and therefore, we provide an implementation for the PATCH method. For example, we can use the PATCH method to update an existing game and set the value for its played_once and played_times field to True and 1. We don't want to use the PUT method because this method is meant to replace an entire game. Remember that the PATCH method is meant to apply a delta to an existing game, and therefore, it is the appropriate method to just change the value of the played_once and played_times fields.

Now we will compose and send an HTTP PATCH request to update an existing game, specifically, to update the value of the played_once and played_times fields and set them to True and 10. Make sure you replace 2 with id of an existing game in your configuration. The code file for the sample is included in the restful_python_2_07_01 folder, in the Django01/cmd/cmd703.txt file:

```
http PATCH ":8000/games/2/" played_once=true played_times=10
```

The following is the equivalent curl command. The code file for the sample is included in the restful_python_2_07_01 folder, in the Django01/cmd/cmd704.txt file:

```
curl -iX PATCH -H "Content-Type: application/json" -d
'{"played_once":"true", "played_times": 10}' "localhost:8000/games/2/"
```

The previous command will compose and send an HTTP PATCH request with the specified JSON key-value pairs. The request has a number after /games/, and therefore, it will match '^games/(?P<pk>[0-9]+)/$' and run the patch method for the views.GameDetail class-based view. Remember that the patch method is defined in the RetrieveUpdateDestroyAPIView superclass and it ends up calling the update method defined in mixins.UpdateModelMixin. If the Game instance with the updated values for the played_once and played_times fields is valid and it was successfully persisted in the database, the call to the method will return the 200 OK status code and the recently updated Game serialized to JSON in the response body.

The following lines show a sample response:

```
HTTP/1.1 200 OK
Allow: GET, PUT, PATCH, DELETE, HEAD, OPTIONS
Content-Length: 204
Content-Type: application/json
Date: Fri, 26 Oct 2018 16:40:51 GMT
Server: WSGIServer/0.2 CPython/3.7.1
Vary: Accept, Cookie
X-Frame-Options: SAMEORIGIN
{
    "esrb_rating": "AO (Adults Only)",
    "name": "Mutant Football League: Dynasty Edition",
    "played_once": true,
    "played_times": 10,
    "release_date": "2018-10-20T03:02:00.776594Z",
    "url": "http://localhost:8000/games/2/"
}
```

Taking advantage of pagination

Our database has a few rows for each of the tables that persist the models we have defined. However, after we start working with our API in a real-life production environment, we will have thousands of player scores, players, and games—although the ESRB ratings will still be few in number. We definitely have to prepare our API to deal with large result sets. Luckily, we can take advantage of the pagination features available in Django REST framework to make it easy to specify how we want large result sets to be split into individual pages of data.

First, we will write commands to compose and send HTTP POST requests to create 10 games that belong to one of the ESRB ratings we have created: T (Teen). This way, we will have a total of 12 games persisted in the database. We had two games and we add 10 more. The code file for the sample is included in the restful_python_2_07_01 folder, in the Django01/cmd/cmd705.txt file:

```
http POST ":8000/games/" name='Heavy Fire: Red Shadow' esrb_rating='T
(Teen)' release_date='2018-06-21T03:02:00.776594Z'
http POST ":8000/games/" name='ARK: Survival Evolved' esrb_rating='T
(Teen)' release_date='2018-06-21T03:02:00.776594Z'
http POST ":8000/games/" name='The Escapists 2' esrb_rating='T (Teen)'
release_date='2018-06-21T03:02:00.776594Z'
http POST ":8000/games/" name='Honor and Duty: D-Day' esrb_rating='T
(Teen)' release_date='2018-06-21T03:02:00.776594Z'
http POST ":8000/games/" name='Speed Brawl' esrb_rating='T (Teen)'
```

```
release_date='2018-06-21T03:02:00.776594Z'
http POST ":8000/games/" name='Unearthing Mars 2' esrb_rating='T (Teen)'
release_date='2018-06-21T03:02:00.776594Z'
http POST ":8000/games/" name='Super Street: The Game' esrb_rating='T
(Teen)' release_date='2019-01-21T03:02:00.776594Z'
http POST ":8000/games/" name='Valkyria Chronicles 4' esrb_rating='T
(Teen)' release_date='2019-01-21T03:02:00.776594Z'
http POST ":8000/games/" name='Tales of Vesperia: Definitive Edition'
esrb_rating='T (Teen)' release_date='2019-01-21T03:02:00.776594Z'
http POST ":8000/games/" name='Moonfall Ultimate' esrb_rating='T (Teen)'
release_date='2019-01-21T03:02:00.776594Z'
```

The following are the equivalent `curl` commands. The code file for the sample is included in the `restful_python_2_07_01` folder, in the `Django01/cmd/cmd706.txt` file:

```
curl -iX POST -H "Content-Type: application/json" -d '{"name":"Heavy Fire:
Red Shadow", "esrb_rating":"T (Teen)", "release_date":
"2018-06-21T03:02:00.776594Z"}'
"localhost:8000/games/"
curl -iX POST -H "Content-Type: application/json" -d '{"name":"ARK:
Survival Evolved", "esrb_rating":"T (Teen)", "release_date":
"2018-06-21T03:02:00.776594Z"}'
"localhost:8000/games/"
curl -iX POST -H "Content-Type: application/json" -d '{"name":"The
Escapists 2", "esrb_rating":"T (Teen)", "release_date":
"2018-06-21T03:02:00.776594Z"}'
"localhost:8000/games/"
curl -iX POST -H "Content-Type: application/json" -d '{"name":"Honor and
Duty: D-Day", "esrb_rating":"T (Teen)", "release_date":
"2018-06-21T03:02:00.776594Z"}'
"localhost:8000/games/"
curl -iX POST -H "Content-Type: application/json" -d '{"name":"Speed
Brawl", "esrb_rating":"T (Teen)", "release_date":
"2018-06-21T03:02:00.776594Z"}'
"localhost:8000/games/"
curl -iX POST -H "Content-Type: application/json" -d '{"name":"Unearthing
Mars 2", "esrb_rating":"T (Teen)", "release_date":
"2018-06-21T03:02:00.776594Z"}'
"localhost:8000/games/"
curl -iX POST -H "Content-Type: application/json" -d '{"name":"Super
Street: The Game", "esrb_rating":"T (Teen)", "release_date":
"2019-01-21T03:02:00.776594Z"}'
"localhost:8000/games/"
curl -iX POST -H "Content-Type: application/json" -d '{"name":"Valkyria
Chronicles 4", "esrb_rating":"T (Teen)", "release_date":
"2019-01-21T03:02:00.776594Z"}'
"localhost:8000/games/"
curl -iX POST -H "Content-Type: application/json" -d '{"name":"Tales of
```

```
Vesperia: Definitive Edition", "esrb_rating":"T (Teen)", "release_date":
"2019-01-21T03:02:00.776594Z"}'
"localhost:8000/games/"
curl -iX POST -H "Content-Type: application/json" -d '{"name":"Moonfall
Ultimate", "esrb_rating":"T (Teen)", "release_date":
"2019-01-21T03:02:00.776594Z"}'
"localhost:8000/games/"
```

The previous commands will compose and send 10 HTTP `POST` requests with the specified JSON key-value pairs. Each request specifies `/games/`, and therefore, it will match `'^games/$'` and run the `post` method for the `views.GameList` class-based view.

Now we have 12 games in our database. However, we don't want to retrieve the 12 games when we compose and send an HTTP `GET` request to `/games/`. We will configure one of the customizable pagination styles included in Django REST framework to include a maximum of four resources in each individual page of data.

 Our API is using the generic views that work with the mixin classes that can handle paginated responses, and therefore, they will automatically take into account the pagination settings we configure in Django REST Framework.

Open the `settings.py` file in the `games_service/games_service` folder. Add the following lines after the last line to declare a dictionary named `REST_FRAMEWORK` with key-value pairs that configure the global pagination settings for Django REST Framework. The code file for the sample is included in the `restful_python_2_07_02` folder, in the `Django01/games-service/games_service/settings.py` file:

```
REST_FRAMEWORK = {
    'DEFAULT_PAGINATION_CLASS':
    'rest_framework.pagination.LimitOffsetPagination',
    'PAGE_SIZE': 4
}
```

The value for the `DEFAULT_PAGINATION_CLASS` settings key specifies a global setting with the default pagination class that the generic views will use to provide paginated responses. In this case, we will use the `rest_framework.pagination.LimitOffsetPagination` class that provides a limit/offset based style. This pagination style works with `limit`, which indicates the maximum number of items to return, and `offset`, which specifies the starting position of the query. The value for the `PAGE_SIZE` settings key specifies a global setting with the default value for `limit`, also known as page size. We can specify a different limit when we perform the HTTP request by specifying the desired value in the `limit` query parameter. We can configure the class to have a maximum `limit` value in order to avoid undesired huge result sets.

Now run the following command to compose and send an HTTP GET request to retrieve all the games; specifically, an HTTP GET method to /games/. The code file for the sample is included in the restful_python_2_07_02 folder, in the Django01/cmd/cmd707.txt file:

```
http GET ":8000/games/"
```

The following is the equivalent curl command. The code file for the sample is included in the restful_python_2_07_02 folder, in the Django01/cmd/cmd708.txt file:

```
curl -iX GET "localhost:8000/games/"
```

The generic views will use the new settings we added to enable the offset/limit pagination. We will receive a 200 OK status code in the response header and the result will provide us values for the following keys:

- results: The value for this key provides the first four-game resources.
- count: The value for this key provides the total number of games for the query. In this case, the value is the total number of games persisted in the database because the query didn't apply any filter criteria.
- next: The value for this key provides the URL for the next page.
- previous: The value for this key provides the URL for the previous page. In this case, the result set is the first page, and therefore, the link to the previous page is null.

The output of the curl command is shown as follows:

```
HTTP/1.1 200 OK
Allow: GET, POST, HEAD, OPTIONS
Content-Length: 812
Content-Type: application/json
Date: Fri, 26 Oct 2018 19:33:50 GMT
Server: WSGIServer/0.2 CPython/3.7.1
Vary: Accept, Cookie
X-Frame-Options: SAMEORIGIN
{
    "count": 12,
    "next": "http://localhost:8000/games/?limit=4&offset=4",
    "previous": null,
    "results": [
        {
            "esrb_rating": "T (Teen)",
            "name": "ARK: Survival Evolved",
            "played_once": false,
            "played_times": 0,
```

```
            "release_date": "2018-06-21T03:02:00.776594Z",
            "url": "http://localhost:8000/games/4/"
    },
    {

            "esrb_rating": "AO (Adults Only)",
            "name": "Battlefield V",
            "played_once": false,
            "played_times": 0,
            "release_date": "2017-05-01T01:02:00.776594Z",
            "url": "http://localhost:8000/games/1/"
    },
    {

            "esrb_rating": "T (Teen)",
            "name": "Heavy Fire: Red Shadow",
            "played_once": false,
            "played_times": 0,
            "release_date": "2018-06-21T03:02:00.776594Z",
            "url": "http://localhost:8000/games/3/"
    },
    {

            "esrb_rating": "T (Teen)",
            "name": "Honor and Duty: D-Day",
            "played_once": false,
            "played_times": 0,
            "release_date": "2018-06-21T03:02:00.776594Z",
            "url": "http://localhost:8000/games/6/"
    }
  ]
}
```

In the previous HTTP GET request, we didn't specify any values for either the limit or offset parameters. However, as we specified the default value for the limit as 4 in the pagination settings, the generic views use this configuration value and provide us with the first page. If we compose and send the following HTTP GET request to retrieve the first page of all the games by specifying 0 for the offset value, the API will provide the same results shown before. Notice that offset is zero-based. The code file for the sample is included in the restful_python_2_07_02 folder, in the Django01/cmd/cmd709.txt file:

```
http GET ":8000/games/?offset=0"
```

The following is the equivalent curl command. The code file for the sample is included in the restful_python_2_07_02 folder, in the Django01/cmd/cmd710.txt file:

```
curl -iX GET "localhost:8000/games/?offset=0"
```

If we compose and send the following HTTP GET request to retrieve the first page of all the games by specifying 0 for the offset value and 4 for limit, the API will also provide the same results shown before. The code file for the sample is included in the restful_python_2_07_02 folder, in the Django01/cmd/cmd711.txt file:

```
http GET ":8000/games/?limit=4&offset=0"
```

The following is the equivalent curl command. The code file for the sample is included in the restful_python_2_07_02 folder, in the Django01/cmd/cmd712.txt file:

```
curl -iX GET "localhost:8000/games/?limit=4&offset=0"
```

Now we will compose and send an HTTP GET request to retrieve the next page, that is, the second page for the games, specifically an HTTP GET method to /games/ with the offset value set to 4. Remember that the value for the next key returned in the JSON body of the previous result provides us with the URL to the next page. The following is the equivalent curl command. The code file for the sample is included in the restful_python_2_07_02 folder, in the Django01/cmd/cmd713.txt file:

```
http GET ":8000/games/?limit=4&offset=4"
```

The following is the equivalent curl command. The following is the equivalent curl command. The code file for the sample is included in the restful_python_2_07_02 folder, in the Django01/cmd/cmd714.txt file:

```
curl -iX GET ":8000/games/?limit=4&offset=4"
```

The result will provide us the second set of 4 game resources in the results key, the total number of games for the query in the count key and a link to the next and previous pages in the next and previous keys. In this case, the result set is the second page, and therefore, the link to the previous page in the previous key is http://localhost:8000/games/?limit=4. We will receive a 200 OK status code in the response header and the four games in the results array:

```
HTTP/1.1 200 OK
Allow: GET, POST, HEAD, OPTIONS
Content-Length: 859
Content-Type: application/json
Date: Fri, 26 Oct 2018 20:25:52 GMT
Server: WSGIServer/0.2 CPython/3.7.1
Vary: Accept, Cookie
X-Frame-Options: SAMEORIGIN
{
    "count": 12,
    "next": "http://localhost:8000/games/?limit=4&offset=8",
```

```
    "previous": "http://localhost:8000/games/?limit=4",
    "results": [
        {
            "esrb_rating": "T (Teen)",
            "name": "Moonfall Ultimate",
            "played_once": false,
            "played_times": 0,
            "release_date": "2019-01-21T03:02:00.776594Z",
            "url": "http://localhost:8000/games/12/"
        },
        {
            "esrb_rating": "AO (Adults Only)",
            "name": "Mutant Football League: Dynasty Edition",
            "played_once": true,
            "played_times": 10,
            "release_date": "2018-10-20T03:02:00.776594Z",
            "url": "http://localhost:8000/games/2/"
        },
        {
            "esrb_rating": "T (Teen)",
            "name": "Speed Brawl",
            "played_once": false,
            "played_times": 0,
            "release_date": "2018-06-21T03:02:00.776594Z",
            "url": "http://localhost:8000/games/7/"
        },
        {
            "esrb_rating": "T (Teen)",
            "name": "Super Street: The Game",
            "played_once": false,
            "played_times": 0,
            "release_date": "2019-01-21T03:02:00.776594Z",
            "url": "http://localhost:8000/games/9/"
        }
    ]
}
```

In the previous HTTP request, we specified values for both the `limit` and `offset` parameters. However, as we specified the default value of `limit` as 4 in the global settings, the following request will produce the same results as the previous request. The code file for the sample is included in the `restful_python_2_07_02` folder, in the `Django01/cmd/cmd715.txt` file:

```
http GET ":8000/games/?offset=4"
```

The following is the equivalent `curl` command. The code file for the sample is included in the `restful_python_2_07_02` folder, in the `Django01/cmd/cmd716.txt` file:

```
curl -iX GET "localhost:8000/games/?offset=4"
```

Finally, we will write a command to compose and send an HTTP GET request to retrieve the last page, that is, the third page for the games, specifically an HTTP GET method to `/games/` with the `offset` value set to 8. Remember that the value for the next key returned in the JSON body of the previous result provides us with the URL to the next page. The code file for the sample is included in the `restful_python_2_07_02` folder, in the `Django01/cmd/cmd717.txt` file:

```
http GET ":8000/games/?limit=4&offset=8"
```

The following is the equivalent `curl` command. The code file for the sample is included in the `restful_python_2_07_02` folder, in the `Django01/cmd/cmd718.txt` file:

```
curl -iX GET "localhost:8000/games/?limit=4&offset=8"
```

The result will provide us the last set with the last 4 game resources in the `results` key, the total number of games for the query in the `count` key, and a link to the next and previous pages in the `next` and `previous` keys. In this case, the result set is the last page, and therefore, the link to the next page in the `next` key is `null`. We will receive a `200 OK` status code in the response header and the last four games in the `results` array:

```
HTTP/1.1 200 OK
Allow: GET, POST, HEAD, OPTIONS
Content-Length: 819
Content-Type: application/json
Date: Fri, 26 Oct 2018 20:33:08 GMT
Server: WSGIServer/0.2 CPython/3.7.1
Vary: Accept, Cookie
X-Frame-Options: SAMEORIGIN
{
    "count": 12,
    "next": null,
    "previous": "http://localhost:8000/games/?limit=4&offset=4",
    "results": [
        {
            "esrb_rating": "T (Teen)",
            "name": "Tales of Vesperia: Definitive Edition",
            "played_once": false,
            "played_times": 0,
            "release_date": "2019-01-21T03:02:00.776594Z",
            "url": "http://localhost:8000/games/11/"
        },
```

```
    {
        "esrb_rating": "T (Teen)",
        "name": "The Escapists 2",
        "played_once": false,
        "played_times": 0,
        "release_date": "2018-06-21T03:02:00.776594Z",
        "url": "http://localhost:8000/games/5/"
    },
    {
        "esrb_rating": "T (Teen)",
        "name": "Unearthing Mars 2",
        "played_once": false,
        "played_times": 0,
        "release_date": "2018-06-21T03:02:00.776594Z",
        "url": "http://localhost:8000/games/8/"
    },
    {
        "esrb_rating": "T (Teen)",
        "name": "Valkyria Chronicles 4",
        "played_once": false,
        "played_times": 0,
        "release_date": "2019-01-21T03:02:00.776594Z",
        "url": "http://localhost:8000/games/10/"
    }
    ]
}
```

Customizing pagination classes

The `rest_framework.pagination.LimitOffsetPagination` class that we are using to provide paginated responses declares a `max_limit` class attribute that defaults to `None`. This attribute allows us to indicate the maximum allowable limit that can be specified by using the `limit` query parameter. With the default setting, there is no limit, and we will be able to process requests that specify a value for `1000000` for the `limit` query parameter.

We definitely don't want our API to be able to generate a response with a million player scores or players with a single request. Unluckily, there is no configuration setting that allows us to change the value that the class assigns to the `max_limit` class attribute. Thus, we are forced to create our customized version of the `limit/offset` pagination style provided by Django REST Framework.

Create a new Python file named `max_limit_pagination.py` within the `games_service/games` folder and enter the following code that declares the new `MaxLimitPagination` class. The code file for the sample is included in the `restful_python_2_07_03` folder, in the `Django01/games-service/games/max_limit_pagination.py` file:

```
from rest_framework.pagination import LimitOffsetPagination

class MaxLimitPagination(LimitOffsetPagination):
    max_limit = 8
```

The previous lines declare the `MaxLimitPagination` class as a subclass of the `rest_framework.pagination.LimitOffsetPagination` superclass and overrides the value specified for the `max_limit` class attribute with 8.

Open the `settings.py` file in the `games_service/games_service` folder and replace the line that specified the value for the `DEFAULT_PAGINATION_CLASS` key in the dictionary named `REST_FRAMEWORK` with the highlighted line. The following lines show the new declaration of the dictionary named `REST_FRAMEWORK`. The code file for the sample is included in the `restful_python_2_07_03` folder, in the `Django01/games-service/games/settings.py` file:

```
REST_FRAMEWORK = {
    'DEFAULT_PAGINATION_CLASS':
    'games.max_limit_pagination.MaxLimitPagination',
    'PAGE_SIZE': 4
}
```

Now the generic views will use the recently declared `games.pagination.MaxLimitPagination` class, which provides a `limit/offset` based style with a maximum `limit` value equal to 8. If a request specifies a value for a limit higher than 8, the class will use the maximum limit value, that is, 8, and we will never return more than 8 items in a paginated response.

Now we will write a command to compose and send an HTTP request to retrieve the first page for the games, specifically, an HTTP GET method to `/games/` with the `limit` value set to 20. The code file for the sample is included in the `restful_python_2_07_03` folder, in the `Django01/cmd/cmd719.txt` file:

```
http GET ":8000/games/?limit=20"
```

The following is the equivalent `curl` command. The code file for the sample is included in the `restful_python_2_07_03` folder, in the `Django01/cmd/cmd720.txt` file:

```
curl -iX GET "localhost:8000/games/?limit=20"
```

The result will use a limit value equal to 8, instead of the indicated 20, because we are using our customized pagination class. The result will provide us the first set with 10 game resources in the `results` key, the total number of games for the query in the `count` key, and a link to the next and previous pages in the `next` and `previous` keys. In this case, the result set is the first page, and therefore, the link to the next page in the `next` key is `http://localhost:8000/games/?limit=8&offset=8`. We will receive a 200 OK status code in the response header and the first eight games in the `results` array. The following lines show the header and the first lines of the output:

```
HTTP/1.1 200 OK
Allow: GET, POST, HEAD, OPTIONS
Content-Length: 1542
Content-Type: application/json
Date: Fri, 26 Oct 2018 21:25:06 GMT
Server: WSGIServer/0.2 CPython/3.7.1
Vary: Accept, Cookie
X-Frame-Options: SAMEORIGIN
{
    "count": 12,
    "next": "http://localhost:8000/games/?limit=8&offset=8",
    "previous": null,
    "results": [
        {
```

 It is a good practice to configure a maximum limit to avoid generating huge responses.

Open a web browser and enter `http://localhost:8000/games/`. Replace `localhost` with the IP of the computer that is running the Django development server if you use another computer or device to run the browser. The Browsable API will compose and send an HTTP GET request to `/games/` and will display the results of its execution, that is, the headers and the JSON games list. Because we have configured pagination, the rendered web page will include the default pagination template associated with the base pagination class we are using, and will display the available page numbers at the upper-right corner of the web page.

The following screenshot shows the rendered web page after entering the URL in a web browser with the resource description **game-list**, and the three pages:

Understanding authentication, permissions, and throttling

Our current version of the API processes all incoming requests without requiring any kind of authentication. Django REST Framework allows us to easily use different authentication schemes to identify the user that originated the request or the token that signed the request. Then, we can use these credentials to apply the permission and throttling policies that will determine whether the request must be permitted or not. In a production environment, we can combine an authentication scheme with an API running under HTTPS. In our development configuration, we will continue working with the API under HTTP, but this is only valid for developing.

As happened with other configurations, we can set the authentication schemes globally and then override them, if necessary, in a class-based view or a function view. A list of classes specifies the authentication schemes that we want to use. Django REST Framework will use all the specified classes in the list to authenticate a request before running the code for the view. The first class in the list that generates a successful authentication will be responsible for setting the values for the following two properties:

- `request.user`: This is a user model instance that provides details about the user that generated the request. We will use an instance of the `django.contrib.auth.User` class, that is, a Django `User` instance, in our examples.
- `request.auth`: Additional authentication information such as an authentication token.

After a successful authentication, we can use the `request.user` property in our class-based view methods, which receive the `request` parameter to retrieve additional information about the user that generated the request.

Django REST Framework provides the following three authentication classes in the `rest_framework.authentication` module. All of them are subclasses of the `BaseAuthentication` superclass:

Class name	Description
`BasicAuthentication`	This class provides a basic HTTP authentication against username and password. If we use this class in production, we must make sure that the API is only available over HTTPS.
`SessionAuthentication`	This class works with Django's session framework for authentication.
`TokenAuthentication`	This class provides a simple token-based authentication. The request must include the token generated for a user in the `Authorization` HTTP header with `"Token "` as a prefix for the token.

First, we will use a combination of the featured provided by the `BasicAuthentication` and `SessionAuthentication` classes. Make sure you quit the Django development server. Remember that you just need to press *Ctrl + C* in the Terminal or Command Prompt window in which it is running.

Open the `settings.py` file in the `games_service/games_service` folder. Add the following highlighted lines to the dictionary named `REST_FRAMEWORK` with a key-value pair that configures the global default authentication classes. The code file for the sample is included in the `restful_python_2_07_04` folder, in the `Django01/games-service/games_service/settings.py` file:

```
REST_FRAMEWORK = {
    'DEFAULT_PAGINATION_CLASS':
    'games.pagination.MaxLimitPagination',
    'PAGE_SIZE': 4,
    'DEFAULT_AUTHENTICATION_CLASSES': (
        'rest_framework.authentication.BasicAuthentication',
        'rest_framework.authentication.SessionAuthentication',)
}
```

The value for the `DEFAULT_AUTHENTICATION_CLASSES` settings key specifies a global setting with a tuple of string whose values indicate the classes that we want to use for authentication.

Permissions use the authentication information included in the `request.user` and `request.auth` properties to determine whether the request should be granted or denied access. Permissions allow us to control which classes of users will be granted or denied access to the different features or parts of our RESTful API.

We will use the permissions features in Django REST framework to configure the following:

- Allow only authenticated users to create games
- Allow unauthenticated users to have read-only access to games
- Allow only the user that created a game to make changes to this game

We will make the necessary changes in our API to make a game have an owner-user. We will use predefined permission classes and a customized permission class to define the explained permission policies.

Throttling also determines whether the request must be authorized. Throttles control the rate of requests that users can make to our API. For example, we want to limit unauthenticated users to a maximum of 5 requests per hour. We want to restrict authenticated users to a maximum of 20 requests to the games related views per day.

Adding security-related data to the models

We will associate a game with a creator or owner. Only the authenticated users will be able to create new games. Only the creator of a game will be able to update it or delete it. All the requests that aren't authenticated will only have read-only access to games.

Open the models.py file in the games_service/games folder. Replace the code that declares the Game class with the following code. The new and edited lines are highlighted in the code listing. The code file for the sample is included in the restful_python_2_07_04 folder, in the Django01/games-service/games/models.py file:

```python
class Game(models.Model):
    created = models.DateTimeField(auto_now_add=True)
    name = models.CharField(max_length=200, unique=True)
    esrb_rating = models.ForeignKey(
        EsrbRating,
        related_name='games',
        on_delete=models.CASCADE)
    release_date = models.DateTimeField()
    played_once = models.BooleanField(default=False)
    played_times = models.IntegerField(default=0)
    owner = models.ForeignKey(
        'auth.User',
        related_name='games',
        on_delete=models.CASCADE)

    class Meta:
        ordering = ('name',)

    def __str__(self):
        return self.name
```

The new version of the `Game` model declares a new `owner` field that uses the `django.db.models.ForeignKey` class to provide a many-to-one relationship to the `auth.User` model, specifically, to the `django.contrib.auth.User` model. This `User` model represents the users within the Django authentication system. The `'games'` value specified for the `related_name` argument creates a backward relation from the `User` model to the `Game` model. This value indicates the name to use to relate a `User` object back to a `Game` object. This way, we will be able to access all the games owned by a specific user. Whenever we delete a user, we want all the games owned by this user to be deleted too, and therefore, we specify the `models.CASCADE` value for the `on_delete` argument.

Now we will run the `createsuperuser` subcommand for `manage.py` to create the superuser for Django that we will use to easily authenticate our requests. We will create more users later:

```
python manage.py createsuperuser
```

The command will ask you for the username you want to use for the superuser. Enter the desired username and press *Enter*. We will use `your_games_super_user` as the username for this example. You will see a line similar to the following one:

```
Username (leave blank to use 'xxxxxxxx'):
```

Then, the command will ask you for the email address:

```
Email address:
```

Enter an email address, such as `your_games_super_user@example.com`, and press *Enter*.

Finally, the command will ask you for the password for the new superuser:

```
Password:
```

Enter your desired password and press *Enter*. In the examples, we will use `WCS3qn!a4ybX#` as the password.

The command will ask you to enter the password again:

```
Password (again):
```

Enter it and press *Enter*. If both entered passwords match, the superuser will be created:

```
Superuser created successfully.
```

Open the `serializers.py` file in the `games_service/games` folder. Add the following code after the last line that declares the imports, before the declaration of the `GameCategorySerializer` class. The code file for the sample is included in the `restful_python_2_07_04` folder, in the `Django01/games-service/games/serializers.py` file:

```
from django.contrib.auth.models import User


class UserGameSerializer(serializers.HyperlinkedModelSerializer):
    class Meta:
        model = Game
        fields = (
            'url',
            'name')


class UserSerializer(serializers.HyperlinkedModelSerializer):
    games = UserGameSerializer(many=True, read_only=True)

    class Meta:
        model = User
        fields = (
            'url',
            'id',
            'username',
            'games')
```

The `UserGameSerializer` class is a subclass of the `HyperlinkedModelSerializer` superclass. We use this new serializer class to serialize the games related to a user. We just want to include the URL and the game's name, and therefore, the code specified `'url'` and `'name'` as members of the field tuple defined in the `Meta` inner class. We don't want to use the `GameSerializer` serializer class for the games related to a user because we want to serialize fewer fields, and therefore, we created the `UserGameSerializer` class.

The `UserSerializer` class is a subclass of the `HyperlinkedModelSerializer` superclass. This serializer class is related to the `django.contrib.auth.models.User` model. The `UserSerializer` class declares a `games` attribute as an instance of the previously explained `UserGameSerializer` with `many` and `read_only` equal to `True` because it is a one-to-many relationship and is read-only. We use the `games` name that we specified as the `related_name` string value when we added the `owner` field as a `models.ForeignKey` instance in the `Game` model. This way, the `games` field will provide us with an array of URLs and names for each game that belongs to the user.

We will make more changes to the `serializers.py` file in the `games_service/games` folder. We will add an `owner` field to the existing `GameSerializer` class. The following lines show the new code for the `GameSerializer` class. The new and edited lines are highlighted. The code file for the sample is included in the `restful_python_2_07_04` folder, in the `Django01/games-service/games/serializers.py` file:

```
class GameSerializer(serializers.HyperlinkedModelSerializer):
    # We want to display the game ESRB rating description instead of
    #



    its id
    esrb_rating = serializers.SlugRelatedField(
        queryset=EsrbRating.objects.all(),
        slug_field='description')
    # We want to display the user name that is the owner
    owner = serializers.ReadOnlyField(source='owner.username')

    class Meta:
        model = Game
        fields = (
            'url',
            'esrb_rating',
            'name',
            'release_date',
            'played_once',
            'played_times',
            'owner')
```

Now the `GameSerializer` class declares an `owner` attribute as an instance of the `serializers.ReadOnlyField` class with `source` equal to `'owner.username'`. This way, we will serialize the value for the `username` field of the related `django.contrib.auth.User` hold in the `owner` field. We use the `ReadOnlyField` class because the owner is automatically populated when an authenticated user creates a game, and therefore, it won't be possible to change the owner after a game has been created. This way, the `owner` field will provide us with the username that created the game. In addition, we added `'owner'` to the `fields` string tuple declared in the `Meta` inner class.

Creating a customized permission class for object-level permissions

Create a new Python file named `customized_permissions.py` within the `games_service/games` folder and enter the following code that declares the new `IsOwnerOrReadOnly` class. The code file for the sample is included in the `restful_python_2_07_04` folder, in the `Django01/games-service/games/customized_permissions.py` file:

```python
from rest_framework import permissions


class IsOwnerOrReadOnly(permissions.BasePermission):
    def has_object_permission(self, request, view, obj):
        if request.method in permissions.SAFE_METHODS:
            return True
        else:
            return obj.owner == request.user
```

The `rest_framework.permissions.BasePermission` class is the base class from which all permission classes should inherit. The previous lines declare the `IsOwnerOrReadOnly` class as a subclass of the `BasePermission` superclass and override the `has_object_permission` method, defined in the superclass, that returns a `bool` value indicating whether the permission should be granted or not.

If the HTTP verb specified in the request, available in the `request.method` attribute is any of the three safe methods specified in `permission.SAFE_METHODS` (GET, HEAD, or OPTIONS), the `has_object_permission` method returns `True` and grants permission to the request. These HTTP verbs do not make changes to the related resources, and therefore, they are included in the `permissions.SAFE_METHODS` tuple of string.

If the HTTP verb specified in the request, available in the `request.method` attribute, is not any of the three safe methods, the code returns `True` and grants permission only when the `owner` attribute of the received `obj`, available in the `obj.owner` attribute, matches the user that originated the request (`request.user`). This way, only the owner of the related resource will be granted permission to requests that include HTTP verbs that aren't safe.

We will use the new `IsOwnerOrReadOnly` permission class to make sure that only the game owners can make changes to an existing game. We will combine this permission class with the `rest_framework.permissions.IsAuthenticatedOrReadOnly` permission class that only allows read-only access to resources when the request is not authenticated as a user.

Persisting the user that makes a request and configuring permission policies

We want to be able to list all the users and retrieve the details for a single user. We will create subclasses of the two following generic class views declared in the `rest_framework.generics` module:

- `ListAPIView`: Implements the `get` method that retrieves a listing of `queryset`
- `RetrieveAPIView`: Implements the `get` method to retrieve a model instance

Open the `views.py` file in the `games_service/games` folder. Add the following code after the last line that declares the imports, before the declaration of the `GameCategoryList` class. The code file for the sample is included in the `restful_python_2_07_04` folder, in the `Django01/games-service/games/views.py` file:

```
from django.contrib.auth.models import User
from rest_framework import permissions
from games.serializers import UserSerializer
from games.customized_permissions import IsOwnerOrReadOnly


class UserList(generics.ListAPIView):
    queryset = User.objects.all()
    serializer_class = UserSerializer
    name = 'user-list'


class UserDetail(generics.RetrieveAPIView):
    queryset = User.objects.all()
    serializer_class = UserSerializer
    name = 'user-detail'
```

Stay editing the `views.py` file in the `games_service/games` folder. Add the following highlighted lines to the `ApiRoot` class declared in the `views.py` file. This way, we will be able to navigate to the users related views through the Browsable API. The code file for the sample is included in the `restful_python_2_07_04` folder, in the `Django01/games-service/games/views.py` file:

```
class ApiRoot(generics.GenericAPIView):
    name = 'api-root'
    def get(self, request, *args, **kwargs):
        return Response({
            'users': reverse(UserList.name, request=request),
            'players': reverse(PlayerList.name, request=request),
            'esrb-ratings': reverse(EsrbRatingList.name, request=request),
            'games': reverse(GameList.name, request=request),
            'scores': reverse(PlayerScoreList.name, request=request)
            })
```

Stay editing the `views.py` file in the `games_service/games` folder. Add the following highlighted lines to the `GameList` class-based view to override the `perform_create` method inherited from the `rest_framework.mixins.CreateModelMixin` superclass. Remember that the `generics.ListCreateAPIView` class inherits from `CreateModelMixin` class and other classes. The code in the new method will populate `owner` before a new `Game` instance is persisted in the database. In addition, the new code overrides the value for the `permission_classes` class attribute to configure permission policies for the class-based view. The code file for the sample is included in the `restful_python_2_07_04` folder, in the `Django01/games-service/games/views.py` file:

```
class GameList(generics.ListCreateAPIView):
    queryset = Game.objects.all()
    serializer_class = GameSerializer
    name = 'game-list'
    permission_classes = (
        permissions.IsAuthenticatedOrReadOnly,
        IsOwnerOrReadOnly)

    def perform_create(self, serializer):
        serializer.save(owner=self.request.user)
```

The code for the overridden `perform_create` method passes an additional `owner` field to the `create` method by setting a value for the `owner` argument for the call to the `serializer.save` method. The code sets the `owner` attribute to the value of `self.request.user`, that is, to the user associated to the request. This way, whenever a new game is persisted, it will save the user associated to the request as its owner.

Stay editing the `views.py` file in the `games_service/games` folder. Add the following highlighted lines to the `GameDetail` class-based view to override the value for the `permission_classes` class attribute to configure permission policies for the class-based view. The code file for the sample is included in the `restful_python_2_07_04` folder, in the `Django01/games-service/games/views.py` file:

```
class GameDetail(generics.RetrieveUpdateDestroyAPIView):
    queryset = Game.objects.all()
    serializer_class = GameSerializer
    name = 'game-detail'
    permission_classes = (
        permissions.IsAuthenticatedOrReadOnly,
        IsOwnerOrReadOnly)
```

We have included the `IsAuthenticatedOrReadOnly` class and our previously created `IsOwnerOrReadOnly` permission class in the `permission_classes` tuple for both the `GameList` and `GameDetail` classes.

Open the `urls.py` file in the `games_service/games` folder. Add the following elements to the `urlpatterns` string list. The new strings define the URL patterns that specify the regular expressions that have to be matched in the request to run a specific method for the previously created class-based views in the `views.py` file: `UserList` and `UserDetail`. The code file for the sample is included in the `restful_python_2_07_04` folder, in the `Django01/games-service/games/serializers.py` file:

```
url(r'^users/$',
    views.UserList.as_view(),
    name=views.UserList.name),
url(r'^users/(?P<pk>[0-9]+)/$',
    views.UserDetail.as_view(),
    name=views.UserDetail.name),
```

Now open the `urls.py` file in the `games_service` folder, specifically, the `games_service/urls.py` file. The file defines the root URL configurations and we want to include the URL patterns to allow the Browsable API to display the login and logout views. The following lines show the new code with the added line highlighted. The code file for the sample is included in the `restful_python_2_07_04` folder, in the `Django01/games-service/games/serializers.py` file:

```
from django.conf.urls import url, include

urlpatterns = [
    url(r'^', include('games.urls')),
    url(r'^api-auth/', include('rest_framework.urls')),
]
```

The new line adds the URL patterns defined in the `rest_framework.urls` module and associates them to the `^api-auth/` pattern. The browsable API uses `api-auth/` as a prefix for all the view related to the user login and logout

Setting a default value for a new required field in migrations

We have persisted many games in our database and we have added a new `owner` field for the games that are a required field. We don't want to delete all the existing games, and therefore, we will take advantage of some features in Django that make it easy for us to make the changes in the underlying database without losing the existing data.

Now we need to retrieve the `id` for the superuser we have created to use it as the default owner for the existing games. Django will allow us to easily update the existing games to set the owner user for them.

Run the following commands to retrieve the `id` from the `auth_user` table for the row whose `username` matches `'superuser'`. Replace `your_games_super_user` with the username you selected for the previously created superuser. In addition, replace `your_games_user_name` in the command with the username you used to create the PostgreSQL 10.5 database and `your_games_password` with your chosen password for this database user. You defined these values in Chapter 6, *Working with Class-Based Views and Hyperlinked APIs in Django 2.1*, in the *Declaring relationships with the models* section. The command assumes that you are running PostgreSQL on the same computer in which you are running the command.

The code file for the sample is included in the `restful_python_2_07_01` folder, in the `Django01/cmd/retrieve_id_for_django_superuser.sql` file:

```
psql --username=your_games_user_name --dbname=django_games --
command="SELECT id FROM auth_user WHERE username =
'your_games_super_user';"
```

The following screenshot shows a sample output for the previous command with the value for the `id` field: `1`:

```
games_service — -bash — 74×40
(Django01) Gastons-MacBook-Pro:games_service gaston$ psql --username=your_
games_user_name --dbname=django_games --command="SELECT id FROM auth_user
WHERE username = 'your_games_super_user';"
 id
----
  1
(1 row)

(Django01) Gastons-MacBook-Pro:games_service gaston$
```

Now run the following Python script to generate the migrations that will allow us to synchronize the database with the new field we added to the `Game` model to persist its owner. Make sure you are in the `games_service` folder within the root folder for the virtual environment (`Django01`). Notice that we use the Django app name, `games`, and not the PostgreSQL database name, `django_games` in the next script:

```
python manage.py makemigrations games
```

Django will display the question shown in the next screenshot:

```
You are trying to add a non-nullable field 'owner' to game without a default; we can't do that (the database needs
 something to populate existing rows).
Please select a fix:
 1) Provide a one-off default now (will be set on all existing rows with a null value for this column)
 2) Quit, and let me add a default in models.py
Select an option:
```

We want to provide the one-off default that will be set on all existing rows in the `games_game` table that persists the `Game` models. Hence, enter `1` to select the first option and press *Enter*.

Django will display the text shown in the next screenshot asking us to enter the default value as a valid Python expression:

```
Select an option: 1
Please enter the default value now, as valid Python
The datetime and django.utils.timezone modules are available, so you can do e.g. timezone.now
Type 'exit' to exit this prompt
>>>
```

Enter the value for the previously retrieved id, 1 in our example, and press *Enter*. The following lines show the output generated after running the previous command:

```
Migrations for 'games':
  games/migrations/0003_game_owner.py
    - Add field owner to game
```

The output indicates that the games_service/games/migrations/0003_game_owner.py file includes the code to add the field named owner to game. The following lines show the code for this file that was automatically generated by Django and its integrated ORM. The code file for the sample is included in the restful_python_2_07_04 folder, in the Django01/games-service/games/migrations/0003_game_owner.py file:

```
# Generated by Django 2.1.2 on 2018-10-27 14:28
from django.conf import settings
from django.db import migrations, models
import django.db.models.deletion
class Migration(migrations.Migration):
    dependencies = [
        migrations.swappable_dependency(settings.AUTH_USER_MODEL),
        ('games', '0002_auto_20181026_0450'),
    ]
    operations = [
        migrations.AddField(
            model_name='game',
            name='owner',
            field=models.ForeignKey(default=1,
on_delete=django.db.models.deletion.CASCADE, related_name='games',
to=settings.AUTH_USER_MODEL),
            preserve_default=False,
        ),
    ]
```

The code declares a subclass of the `django.db.migrations.Migration` class named `Migration` that defines an `operations` list with `migrations.AddField` that will add the `owner` field to the table related to the `game` model. Notice that the code defines a dependency with the previously executed migration.

Now run the following Python script to apply all the generated migrations and execute the changes in the database tables:

```
python manage.py migrate
```

The following lines show the output generated after running the previous command:

```
Operations to perform:
  Apply all migrations: admin, auth, contenttypes, games, sessions
Running migrations:
  Applying games.0003_game_owner... OK
```

After we run the previous command, we will have a new `owner_id` field added to the `games_game` table in the PostgreSQL 10.5 database. The existing rows in the `games_game` table will use the default value we indicated Django to use for the new `owner_id` field. We can use the PostgreSQL command line or any other application to easily check the contents of the `games_game` table that Django updated. The following screenshot shows all the rows for the `games_game` table with the owner field set to 1:

Run the following command to launch the interactive shell. Make sure you are in the `games_service` folder within the root folder for the virtual environment (`Django01`):

```
python manage.py shell
```

You will notice that a line that says (`InteractiveConsole`) is displayed after the usual lines that introduce your default Python interactive shell. Enter the following code in the Python interactive shell to create another user that is not a superuser. We will use this user and the superuser to test our changes in the permissions policies. Replace `gaston-hillar` with your desired username, `testuser@example.com` with the email, and `FG$gI^76q#yA3v` with the password you want to use for this user. Take into account that we will be using these credentials in the following sections. Make sure you always replace the credentials with your own credentials. The code file for the sample is included in the `restful_python_2_07_04` folder, in the `Django01/cmd/create_test_user.py` file:

```
from django.contrib.auth.models import User
user = User.objects.create_user('gaston-hillar', 'testuser@example.com',
'FG$gI^76q#yA3v')
user.save()
```

Finally, quit the interactive console by entering the following command:

```
quit()
```

Now we can launch Django's development server to compose and send HTTP requests. Execute any of the following two commands based on your needs to access the API in other devices or computers connected to your LAN:

```
python manage.py runserver
python manage.py runserver 0.0.0.0:8000
```

Composing requests with the necessary authentication

Now we will write a command to compose and send an HTTP `POST` request to create a new game without authentication credentials. The code file for the sample is included in the `restful_python_2_07_04` folder, in the `Django01/cmd/cmd721.txt` file:

```
http POST ":8000/games/" name='Super Mario Odyssey' esrb_rating='T (Teen)'
release_date='2017-10-27T01:00:00.776594Z'
```

The following is the equivalent `curl` command. The code file for the sample is included in the `restful_python_2_07_04` folder, in the `Django01/cmd/cmd722.txt` file:

```
curl -iX POST -H "Content-Type: application/json" -d '{"name":"Super Mario
Odyssey", "esrb_rating":"T (Teen)", "release_date":
"2017-10-27T01:00:00.776594Z"}'
"localhost:8000/games/"
```

We will receive a `403 Forbidden` status code in the response header and a detailed message indicating that we didn't provide authentication credentials in the JSON body. The following lines show a sample response:

```
HTTP/1.1 403 Forbidden
Allow: GET, POST, HEAD, OPTIONS
Content-Length: 58
Content-Type: application/json
Date: Sat, 27 Oct 2018 15:03:53 GMT
Server: WSGIServer/0.2 CPython/3.7.1
Vary: Accept, Cookie
X-Frame-Options: SAMEORIGIN
{
    "detail": "Authentication credentials were not provided."
}
```

If we want to create a new game, that is, to make a `POST` request to `/games/`, we need to provide authentication credentials by using HTTP authentication. Now we will compose and send an HTTP request to create a new game with authentication credentials, that is, with the superuser name and their password. Remember to replace `your_games_super_user` with the name you used for the superuser and `WCS3qn!a4ybX#` with the password you configured for this user. The code file for the sample is included in the `restful_python_2_07_04` folder, in the `Django01/cmd/cmd723.txt` file:

```
http -a your_games_super_user:'WCS3qn!a4ybX#' POST ":8000/games/"
name='Super Mario Odyssey' esrb_rating='T (Teen)'
release_date='2017-10-27T01:00:00.776594Z'
```

The following is the equivalent `curl` command. The code file for the sample is included in the `restful_python_2_07_04` folder, in the `Django01/cmd/cmd724.txt` file:

```
curl --user your_games_super_user:'password' -iX POST -H "Content-Type:
application/json" -d '{"name":"Super Mario Odyssey", "esrb_rating":"T
(Teen)", "release_date": "2017-10-27T01:00:00.776594Z"}'
"localhost:8000/games/"
```

If the new `Game` with the user named `your_games_super_user` as its owner was successfully persisted in the database, the function returns an HTTP `201 Created` status code and the recently-persisted `Game` serialized to JSON in the response body. The following lines show an example response for the HTTP request, with the new `Game` object in the JSON response:

```
HTTP/1.1 201 Created
Allow: GET, POST, HEAD, OPTIONS
Content-Length: 209
Content-Type: application/json
```

```
Date: Sat, 27 Oct 2018 15:17:40 GMT
Location: http://localhost:8000/games/13/
Server: WSGIServer/0.2 CPython/3.7.1
Vary: Accept, Cookie
X-Frame-Options: SAMEORIGIN
{
    "esrb_rating": "T (Teen)",
    "name": "Super Mario Odyssey",
    "owner": "your_games_super_user",
    "played_once": false,
    "played_times": 0,
    "release_date": "2017-10-27T01:00:00.776594Z",
    "url": "http://localhost:8000/games/13/"
}
```

Now we will compose and send an HTTP PATCH request to update the played_once and played_times field values for the previously created game with authentication credentials. However, in this case, we will use the other user we created in Django to authenticate the request. Remember to replace gaston-hillar with the name you used for the user and FG$gI^76q#yA3v with their password. In addition, replace 13 with the id generated for the previously-created game in your configuration. The code file for the sample is included in the restful_python_2_07_04 folder, in the Django01/cmd/cmd725.txt file:

```
http -a 'gaston-hillar':'FG$gI^76q#yA3v' PATCH ":8000/games/13/"
played_once=true played_times=15
```

The following is the equivalent curl command. The code file for the sample is included in the restful_python_2_07_04 folder, in the Django01/cmd/cmd726.txt file:

```
curl --user 'gaston-hillar':'FG$gI^76q#yA3v' -iX PATCH -H "Content-Type:
application/json" -d '{"played_once": "true", "played_times": 15}'
"localhost:8000/games/13/"
```

We will receive a 403 Forbidden status code in the response header and a detailed message indicating that we do not have permission to perform the action in the JSON body. The owner for the game we want to update is your_games_super_user and the authentication credentials for this request use a different user. Hence, the operation is rejected by the has_object_permission method in the IsOwnerOrReadOnly class. The following lines show a sample response:

```
HTTP/1.1 403 Forbidden
Allow: GET, PUT, PATCH, DELETE, HEAD, OPTIONS
Content-Length: 63
Content-Type: application/json
Date: Sat, 27 Oct 2018 15:23:45 GMT
```

```
Server: WSGIServer/0.2 CPython/3.7.1
Vary: Accept, Cookie
X-Frame-Options: SAMEORIGIN
{
    "detail": "You do not have permission to perform this action."
}
```

If we compose and send an HTTP request with the same authentication credentials for that resource with the GET method, we will be able to retrieve the game that the specified user doesn't own. The request will work because GET is one of the safe methods and a user that is not the owner is allowed to read the game. Remember to replace gaston-hillar with the name you used for the user and FG$gI^76q#yA3v with their password. In addition, replace 13 with the ID generated for the previously created game in your configuration. The code file for the sample is included in the restful_python_2_07_04 folder, in the Django01/cmd/cmd727.txt file:

```
http -a 'gaston-hillar':'FG$gI^76q#yA3v' GET ":8000/games/13/"
```

The following is the equivalent curl command. The code file for the sample is included in the restful_python_2_07_04 folder, in the Django01/cmd/cmd728.txt file:

```
curl --user 'gaston-hillar':'FG$gI^76q#yA3v' -iX GET
"localhost:8000/games/13/"
```

Browsing the API with authentication credentials

Open a web browser and enter http://localhost:8000/. Replace localhost with the IP of the computer that is running the Django development server if you use another computer or device to run the browser. The Browsable API will compose and send a GET request to / and will display the results of its execution, that is, the API root. You will notice there is a **Log in** hyperlink at the upper-right corner.

Click **Log in** and the browser will display the Django REST Framework login page. Enter gaston-hillar in the username field, enter FG$gI^76q#yA3v in the password field, and click **Log In**. Now, you will be logged in as gaston-hillar and all the requests you compose and send through the Browsable API will use this user.

You will be redirected again to the **api-root** and you will notice the **Log In** hyperlink is replaced with the username (**gaston-hillar**) and a drop-down menu that allows you to log out. The following screenshot shows the **api-root** after we are logged in as gaston-hillar:

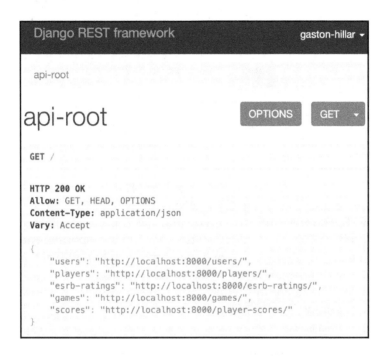

Click or tap on the URL displayed next to "users". If you are browsing in localhost, the URL will be http://localhost:8000/users/. The Browsable API will render the web page for the **Users List**. The following lines show the JSON body with the results for the GET request to localhost:8000/users/. The games array includes the URL and the name for each game that the user owns because the UserGameSerializer class is serializing the content for each game. The next lines show the first lines of the output:

```
HTTP 200 OK
Allow: GET, HEAD, OPTIONS
Content-Type: application/json
Vary: Accept
{
    "count": 2,
    "next": null,
    "previous": null,
    "results": [
        {
            "url": "http://localhost:8000/users/1/",
```

```
        "id": 1,
        "username": "your_games_super_user",
        "games": [
            {
                "url": "http://localhost:8000/games/4/",
                "name": "ARK: Survival Evolved"
            },
            {
                "url": "http://localhost:8000/games/1/",
                "name": "Battlefield V"
            },
            {
                "url": "http://localhost:8000/games/3/",
                "name": "Heavy Fire: Red Shadow"
            },
```

Click or tap on one of the URLs for the games listed as owned by the your_games_super_user user, that is, the other user. The Browsable API will render the web page for **game-detail**. Click or tap **OPTIONS** and the **DELETE** button will appear. Click or tap **DELETE**. The web browser will display a confirmation dialog box. Click or tap **Delete**. We will receive a 403 Forbidden status code in the response header and a detailed message indicating that we do not have permission to perform the action in the JSON body. The owner for the game we want to delete is your_games_super_user and the authentication credentials for this request use a different user, specifically, gaston-hillar. Thus, the operation is rejected by the has_object_permission method in the IsOwnerOrReadOnly class. The following screenshot shows a sample response:

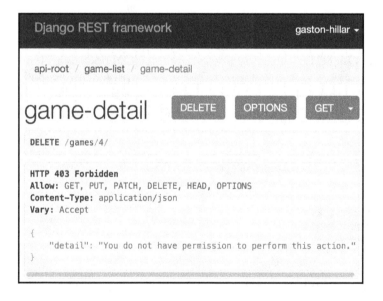

Django REST framework has many additional authentication plugins that can be useful for user security goals. In addition, there are third-party authentication packages. You can read more details about all the possibilities that the framework provides us for authentication at `http://www.django-rest-framework.org/api-guide/authentication/`.

Test your knowledge

Let's see whether you can answer the following questions correctly:

1. Which of the following lines define a field named `title` in a model that will generate a unique constraint on this field?
    1. `title = django.db.models.CharField(max_length=250, unique=True)`
    2. `title = django.db.models.UniqueCharField(max_length=250)`
    3. `title = django.db.models.CharField(max_length=250, options=django.db.models.unique_constraint)`

2. Which of the following lines define a field named `title` in a model that won't generate a unique constraint on this field?
    1. `title = django.db.models.CharField(max_length=250, unique=False)`
    2. `title = django.db.models.NonUniqueCharField(max_length=250)`
    3. `title = django.db.models.CharField(max_length=250, options=django.db.models.allow_duplicates)`

3. Which of the following setting's keys in the `REST_FRAMEWORK` dictionary specifies a global setting with the default pagination class that the generic views will use to provide paginated responses?
    1. `DEFAULT_PAGINATED_RESPONSE_PARSER`
    2. `DEFAULT_PAGINATION_CLASS`
    3. `DEFAULT_PAGINATED_RESPONSE_CLASS`

4. Which of the following pagination classes provides a limit/offset-based style in Django REST framework?
     1. `rest_framework.pagination.LimitOffsetPaging`
     2. `rest_framework.styles.LimitOffsetPagination`
     3. `rest_framework.pagination.LimitOffsetPagination`

5. The `rest_framework.authentication.BasicAuthentication` class:
     1. Works with Django's session framework for authentication
     2. Provides an HTTP basic authentication against username and password
     3. Provides a simple token-based authentication

6. The `rest_framework.authentication.SessionAuthentication` class:
     1. Works with Django's session framework for authentication
     2. Provides an HTTP basic authentication against username and password
     3. Provides a simple token-based authentication

7. Which of the following setting's keys in the `REST_FRAMEWORK` dictionary specifies a global setting with a tuple of string that indicates the classes we want to use for authentication?:
     1. `DEFAULT_AUTH_CLASSES`
     2. `AUTHENTICATION_CLASSES`
     3. `DEFAULT_AUTHENTICATION_CLASSES`

Summary

In this chapter, we improved the RESTful API in many ways. We added unique constraints to the model and updated the database, we made it easy to update single fields with the PATCH method, and we took advantage of pagination.

Then, we started working with authentication, permissions, and throttling. We added security-related data to the models and we updated the database. We made many changes in the different pieces of code to achieve a specific security goal and we took advantage of Django REST Framework's authentication and permissions features.

Now that we have built an improved and complex API that takes into account authentication and uses permission policies, we will use additional abstractions included in the framework, adding throttling and tests, which are the topics of the next chapter.

8
Throttling, Filtering, Testing, and Deploying an API with Django 2.1

In this chapter, we will use additional features included in Django 2.1 and Django REST Framework to improve our RESTful API. We will also write, execute, and improve unit tests and learn a few things related to deployment. We will look at the following:

- Install packages with the `requirements.txt` file to work with filters, throttling, and tests
- Understand filtering, searching, and ordering classes
- Configure filtering, searching, and ordering for views
- Execute HTTP requests to test filtering, searching, and ordering features
- Filter, search, and order in the Browsable API
- Understand throttling classes and goals
- Configure throttling policies
- Execute HTTP requests to test throttle policies
- Setting up unit tests with `pytest`
- Write the first round of unit tests
- Run unit tests with `pytest`
- Improve testing coverage
- Run Django RESTful APIs on the cloud

Installing packages with the requirements.txt file to work with filters, throttling, and tests

Make sure you quit Django development server. You just need to press *Ctrl + C* in the Terminal or Command Prompt window in which it is running.

Now, we will install many additional packages to work with filtering capabilities and to be able to easily run tests and measure their code coverage. Make sure you have activated the virtual environment we have created in the previous chapter, named Django01. After you activate the virtual environment, it is time to run many commands that will be the same for macOS, Linux, and Windows.

Now, we will edit the existing requirements.txt file to specify the additional packages that our application requires to be installed on any supported platform. This way, it will be extremely easy to repeat the installation of the specified packages with their versions in any new virtual environment.

Use your favorite editor to edit the existing text file, named requirements.txt, within the root folder for the virtual environment. Add the following lines after the last line to declare the additional packages and the versions that our new version of the API requires. The code file for the sample is included in the restful_python_2_08_01 folder, in the Django01/requirements.txt file:

```
django-filter==2.0.0
pytest==4.0.2
coverage==4.5.2
pytest-cov==2.6.0
pytest-django==3.4.4
```

Each additional line added to the requirements.txt file indicates the package and the version that needs to be installed.

The following table summarizes the packages and the version numbers that we specified as additional requirements to the previously included packages:

Package name	Version to be installed
django-filter	2.0.0
pytest	4.0.2
coverage	4.5.2
pytest-cov	2.6.0
pytest-django	3.4.4

We will install the following Python packages in our virtual environment:

- django-filter: This Django application provides a filter backend for its usage in Django REST Framework that allows us to easily add dynamic QuerySet filtering from URL parameters.
- pytest: This is a very popular Python unit test framework that makes testing easy and reduces boilerplate code.
- coverage: This tool measures the code coverage of Python programs. We will use it to determine which parts of the code are being executed by unit tests and which parts aren't.
- pytest-cov: This plugin for pytest makes it easy to produce coverage reports that use the coverage tool under the hood, and provides some additional features.
- pytest-django: This plugin for pytest provides a set of tools to make it easier to test Django projects with pytest, including the useful client fixture.

Now we must run the following command on macOS, Linux, or Windows to install the additional packages of the versions outlined in the previous table with pip using the recently edited requirements.txt file. Make sure you are located in the folder that contains the requirements.txt file before running the following command:

```
pip install -r requirements.txt
```

The last lines for the output will indicate that all the new packages and their dependencies have been successfully installed. If you downloaded the source code for the example and you didn't work with the previous version of the API, `pip` will also install the other packages included in the `requirements.txt` file:

```
Installing collected packages: django-filter, atomicwrites, pluggy, six,
more-itertools, py, attrs, pytest, coverage, pytest-cov, pytest-django
Successfully installed atomicwrites-1.2.1 attrs-18.2.0 coverage-4.5.2
django-filter-2.0.0 more-itertools-4.3.0 pluggy-0.8.0 py-1.7.0 pytest-4.0.2
pytest-cov-2.6.0 six-1.11.0 pytest-django-3.4.4
```

Understanding filtering, searching, and ordering classes

In the previous chapter, we took advantage of the pagination features available in Django REST Framework to specify how we wanted large results sets to be split into individual pages of data. However, we have always been working with the entire `queryset` as the result set; that is, we didn't apply any filter.

 Django REST Framework makes it easy to customize filtering, searching, and sorting capabilities for the views we have already coded.

Open the `settings.py` file in the `games_service/games_service` folder. Add the following highlighted lines after the first line that declares the dictionary named `REST_FRAMEWORK` to add the new `'DEFAULT_FILTER_BACKENDS'` setting key. Don't remove the lines that will appear after the new highlighted lines. We don't show them to avoid repeating code. The code file for the sample is included in the `restful_python_2_08_01` folder, in the `Django01/games-service/games_service/settings.py` file:

```
REST_FRAMEWORK = {
    'DEFAULT_FILTER_BACKENDS': (
        'django_filters.rest_framework.DjangoFilterBackend',
        'rest_framework.filters.SearchFilter',
        'rest_framework.filters.OrderingFilter'),
```

The value for the `'DEFAULT_FILTER_BACKENDS'` settings key specifies a global setting with a tuple of string whose values indicate the default classes that we want to use for filter backends. We will use the following three classes:

Module	Class name	Owner
`django_filters.rest_framework`	`DjangoFilterBackend`	Django filter
`rest_framework.filters`	`SearchFilter`	Django REST Framework
`rest_framework.filters`	`OrderingFilter`	Django REST Framework

The `DjangoFilterBackend` class provides field-filtering capabilities through the recently installed `django-filer` package. We can specify the set of fields we want to be able to filter against or create a `django_filters.rest_framework.FilterSet` class with more customized settings and associate it with the desired view.

The `SearchFilter` class provides single query parameter-based searching capabilities and is based on the Django admin's search function. We can specify the set of fields we want to include for the search, and the client will be able to filter items by making queries that search on these fields with a single query. This is useful when we want to make it possible for a request to search on multiple fields with a single query.

The `OrderingFilter` class allows the client that composes the request to control how the results are ordered with a single query parameter. We can specify which fields may be ordered against.

> Note that we can also configure the filter backends by including any of the previously enumerated classes in a tuple and assigning it to the `filter_backends` class attribute for the desired generic view. However, in this case, we will use the default configuration for all our class-based views.

Whenever we design a RESTful API, we have to make sure we provide the required features with a properly optimized usage of the available resources. Hence, we have to be careful to make the fields we configure available in the filtering, searching, and ordering features. The configurations we make in these features will have an impact on the queries that Django's integrated ORM will generate and execute on the database. We must definitely make sure that we have the appropriate database optimizations that take into account the queries that will be executed.

Stay in the `settings.py` file in the `games_service/games_service` folder. Add the following highlighted lines after the first line that declares the dictionary, named `INSTALLED_APPS`, to add `'django_filters'` as a newly installed application for the Django project.

Don't remove the lines that will appear after the new highlighted lines. We don't show them to avoid repeating code. The code file for the sample is included in the `restful_python_2_08_01` folder, in the `Django01/games-service/games_service/settings.py` file:

```
INSTALLED_APPS = [
    # Django Filters
    'django_filters',
```

Configuring filtering, searching, and ordering for views

Open the `views.py` file in the `games_service/games` folder. Add the following code after the last line that declares the imports, before the declaration of the `UserList` class. The code file for the sample is included in the `restful_python_2_08_01` folder, in the `Django01/games-service/games/views.py` file:

```
from rest_framework import filters
from django_filters import AllValuesFilter, DateTimeFilter, NumberFilter
from django_filters.rest_framework import FilterSet
```

Stay editing the `views.py` file in the `games_service/games` folder. Add the following highlighted lines to the `EsrbRatingList` class declared in the `views.py` file. Don't remove the existing lines for this class that isn't shown to avoid repeating code. The code file for the sample is included in the `restful_python_2_08_01` folder, in the `Django01/games-service/games/views.py` file:

```
class EsrbRatingList(generics.ListCreateAPIView):
    filterset_fields = ('description',)
    search_fields = ('^description',)
    ordering_fields = ('description',)
```

The added lines declare the following three attributes of the `EsrbRatingList` class:

- `filterset_fields`: This attribute specifies a tuple of string whose values indicate the field names that we want to be able to filter against. Under the hood, Django filters and its Django REST Framework integration will automatically create a `django_filters.rest_framework.FilterSet` class and associate it to the `EsrbRatingList` view. This way, we will be able to filter against the `name` field with our HTTP requests.

- `search_fields`: This attribute specifies a tuple of string whose values indicate the text-type field names that we want to include in the search feature. In this case, we want to search only against the name field and perform a starts-with match. The `'^'` included as a prefix of the field name indicates that we want to restrict the search behavior to a starts-with match.
- `ordering_fields`: This attribute specifies a tuple of string whose values indicate the field names that the client can specify to sort the results. If the client doesn't specify a field for ordering, the response will use the default ordering fields indicated in the model related to the view.

Notice that the previously explained configuration limits the options that we will enable for filtering, searching, and ordering views with the query parameters included in the HTTP requests. This way, we have full control over what the API clients will be able to do in relation to these options. Now, we will continue adding those three class attributes to other existing class-based views to specify the fields to be used in the filter, search, and ordering features.

Stay editing the `views.py` file in the `games_service/games` folder. Add the following highlighted lines to the `GameList` class declared in the `views.py` file. Don't remove the existing lines for this class that isn't shown to avoid repeating code. The code file for the sample is included in the `restful_python_2_08_01` folder, in the `Django01/games-service/games/views.py` file:

```
class GameList(generics.ListCreateAPIView):
    filterset_fields = (
        'name',
        'esrb_rating',
        'release_date',
        'played_times',
        'owner',)
    search_fields = (
        '^name',)
    ordering_fields = (
        'name',
        'release_date',
        'played_times',)
```

In this case, we specified many field names in the `filterset_fields` attribute. We included `'esrb_rating'` and `'owner'` in the string tuple, and therefore, the client will be able to include the `id` values for any of these two fields in the filter. We will take advantage of other options for related models that will allow us to filter by the fields of the related model later. This way, we will understand the different customizations available for Django filters.

The `ordering_fields` attribute specifies three field names for the tuple of string, and therefore, the client will be able to sort the results by `name`, `release_date`, or `played_times`.

Stay editing the `views.py` file in the `games_service/games` folder. Add the following highlighted lines to the `PlayerList` class declared in the `views.py` file. Don't remove the existing lines for this class that isn't shown to avoid repeating code. The code file for the sample is included in the `restful_python_2_08_01` folder, in the `Django01/games-service/games/views.py` file:

```
class PlayerList(generics.ListCreateAPIView):
    filterset_fields = (
        'name',
        'gender',)
    search_fields = (
        '^name',)
    ordering_fields = (
        'name',)
```

Stay editing the `views.py` file in the `games_service/games` folder. Add the following code to create the new `PlayerScoreFilter` class in the `views.py` file, before the declaration of the `PlayerScoreList` class. The code file for the sample is included in the `restful_python_2_08_01` folder, in the `Django01/games-service/games/views.py` file:

```
class PlayerScoreFilter(FilterSet):
    player_name = AllValuesFilter(field_name='player__name')
    game_name = AllValuesFilter(field_name='game__name')
    min_score = NumberFilter(field_name='score', lookup_expr='gte')
    max_score = NumberFilter(field_name='score', lookup_expr='lte')
    from_score_date = DateTimeFilter(field_name='score_date',
lookup_expr='gte')
    to_score_date = DateTimeFilter(field_name='score_date',
lookup_expr='lte')

    class Meta:
        model = PlayerScore
        fields = (
            'game_name',
            'player_name',
            'score',
            'from_score_date',
            'to_score_date',
            'min_score',
            'max_score',)
```

The `PlayerScoreFilter` is a subclass of the `FilterSet` superclass and allows us to customize settings for the fields that we will use for filtering in the `PlayerScoreList` class-based view. The class declares the following six class attributes:

- `player_name`: This class attribute is an `AllValuesFilter` instance that allows the client to filter the player scores whose player's name matches the specified string value. The value for `field_name` indicates the field to which the filter is applied, `'player__name'`. Notice that the value has a double underscore (__): you can read it as the `name` field for the `player` model, or simply replace the double underscore with a dot (.) and read `player.name`. The name uses Django's double-underscore syntax. However, we don't want the client to use `player__name` to specify the filter for the player's name. Thus, the instance is stored in the class attribute named `player_name`, with just a single underscore between player and name. The Browsable API will display a drop-down menu with all the possible values for the player's name to be used as filters. The drop-down menu will only include the player's names that have registered scores because we used the `AllValuesFilter` class.

- `game_name`: This class attribute is an `AllValuesFilter` instance that allows the client to filter the player scores whose game's name matches the specified string value. The value for `field_name` indicates the field to which the filter is applied, `'game__name'`. The name uses the previously explained double-underscore syntax of Django. As happened with `player_name`, we don't want the client to use `game__name` to specify the filter for the game's name, and therefore, we store the instance in the class attribute named `game_name`, with just a single underscore between game and name. The Browsable API will display a drop-down menu with all the possible values for the game's name for use as a filter. The drop-down menu will only include the game's names that have registered scores because we used the `AllValuesFilter` class.

- `min_score`: This class attribute is a `NumberFilter` instance that allows the client to filter the player scores whose `score` numeric value is greater than or equal to the specified number. The value for `field_name` indicates the field to which the numeric filter is applied, `'score'`, and the `lookup_expr` value indicates the lookup expression, `'gte'`, which means greater than or equal to.

- `max_score`: This class attribute is a `NumberFilter` instance that allows the client to filter the player scores whose `score` numeric value is less than or equal to the specified number. The value for `field_name` indicates the field to which the numeric filter is applied, `'score'`, and the `lookup_expr` value indicates the lookup expression, `'lte'`, which means less than or equal to.

- `from_score_date`: This class attribute is a `DateTimeFilter` instance that allows the client to filter the player scores whose `score_date` date-time value is greater than or equal to the specified date-time value. The value for `field_name` indicates the field to which the date-time filter is applied, `'score_date'`, and the `lookup_expr` value indicates the lookup expression, `'gte'`.
- `to_score_date`: This class attribute is a `DateTimeFilter` instance that allows the client to filter the player scores whose `score_date` date-time value is less than or equal to the specified date-time value. The value for `field_name` indicates the field to which the date-time filter is applied, `'score_date'`, and the `lookup_expr` value indicates the lookup expression, `'lte'`.

In addition, the `PlayerScoreFilter` class declares a `Meta` inner class that declares two attributes:

- `model`: This attribute specifies the model related to the filter set; that is, the `PlayerScore` class.
- `fields`: This attribute specifies a tuple of string whose values indicate the field names and filter names that we want to include in the filters for the related model. We included `'scores'` and the names for all the previously declared filters. The `'scores'` string refers to the `score` field name; we want to apply the default numeric filter that will be built under the hood to allow the client to filter by an exact match in the `score` field.

Stay editing the `views.py` file in the `games_service/games` folder. Add the following highlighted lines to the `PlayerScoreList` class declared in the `views.py` file. Don't remove the existing lines for this class that isn't shown to avoid repeating code. The code file for the sample is included in the `restful_python_2_08_01` folder, in the `Django01/games-service/games/views.py` file:

```
class PlayerScoreList(generics.ListCreateAPIView):
    ordering_fields = (
        'score',
        'score_date',)
    filterset_class = PlayerScoreFilter
```

The `filterset_class` attribute specifies the `FilterSet` subclass that we want to use for this class-based view: `PlayerScoreFilter`. In addition, we specified the two field names that the client will be able to use for sorting features in the `ordering_fields` tuple of string.

Executing HTTP requests to test filtering, searching, and ordering

Now, we can launch Django's development server to compose and send HTTP requests. Execute any of the following two commands, based on your needs to access the API in other devices or computers connected to your LAN:

```
python manage.py runserver
python manage.py runserver 0.0.0.0:8000
```

After we run any of the previous commands, the development server will start listening at port `8000`.

Now, we will write a command to compose and send an HTTP GET request to retrieve all the ESRB ratings whose description matches T (Teen). The code file for the sample is included in the `restful_python_2_08_01` folder, in the `Django01/cmd/cmd801.txt` file:

```
http ":8000/esrb-ratings/?description=T+(Teen)"
```

The following is the equivalent `curl` command. The code file for the sample is included in the `restful_python_2_08_01` folder, in the `Django01/cmd/cmd802.txt` file:

```
curl -iX GET "localhost:8000/esrb-ratings/?description=T+(Teen)"
```

The following lines show a sample response with the single ESRB rating whose description matches the specified description in the filter. The following lines only show the JSON body without the headers:

```
{
    "count": 1,
    "next": null,
    "previous": null,
    "results": [
        {
            "description": "T (Teen)",
            "games": [
                "http://localhost:8000/games/4/",
```

```
                        "http://localhost:8000/games/3/",
                        "http://localhost:8000/games/6/",
                        "http://localhost:8000/games/12/",
                        "http://localhost:8000/games/7/",
                        "http://localhost:8000/games/13/",
                        "http://localhost:8000/games/9/",
                        "http://localhost:8000/games/11/",
                        "http://localhost:8000/games/5/",
                        "http://localhost:8000/games/8/",
                        "http://localhost:8000/games/10/"
                ],
                "id": 2,
                "url": "http://localhost:8000/esrb-ratings/2/"
            }
        ]
    }
```

Now, we will write a command to compose and send an HTTP GET request to retrieve all the games whose related ESRB rating is 1 and the value for the played_times field is equal to 10. We want to sort the results by release_date in descending order, and therefore, we specify -release_date in the value for ordering. The hyphen (-) before the field name specifies the ordering feature to use descending order, instead of the default ascending order. Make sure you replace 1 with the id value of the ESRB rating whose description is AO (Adults Only). The code file for the sample is included in the restful_python_2_08_01 folder, in the Django01/cmd/cmd803.txt file:

```
http ":8000/games/?esrb_rating=1&played_times=10&ordering=-release_date"
```

The following is the equivalent curl command. The code file for the sample is included in the restful_python_2_08_01 folder, in the Django01/cmd/cmd804.txt file:

```
curl -iX GET
"localhost:8000/games/?esrb_rating=1&played_times=10&ordering=-
release_date"
```

The following lines show a sample response with the single game that matches the specified criteria in the filter. The following lines only show the JSON body without the headers:

```
    {
        "count": 1,
        "next": null,
        "previous": null,
        "results": [
            {
                "esrb_rating": "AO (Adults Only)",
```

```
            "name": "Mutant Football League: Dynasty Edition",
            "owner": "your_games_super_user",
            "played_once": true,
            "played_times": 10,
            "release_date": "2018-10-20T03:02:00.776594Z",
            "url": "http://localhost:8000/games/2/"
        }
    ]
}
```

In the `GameList` class, we specified `'esrb_rating'` as one of the strings in the `filterset_fields` tuple of string. Thus, we had to use the ESRB rating `id` in the filter.

Now, we will run a command that will compose and send an HTTP `GET` request that uses a filter on the game's name related to a registered score. The `PlayerScoreFilter` class provides us a filter to the name of the related game in `game_name`. We will combine the filter with another filter on the player's name related to a registered score. The `PlayerScoreFilter` class provides us a way to filter to the name of the related player in `player_name`. Both conditions specified in the criteria must be met, and therefore, the filters are combined with the `AND` operator. The code file for the sample is included in the `restful_python_2_08_01` folder, in the `Django01/cmd/cmd805.txt` file:

```
http ":8000/player-
scores/?player_name=Enzo+Scocco&game_name=Battlefield+V"
```

The following is the equivalent `curl` command. The code file for the sample is included in the `restful_python_2_08_01` folder, in the `Django01/cmd/cmd806.txt` file:

```
curl -iX GET "localhost:8000/player-
scores/?player_name=Enzo+Scocco&game_name=Battlefield+V"
```

The following lines show a sample response with the score that matches the specified criteria in the filters. The following lines only show the JSON body without the headers:

```
{
    "count": 1,
    "next": null,
    "previous": null,
    "results": [
        {
            "game": "Battlefield V",
            "id": 3,
            "player": "Enzo Scocco",
            "score": 43200,
            "score_date": "2019-01-01T03:02:00.776594Z",
            "url": "http://localhost:8000/player-scores/3/"
```

```
        }
    ]
}
```

We will compose and send an HTTP GET request to retrieve all the scores that match the following criteria, sorted by `score` in descending order:

- The `score` value is between 17,000 and 45,000
- The `score_date` value is between 2019-01-01 and 2019-01-31

The following command composes and sends the previously explained HTTP GET request. The code file for the sample is included in the `restful_python_2_08_01` folder, in the `Django01/cmd/cmd807.txt` file:

```
http ":8000/player-
scores/?from_score_date=2019-01-01&to_score_date=2019-01-
31&min_score=17000&max_score=45000&ordering=-score"
```

The following is the equivalent `curl` command. The code file for the sample is included in the `restful_python_2_08_01` folder, in the `Django01/cmd/cmd808.txt` file:

```
curl -iX GET "localhost:8000/player-
scores/?from_score_date=2019-01-01&to_score_date=2019-01-
31&min_score=17000&max_score=45000&ordering=-score"
```

The following lines show a sample response with the three games that match the specified criteria in the filters. The following lines only show the JSON body without the headers:

```
{
    "count": 3,
    "next": null,
    "previous": null,
    "results": [
        {
            "game": "Battlefield V",
            "id": 3,
            "player": "Enzo Scocco",
            "score": 43200,
            "score_date": "2019-01-01T03:02:00.776594Z",
            "url": "http://localhost:8000/player-scores/3/"
        },
        {
            "game": "Battlefield V",
            "id": 1,
            "player": "Gaston Hillar",
            "score": 17500,
            "score_date": "2019-01-01T03:02:00.776594Z",
```

```
                "url": "http://localhost:8000/player-scores/1/"
        },
        {

                "game": "Mutant Football League: Dynasty Edition",
                "id": 4,
                "player": "Enzo Scocco",
                "score": 17420,
                "score_date": "2019-01-01T05:02:00.776594Z",
                "url": "http://localhost:8000/player-scores/4/"
        }
    ]
}
```

> In the previous requests, none of the responses had more than one page. If the response requires more than one page, the values for the previous and next keys will display the URLs that include the combination of the filters, search, ordering, and pagination. Django combines all the features to build the appropriate URLs.

We will compose and send an HTTP request to retrieve all the games whose name starts with 'S'. We will use the search feature that we configured to restrict the search behavior to a starts-with match on the name field. The code file for the sample is included in the restful_python_2_08_01 folder, in the Django01/cmd/cmd809.txt file:

```
http ":8000/games/?search=H"
```

The following is the equivalent curl command. The code file for the sample is included in the restful_python_2_08_01 folder, in the Django01/cmd/cmd810.txt file:

```
curl -iX GET "localhost:8000/games/?search=H"
```

The following lines show a sample response with the two games that match the specified search criteria; that is, those games whose names start with 'H'. The following lines only show the JSON body without the headers:

```
{
    "count": 2,
    "next": null,
    "previous": null,
    "results": [
        {
            "esrb_rating": "T (Teen)",
            "name": "Heavy Fire: Red Shadow",
            "owner": "your_games_super_user",
            "played_once": false,
            "played_times": 0,
```

```
                "release_date": "2018-06-21T03:02:00.776594Z",
                "url": "http://localhost:8000/games/3/"
        },
        {

                "esrb_rating": "T (Teen)",
                "name": "Honor and Duty: D-Day",
                "owner": "your_games_super_user",
                "played_once": false,
                "played_times": 0,
                "release_date": "2018-06-21T03:02:00.776594Z",
                "url": "http://localhost:8000/games/6/"
        }
    ]
}
```

So far, we have been using the default search and ordering query parameters: `'search'` and `'ordering'`. We just need to specify the desired names as strings in the SEARCH_PARAM and the ORDERING_PARAM settings in the `settings.py` file in the `games_service/games_service` folder.

Filtering, searching and ordering in the Browsable API

We can take advantage of the Browsable API to easily test filtering, searching, and ordering features through a web browser. Open a web browser and enter `http://localhost:8000/player-scores/`. Replace `localhost` with the IP of the computer that is running the Django development server if you use another computer or device to run the browser.

The Browsable API will compose and send an HTTP GET request to `/player-scores/` and will display the results of its execution; that is, the headers and the JSON player scores list. You will notice there is a new **Filters** button located at the left-hand side of the **OPTIONS** button.

Click on **Filters** and the Browsable API will display the **Filters** dialog box, with the appropriate controls for each filter that you can apply underneath **Field Filters,** and the different ordering options below **Ordering**.

The following screenshot shows the **Filters** dialog box:

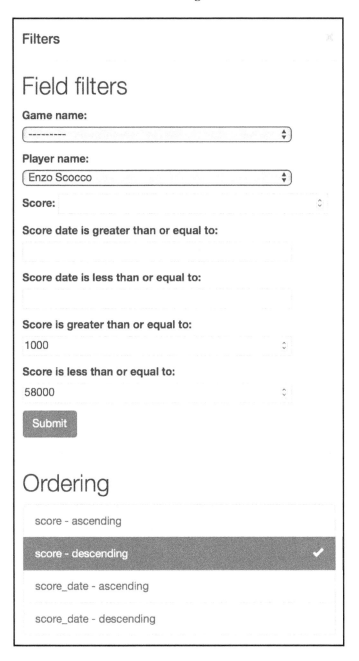

Both the **Player name** and **Game name** drop-downs menu will only include the related player's names and game's names that have registered scores because we used the `AllValuesFilter` class for both filters. After we enter all the values for the filters, we can select the desired ordering option or click **Submit**. The Browsable API will compose and send the appropriate HTTP request and will render a web page with the results of its execution:

```
GET /player-
scores/from_score_date=&game_name=&max_score=58000&min_score=1000&or
dering=-score&player_name=Enzo+Scocco&score=&to_score_date=
```

The results will include the HTTP request that was made to the Django server. The following screenshot shows an example of the results of executing the next request that is, the request we built by using the Browsable API. The following screenshot shows the output:

```
playerscore-list                                      ✦Filters   OPTIONS   GET ▾

GET /player-scores/?from_score_date=&game_name=&max_score=58000&min_score=1000&ordering=-score&player_name=Enzo+Scocco&score=&to_score_date=

HTTP 200 OK
Allow: GET, POST, HEAD, OPTIONS
Content-Type: application/json
Vary: Accept

{
    "count": 2,
    "next": null,
    "previous": null,
    "results": [
        {
            "url": "http://localhost:8000/player-scores/3/",
            "id": 3,
            "score": 43200,
            "score_date": "2019-01-01T03:02:00.776594Z",
            "player": "Enzo Scocco",
            "game": "Battlefield V"
        },
        {
            "url": "http://localhost:8000/player-scores/4/",
            "id": 4,
            "score": 17420,
            "score_date": "2019-01-01T05:02:00.776594Z",
            "player": "Enzo Scocco",
            "game": "Mutant Football League: Dynasty Edition"
        }
    ]
}
```

Understanding throttling classes and goals

So far, we haven't established any limits on the usage of our API, and therefore, both authenticated and unauthenticated users can compose and send as many requests as they want to. We only took advantage of the pagination features available in Django REST Framework to specify how we wanted large result sets to be split into individual pages of data. However, any user can compose and send thousands of requests to be processed without any kind of limitation.

Obviously, it is not a good idea to deploy such an API encapsulated in a microservice in a cloud platform. A wrong usage of the API by any user could cause the microservice to consume a huge amount of resources, and the cloud platform bills would reflect this situation.

We will use the throttling capabilities available in Django REST Framework to configure the following global limitations to the usage of our API, based on whether the requests come from unauthenticated or authenticated users. We will define the following configuration:

- **Unauthenticated users**: They will be able to run a maximum of 5 requests per hour
- **Authenticated users**: They will be able to run a maximum of 20 requests per hour

In addition, we want to configure a maximum of 25 requests per hour to the ESRB ratings-related views, no matter whether the user is authenticated or not.

Django REST Framework provides three throttling classes (as listed in the following table), in the `rest_framework.throttling` module. All of them are subclasses of the `SimpleRateThrottle` superclass, which is a subclass of the `BaseThrottle` superclass. The classes allow us to set the maximum number of requests per period that will be computed based on different mechanisms to determine the previous request information to specify the scope. The previous request information for throttling is stored in the cache and the classes override the `get_cache_key` method that determines the scope:

Throttling class name	Description
AnonRateThrottle	This class limits the rate of requests that an anonymous user can make. The IP address of the request is the unique cache key. Hence, bear in mind that all the requests coming from the same IP address will accumulate the total number of requests.

`UserRateThrottle`	This class limits the rate of requests that a specific user can make. For authenticated users, the authenticated user `id` is the unique cache key. For anonymous users, the IP address of the request is the unique cache key.
`ScopedRateThrottle`	This class limits the rate of requests for specific parts of the API identified with the value assigned to the `throttle_scope` property. The class is useful when we want to restrict access to specific parts of the API with different rates.

Configuring throttling policies

We will use a combination of the three throttling classes to achieve our previously explained goals. Make sure you quit the Django development server. Remember that you just need to press *Ctrl* + *C* in the Terminal or Command Prompt window in which it is running.

Open the `settings.py` file in the `games_service/games_service` folder. Add the following highlighted lines after the first line that declares the dictionary named `REST_FRAMEWORK` to add the new `'DEFAULT_THROTTLE_CLASSES'` and `'DEFAULT_THROTTLE_RATES'` setting keys. Don't remove the lines that will appear after the new highlighted lines. We don't show them to avoid repeating code. The code file for the sample is included in the `restful_python_2_08_02` folder, in the `Django01/games-service/games_service/settings.py` file:

```
REST_FRAMEWORK = {
    'DEFAULT_THROTTLE_CLASSES': (
        'rest_framework.throttling.AnonRateThrottle',
        'rest_framework.throttling.UserRateThrottle',
    ),
    'DEFAULT_THROTTLE_RATES': {
        'anon': '5/hour',
        'user': '20/hour',
        'esrb-ratings': '25/hour',
    },
```

The value for the `DEFAULT_THROTTLE_CLASSES` settings key specifies a global setting with a tuple of string whose values indicate the default classes that we want to use for throttling: `AnonRateThrottle` and `UserRateThrottle`.

The value for the `DEFAULT_THROTTLE_RATES` settings key specifies a dictionary with the default throttle rates. The previous code specifies the following values for the keys:

Key	Value	Description
`'anon'`	`'5/hour'`	The API will allow a maximum of 5 requests per hour for anonymous users
`'user'`	`'20/hour'`	The API will allow a maximum of 20 requests per hour for authenticated users
`'esrb-ratings'`	`'25/hour'`	The API will allow a maximum of 25 requests per hour for the scope that matches the `'esrb-ratings'` name

The maximum rate is a string that specifies the number of requests per period with the following format: `'number_of_requests/period'`, where period can be any of the following:

- s or sec: second
- m or min: minute
- h or hour: hour
- d or day: day

Now, we will configure throttling policies for the class-based views related to ESRB ratings. We will override the value for the `throttle_scope` and `throttle_classes` class attributes for the `EsrbRatingList` and `EsrbRatingDetail` classes.

Open the `views.py` file in the `games_service/games` folder. Add the following code after the last line that declares the imports, before the declaration of the `UserList` class. The code file for the sample is included in the `restful_python_2_08_02` folder, in the `Django01/games-service/games/views.py` file:

```
from rest_framework.throttling import ScopedRateThrottle
```

Stay editing the `views.py` file in the `games_service/games` folder. Add the following highlighted lines to the `EsrbRatingList` class declared in the `views.py` file. Don't remove the existing lines for this class, which aren't shown to avoid repeating code. The code file for the sample is included in the `restful_python_2_08_02` folder, in the `Django01/games-service/games/views.py` file:

```
class EsrbRatingList(generics.ListCreateAPIView):
    throttle_scope = 'esrb-ratings'
    throttle_classes = (ScopedRateThrottle,)
```

Stay editing the `views.py` file in the `games_service/games` folder. Add the following highlighted lines to the `EsrbRatingDetail` class declared in the `views.py` file. Don't remove the existing lines for this class that isn't shown to avoid repeating code. The code file for the sample is included in the `restful_python_2_08_02` folder, in the `Django01/games-service/games/views.py` file;

```
class EsrbRatingDetail(generics.RetrieveUpdateDestroyAPIView):
    throttle_scope = 'esrb-ratings'
    throttle_classes = (ScopedRateThrottle,)
```

We added the same two lines of code in the two classes. We assigned `'esrb-ratings'` as the value for the `throttle_scope` class attribute and we included `ScopedRateThrottle` in the tuple that defines the value for the `throttle_classes` class attribute. This way, the two class-based views will use the settings specified for the `'esrb-ratings'` scope and the `ScopeRateThrottle` class for throttling. These views will be able to serve 25 requests per hour and won't take into account the global settings that apply to the default classes that we use for throttling: `AnonRateThrottle` and `UserRateThrottle`.

 Before Django runs the main body of a view, it performs the checks for each throttle class specified in the throttle classes. In the ESRB ratings-related views, we wrote code that overrides the default settings. If a single throttle check fails, the code will raise a `Throttled` exception and Django won't execute the main body of the view. The cache is responsible for storing information on previous requests for throttling checking.

Executing HTTP requests to test throttling policies

Launch Django's development server to compose and send HTTP requests. Execute either of the following two commands based on your needs:

```
python manage.py runserver
python manage.py runserver 0.0.0.0:8000
```

Now, we will write commands to compose and send HTTP requests many times. In order to do so, we will learn how to achieve this goal with any of the following options combined with `http` and `curl` commands. Select the most appropriate one based on your needs. Don't forget that you will need to have the virtual environment activated in any of the options you select to run the commands when you use the `http` command:

- macOS: Terminal with a Bash shell.
- Linux: Terminal with a Bash shell.
- Windows: Cygwin Terminal or Linux Bash Shell (also known as the Windows Subsystem for Linux). The steps are the same for a Terminal with a Bash shell.
- Windows: Windows PowerShell.

We will run the following command six times to compose and send an HTTP GET request to retrieve all the player scores without authentication:

```
http ":8000/player-scores/"
```

In a Terminal with a Bash shell, run the next line. The code file for the sample is included in the `restful_python_2_08_01` folder, in the `Django01/cmd/cmd811.txt` file:

```
for i in {1..6}; do http ":8000/player-scores/"; done;
```

In Windows PowerShell, run the next line. The code file for the sample is included in the `restful_python_2_08_01` folder, in the `Django01/cmd/cmd812.txt` file:

```
1..6 | foreach { http ":8000/player-scores/" }
```

The following is the equivalent `curl` command that we must execute six times:

```
curl -iX GET "localhost:8000/player-scores/"
```

In a Terminal with a Bash shell, run the next line for `curl`. The code file for the sample is included in the `restful_python_2_08_01` folder, in the `Django01/cmd/cmd813.txt` file:

```
for i in {1..6}; do curl -iX GET "localhost:8000/player-scores/"; done;
```

In Windows PowerShell, run the next line for `curl`. The code file for the sample is included in the `restful_python_2_08_01` folder, in the `Django01/cmd/cmd814.txt` file:

```
1..6 | foreach { curl -iX GET "localhost:8000/player-scores/" }
```

Django won't process the sixth request because the `AnonRateThrottle` class is configured as one of the default throttle classes, and its throttle settings specify `5` requests per hour. Thus, we will receive a `429 Too Many Requests` status code in the response header, a message indicating that the request was throttled, and the time in which the server will be able to process an additional request. The `Retry-After` key in the response header provides the number of seconds that it is necessary to wait until the next request: `3598`. The following lines show a sample response for the last request:

```
HTTP/1.1 429 Too Many Requests
Allow: GET, POST, HEAD, OPTIONS
Content-Length: 71
Content-Type: application/json
Date: Mon, 29 Oct 2018 17:07:41 GMT
Retry-After: 3598
Server: WSGIServer/0.2 CPython/3.6.6
Vary: Accept, Cookie
X-Frame-Options: SAMEORIGIN
{
    "detail": "Request was throttled. Expected available in 3598
seconds."
}
```

We will run the following command six times to compose and send an HTTP `GET` request to retrieve all the player scores with authentication credentials; that is, with the superuser name and his password. We will execute the same request six times. Remember to replace `your_games_super_user` with the name you used for the superuser and `WCS3qn!a4ybX#` with the password you configured for this user in Chapter 7, *Improving Our API and Adding Authentication to it with Django*, in the *Adding security-related data to the models* section:

```
http -a your_games_super_user:'WCS3qn!a4ybX#' ":8000/player-scores/"
```

In a Terminal with a Bash shell, run the next line. The code file for the sample is included in the `restful_python_2_08_01` folder, in the `Django01/cmd/cmd815.txt` file:

```
for i in {1..6}; do http -a your_games_super_user:'WCS3qn!a4ybX#'
":8000/player-scores/"; done;
```

In Windows PowerShell, run the next line. The code file for the sample is included in the `restful_python_2_08_01` folder, in the `Django01/cmd/cmd816.txt` file:

```
1..6 | foreach { http http -a your_games_super_user:'WCS3qn!a4ybX#'
":8000/player-scores/" }
```

The following is the equivalent `curl` command that we must execute six times:

```
curl --user your_games_super_user:'WCS3qn!a4ybX#' -iX GET
"localhost:8000/player-scores/"
```

In a Terminal with a Bash shell, run the next line for `curl`. The code file for the sample is included in the `restful_python_2_08_01` folder, in the `Django01/cmd/cmd817.txt` file:

```
for i in {1..6}; do curl --user your_games_super_user:'WCS3qn!a4ybX#' -iX
GET "localhost:8000/player-scores/"; done;
```

In Windows PowerShell, run the next line for `curl`. The code file for the sample is included in the `restful_python_2_08_01` folder, in the `Django01/cmd/cmd818.txt` file:

```
1..6 | foreach { curl --user your_games_super_user:'WCS3qn!a4ybX#' -
iX GET "localhost:8000/player-scores/" }
```

Django will process the sixth request because we have composed and sent six authenticated requests with the same user. The `UserRateThrottle` class is configured as one of the default throttle classes and its throttle settings specify `20` requests per hour; we still have `14` requests available.

If we run the previous commands 15 times more, we will accumulate `21` requests and we will receive a `429 Too many requests` status code in the response header, a message indicating that the request was throttled, and the time in which the server will be able to process an additional request after the last execution.

Now we will run the following command 25 times to compose and send an HTTP `GET` request to retrieve all the ESRB ratings without authentication credentials:

```
http ":8000/esrb-ratings/"
```

In a Terminal with a Bash shell, run the next line. The code file for the sample is included in the `restful_python_2_08_01` folder, in the `Django01/cmd/cmd819.txt` file:

```
for i in {1..25}; do http ":8000/esrb-ratings/"; done;
```

In Windows PowerShell, run the next line. The code file for the sample is included in the `restful_python_2_08_01` folder, in the `Django01/cmd/cmd820.txt` file:

```
1..25 | foreach { http ":8000/esrb-ratings/" }
```

The following is the equivalent `curl` command that we must execute 25 times:

```
curl -iX GET "localhost:8000/esrb-ratings/"
```

In a Terminal with a Bash shell, run the next line for `curl`. The code file for the sample is included in the `restful_python_2_08_01` folder, in the `Django01/cmd/cmd821.txt` file:

```
for i in {1..25}; do curl -iX GET "localhost:8000/esrb-ratings/"; done;
```

In Windows PowerShell, run the next line for `curl`. The code file for the sample is included in the `restful_python_2_08_01` folder, in the `Django01/cmd/cmd822.txt` file:

```
1..25 | foreach { curl -iX GET "localhost:8000/esrb-ratings/" }
```

Django will process the `25` requests because we have composed and sent `25` unauthenticated requests to a URL that is identified with the `'esrb-ratings'` throttle scope and uses the `ScopedRateThrottle` class for throttle permission control. The throttle settings for the throttle scope identified with `'esrb-ratings'` is configured to `25` requests per hour.

If we run the previous command once again, we will accumulate `26` requests and will receive a `429 Too Many Requests` status code in the response header, a message indicating that the request was throttled, and the time in which the server will be able to process an additional request after the last execution.

Setting up unit tests with pytest

Create a new `pytest.ini` file within the `games_service` folder (the same folder that has the `manage.py` file). The following lines show the code that specifies the desired configuration for Pytest. The code file for the sample is included in the `restful_python_2_08_02` folder, in the `Django01/game_service/manage.py` file:

```
[pytest]
DJANGO_SETTINGS_MODULE = games_service.settings
python_files = tests.py test_*.py *_tests.py
```

The `DJANGO_SETTINGS_MODULE` configuration variable specifies that we want to use the `settings.py` file located in the `games_service/games_service` folder as the settings module for Django when tests are executed.

The `python_files` configuration variable indicates the filters that `pytest` will use to find modules with test functions.

Writing the first round of unit tests

Now, we will write the first round of unit tests. Specifically, we will write unit tests related to the ESRB rating class-based views: `EsrbRatingList` and `EsrbRatingDetail`.

Open the `tests.py` file in the `games_service/games` folder. Replace the existing code with the following lines that declare many `import` statements and two functions. The code file for the sample is included in the `restful_python_2_08_02` folder, in the `Django01/games-service/games/tests.py` file:

```python
import pytest
from django.urls import reverse
from django.utils.http import urlencode
from rest_framework import status
from games import views
from games.models import EsrbRating


def create_esrb_rating(client, description):
    url = reverse(views.EsrbRatingList.name)
    esrb_rating_data = {'description': description}
    esrb_rating_response = client.post(url, esrb_rating_data,
format='json')
    return esrb_rating_response


@pytest.mark.django_db def test_create_and_retrieve_esrb_rating(client):
    """
    Ensure we can create a new EsrbRating and then retrieve it
    """
    new_esrb_rating_description = 'E (Everyone)'
    response = create_esrb_rating(client, new_esrb_rating_description)
    assert response.status_code == status.HTTP_201_CREATED
    assert EsrbRating.objects.count() == 1
    assert EsrbRating.objects.get().description ==
new_esrb_rating_description
```

The code declares the `create_esrb_rating` function that receives the desired `description` for the new ESRB rating as an argument. The method builds the URL and the data dictionary to compose and send an HTTP `POST` method to the view associated with the `esrbrating-list` view name and then returns the response generated by this request.

The code uses the received `client` to access the `APIClient` instance that allows us to easily compose and send HTTP requests for testing. In this case, the code calls the `post` method with the built `url`, the `esrb_rating_data` dictionary, and the desired format for the data: `'json'`. Many test functions will call the `create_esrb_rating` function to create an ESRB rating, and then compose and send other HTTP requests to the API.

The `test_create_and_retrieve_esrb_rating` test function tests whether we can create a new `EsrbRating` object and then retrieve it. The method calls the previously explained `create_esrb_rating` function and then uses `assert` to check for the following expected results:

- The `status_code` for the response is HTTP `201 Created` (`status.HTTP_201_CREATED`)
- The total number of `EsrbRating` objects retrieved from the database is 1
- The `description` attribute of the `EsrbRating` object retrieved from the database matches the description specified when we created the object

The `test_create_and_retrieve_esrb_rating` test function uses the `client` test fixture that the `pytest-django` plugin provides us for easy access to an `APIClient` instance, where we can compose and send HTTP requests for testing. Whenever we use `client` as an argument in a test function, Pytest will make the fixture function that `pytest-django` declares to provide the `APIClient` instance in this argument.

 Notice that the `test_create_and_retrieve_esrb_rating` test function uses the `@pytest.mark.django_db` decorator, declared by `pytest-django`, to indicate that the test function needs to work with the test database. This way, the test runs its own transaction that will be rolled back when the test function finishes its execution.

Stay in the `tests.py` file in the `games_service/games` folder. Add the following code after the last line to declare new test functions. The code file for the sample is included in the `restful_python_2_08_02` folder, in the `Django01/games-service/games/tests.py` file:

```
@pytest.mark.django_db
def test_create_duplicated_esrb_rating(client):
    """
    Ensure we can create a new EsrbRating
    """
    url = reverse('esrbrating-list')
    new_esrb_rating_description = 'T (Teen)'
    post_response_1 = create_esrb_rating(client,
new_esrb_rating_description)
    assert post_response_1.status_code == status.HTTP_201_CREATED
    post_response_2 = create_esrb_rating(client,
new_esrb_rating_description)
    assert post_response_2.status_code == status.HTTP_400_BAD_REQUEST


@pytest.mark.django_db
def test_retrieve_esrb_ratings_list(client):
    """
    Ensure we can retrieve an ESRB rating
    """
    new_esrb_rating_description = 'AO (Adults Only)'
    post_response = create_esrb_rating(client, new_esrb_rating_description)
    url = reverse('esrbrating-list')
    get_response = client.get(url, format='json')
    assert get_response.status_code == status.HTTP_200_OK
    assert get_response.data['count'] == 1
    assert get_response.data['results'][0]['description'] ==
new_esrb_rating_description
```

We added the following test functions whose names start with the `test_` prefix:

- `test_create_duplicated_game_category`: This test function tests whether the unique constraints make it possible for us to create two ESRB ratings with the same description. The second time we compose and send an HTTP POST request with a duplicate category name, we must receive an HTTP 400 Bad Request status code (`status.HTTP_400_BAD_REQUEST`).

- `test_retrieve_game_categories_list`: This test function tests whether we can retrieve a specific ESRB rating by its `id` with an HTTP GET request.

The `test_retrieve_game_categories_list` function checks the data included in the response JSON body by inspecting the `data` attribute for the response. The first line checks whether the value for `count` is equal to `1`. The next lines check whether the `description` key for the first element in the `results` array is equal to the value held in the `new_esrb_rating_description` variable:

```
assert get_response.data['count'] == 1
assert get_response.data['results'][0]['description'] ==
new_esrb_rating_description
```

Note that each test function that requires a specific condition in the database must execute all the necessary code for the database to be in this specific condition. For example, in order to update an existing ESRB rating, first we must create a new ESRB rating, and only then we can update it. Each test method will be executed without data from the previously executed test methods in the database; that is, each test will run with a database cleaned of data from previous tests.

Stay in the `tests.py` file in the `games_service/games` folder. Add the following code after the last line to declare new test functions. The code file for the sample is included in the `restful_python_2_08_02` folder, in the `Django01/games-service/games/tests.py` file:

```python
@pytest.mark.django_db
def test_update_game_category(client):
    """
    Ensure we can update a single field for an ESRB rating
    """
    new_esrb_rating_description = 'M (Mature)'
    post_response = create_esrb_rating(client, new_esrb_rating_description)
    url = reverse('esrbrating-detail', None, {post_response.data['id']})
    updated_esrb_rating_description = 'M10 (Mature - 10)'
    data = {'description': updated_esrb_rating_description}
    patch_response = client.patch(url,
        data,
        content_type='application/json',
        format='json')
    assert patch_response.status_code == status.HTTP_200_OK
    assert patch_response.data['description'] ==
updated_esrb_rating_description


@pytest.mark.django_db
def test_filter_esrb_rating_by_description(client):
    """
    Ensure we can filter an ESRB rating by description
```

```
"""
    esrb_rating_description1 = 'T (Teen)'
    create_esrb_rating(client, esrb_rating_description1)
    esrb_rating_description2 = 'M (Mature)'
    create_esrb_rating(client, esrb_rating_description2)
    filter_by_description = { 'description' : esrb_rating_description1 }
    url = '{0}?{1}'.format(reverse('esrbrating-list'),
        urlencode(filter_by_description))
    get_response = client.get(url, format='json')
    assert get_response.status_code == status.HTTP_200_OK
    assert get_response.data['count'] == 1
    assert get_response.data['results'][0]['description'] ==
esrb_rating_description1
```

We added the following test functions whose name start with the `test_` prefix:

- `test_update_esrb_rating`: This test function tests whether we can update a single field for an ESRB rating by using the HTTP `PATCH` method
- `test_filter_esrb_rating_by_description`: This test function tests whether we can filter an ESRB rating by description

The `test_filter_esrb_rating_by_description` function calls the `django.utils.http.urlencode` function to generate an encoded URL from the `filter_by_description` dictionary that specifies the field name and the value we want to use to filter the retrieved data. The following lines show the code that generates the URL and saves it in the `url` variable. If `esrb_rating_description1` is `'T (Teen)'`, the result of the call to the `urlencode` function will be `'description=T+(Teen)'`:

```
filter_by_description = { 'description' : esrb_rating_description1 }
url = '{0}?{1}'.format(reverse('esrbrating-list'),
    urlencode(filter_by_description))
```

Running unit tests with pytest

Now, run the following command to create a test database, run all the migrations, and use `pytest`, in combination with the `pytest-django` plugin, to discover and execute all the tests we created. The test runner will execute all the methods that start with the `test_` prefix in the `tests.py` file and will display the results. Make sure you run the command in the Terminal or Command Prompt window in which you have activated the virtual environment, and that you are located within the `games_service` folder that has the `manage.py` file:

```
pytest -v
```

The tests won't make changes to the database we have been using when running request on the API through `pytest`.

The test runner will execute all the functions defined in the `tests.py` that start with the `test_` prefix and will display the results. We use the `-v` option to instruct `pytest` to print the test function names and statuses in the verbose mode.

The following lines show the sample output:

```
=============================== test session starts
===============================
platform darwin -- Python 3.6.6, pytest-3.9.3, py-1.7.0, pluggy-
0.8.0 -- /Users/gaston/HillarPythonREST2/Django01/bin/python3
cachedir: .pytest_cache
Django settings: games_service.settings (from ini file)
rootdir: /Users/gaston/HillarPythonREST2/Django01/games_service,
inifile: pytest.ini
plugins: django-3.4.3, cov-2.6.0
collected 5 items
games/tests.py::test_create_and_retrieve_esrb_rating PASSED
[ 20%]
games/tests.py::test_create_duplicated_esrb_rating PASSED
[ 40%]
games/tests.py::test_retrieve_esrb_ratings_list PASSED
[ 60%]
games/tests.py::test_update_game_category PASSED
[ 80%]
games/tests.py::test_filter_esrb_rating_by_description PASSED
[100%]
============================ 5 passed in 1.68 seconds
============================
```

The output provides details indicating that the test runner executed 5 tests, and all of them passed.

Improving testing coverage

Now, we will write additional test functions to improve the testing coverage. Specifically, we will write unit tests related to the player class-based views: `PlayerList` and `PlayerDetail`. Stay in the `tests.py` file in the `games_service/games` folder. Add the following code after the last line to declare a new function and new test functions. The code file for the sample is included in the `restful_python_2_08_03` folder, in the `Django01/games-service/games/tests.py` file:

```python
def create_player(client, name, gender):
    url = reverse('player-list')
    player_data = {'name': name, 'gender': gender}
    player_response = client.post(url, player_data, format='json')
    return player_response


@pytest.mark.django_db
def test_create_and_retrieve_player(client):
    """
    Ensure we can create a new Player and then retrieve it
    """
    new_player_name = 'Will.i.am'
    new_player_gender = Player.MALE
    response = create_player(client, new_player_name, new_player_gender)
    assert response.status_code == status.HTTP_201_CREATED
    assert Player.objects.count() == 1
    assert Player.objects.get().name == new_player_name
```

The code declares the `create_player` function that receives the desired `name` and `gender` for the new player as arguments. The method builds the URL and the data dictionary to compose and send an HTTP `POST` method to the view associated with the `player-list` view name, and returns the response generated by this request. The code uses the received `client` to access the `APIClient` instance that allows us to easily compose and send HTTP requests for testing. Many test functions will call the `create_player` function to create a player, and then compose and send other HTTP requests to the API.

The `test_create_and_retrieve_player` test function tests whether we can create a new `Player` object and then retrieve it. The method calls the previously explained `create_player` function and then uses `assert` to check for the following expected results:

- The `status_code` for the response is HTTP `201 Created` (`status.HTTP_201_CREATED`)
- The total number of `Player` objects retrieved from the database is 1

- The `name` attribute of the `Player` object retrieved from the database matches the description specified when we created the object
- The `gender` attribute of the `Player` object retrieved from the database matches the description specified when we created the object

Stay in the `tests.py` file in the `games_service/games` folder. Add the following code after the last line to declare new test functions. The code file for the sample is included in the `restful_python_2_08_03` folder, in the `Django01/games-service/games/tests.py` file:

```python
@pytest.mark.django_db
def test_create_duplicated_player(client):
    """
    Ensure we can create a new Player and we cannot create a duplicate
    """
    url = reverse('player-list')
    new_player_name = 'Fergie'
    new_player_gender = Player.FEMALE
    post_response1 = create_player(client, new_player_name,
new_player_gender)
    assert post_response1.status_code == status.HTTP_201_CREATED
    post_response2 = create_player(client, new_player_name,
new_player_gender)
    assert post_response2.status_code == status.HTTP_400_BAD_REQUEST


@pytest.mark.django_db
def test_retrieve_players_list(client):
    """
    Ensure we can retrieve a player
    """
    new_player_name = 'Vanessa Perry'
    new_player_gender = Player.FEMALE
    create_player(client, new_player_name, new_player_gender)
    url = reverse('player-list')
    get_response = client.get(url, format='json')
    assert get_response.status_code == status.HTTP_200_OK
    assert get_response.data['count'] == 1
    assert get_response.data['results'][0]['name'] == new_player_name
    assert get_response.data['results'][0]['gender'] == new_player_gender
```

The code declares the following test functions whose names start with the `test_` prefix:

- `test_create_duplicated_player`: This test function tests whether the unique constraints make it possible for us to create two players with the same name. The second time we compose and send an HTTP `POST` request with a duplicate player name, we should receive an HTTP `400 Bad Request` status code (`status.HTTP_400_BAD_REQUEST`).
- `test_retrieve_player_list`: This test function tests whether we can retrieve a specific player by its `id` with an HTTP `GET` request.

We just coded a few tests related to players to improve test coverage. However, we should definitely write more tests to cover all the features included in our API.

Now, we will use the `pytest` command to run the tests again. Make sure you run the following command in the Terminal or Command Prompt window in which you have activated the virtual environment, and that you are located within the `games_service` folder that has the `manage.py` file:

```
pytest -v
```

The following lines show the sample output:

```
=============================== test session starts
===============================
platform darwin -- Python 3.6.6, pytest-3.9.3, py-1.7.0, pluggy-
0.8.0 -- /Users/gaston/HillarPythonREST2/Django01/bin/python3
cachedir: .pytest_cache
Django settings: games_service.settings (from ini file)
rootdir: /Users/gaston/HillarPythonREST2/Django01/games_service,
inifile: pytest.ini
plugins: django-3.4.3, cov-2.6.0
collected 8 items
games/tests.py::test_create_and_retrieve_esrb_rating PASSED
[ 12%]
games/tests.py::test_create_duplicated_esrb_rating PASSED
[ 25%]
games/tests.py::test_retrieve_esrb_ratings_list PASSED
[ 37%]
games/tests.py::test_update_game_category PASSED
[ 50%]
games/tests.py::test_filter_esrb_rating_by_description PASSED
[ 62%]
games/tests.py::test_create_and_retrieve_player PASSED
[ 75%]
games/tests.py::test_create_duplicated_player PASSED
```

```
[ 87%]
games/tests.py::test_retrieve_players_list PASSED
[100%]
============================ 8 passed in 1.48 seconds
============================
```

The output provided details indicating that `pytest` executed 8 tests and all of them passed. It is possible to work with `pytest` fixtures to reduce boilerplate code in the previously coded functions. However, we are focused on making the functions easy to understand. Then, you can use the code as a baseline and improve it by taking full advantage of additional features provided by Pytest fixtures and `pytest-django`.

We just created a few unit tests to understand how we can code them. However, of course, it would be necessary to write more tests to provide appropriate coverage of all the featured and execution scenarios included in the API.

Running Django RESTful APIs on the cloud

One of the biggest drawbacks related to Django and Django REST Framework is that each HTTP request is blocking. Thus, whenever the Django server receives an HTTP request, it doesn't start working on any other HTTP requests in the incoming queue until the server sends the response for the first HTTP request is received.

However, one of the great advantages of RESTful Web Services is that they are stateless; that is, they shouldn't keep a client state on any server. Our API is a good example of a stateless RESTful Web Service. Thus, we can make the API run on as many servers as necessary to achieve our scalability goals. Obviously, we must take into account that we can easily transform the database server in our scalability bottleneck.

Nowadays, we have a huge number of cloud-based alternatives with which to deploy a RESTful Web Service that uses Django and Django REST Framework and make it extremely scalable. Just to mention a few examples, we have Heroku, PythonAnywhere, Google App Engine, OpenShift, AWS Elastic Beanstalk, and Microsoft Azure.

There are dozens of deployment options for Django and Django REST Framework, and the different coverages for stacks and procedures offered by each option are out of the scope of this book, which is focused on development tasks for RESTful APIs with the most popular Python frameworks. The most important cloud providers include instructions on how to deploy Django applications with diverse possible configurations. In addition, there are many options to use **WSGI** (short for **Web Server Gateway Interface**) servers that implement the web server side of the WSGI interface, which allow us to run Python web applications such as Django applications in production.

> Of course, in a production environment, we will want to work with HTTPS instead of HTTP. We will have to configure the appropriate TLS certificates, also known as SSL certificates.

Our API is a good example of a stateless RESTful Web Service with Django, Django REST Framework, and PostgreSQL 10.5 that can be containerized in a Docker container. For example, we can produce an image with our application configured to run with NGINX, uWSGI, Redis, and Django. Thus, we can make the API run as a microservice.

We always have to make sure that we profile the API and the database before we deploy our first version of our API. It is very important to make sure that the generated queries run properly on the underlying database, and that the most popular queries do not end up in sequential scans. It is usually necessary to add the appropriate indexes to the tables in the database.

We have been using basic HTTP authentication. We can improve it with token-based authentication and configure additional authentication plugins available for Django and Django REST Framework.

Each platform includes detailed instructions to deploy our application. All of them will require us to generate the `requirements.txt` file that lists the application dependencies, together with their versions. This way, the platforms will be able to install all the necessary dependencies listed in the file. We have been updating this file each time we needed to install a new package in our virtual environment. However, it is a good idea to run the following `pip freeze` within the root folder of our virtual environment, `Django01`, to generate the final `requirements.txt` file.

Run the following `pip freeze` to generate the `requirements.txt` file:

```
pip freeze > requirements.txt
```

The following lines show the contents of a sample generated `requirements.txt` file. Notice that the generated file also includes all the dependencies that were installed by the packages we specified in the original `requirements.txt` file:

```
atomicwrites==1.2.1
attrs==18.2.0
certifi==2018.10.15
chardet==3.0.4
coverage==4.5.2
Django==2.1.4
django-filter==2.0.0
djangorestframework==3.9.0
httpie==1.0.2
idna==2.7
more-itertools==4.3.0
pluggy==0.8.0
psycopg2==2.7.5
py==1.7.0
Pygments==2.2.0
pytest==4.0.2
pytest-cov==2.6.0
pytest-django==3.4.4
pytz==2018.6
requests==2.20.0
six==1.11.0
urllib3==1.24
```

We must make sure that we change the following line in the `settings.py` file:

```
DEBUG = True
```

We must always turn off the debug mode in production, and therefore, we must replace the previous line with the following one:

```
DEBUG = False
```

Test your knowledge

Let's see whether you can answer the following questions correctly:

1. Which of the following fixtures provided by the `pytest-django` plugin allow us to access the `APIClient` instance that makes it easy for us to compose and send HTTP requests for testing?

    1. `client`
    2. `api_client`
    3. `http`

2. Which of the following decorators declared in `pytest-django` indicate that a test function needs to work with the test database?

    1. `@pytest.django.db`
    2. `@pytest.mark.django_db`
    3. `@pytest.mark.db`

3. The `ScopedRateThrottle` class:

    1. Limits the rate of requests that a specific user can make
    2. Limits the rate of requests for specific parts of the API identified with the value assigned to the `throttle_scope` property
    3. Limits the rate of requests that an anonymous user can make

4. The `UserRateThrottle` class:

    1. Limits the rate of requests that a specific user can make
    2. Limits the rate of requests for specific parts of the API identified with the value assigned to the `throttle_scope` property
    3. Limits the rate of requests that an anonymous user can make

5. The `DjangoFilterBackend` class:

    1. Provides single query parameter-based searching capabilities and is based on the Django admin's search function
    2. Allows the client to control how the results are ordered with a single query parameter
    3. Provides field filtering capabilities

6. The `SearchFilter` class:
   1. Provides single query parameter-based searching capabilities and is based on the Django admin's search function
   2. Allows the client to control how the results are ordered with a single query parameter
   3. Provides field filtering capabilities

7. Which of the following class attributes specifies the `FilterSet` subclass that we want to use for a class-based view?
   1. `filters_class`
   2. `filtering_class`
   3. `filterset_class`

Summary

In this chapter, we took advantage of many features included in Django REST Framework to define throttling policies. We used the filtering, searching, and ordering of classes to make it easy to configure filters, search queries, and the desired order for the results in HTTP requests. We used the Browsable API feature to test these new features included in our API.

We wrote the first round of unit tests and set the necessary configuration to use the popular and modern `pytest` Python unit test framework with Django REST Framework. Then, we wrote additional unit tests to improve test coverage. Finally, we understood many considerations for deployment and scalability in the cloud.

Now that we have built a complex API with Django REST Framework and tested it, we will move to another popular Python Web framework, Pyramid, which is the topic of the next chapter.

9
Developing RESTful APIs with Pyramid 1.10

In this chapter, we will work with Pyramid 1.10 to create a RESTful Web API that performs CRUD operations on a simple data source. We will look at the following topics:

- Design a RESTful API to interact with a simple data source
- Understand the tasks performed by each HTTP method
- Set up the virtual environment with Pyramid 1.10
- Create a new Pyramid project based on a template
- Create the model
- Use a dictionary as a repository
- Create a Marshmallow schema to validate, serialize, and deserialize the model
- Work with view callables and view configurations
- Understand and configure view handlers
- Make HTTP requests to the API with command-line tools

Designing a RESTful API to interact with a simple data source

A surfer who won dozens of international surfing competitions became a surfing coach and wants to build a new tool to help surfers train for the Olympic Games. The development team that works with the surfing coach has years of experience working with the Pyramid web framework, and therefore, he wants us to build a simple RESTful API with Pyramid to work with the data provided by an IoT board connected to multiple sensors in the surfboards.

Each IoT board will provide the following data:

- **Status**: Many wearable wireless sensors embedded in each surfer's wetsuit and other sensors included in the surfboard will provide data, and the IoT board will perform a real-time analysis to indicate the action that the surfer is performing
- **Speed**: A sensor will measure the surfboard's speed in **miles per hour** (**MPH**)
- **Altitude**: A sensor will measure the surfboard's altitude in feet
  - **Water temperature**: A sensor located in one of the surfboard's fins will measure the water temperature in degrees Fahrenheit

Some third-party software is running on the IoT board and makes calls to a RESTful API. There is a team writing code to interact with the RESTful API and retrieve the previously explained surfing metrics provided by the IoT board. Hence, we will have an IoT board and an application interacting with the RESTful API. Another team has to start working on a mobile app and a website that has to interact with the RESTful API to perform create, read, and delete operations with surfing metrics.

We don't need an **ORM** (short for **Object-Relational Mapping**) because we won't persist the metrics on a database. We will just work with an in-memory dictionary as our data source. It is one of the requirements we have for this RESTful API. In this case, the RESTful web service will be running on a low-power IoT device capable of running Python 3.6.6 and Pyramid.

 This example is going to allow us to understand how we can easily develop a RESTful API with Pyramid. Then, we can use the code as a baseline to build an API with other kinds of data sources, such as relational and NoSQL databases.

The team has chosen Pyramid because they already have experience building web applications with this framework and they want to be able to easily maintain the code for the RESTful API. Pyramid is a lightweight and simple framework; we don't need to configure an ORM and we want to start running the RESTful API on the IoT device as soon as possible to allow all the teams to interact with it.

The IoT board and its connected sensors are capable of distinguishing between the following five possible statuses of a surfer and their surfboard:

Status key	Meaning
0	Idle
1	Paddling
2	Riding
3	Ride finished
4	Wiped out

First, we must specify the requirements for our main resource: a surfboard metric. We need the following attributes or fields for a surfboard metric:

- An integer identifier
- A string status
- A speed expressed in MPH
- An altitude (expressed in feet)
- A water temperature (expressed in degrees Fahrenheit)

The following table shows the HTTP verbs, the scope, and the semantics for the methods that our API must support. Each method is composed by an HTTP verb and a scope, and all the methods have a well-defined meaning for all metrics and collections. In our API, each metric has its own unique URL:

HTTP verb	Scope	Semantics
GET	Collection of metrics	Retrieves all the stored metrics in the collection
GET	Metric	Retrieves a single metric
POST	Collection of metrics	Creates a new metric in the collection
DELETE	Metric	Deletes an existing metric

In the previous table, we have many methods and scopes. The following list enumerates the URIs for each scope mentioned in the previous table, where {id} has to be replaced with the numeric id of the resource. We want our API to differentiate collections from a single resource of the collection in the URLs.

When we refer a collection, we will use a slash (/) as the last character for the URL, and when we refer a single resource of the collection, we will omit this slash (/):

- Collection of metrics: `/metrics/`
- Metric: `/metrics/{id}`

Let's consider that `http://localhost:6543/` is the URL for the API running on the Pyramid development server. We have to compose and send an HTTP request with the following HTTP verb (`GET`) and request URL (`http://localhost:6543/metrics/`) to retrieve all the stored metrics in the collection:

```
GET http://localhost:6543/metrics/
```

We will always provide the request body in JSON, and all the response bodies will be in JSON. We don't need additional parsers or renderers. Notice that we support neither `PATCH` nor `PUT` methods because we don't need them in this API.

Setting up the virtual environment with Pyramid 1.10

In `Chapter 1`, *Developing RESTful APIs and Microservices with Flask 1.0.2*, we learned that, throughout this book, we were going to work with the lightweight virtual environments that were introduced and improved on in Python 3.4. Now, we will follow many steps to create a new lightweight virtual environment to work with Pyramid 1.10. It is highly recommended to read the section named *Working with lightweight virtual environments* in `Chapter 1`, *Developing RESTful APIs and Microservices with Flask 1.0.2*, if you don't have experience with lightweight virtual environments in modern Python. This chapter includes all the detailed explanations about the effects of the steps we are going to follow.

The following commands assume that you have Python 3.6.6 installed on Linux, macOS, or Windows.

First, we have to select the target folder or directory for our lightweight virtual environment. The following is the path we will use in the example for Linux and macOS:

```
~/HillarPythonREST2/Pyramid01
```

The target folder for the virtual environment will be the `HillarPythonREST2/Pyramid01` folder within our home directory. For example, if our home directory in macOS or Linux is `/Users/gaston`, the virtual environment will be created within `/Users/gaston/HillarPythonREST2/Pyramid01`. You can replace the specified path with your desired path in each command.

The following is the path we will use in the example for Windows:

> **%USERPROFILE%\HillarPythonREST2\Pyramid01**

The target folder for the virtual environment will be the `HillarPythonREST2\Pyramid01` folder within our user profile folder. For example, if our user profile folder is `C:\Users\gaston`, the virtual environment will be created within `C:\Users\gaston\HillarPythonREST2\Pyramid01`. Of course, you can replace the specified path with your desired path in each command.

In Windows PowerShell, the previous path would be the following:

> **$env:userprofile\HillarPythonREST2\Pyramid01**

Now, we have to use the `-m` option followed by the `venv` module name and the desired path to make Python run this module as a script and create a virtual environment at the specified path. The instructions are different depending on the platform in which we are creating the virtual environment. Thus, make sure you follow the instructions for your operating system:

1. Open a Terminal in Linux or macOS and execute the following command to create a virtual environment:

    > **python3 -m venv ~/HillarPythonREST2/Pyramid01**

2. In Windows, execute the following command in the Command Prompt to create a virtual environment:

    > **python -m venv %USERPROFILE%\HillarPythonREST2\Pyramid01**

3. If you want to work with Windows PowerShell, execute the following command to create a virtual environment:

    > **python -m venv $env:userprofile\HillarPythonREST2\Pyramid01**

    The previous commands don't produce any output. Now that we have created a virtual environment, we will run a platform-specific script to activate it. After we activate the virtual environment, we will install packages that will only be available in this virtual environment.

4. If your Terminal is configured to use the `bash` shell in macOS or Linux, run the following command to activate the virtual environment. The command also works for the `zsh` shell:

```
source ~/HillarPythonREST2/Pyramid01/bin/activate
```

5. If your Terminal is configured to use either the `csh` or `tcsh` shell, run the following command to activate the virtual environment:

```
source ~/HillarPythonREST2/Pyramid01/bin/activate.csh
```

6. If your Terminal is configured to use the `fish` shell, run the following command to activate the virtual environment:

```
source ~/HillarPythonREST2/Pyramid01/bin/activate.fish
```

7. In Windows, you can run either a batch file in the Command Prompt or a Windows PowerShell script to activate the virtual environment. If you prefer the Command Prompt, run the following command in the Windows command line to activate the virtual environment:

```
%USERPROFILE%\HillarPythonREST2\Pyramid01\Scripts\activate.bat
```

8. If you prefer Windows PowerShell, launch it and run the following commands to activate the virtual environment. However, notice that you should have script execution enabled in Windows PowerShell to be able to run the script:

```
cd $env:USERPROFILE
HillarPythonREST2\Pyramid01\Scripts\Activate.ps1
```

After you activate the virtual environment, the command prompt will display the virtual environment's root folder name, enclosed in parenthesis as a prefix of the default prompt, to remind us that we are working in the virtual environment. In this case, we will see (`Pyramid01`) as a prefix for the Command Prompt because the root folder for the activated virtual environment is `Pyramid01`.

We have followed the necessary steps to create and activate a virtual environment. Now, we will create a `requirements.txt` file to specify the set of packages that our application requires to be installed on any supported platform. This way, it will be extremely easy to repeat the installation of the specified packages with their versions in any new virtual environment.

Use your favorite editor to create a new text file named `requirements.txt` within the root folder for the recently created virtual environment. The following lines show the contents for the file that declares the packages and the versions that our API requires. The code file for the sample is included in the `restful_python_2_11_01` folder, in the `Pyramid01/requirements.txt` file:

```
pyramid==1.10
cookiecutter==1.6.0
httpie==1.0.2
```

Each line in the `requirements.txt` file indicates the package and the version that needs to be installed. In this case, we are working with exact versions by using the `==` operator because we want to make sure that the specified version is installed. The following table summarizes the packages and the version numbers that we specified as requirements:

Package name	Version to be installed
pyramid	1.10.1
cookiecutter	1.6.0
httpie	1.0.2

The `cookiecutter` package installs a command-line utility that makes it possible to create Pyramid projects from project templates. We will use this utility to create a basic Pyramid 1.10 project and then make the necessary changes to build our RESTful API without writing all the code from scratch. Notice that we will install additional packages later by specifying additional required packages in the Pyramid `setup.py` file.

Go to the root folder for the virtual environment: `Pyramid01`. In macOS or Linux, enter the following command:

```
cd ~/HillarPythonREST2/Pyramid01
```

In Windows Command Prompt, enter the following command:

```
cd /d %USERPROFILE%\HillarPythonREST2\Pyramid01
```

In Windows PowerShell, enter the following command:

```
cd $env:USERPROFILE
cd HillarPythonREST2\Pyramid01
```

Now, we must run the following command on macOS, Linux, or Windows to install the packages and the versions explained in the previous table with `pip` by using the recently created `requirements.txt` file. Make sure you are located in the folder that contains the `requirements.txt` file before running the command (`Pyramid01`):

```
pip install -r requirements.txt
```

The last lines for the output will indicate that `pyramid`, `cookiecutter`, `httpie`, and their dependencies have been successfully installed:

```
Installing collected packages: translationstring, plaster, PasteDeploy,
plaster-pastedeploy, zope.deprecation, venusian, zope.interface, webob,
hupper, pyramid, future, six, python-dateutil, arrow, MarkupSafe, jinja2,
jinja2-time, click, chardet, binaryornot, poyo, urllib3, certifi, idna,
requests, whichcraft, cookiecutter, Pygments, httpie
      Running setup.py install for future ... done
      Running setup.py install for arrow ... done
Successfully installed MarkupSafe-1.1.0 PasteDeploy-1.5.2 Pygments-2.2.0
arrow-0.12.1 binaryornot-0.4.4 certifi-2018.10.15 chardet-3.0.4 click-7.0
cookiecutter-1.6.0 future-0.17.1 httpie-1.0.2 hupper-1.4 idna-2.7
jinja2-2.10 jinja2-time-0.2.0 plaster-1.0 plaster-pastedeploy-0.6
poyo-0.4.2 pyramid-1.10.1 python-dateutil-2.7.5 requests-2.20.0 six-1.11.0
translationstring-1.3 urllib3-1.24.1 venusian-1.1.0 webob-1.8.3
whichcraft-0.5.2 zope.deprecation-4.3.0 zope.interface-4.6.0
```

Creating a new Pyramid project based on a template

Now, we will generate a Pyramid project by using an app template, also known as **scaffold**. Notice that you need Git installed on your development computer to use the next command. You can visit the following web page for more information about Git: `https://git-scm.com`.

Run the following command to use `cookiecutter` to generate a new project based on the `pyramid-cookiecutter-starter` template. We use the `--checkout 1.10-branch` option to use a specific branch that makes sure that the template is compatible with Pyramid 1.10:

```
cookiecutter gh:Pylons/pyramid-cookiecutter-starter --checkout 1.10-branch
```

The command will ask you for the project's name. Enter `metrics` and press *Enter*. You will see a line similar to the following one:

```
project_name [Pyramid Scaffold]:
```

Then, the command will ask you for the repository name and will specify `metrics` as the default option. Just press *Enter*:

```
repo_name [metrics]:
```

The command will ask you for the template language you want to use. Enter `1` to select `jinja2` and press *Enter*:

```
Select template_language:
1 - jinja2
2 - chameleon
3 - mako
Choose from 1, 2, 3 (1, 2, 3) [1]:
```

Finally, the command will ask you for the backend. Enter `1` to select `none` and press *Enter*:

```
Select backend:
1 - none
2 - sqlalchemy
3 - zodb
Choose from 1, 2, 3 (1, 2, 3) [1]:
```

The command will create the project in a new `metrics` subfolder and it will display instructions to get started. We won't follow these instructions because we already created a virtual environment:

```
================================================================================
====
Documentation:
https://docs.pylonsproject.org/projects/pyramid/en/latest/
Tutorials:
https://docs.pylonsproject.org/projects/pyramid_tutorials/en/latest/
Twitter:        https://twitter.com/PylonsProject
Mailing List:  https://groups.google.com/forum/#!forum/pylons-discuss
Welcome to Pyramid.  Sorry for the convenience.
================================================================================
====
    Change directory into your newly created project.
        cd metrics
    Create a Python virtual environment.
        python3 -m venv env
    Upgrade packaging tools.
```

```
    env/bin/pip install --upgrade pip setuptools
Install the project in editable mode with its testing requirements.
    env/bin/pip install -e ".[testing]"
Run your project's tests.
    env/bin/pytest
Run your project.
    env/bin/pserve development.ini
```

The specified app template is focused on building a starter Pyramid web application. We want to develop a RESTful API, and therefore we don't need many of the elements provided by the template. We will remove the unnecessary elements later.

Now, run the following commands to install the Python packages required by our new Pyramid web application. These commands will install the packages specified in the requires and tests_require string lists in the metrics/setup.py file:

```
cd metrics
pip install -e ".[testing]"
```

The last lines for the output will indicate that the specified packages and their dependencies have been successfully installed:

```
Installing collected packages: pyramid-jinja2, Mako, pyramid-mako,
repoze.lru, pyramid-debugtoolbar, waitress, beautifulsoup4, WebTest, more-
itertools, atomicwrites, pluggy, attrs, py, pytest, coverage, pytest-cov,
metrics
    Running setup.py install for Mako ... done
    Running setup.py install for pyramid-mako ... done
    Running setup.py develop for metrics
Successfully installed Mako-1.0.7 WebTest-2.0.32 atomicwrites-1.2.1
attrs-18.2.0 beautifulsoup4-4.6.3 coverage-4.5.1 metrics more-
itertools-4.3.0 pluggy-0.8.0 py-1.7.0 pyramid-debugtoolbar-4.5 pyramid-
jinja2-2.7 pyramid-mako-1.0.2 pytest-3.10.0 pytest-cov-2.6.0 repoze.lru-0.7
waitress-1.1.0
```

The metrics/setup.py file is a Python module with module-level variables that define the setup of the Pyramid for the metrics project. We will make some changes to this Pyramid setup.py file.

Open the `metrics/setup.py` file and locate the following lines that specify the strings list, which declares the required packages and saves the list in the `requires` variable:

```
requires = [
    'plaster_pastedeploy',
    'pyramid',
    'pyramid_jinja2',
    'pyramid_debugtoolbar',
    'waitress',
]
```

Add the following two strings to the `requires` strings list and save the changes to the `metrics/setup.py` file:

- `'marshmallow == 2.16.3'`
- `'marshmallow_enum == 1.4.1'`

The following lines show the new code that declares the `requires` strings list with the added lines highlighted. The code file for the sample is included in the `restful_python_2_09_01` folder, in the `Pyramid01/metrics/setup.py` file:

```
requires = [
    'plaster_pastedeploy',
    'pyramid',
    'pyramid_jinja2',
    'pyramid_debugtoolbar',
    'waitress',
    'marshmallow == 2.16.3',
    'marshmallow_enum == 1.4.1',
]
```

Each additional string added to the `requires` string list indicates the package and the version that needs to be installed. The following table summarizes the packages and the version numbers that we specified as additional requirements to the previously included packages:

Package name	Version to be installed
marshmallow	2.16.3
marshmallow_enum	1.4.1

Marshmallow is a lightweight library for converting complex datatypes to and from native Python datatypes. Marshmallow provides schemas that we can use to validate input data, deserialize input data to app-level objects, and serialize app-level objects to Python primitive types.

`marshmallow_enum` is a simple library that adds `Enum` fields support for their usage with Marshmallow. We will use an `Enum` field to represent the different status of the surfer.

Now, run the following command on macOS, Linux, or Windows to install the recently added Python packages required by our new Pyramid web application. The command will install the two packages and the versions specified in the `requires` list in the `metrics/setup.py` file:

```
pip install -e ".[testing]"
```

The last lines for the output will indicate that the specified packages and their dependencies have been successfully installed:

```
Successfully installed marshmallow-2.16.3 marshmallow-enum-1.4.1 metrics
```

Our RESTful API won't be using templates, and therefore we can delete the `metrics/metrics/static` and `metrics/metrics/templates` folders.

Creating the model

Now, we will create a simple `SurfboardMetricModel` class that we will use to represent metrics. Remember that we won't be persisting the model in any database or file, and therefore, in this case, our class will just provide the required attributes and no mapping information.

Create a new `models` subfolder within the `metrics/metrics` folder. Then, create a new `metrics.py` file in the `metrics/metrics/models` subfolder. The following lines show the code that declares the necessary imports that we will require for many classes. This will then create a `SurfboardMetricModel` class in this file. The code file for the sample is included in the `restful_python_2_09_01` folder, in the `Pyramid01/metrics/metrics/models/metrics.py` file:

```python
from enum import Enum
from marshmallow import Schema, fields
from marshmallow_enum import EnumField


class SurfboardMetricModel:
    def __init__(self, status, speed_in_mph, altitude_in_feet,
water_temperature_in_f):
        # We will automatically generate the new id
        self.id = 0
        self.status = status
```

```
self.speed_in_mph = speed_in_mph
self.altitude_in_feet = altitude_in_feet
self.water_temperature_in_f = water_temperature_in_f
```

The SurfboardMetricModel class just declares a constructor; that is, the __init__ method. This method receives many arguments and uses them to initialize the attributes with the same names: status, speed_in_mph, altitude_in_feet, and water_temperature_in_f. The id attribute is set to 0. We will automatically increment the identifier for each new surfboard metric generated with an API call.

Using a dictionary as a repository

Now, we will create a SurfboardMetricManager class that we will use to persist the SurfboardMetricModel instances in an in-memory dictionary. Our API methods will call methods for the SurfboardMetricManager class to retrieve, insert, and delete SurfboardMetricModel instances.

Stay in the metrics.py file in the metrics/metrics/models subfolder. Add the following lines to declare the SurfboardMetricManager class. The code file for the sample is included in the restful_python_2_09_01 folder, in the Pyramid01/metrics/metrics/models/metrics.py file:

```
class SurfboardMetricManager():
    last_id = 0
    def __init__(self):
        self.metrics = {}

    def insert_metric(self, metric):
        self.__class__.last_id += 1
        metric.id = self.__class__.last_id
        self.metrics[self.__class__.last_id] = metric

    def get_metric(self, id):
        return self.metrics[id]

    def delete_metric(self, id):
        del self.metrics[id]
```

The SurfboardMetricManager class declares a last_id class attribute and initializes it as 0. This class attribute stores the last id that has been generated and assigned to a SurfboardMetricModel instance that's stored in a dictionary. The constructor—that is, the __init__ method—creates and initializes the metrics attribute as an empty dictionary.

The code declares the following three methods for the class:

- `insert_metric`: This method receives a recently created `SurfboardMetricModel` instance in the `metric` argument. The code increases the value for the `last_id` class attribute and then assigns the resulting value to the ID for the received metric. The code uses `self.__class__` to reference the type of the current instance. Finally, the code adds the `metric` as a value to the key identified with the generated `id`, and `last_id` to the `self.metrics` dictionary.
- `get_metric`: This method receives the `id` of the message that has to be retrieved from the `self.metrics` dictionary. The code returns the value related to the key that matches the received `id` in the `self.metrics` dictionary that we are using as our data source.
- `delete_metric`: This method receives the `id` of the metric that has to be removed from the `self.metrics` dictionary. The code deletes the key-value pair whose key matches the received `id` in the `self.metrics` dictionary that we are using as our data source.

Creating a Marshmallow schema to validate, serialize, and deserialize the model

Now, we will create a simple Marshmallow schema that we will use to validate, serialize, and deserialize the previously declared `SurfboardMetricModel` model.

Stay in the `metrics.py` file in the `metrics/metrics/models` subfolder. Add the following lines to declare `SurferStatus Enum` and the `SurfboardMetricSchema` class. The code file for the sample is included in the `restful_python_2_09_01` folder, in the `Pyramid01/metrics/metrics/models/metrics.py` file:

```
class SurferStatus(Enum):
    IDLE = 0
    PADDLING = 1
    RIDING = 2
    RIDE_FINISHED = 3
    WIPED_OUT = 4


class SurfboardMetricSchema(Schema):
    id = fields.Integer(dump_only=True)
    status = EnumField(SurferStatus, required=True)
```

```
speed_in_mph = fields.Integer(required=True)
altitude_in_feet = fields.Integer(required=True)
water_temperature_in_f = fields.Integer(required=True)
```

First, the code declares the `SurferStatus Enum` that we will use to map description to an integer for the surfer status. We want the users of the API to be able to specify the status as a string that matches one of the `Enum` descriptions. For example, if the user wants to create a new metric with its status set to `SurferStatus.PADDLING`, they should use `'PADDLING'` as the value for the status key in the provided JSON body.

Then, the code declares the `SurfboardMetricSchema` class as a subclass of the `marshmallow.Schema` class. We declare the attributes that represent fields as instances of the appropriate classes declared in the `marshmallow.fields` module. Whenever we specify the `True` value for the `dump_only` argument, it means that we want the field to be read-only. For example, we won't be able to provide a value for the `id` field in the schema. The value for this field will be automatically generated by the `SurfboardMetricManager` class.

The `SurfboardMetricSchema` class declares the `status` attribute as an instance of the `marshmallow_enum.EnumField` class. The enum argument is set to `SurferStatus` to specify that only the members of this `Enum` will be considered valid values. As a result of this setting, only a string that matches the descriptions in `SurferStatus Enum` will be accepted as a valid value for this field during deserialization. In addition, whenever this field is serialized, the string representation of the `Enum` description will be used.

The `speed_in_mph`, `altitude_in_feet`, and `water_temperature_in_f` attributes are instances of the `fields.Integer` class, with the `required` argument set to `True`.

Working with view callables and view configurations

Our RESTful API won't be using the two modules included in the `metrics/metrics/views` subfolder that was generated by the app template. Thus, we must delete the `metrics/metrics/views/default.py` and `metrics/metrics/views/notfound.py` files.

Pyramid uses view callables as the main building blocks for a RESTful API. Whenever a request arrives, Pyramid finds and invokes the appropriate view callable to process the request and return an appropriate response.

> View callables are callable Python objects such as functions, classes, or instances that implement a __call__ method. Any view callable receives an argument named request that will provide the pyramid.request.Request instance that represents an HTTP request.

In this case, we will work with view callable functions to process the requests related to metrics and metrics collections. In addition, we will take advantage of the @view_config decorator to associate view configuration information with each function that acts as a Pyramid view callable.

Create a new metrics.py file in the metrics/metrics/views subfolder. The following lines show the code that declares the necessary imports we will require for all the functions we will declare, creates two instances, and declares a get_metric_or_not_found function in this file. The code file for the sample is included in the restful_python_2_09_01 folder, in the Pyramid01/metrics/metrics/views/metrics.py file:

```
from pyramid.httpexceptions import HTTPCreated, HTTPNotFound,
HTTPBadRequest, HTTPMethodNotAllowed, HTTPNoContent
from pyramid.response import Response
from pyramid.view import view_config
from metrics.models.metrics import SurfboardMetricModel,
SurfboardMetricManager, SurferStatus, SurfboardMetricSchema


metric_manager = SurfboardMetricManager()
metric_schema = SurfboardMetricSchema()


def get_metric_or_not_found(id):
    if id in metric_manager.metrics:
        return metric_manager.metrics[id]
    else:
        raise HTTPNotFound("Metric {0} doesn't exist".format(id))
```

The first lines declare the imports and create the following instances that we will use in the different functions:

- metric_manager: This is an instance of the previously created SurfboardMetricManager class. We will use this instance to create, retrieve, and delete SurfboardMetricModel instances.

- `metric_schema`: This is an instance of the previously created `SurfboardMetricSchema` class. We will use this instance to validate, serialize, and deserialize metrics.

Then, the code creates the `get_metric_or_not_found` function that receives `id` for an existing `SurfboardMetricModel` instance in the `id` argument. If the received `id` is not in the keys of the `metric_manager.metrics` dictionary, the method raises a `pyramid.httpexceptions.HTTPNotFound` exception with a message indicating that the metric with the specified `id` doesn't exist. In this case, we generate an HTTP `404 Not Found` status code.

Stay in the `metrics.py` file in the `metrics/metrics/views` subfolder. Add the following lines to declare the `metrics_collection` function. The highlighted lines show the expressions that evaluate the value of the `request.method` attribute to determine the actions to be performed based on the HTTP verb. The code file for the sample is included in the `restful_python_2_09_01` folder, in the `Pyramid01/metrics/metrics/views/metrics.py` file:

```
"""
Metrics collection
"""
@view_config(route_name='metrics',
    accept='application/json')
def metrics_collection(request):
    if request.method == 'GET':
        metrics = metric_manager.metrics.values()
        dump_result = metric_schema.dump(metrics, many=True).data
        return dump_result
    elif request.method == 'POST':
        if not request.json_body:
            raise HTTPBadRequest('No input data provided')
        errors = metric_schema.validate(request.json_body)
        if errors:
            raise HTTPBadRequest(errors)
        metric = SurfboardMetricModel(
            status = SurferStatus[request.json_body['status']],
            speed_in_mph = request.json_body['speed_in_mph'],
            altitude_in_feet = request.json_body['altitude_in_feet'],
            water_temperature_in_f =
request.json_body['water_temperature_in_f'])
        metric_manager.insert_metric(metric)
        dumped_metric = metric_schema.dump(metric).data
        response = Response()
        response.status_code=HTTPCreated.code
        # It is necessary to set the content_type
```

```
            # The default is text/html; charset=UTF-8
            response.content_type='application/json; charset=UTF-8'
            response.json_body = dumped_metric
            return response
    else:
            # The method is neither GET nor POST
            raise HTTPMethodNotAllowed()
```

When Pyramid receives an HTTP request, Pyramid creates a `Request` instance, specifically a `pyramid.request.Request` object. This instance contains metadata about the request, including the HTTP verb. The `method` attribute provides a string representing the HTTP verb or method used in the request.

When Pyramid invokes the appropriate view callable that will process the request, it passes the `Request` instance as the first argument to the view callable. The view callable can return any object that will be rendered with the renderer specified in the view configuration. We will analyze this configuration later. In this case, we will configure all the views to use a JSON renderer, and therefore all the values returned by the view callable functions will be rendered to JSON.

The `metrics_collection` function uses the `@view_config` decorator with values for the `route_name` and `accept` arguments. This way, some details about the view registration are near to the view callable function definition. This function will be invoked only when the named route matches the value specified for the `route_name` argument: `'metrics'`. The value for the accept argument specifies that the function will only accept `application/json` as the content type.

The `metrics_collection` function lists all the metrics or creates a new metric. The function receives a `Request` instance in the `request` argument. The function is capable of processing two HTTP verbs for the metrics collection resource: `GET` and `POST`. The code checks the value of the `request.method` attribute to determine the code to be executed based on the HTTP verb.

If the HTTP verb is `GET`, the expression `request.method == 'GET'` will evaluate to `True` and the code has to list all the metrics. The code calls the `metric_manager.metrics.values` method to retrieve all the `SurfboardMetricModel` instances persisted in the dictionary. Then, the code calls the `notification_schema.dump` method with the retrieved metrics and the `many` argument set to `True` to serialize the iterable collection of objects.

The `dump` method will take each `SurfboardMetricModel` instance retrieved from the dictionary and apply the field filtering and output formatting specified by the `SurfboardMetricSchema` class. The code returns the `data` attribute of the result returned by the `dump` method; that is, the serialized metrics in JSON format as the body, with the default HTTP `200 OK` status code.

If the HTTP verb is `POST`, the expression `request.method == 'POST'` will evaluate to `True`. The code has to create a new metric based on the JSON data that is included in the HTTP request body and is accessed with the `request.json_body` attribute. If no content is provided in the HTTP request body, the code raises an `HTTPBadRequest` exception with a message indicating that no input data has been provided. This way, the code returns an HTTP `400 Bad Request` status code.

The `request.json_body` attribute allows us to retrieve the key-value pairs received as arguments with the request. The code calls the `metric_schema.validate` method to validate the new metric built with the retrieved key-value pairs. If there are validation errors, the code raises an `HTTPBadRequest` exception with the validation errors. This way, the code returns an HTTP `400 Bad Request` status code and provides details about the errors that caused the validation to fail.

If the validation is successful, the code creates a new metric with the values retrieved from the `request.json_body` dictionary. Notice that the code uses the value of the `status` key in the `request.json_body` dictionary to create a `SurferStatusEnum` based on this string value. The `metric_schema.validate` method made sure that we have a valid value for the related `Enum` which is a required field in the Marshmallow schema. The code persists the validated metric in the dictionary.

In this case, we don't want to return the default HTTP `200 OK` status code, and therefore the code creates a new `pyramid.response.Response` instance to build a customized response for the request and sets its `status_code` attribute to `HTTPCreated.code` to specify an HTTP `201 Created` status code. Then, the code sets the `content_type` attribute to `'application/json; charset=UTF-8'` to override the default content type of `'text/html; charset=UTF-8'`. We want to return a JSON response body.

The next line assigns the `data` attribute of the result returned by the `metric_schema.dump` method for the inserted metric to the `response.json_body` attribute. This way, the serialized metric in JSON format will become the body for the response. Finally, the code returns the `response` instance.

If the `request.method` doesn't match either `'GET'` or `'POST'`, the code raises an `HTTPMethodNotAllowed` exception to return an HTTP `405 Method Not Allowed` status code.

Stay in the `metrics.py` file in the `metrics/metrics/views` subfolder. Add the following lines to declare the `metric` function. The highlighted lines show the expressions that evaluate the value of the `request.method` attribute to determine the actions to be performed based on the HTTP verb. The code file for this sample is included in the `restful_python_2_09_01` folder, in the `Pyramid01/metrics/metrics/views/metrics.py` file:

```
"""
Metric resource
"""
@view_config(route_name='metric',
    accept='application/json')
def metric(request):
    id = int(request.matchdict['id'])
    metric = get_metric_or_not_found(id)
    if request.method == 'GET':
        dumped_metric = metric_schema.dump(metric).data
        return dumped_metric
    elif request.method == 'DELETE':
        metric_manager.delete_metric(id)
        return HTTPNoContent()
    else:
        # The method is neither GET nor DELETE
        raise HTTPMethodNotAllowed()
```

The `metric` function uses the `@view_config` decorator with values for the `route_name` and `accept` arguments. This function will be invoked only when the named route matches the value specified for the `route_name` argument: `'metric'`. The value for the `accept` argument specifies that the function will only accept `application/json` as the content type.

The `metric` function retrieves or deletes an existing metric. The function receives a `Request` instance in the `request` argument. The function is capable of processing two HTTP verbs for a metric resource: GET and DELETE. The code checks the value of the `request.method` attribute to determine the code to be executed based on the HTTP verb.

First, the code retrieves the `id` value specified in the request, available in the `request.matchdict` dictionary, and saves it in the `id` variable.

After a request matches a route, the `request.matchdict` dictionary contains the key-value pairs with the keys that matched the URL pattern associated with the route and the values retrieved from the request.

The next line calls the code calls the `get_metric_or_not_found` function to return an HTTP `404 Not Found` status in case there is no metric with the requested `id` in the in-memory dictionary.

If the metric exists and the HTTP verb is `GET`, the code calls the `metric_schema.dump` method with the retrieved metric as an argument to use the `SurfboardMetricSchema` instance to serialize the `SurfboardMetricModel` instance whose `id` matches the specified `id`. The `dump` method takes the `SurfboardMetricModel` instance and applies the field filtering and output formatting specified in the `SurfboardMetricSchema` class. The code returns the `data` attribute of the result returned by the `dump` method, that is, the serialized metric in JSON format as the body, with the default HTTP `200 OK` status code.

If the metric exists and the HTTP verb is `DELETE`, the code calls the `metric_manager.delete_metric` method with the `id` as an argument to erase the metric from the in-memory dictionary. Then, the code returns an instance of the `HTTPNoContent` class to make the request return an empty response body and an HTTP `204 No Content` status code.

If the `request.method` doesn't match either `'GET'` or `'DELETE'`, the code raises an `HTTPMethodNotAllowed` exception, returning an HTTP `405 Method Not Allowed` status code.

Understanding and configuring view handlers

The following table shows the function that we want to be executed for each combination of HTTP verb and scope, and the route name that identifies each resource:

HTTP verb	Scope	Route name	Function
GET	Collection of metrics	'metrics'	metrics_collection
GET	Metric	'metric'	metric
POST	Collection of metrics	'metrics'	metrics_collection
DELETE	Metric	'metrics'	metric

We must make the necessary resource routing configurations to call the appropriate functions, pass them all the necessary arguments by defining the appropriate routes, and match the appropriate view callable with the route.

First, we will check how the application template we used configures and returns a Pyramid WSGI application that will run our RESTful API. The following lines show the code for the __init__.py file within the metrics/metrics folder:

```
from pyramid.config import Configurator


def main(global_config, **settings):
    """ This function returns a Pyramid WSGI application.
    """
    with Configurator(settings=settings) as config:
        config.include('pyramid_jinja2')
        config.include('.routes')
        config.scan()
    return config.make_wsgi_app()
```

We have already removed the usage of the jinja2 template, and therefore remove the highlighted line from the previous code. The code file for the sample is included in the restful_python_2_09_01 folder, in the Pyramid01/metrics/metrics/__init__.py file.

The code defines a main function that creates a pyramid.config.Configurator instance named config, with the settings received as an argument. The main function calls the config.include method with '.routes' as an argument to include the configuration callable that accepts a single argument named config from the routes module. This callable will receive the instance of Configurator in the config argument and will be able to call its methods to perform the appropriate configuration for routes. We will replace the existing code for the routes module after we finish analyzing the previous code.

Then, the code calls the config.scan method to scan the Python packages and subpackages for callables that have specific decorator objects that perform configurations, such as the functions that we declared with the @view.config decorator.

Finally, the code calls the config.make_wsgi_app method to commit any pending configuration statements and return the Pyramid WSGI application that represent the committed configuration state. This way, Pyramid completes with the configuration process and launches the server.

Open the existing `routes.py` file within the `metrics/metrics` folder and replace the existing code with the following lines. The code file for the sample is included in the `restful_python_2_09_01` folder, in the `Pyramid01/metrics/metrics/routes.py` file:

```
from metrics.views.metrics import metric, metrics_collection


def includeme(config):
    # Define the routes for metrics
    config.add_route('metrics', '/metrics/')
    config.add_route('metric', '/metrics/{id:\d+}/')
    # Match the metrics views with the appropriate routes
    config.add_view(metrics_collection,
        route_name='metrics',
        renderer='json')
    config.add_view(metric,
        route_name='metric',
        renderer='json')
```

The code defines an `includeme` function which receives the previously explained `pyramid.config.Configurator` instances in the `config` argument. First, the code calls the `config.add_route` method twice to associate the route named `'metrics'` with the `'/metrics/'` pattern and the route named `'metric'` with the `'metrics/{id:\d+}/'` pattern. Notice that the semicolon (`:`) after `id` is followed by a regular expression that makes sure that `id` is only composed of digits.

Then, the code calls the `config.add_view` method twice to specify the view callable `metrics_collection` as the function that must be called when the route name is equal to `'metrics'` and the view callable `metric` as the function that must be called when the route name is equal to `'metric'`. In both cases, the `config.add_view` method specifies that we want to use `'json'` as the renderer for the responses.

Making HTTP requests to the API with command-line tools

The `metrics/development.ini` file is a settings file that defines the Pyramid app and server configuration for the development environment. As happens in most `.ini` files, the configuration settings are organized in sections. For example, the `[server:main]` section specifies the value for the listen setting as `localhost:6543` to make the `waitress` server `listen` on port `6543` and bind it to the localhost address.

This file was included when we created a new app based on a template. Open the metrics/development.ini file and locate the following line that specifies the bool value for the pyramid.debug_routematch setting. The code file for the sample is included in the restful_python_2_09_01 folder, in the Pyramid01/metrics/development.ini.py file:

```
pyramid.debug_routematch = false
```

Replace the false value with true, as shown in the following line. Make sure you use true (lowercase) and not True, we use in Python code. This way, the server will print the details of the route-matching decision for each request in the console output:

```
pyramid.debug_routematch = true
```

Now, we will use the pserve command to serve a web application with the previously introduced development configuration file provided by the application template, development.ini. This way, we will be able to compose and send HTTP requests to our RESTful API. Execute the following command within the metrics folder (Pyramid01/metrics):

```
pserve development.ini
```

The following lines show the output after we execute the previous command. The server is listening at port 6543:

```
Starting server in PID 9311.
Serving on http://localhost:6543
```

With the previous command, we will start the waitress server and will only be able to access it in our development computer. The previous command starts the development server at the default IP address, that is, 127.0.0.1 (localhost). It is not possible to access this IP address from other computers or devices connected on our LAN. Thus, if we want to make HTTP requests to our API from other computers or devices connected to our LAN, we have to change the value for the listen setting in the previously explained [server:main] section in the development.ini file.

We will start composing and sending HTTP requests with the curl and HTTPie command-line tools that we introduced in Chapter 1, *Developing RESTful APIs and Microservices with Flask 1.0.2*, in the section named *Working with command-line tools - curl and httpie*. Make sure you read this section before executing the following examples.

Whenever we compose HTTP requests with the command-line, we will use two versions of the same command: the first one with HTTPie, and the second one with curl. This way, you will be able to use the most convenient for you.

Make sure you leave the Pyramid application running. Don't close the Terminal or Command Prompt that is running the development server. Open a new Terminal in macOS or Linux, or a Command Prompt in Windows, and run the following command. The code file for the sample is included in the `restful_python_2_09_01` folder, in the `Pyramid01/cmd/cmd901.txt` file:

```
http POST ":6543/metrics/" status='IDLE' speed_in_mph=1
altitude_in_feet=2 water_temperature_in_f=58
```

The following is the equivalent `curl` command. It is very important to use the `-H "Content-Type: application/json"` option to tell `curl` to send the data specified after the -d option as `application/json` instead of the default `application/x-www-form-urlencoded`. The code file for the sample is included in the `restful_python_2_09_01` folder, in the `Pyramid01/cmd/cmd902.txt` file:

```
curl -iX POST -H "Content-Type: application/json" -d '{"status":"IDLE",
"speed_in_mph":1, "altitude_in_feet": 2, "water_temperature_in_f": 58}'
"localhost:6543/metrics/"
```

The previous commands will compose and send the following HTTP request: `POST` `http://localhost:6543/metrics/` with the following JSON key-value pairs:

```
{
    "status": "IDLE",
    "speed_in_mph": 1,
    "altitude_in_feet": 2,
    "water_temperature_in_f": 58
}
```

Notice that the value for the `status` key is the description for the desired status. The request specifies `/metrics/`, and therefore, it will match the `'/metrics/'` pattern and run the `metrics_collection` function. The function just receives `request` as a parameter. As the HTTP verb for the request is `POST`, the `request.method` property is equal to `'POST'`, and therefore the function will execute the code that validates and deserializes the JSON data received in the request, create a new `SurfboardMetricModel`, and insert it in the in-memory dictionary. The function returns an HTTP `201 Created` status code and the recently persisted `SurfboardMetricModel` serialized to JSON in the response body.

The following lines show an example response for the HTTP request, with the new `SurfboardMetricModel` object in the JSON response:

```
HTTP/1.1 201 Created
Content-Length: 90
Content-Type: application/json; charset=UTF-8
Date: Fri, 09 Nov 2018 02:03:23 GMT
Server: waitress
{
    "altitude_in_feet": 2,
    "id": 1,
    "speed_in_mph": 1,
    "status": "IDLE",
    "water_temperature_in_f": 58
}
```

Now, we will write another command to compose an HTTP POST request to add another metric. Run the following command. The code file for the sample is included in the `restful_python_2_09_01` folder, in the `Pyramid01/cmd/cmd903.txt` file:

```
http POST ":6543/metrics/" status='PADDLING' speed_in_mph=3
altitude_in_feet=3 water_temperature_in_f=59
```

The following is the equivalent `curl` command. The code file for the sample is included in the `restful_python_2_09_01` folder, in the `Pyramid01/cmd/cmd904.txt` file:

```
curl -iX POST -H "Content-Type: application/json" -d
'{"status":"PADDLING", "speed_in_mph":3, "altitude_in_feet": 3,
"water_temperature_in_f": 59}' "localhost:6543/metrics/"
```

The previous commands will compose and send the following HTTP request, POST `http://localhost:6543/metrics/`, with the following JSON key-value pairs:

```
{
    "status": "PADDLING",
    "speed_in_mph": 3,
    "altitude_in_feet": 3,
    "water_temperature_in_f": 59
}
```

The following lines show an example response for the HTTP request, with the new
SurfboardMetricModel object in the JSON response:

```
HTTP/1.1 201 Created
Content-Length: 94
Content-Type: application/json; charset=UTF-8
Date: Fri, 09 Nov 2018 02:46:37 GMT
Server: waitress
{
    "altitude_in_feet": 3,
    "id": 1,
    "speed_in_mph": 3,
    "status": "PADDLING",
    "water_temperature_in_f": 59
}
```

Now, we will write a command to compose and send an HTTP GET request to retrieve all
the metrics. Run the following command. The code file for the sample is included in the
restful_python_2_09_01 folder, in the Pyramid01/cmd/cmd905.txt file:

```
http ":6543/metrics/"
```

The following is the equivalent curl command. The code file for the sample is included in
the restful_python_2_09_01 folder, in the Pyramid01/cmd/cmd904.txt file:

```
curl -iX GET "localhost:6543/metrics/"
```

The previous commands will compose and send the following HTTP request: GET
http://localhost:6543/metrics/. The request specifies /metrics/, and therefore, it
will match the '/metrics/' pattern and run the metrics_collection function. In this
case, the HTTP verb for the request is GET, and the request.method property is equal to
'GET', and therefore the function will execute the code that retrieves all the
SurfboardMetricModel instances from the dictionary and generate a JSON response with
all of these SurfboardMetricModel objects serialized.

The following lines show an example response for the HTTP request. The first lines show
the HTTP response headers, including the status (200 OK) and the Content-type
(application/json). After the HTTP response headers, we can see the details for the
two SurfboardMetricModel objects in the JSON response:

```
HTTP/1.1 200 OK
Content-Length: 206
Content-Type: application/json
Date: Fri, 09 Nov 2018 02:56:18 GMT
Server: waitress
```

```
[
    {
        "altitude_in_feet": 2,
        "id": 1,
        "speed_in_mph": 1,
        "status": "IDLE",
        "water_temperature_in_f": 58
    },
    {
        "altitude_in_feet": 3,
        "id": 2,
        "speed_in_mph": 3,
        "status": "PADDLING",
        "water_temperature_in_f": 59
    }
]
```

After we run the three requests, we will see the following lines in the window that is running the Pyramid application server. The output indicates that the service received three HTTP requests, specifically two POST requests and one GET request with /metrics/ as the URI. The service processed the three HTTP requests, returning the status code 201 for the first two requests and 200 for the last request. Notice that the server displays the route name that matched each URL and the pattern:

```
2018-11-08 23:56:09,506 DEBUG [metrics:104][waitress] route matched for url
http://localhost:6543/metrics/; route_name: 'metrics', path_info:
'/metrics/', pattern: '/metrics/', matchdict: {}, predicates: ''
4
2018-11-08 23:56:13,699 DEBUG [metrics:104][waitress] route matched for url
http://localhost:6543/metrics/; route_name: 'metrics', path_info:
'/metrics/', pattern: '/metrics/', matchdict: {}, predicates: ''
 4
2018-11-08 23:56:18,877 DEBUG [metrics:104][waitress] route matched for url
http://localhost:6543/metrics/; route_name: 'metrics', path_info:
'/metrics/', pattern: '/metrics/', matchdict: {}, predicates: ''
```

The following screenshot shows two Terminal windows side-by-side on macOS. The Terminal window on the left-hand side is running the Pyramid application server and displays the routes that each HTTP request has matched. The Terminal window on the right-hand side is running http commands to generate the HTTP requests. It is a good idea to use a similar configuration to check the output while we compose and send the HTTP requests:

Now, we will write a command to compose an HTTP GET request to retrieve an existing metric. Run the following command. Make sure you replace 2 with the id value of an existing metric. The code file for the sample is included in the restful_python_2_09_01 folder, in the Pyramid01/cmd/cmd907.txt file:

```
http ":6543/metrics/2/"
```

The following is the equivalent curl command. The code file for the sample is included in the restful_python_2_09_01 folder, in the Pyramid01/cmd/cmd908.txt file:

```
curl -iX GET -H "localhost:6543/metrics/2/"
```

The previous command will compose and send a GET HTTP request. The request has a number after /metrics/, and therefore it will match the '/metrics/{id:\d+}/' pattern and run the metric function. This function just receives request as a parameter. As the HTTP verb for the request is GET, the request.method property is equal to 'GET', and therefore the function will execute the code that returns the SurfboardMetricModel instance whose ID matches the id value specified in the request.

Now, we will write a command to compose and send an HTTP request to delete an existing metric, specifically, the last one we added. As happened in our last HTTP request, we have to check the value assigned to id in the previous response and replace 2 in the command with the returned value. The code file for the sample is included in the restful_python_2_09_01 folder, in the Pyramid01/cmd/cmd909.txt file:

```
http DELETE ":6543/metrics/2"
```

The following is the equivalent curl command. The code file for the sample is included in the restful_python_2_09_01 folder, in the Pyramid01/cmd/cmd910.txt file:

```
curl -iX DELETE "localhost:6543/metrics/2"
```

The previous commands will compose and send the following HTTP request: DELETE http://localhost:6543/metrics/2. The request has a number after /metrics/, and therefore, it will match the '/metrics/{id:\d+}/' pattern and run the metric function. As the HTTP verb for the request is DELETE, the request.method property is equal to 'DELETE', and therefore the function will execute the code that removes the SurfboardMetricModel instance whose id matches the id value specified in the request from the in-memory dictionary and return an HTTP 204 No Content status code. The following lines show a sample response:

```
HTTP/1.1 204 No Content
Content-Length: 0
Date: Fri, 09 Nov 2018 03:31:39 GMT
Server: waitress
```

Test your knowledge

Let's see whether you can answer the following questions correctly:

1. In Pyramid, view callables are which of the following?
    1. Python objects such as functions, classes, or instances that implement a __call__ method
    2. Classes that inherit from the pyramid.views.Callable superclass
    3. Instances of the pyramid.views.Callable class

2. The `request` argument that any view callable receives represents an HTTP request, and is an instance of which of the following classes?
   1. `pyramid.web.Request`
   2. `pyramid.request.Request`
   3. `pyramid.callable.Request`

3. Which of the following attributes allows us to specify the status code for the response in a `pyramid.response.Response` instance?
   1. `status`
   2. `http_status_code`
   3. `status_code`

4. Which of the following classes, declared in the `pyramid.httpexceptions` module, represent an HTTP `201 Created` status code for a response?
   1. `HTTP_201_Created`
   2. `HTTP_Created`
   3. `HTTPCreated`

5. Which of the following attributes allows us to specify the response body for a JSON response in a `pyramid.response.Response` instance?
   1. `json_body`
   2. `body`
   3. `body_as_json`

Summary

In this chapter, we designed a RESTful API to interact with a simple data source with Pyramid 1.10. We defined the requirements for our API and understood the tasks performed by each HTTP method. We set up a virtual environment with Pyramid, built a new application from an existing template, and added additional required packages to the Pyramid application.

We created a class that represented a surfboard metric, and additional classes to make it possible to generate a simple data source to allow us to focus on specific Pyramid features to build a RESTful API.

We then created a Marshmallow schema to validate, serialize, and deserialize the metric model. Then, we started working with view callable functions to process specific HTTP verbs on certain resources. We understood and configured view handlers in our Pyramid application.

Finally, we started the Pyramid application in development mode, used command-line tools to compose and send HTTP requests to our RESTful API, and analyzed how each HTTP request was processed in our code.

Now that we understand the basics of the Pyramid for creating simple RESTful APIs, we will start working with Tornado, which is the topic of the next chapter.

10
Developing RESTful APIs with Tornado 5.1.1

In this chapter, we will work with Tornado 5.1.1 to create a RESTful Web API. We will start working with this lightweight web framework. We will look at the following:

- Design a RESTful API to interact with slow sensors and actuators
- Understand the tasks performed by each HTTP method
- Set up a virtual environment with Tornado 5.1.1
- Create classes that represent a drone
- Write request handlers
- Map URL patterns to request handlers
- Make HTTP requests to the Tornado API
- Work with command-line tools—`curl` and `httpie`
- Work with GUI tools—Postman and others

Designing a RESTful API to interact with slow sensors and actuators

Imagine that we have to create a RESTful API to control a drone, also known as a **UAV** (short for **Unmanned Aerial Vehicle**). The drone is an IoT device that interacts with many sensors and actuators, including digital electronic speed controllers linked to engines, propellers, and servomotors.

The IoT device has limited resources, and therefore we have to use a lightweight web framework. Our API doesn't need to interact with a database. We don't need a heavyweight web framework such as Django, with all its features and its integrated ORM. We want to be able to process many requests without blocking the web server. We need the web server to provide us with nice scalability while consuming limited resources. Thus, our choice is to use Tornado, the open source version of FriendFeed's web server.

The IoT device is capable of running Python 3.7.1, Tornado 5.1.1, and other Python packages. Tornado is a Python web framework and asynchronous networking library that provides excellent scalability due to its non-blocking network I/O. In addition, Tornado will allow us to easily and quickly build a really lightweight RESTful API.

We have chosen Tornado because it is more lightweight than Django, and makes it easy for us to create an API that takes advantage of the non-blocking network I/O. We don't need to use an ORM, and we want to start running the RESTful API on the IoT device as soon as possible to allow all the teams to interact with it.

We will interact with a library that allows us to run the slow I/O operations that interact with the sensors and actuators in an execution that happens outside the **GIL** (short for **Global Interpreter Lock**). Thus, we will be able to take advantage of the non-blocking feature in Tornado when a request needs to execute any of these slow I/O operations.

In our first version of the API, we will work with synchronous execution, and therefore, when an HTTP request to our API requires running a slow I/O operation, we will block the request processing queue until the slow I/O operation is complete, with either a sensor or an actuator providing a response. We will execute the I/O operation with synchronous execution and Tornado won't be able to continue processing other incoming HTTP requests until a response is sent to the HTTP request.

Then, we will create a second version of our API that will take advantage of the non-blocking features included in Tornado, in combination with asynchronous operations. In the second version, when an HTTP request sent to our API requires running a slow I/O operation, we won't block the request processing queue until the slow I/O operation provides a response from either a sensor or an actuator. We will execute the I/O operation with an asynchronous execution and Tornado will be able to continue processing other incoming HTTP requests.

In order to keep the example simple, we won't use a library to interact with sensors and actuators. We will just print information about the operations that will be performed by these sensors and actuators. However, in the second version of our API, we will write our code to make asynchronous calls in order to understand the advantages of the non-blocking features in Tornado. We will use a simplified set of sensors and actuators. Bear in mind that drones usually have more sensors and actuators. Our goal is to learn how to work with Tornado to build a RESTful API; we don't want to become experts in building drones.

Each of the following sensors and actuators will be a resource in our RESTful API:

- A hexacopter, that is, a six-rotor helicopter
- An altimeter (altitude sensor)
- A red **LED** (short for **Light-Emitting Diode**)
- A green LED
- A blue LED

The following table shows the HTTP verbs, the scope, and the semantics for the methods that our first version of the API must support. Each method is composed by an HTTP verb and a scope, and all the methods have well-defined meanings for all sensors and actuators. In our API, each sensor or actuator has its own unique URL. Notice that our API will only support a specific set of verbs for the different scopes:

HTTP verb	Scope	Semantics
GET	Hexacopter	Retrieve the current hexacopter's motor speed in RPMs and its status (turned on or off)
PATCH	Hexacopter	Set the current hexacopter's motor speed in RPMs
GET	LED	Retrieve the brightness level for a single LED
PATCH	LED	Update the brightness level for a single LED
GET	Altimeter	Retrieve the current altitude in feet or meters based on the value specified in the unit query parameter

Understanding the tasks performed by each HTTP method

Let's consider that `http://localhost:8888/hexacopters/1` is the URL that identifies the hexacopter for our drone.

```
PATCH http://localhost:8888/hexacopters/1
```

We have to compose and send an HTTP request with the HTTP verb (`PATCH`) and request URL (`http://localhost:8888/hexacopters/1`) to set the hexacopter's status and motor speed in RPMs. In addition, we have to provide the JSON key-value pairs with the necessary field name and the value to specify the desired speed. As a result of the request, the server will validate the provided values for the field, make sure that it is a valid speed, and make the necessary calls to adjust the speed with an asynchronous execution. After the speed for the hexacopter is set, the server will return an HTTP `200 OK` status code and a JSON body with the recently updated hexacopter values serialized to JSON:

```
GET http://localhost:8888/hexacopters/1
```

We have to compose and send an HTTP request with the HTTP verb (`GET`) and request URL (`http://localhost:8888/hexacopter/1`) to retrieve the current values for the hexacopter. The server will make the necessary calls to retrieve the status and the speed for the hexacopter with an asynchronous execution. As a result of the request, the server will return an HTTP `200 OK` status code and a JSON body with the serialized key-value pairs that specify the status and speed for the hexacopter. If a number different than 1 is specified, the server will return just an HTTP `404 Not Found` status:

```
PATCH http://localhost:8888/led/{id}
```

We have to compose and send an HTTP request with the HTTP verb (`PATCH`) and request URL (`http://localhost:8888/led/{id}`) to set the brightness level for a specific LED whose `id` matches the specified numeric value in the place where `{id}` is written. For example, if we use the request URL `http://localhost:8888/led/1`, the server will set the brightness level for the LED whose `id` matches 1. In addition, we have to provide the JSON key-value pairs with the necessary field name and the value to specify the desired brightness level. As a result of the request, the server will validate the provided values for the field, making sure that it is a valid brightness level and making the necessary calls to adjust the brightness level with an asynchronous execution. After the brightness level for the LED is set, the server will return a `200 OK` status code and a JSON body with the recently updated LED values serialized to JSON:

```
GET http://localhost:8888/led/{id}
```

We have to compose and send an HTTP request with the HTTP verb (`GET`) and request URL (`http://localhost:8888/led/{id}`) to retrieve the current values for the LED whose `id` matches the specified numeric value in the place where `{id}` is written. For example, if we use the request URL `http://localhost:8888/led/1`, the server will retrieve the LED whose `id` matches `1`, that is, the green LED. The server will make the necessary calls to retrieve the values for the LED with an asynchronous execution. As a result of the request, the server will return an HTTP `200 OK` status code and a JSON body with the serialized key-value pairs that specify the values for the LED. If no LED matches the specified `id`, the server will just return an HTTP `404 Not Found` status:

```
GET http://localhost:8888/altimeter/1?unit=feet
```

We have to compose and send an HTTP request with the HTTP verb (`GET`) and request URL (`http://localhost:8888/altimeter/1?unit=feet`) to retrieve the current value for the altimeter in feet. The server will make the necessary calls to retrieve the value for the altimeter with an asynchronous execution. As a result of the request, the server will return an HTTP `200 OK` status code and a JSON body with the serialized key-value pairs that specify the value for the altimeter. If a number different than `1` is specified, the server will return just an HTTP `404 Not Found` status:

```
GET http://localhost:8888/altimeter/1?unit=meters
```

If we want to retrieve the value for the altimeter in meters, we have to compose and send an HTTP request with the HTTP verb (`GET`) and request URL (`http://localhost:8888/altimeter/1?unit=meters`).

Setting up a virtual environment with Tornado 5.1.1

In `Chapter 1`, *Developing RESTful APIs and Microservices with Flask 1.0.2*, we learned that throughout this book we are going to work with the lightweight virtual environments introduced and improved in Python 3.4. Now, we will follow many steps to create a new lightweight virtual environment to work with Tornado 5.1.1. It is highly recommended to read the section named *Working with lightweight virtual environments* in `Chapter 1`, *Developing RESTful APIs and Microservices with Flask 1.0.2*, if you don't have experience with lightweight virtual environments in modern Python. The chapter includes all the detailed explanations about the effects of the steps we are going to follow.

The following commands assume that you have Python 3.7.1 installed on Linux, macOS, or Windows.

First, we have to select the target folder or directory for our lightweight virtual environment. The following is the path we will use in the example for Linux and macOS:

`~/HillarPythonREST2/Tornado01`

The target folder for the virtual environment will be the `HillarPythonREST2/Tornado01` folder within our home directory. For example, if our home directory in macOS or Linux is `/Users/gaston`, the virtual environment will be created within `/Users/gaston/HillarPythonREST2/Tornado01`. You can replace the specified path with your desired path in each command.

The following is the path we will use in the example for Windows:

`%USERPROFILE%\HillarPythonREST2\Tornado01`

The target folder for the virtual environment will be the `HillarPythonREST2\Tornado01` folder within our user profile folder. For example, if our user profile folder is `C:\Users\gaston`, the virtual environment will be created within `C:\Users\gaston\HillarPythonREST2\Tornado01`. Of course, you can replace the specified path with your desired path in each command.

In Windows PowerShell, the previous path would be the following:

`$env:userprofile\HillarPythonREST2\Tornado01`

Now, we have to use the `-m` option, followed by the `venv` module name and the desired path, to make Python run this module as a script and create a virtual environment in the specified path. The instructions are different depending on the platform in which we are creating the virtual environment. So, make sure you follow the instructions for your operating system:

1. Open a Terminal in Linux or macOS and execute the following command to create a virtual environment:

    `python3 -m venv ~/HillarPythonREST2/Tornado01`

2. In Windows, in the Command Prompt, execute the following command to create a virtual environment:

    `python -m venv %USERPROFILE%\HillarPythonREST2\Tornado01`

3. If you want to work with Windows PowerShell, execute the following command to create a virtual environment:

    `python -m venv $env:userprofile\HillarPythonREST2\Tornado01`

The previous commands don't produce any output. Now that we have created a virtual environment, we will run a platform-specific script to activate it. After we activate the virtual environment, we will install packages that will only be available in this virtual environment.

4. If your Terminal is configured to use the `bash` shell in macOS or Linux, run the following command to activate the virtual environment. The command also works for the `zsh` shell:

    ```
    source ~/HillarPythonREST2/Tornado01/bin/activate
    ```

5. If your Terminal is configured to use the `csh` or `tcsh` shell, run the following command to activate the virtual environment:

    ```
    source ~/HillarPythonREST2/Tornado01/bin/activate.csh
    ```

6. If your Terminal is configured to use either the `fish` shell, run the following command to activate the virtual environment:

    ```
    source ~/HillarPythonREST2/Tornado01/bin/activate.fish
    ```

7. In Windows, you can run either a batch file in the Command Prompt or a Windows PowerShell script to activate the virtual environment. If you prefer the Command Prompt, run the following command in the Windows command line to activate the virtual environment:

    ```
    %USERPROFILE%\HillarPythonREST2\Tornado01\Scripts\activate.bat
    ```

8. If you prefer Windows PowerShell, launch it and run the following commands to activate the virtual environment. However, note that you should have script execution enabled in Windows PowerShell to be able to run the script:

    ```
    cd $env:USERPROFILE
    HillarPythonREST2\Tornado01\Scripts\Activate.ps1
    ```

After you activate the virtual environment, the Command Prompt will display the virtual environment root folder name enclosed in parentheses as a prefix of the default prompt, to remind us that we are working in the virtual environment. In this case, we will see (`Tornado01`) as a prefix for the Command Prompt because the root folder for the activated virtual environment is `Tornado01`.

We have followed the necessary steps to create and activate a virtual environment. Now, we will create a `requirements.txt` file to specify the set of packages that our application requires to be installed on any supported platform. This way, it will be extremely easy to repeat the installation of the specified packages with their versions in any new virtual environment.

Use your favorite editor to create a new text file named `requirements.txt` within the root folder for the recently created virtual environment. The following lines show the content of the file which declares the packages and the versions that our API requires. The code file for the sample is included in the `restful_python_2_10_01` folder, in the `Tornado01/requirements.txt` file:

```
tornado==5.1.1
httpie==0.9.9
```

Each line in the `requirements.txt` file indicates the package and the version that needs to be installed. In this case, we are working with exact versions by using the == operator because we want to make sure that the specified version is installed. The following table summarizes the packages and the version numbers that we specified as requirements:

Package name	Version to be installed
tornado	5.1.1
httpie	0.9.9

Go to the root folder for the virtual environment: `Tornado01`. In macOS or Linux, enter the following command:

cd ~/HillarPythonREST2/Tornado01

In Windows Command Prompt, enter the following command:

cd /d %USERPROFILE%\HillarPythonREST2\Tornado01

In Windows PowerShell, enter the following command:

cd $env:USERPROFILE
cd HillarPythonREST2\Tornado01

Now, we must run the following command on macOS, Linux, or Windows to install the packages and the versions explained in the previous table with `pip` by using the recently created `requirements.txt` file. Make sure you are located in the folder that has the `requirements.txt` file before running the command (`Tornado01`):

```
pip install -r requirements.txt
```

The last lines for the output will indicate that `tornado` and `httpie` have been successfully installed:

```
Installing collected packages: tornado, httpie
  Running setup.py install for tornado ... done
Successfully installed httpie-0.9.9 tornado-5.1.1
```

Creating classes that represent a drone

We will create the following classes that we will use to represent the different components of a drone:

Class name	Description
HexacopterStatus	This class stores status data for the hexacopter
Hexacopter	This class represents a hexacopter
LightEmittingDiode	This class represents an LED connected to the drone
Altimeter	This class represents the altimeter that measures the current altitude for the drone
Drone	This class represents the drone with its different sensors and actuators

In a real-life example, these classes would interact with a library that interacts with sensors and actuators. In order to keep our example simple, we will make calls to `time.sleep` to simulate interactions that take some time to write values to interfaces with sensors and actuators. We will use the same procedure to simulate interactions that take some time to retrieve values from interfaces with sensors.

First, we will create the `Hexacopter` class, which we will use to represent the hexacopter, and a `HexacopterStatus` class, which we will use to store status data for the hexacopter.

Create a new Python file named `drone.py` in the root folder of the virtual environment (`Tornado01`). The following lines show all the necessary imports for the classes that we will create and the code that declares the `Hexacopter` and `HexacopterStatus` classes in this file. The code file for the sample is included in the `restful_python_2_10_01` folder, in the `Django01/drone.py` file:

```
from time import sleep
from random import randint


class HexacopterStatus:
```

```
        def __init__(self, motor_speed, is_turned_on):
            self.motor_speed = motor_speed
            self.is_turned_on = is_turned_on


    class Hexacopter:
        MIN_MOTOR_SPEED = 0
        MAX_MOTOR_SPEED = 500

        def __init__(self):
            self._motor_speed = self.__class__.MIN_MOTOR_SPEED
            self._is_turned_on = False

        @property
        def motor_speed(self):
            return self._motor_speed

        @motor_speed.setter
        def motor_speed(self, value):
            if value < self.__class__.MIN_MOTOR_SPEED:
                raise ValueError('The minimum speed is
    {0}'.format(self.__class__.MIN_MOTOR_SPEED))
            if value > self.__class__.MAX_MOTOR_SPEED:
                raise ValueError('The maximum speed is
    {0}'.format(self.__class__.MAX_MOTOR_SPEED))
            sleep(2)
            self._motor_speed = value
            self._is_turned_on = (self.motor_speed is not 0)

        @property
        def is_turned_on(self):
            return self._is_turned_on

        @property
        def status(self):
            sleep(3)
            return HexacopterStatus(self.motor_speed, self.is_turned_on)
```

The HexacopterStatus class just declares a constructor, the __init__ method. This method receives many arguments and uses them to initialize the attributes with the same names: motor_speed and is_turned_on.

The Hexacopter class declares two class attributes that specify the minimum and maximum speed values for its motor: MIN_MOTOR_SPEED and MAX_MOTOR_SPEED. The constructor, the __init__ method, initializes the _motor_speed attribute with the MIN_MOTOR_SPEED value and sets the _is_turned_on attribute to False.

The `motor_speed` property getter, the `motor_speed` method that has the `@property` decorator, returns the value of the `_motor_speed` attribute. The `motor_speed` property setter, which is the `motor_speed` method that has the `@motor_speed.setter` decorator, checks whether the value for the `value` argument is in the valid range. If the validation fails, the method raises a `ValueError` exception. Otherwise, the method sets the value of the `_motor_speed` attribute with the received value and sets the value for the `_is_turned_on` attribute to `True` if the `motor_speed` property is greater than 0. Finally, the method calls `sleep` to simulate that it takes two seconds to complete these operations.

The `is_turned_on` property getter, the `is_turned_on` method that has the `@property` decorator, returns the value of the `_is_turned_on` attribute. The `status` property getter calls `sleep` to simulate that it takes three seconds to retrieve the hexacopter status and then returns a `HexacopterStatus` instance initialized with the `motor_speed` and `turned_on` property values.

Stay in the `drones.py` file in the root folder for the virtual environment (`Tornado01`). Add the following lines to declare a `LightEmittingDiode` class that we will use to represent each LED. The code file for the sample is included in the `restful_python_2_10_01` folder, in the `Django01/drone.py` file:

```
class LightEmittingDiode:
    MIN_BRIGHTNESS_LEVEL = 0
    MAX_BRIGHTNESS_LEVEL = 255

    def __init__(self, id, description):
        self.id = id
        self.description = description
        self._brightness_level = self.__class__.MIN_BRIGHTNESS_LEVEL

    @property
    def brightness_level(self):
        sleep(1)
        return self._brightness_level

    @brightness_level.setter
    def brightness_level(self, value):
        if value < self.__class__.MIN_BRIGHTNESS_LEVEL:
            raise ValueError('The minimum brightness level is
{0}'.format(self.__class__.MIN_BRIGHTNESS_LEVEL))
        if value > self.__class__.MAX_BRIGHTNESS_LEVEL:
            raise ValueError('The maximum brightness level is
{0}'.format(self.__class__.MAX_BRIGHTNESS_LEVEL))
        sleep(2)
        self._brightness_level = value
```

The `LightEmittingDiode` class declares two class attributes that specify the minimum and maximum brightness level values for an LED: `MIN_BRIGHTNESS_LEVEL` and `MAX_BRIGHTNESS_LEVEL`. The constructor, the `__init__` method, initializes the `_brightness_level` attribute with the `MIN_BRIGHTNESS_LEVEL` and the `id` and `description` attributes with the values received in the arguments with the same names.

The `brightness_level` property getter, the `brightness_level` method that has the `@property` decorator, calls `sleep` to simulate it taking 1 second to retrieve the brightness level for the wired LED, and then returns the value of the `_brightness_level` attribute.

The `brightness_level` property setter, the `brightness_level` method that has the `@brightness_level.setter` decorator, checks whether the value for the `value` argument is in the valid range. If the validation fails, the method raises a `ValueError` exception. Otherwise, the method calls `sleep` to simulate it taking two seconds to set the new brightness level and finally sets the value of the `_brightness_level` attribute with the received value.

Stay in the `drones.py` file in the root folder for the virtual environment (`Tornado01`). Add the following lines to declare an `Altimeter` class that we will use to represent the altimeter. The code file for the sample is included in the `restful_python_2_10_01` folder, in the `Django01/drone.py` file:

```
class Altimeter:
    @property
    def altitude(self):
        sleep(1)
        return randint(0, 3000)
```

The `Altimeter` class declares an `altitude` property setter that calls `sleep` to simulate it taking one second to retrieve the altitude from the altimeter, and finally generates a random integer from 0 to 3000 (inclusive) and returns it.

Stay in the `drones.py` file in the root folder for the virtual environment (`Tornado01`). Add the following lines to declare a `Drone` class, which we will use to represent the drone with its sensors and actuators. The code file for the sample is included in the `restful_python_2_10_01` folder, in the `Django01/drone.py` file:

```
class Drone:
    def __init__(self):
        self.hexacopter = Hexacopter()
        self.altimeter = Altimeter()
        self.red_led = LightEmittingDiode(1, 'Red LED')
        self.green_led = LightEmittingDiode(2, 'Green LED')
        self.blue_led = LightEmittingDiode(3, 'Blue LED')
```

```
self.leds = {
    self.red_led.id: self.red_led,
    self.green_led.id: self.green_led,
    self.blue_led.id: self.blue_led}
```

The `Drone` class just declares a constructor, the `__init__` method, which creates instances of the previously declared classes that represent the different components for the drone. The `leds` attribute saves a dictionary that has a key-value pair for each `LightEmittingDiode` instance with its `id` and its instance.

Writing request handlers

The main building blocks for a RESTful API in Tornado are subclasses of the `tornado.web.RequestHandler` class, that is, the base class for HTTP request handlers in Tornado. We just need to perform the following tasks to build our RESTful API that interacts with a drone:

1. Create a subclass of the `RequestHandler` class and declare the methods for each supported HTTP verb
2. Override the methods to handle HTTP requests
3. Map the URL patterns to each subclass of the `RequestHandler` superclass in the `tornado.web.Application` instance that represents the Tornado web application

We will create the following subclasses of the `RequestHandler` class:

Class name	Description
`HexacopterHandler`	This class processes the HTTP `GET` and `PATCH` methods for a hexacopter resource.
`LedHandler`	This class processes the HTTP `GET` and `PATCH` methods for an LED resource.
`AltimeterHandler`	This class processes the HTTP `GET` method for an altimeter resource.

In order to set the status codes returned by each method that processes HTTP requests, we will use the HTTPStatus enum defined in the Python http module. For example, instead of using 200 for the HTTP 200 OK status code, we will use HTTPStatus.OK. The only drawback of this enum is that it doesn't include the status code numbers.

Create a new Python file named drone_service.py in the root folder for the virtual environment (Tornado01). The following lines show all the necessary imports for the classes that we will create and the code that declares the HexacopterHandler class in this file. The code file for the sample is included in the restful_python_2_10_01 folder, in the Django01/drone_service.py file:

```python
from http import HTTPStatus
from datetime import date
from tornado import web, escape, ioloop, httpclient, gen
from drone import Altimeter, Hexacopter, LightEmittingDiode, Drone


drone = Drone()


class HexacopterHandler(web.RequestHandler):
    SUPPORTED_METHODS = ("GET", "PATCH")
    HEXACOPTER_ID = 1

    def get(self, id):
        if int(id) is not self.__class__.HEXACOPTER_ID:
            self.set_status(HTTPStatus.NOT_FOUND)
            return
        print("I've started retrieving the hexacopter's status")
        hexacopter_status = drone.hexacopter.status
        print("I've finished retrieving the hexacopter's status")
        response = {
            'motor_speed_in_rpm': hexacopter_status.motor_speed,
            'is_turned_on': hexacopter_status.is_turned_on, }
        self.set_status(HTTPStatus.OK)
        self.write(response)
    def patch(self, id):
        if int(id) is not self.__class__.HEXACOPTER_ID:
            self.set_status(HTTPStatus.NOT_FOUND)
            return
        request_data = escape.json_decode(self.request.body)
        if ('motor_speed_in_rpm' not in request_data.keys()) or \
            (request_data['motor_speed_in_rpm'] is None):
            self.set_status(HTTPStatus.BAD_REQUEST)
            return
```

```
try:
    motor_speed = int(request_data['motor_speed_in_rpm'])
    print("I've started setting the hexacopter's motor speed")
    drone.hexacopter.motor_speed = motor_speed
    hexacopter_status = drone.hexacopter.status
    print("I've finished setting the hexacopter's motor speed")
    response = {
        'motor_speed_in_rpm': hexacopter_status.motor_speed,
        'is_turned_on': hexacopter_status.is_turned_on,}
    self.set_status(HTTPStatus.OK)
    self.write(response)
except ValueError as e:
    print("I've failed setting the hexacopter's motor speed")
    self.set_status(HTTPStatus.BAD_REQUEST)
    response = {
        'error': e.args[0]}
    self.write(response)
```

The `HexacopterHandler` class is a subclass of the `tornado.web.RequestHandler` superclass and declares the following two methods, which will be called when the HTTP method with the same name arrives as a request on this HTTP handler:

- `get`: This method receives `id` of the hexacopter whose status has to be retrieved in the `id` argument. If the received `id` doesn't match the value of the `HEXACOPTER_ID` class attribute, the code calls the `self.set_status` method with `HTTPStatus.NOT_FOUND` as an argument to set the status code for the response to HTTP `404 Not Found`. Otherwise, the code prints a message indicating that it has started retrieving the hexacopter's status, calls the `drone.hexacopter.get_hexacopter_status` method with a synchronous execution, and saves the result in the `hexacopter_status` variable. Then, the code writes a message indicating that it has finished retrieving the status, and generates a `response` dictionary with `'motor_speed_in_rpm'` and `'is_turned_on'` keys and their values. Finally, the code calls the `self.set_status` method with `HTTPStatus.OK` as an argument to set the status code for the response to HTTP `200 OK`, and calls the `self.write` method with the `response` dictionary as an argument. Because `response` is a dictionary, Tornado automatically writes the chunk as JSON and sets the value of the `Content-Type` header to `application/json`.

- `patch`: This method receives the `id` of the hexacopter that has to be updated or patched in the `id` argument. As in the previously explained `get` method, the code returns an HTTP `404 Not Found` if the received `id` doesn't match the value of the `HEXACOPTER_ID` class attribute. Otherwise, the code calls the `tornado.escape.json_decode` method with `self.request.body` as an argument to generate Python objects for the JSON string of the request body, and saves the generated dictionary in the `request_data` variable. If the dictionary doesn't include a key named `'motor_speed_in_rpm'`, the code returns an HTTP `400 Bad Request` status code. If there is a key, the code prints a message indicating that it started setting the hexacopter's speed, sets the new value for the `drone.hexacopter.motor_speed` property with a synchronous execution, and saves the value of the `drone.hexacopter.status` property in the `hexacopter_status` variable. If the value specified for the motor speed is not valid, a `ValueError` exception will be caught and the code will return an HTTP `400 Bad Request` status code and the validation error messages as the response body. Otherwise, the code writes a message indicating it finished setting the motor speed and generates a `response` dictionary with the `'motor_speed_in_rpm'` and `'is_turned_on'` keys and their values. Finally, the code calls the `self.set_status` method with `HTTPStatus.OK` as an argument to set the status code for the response to HTTP `200 OK`, and calls the `self.write` method with the `response` dictionary as an argument. Because `response` is a dictionary, Tornado automatically writes the chunk as JSON and sets the value of the `Content-Type` header to `application/json`.

The class overrides the `SUPPORTED_METHODS` class variable with a tuple that indicates the class just supports the `GET` and `PATCH` methods. This way, in case the handler has requested a method that isn't included in the `SUPPORTED_METHODS` tuple, the server will automatically return an HTTP `405 Method Not Allowed` status code.

Stay in the `drone_service.py` file in the root folder for the virtual environment (`Tornado01`). Add the following lines to declare a `LedHandler` class that we will use to represent the LED resources. The code file for the sample is included in the `restful_python_2_10_01` folder, in the `Django01/drone_service.py` file:

```
class LedHandler(web.RequestHandler):
    SUPPORTED_METHODS = ("GET", "PATCH")

    def get(self, id):
        int_id = int(id)
        if int_id not in drone.leds.keys():
            self.set_status(HTTPStatus.NOT_FOUND)
            return
        led = drone.leds[int_id]
        print("I've started retrieving {0}'s
status".format(led.description))
        brightness_level = led.brightness_level
        print("I've finished retrieving {0}'s
status".format(led.description))
        response = {
            'id': led.id,
            'description': led.description,
            'brightness_level': brightness_level}
        self.set_status(HTTPStatus.OK)
        self.write(response)

    def patch(self, id):
        int_id = int(id)
        if int_id not in drone.leds.keys():
            self.set_status(HTTPStatus.NOT_FOUND)
            return
        led = drone.leds[int_id]
        request_data = escape.json_decode(self.request.body)
        if ('brightness_level' not in request_data.keys()) or \
            (request_data['brightness_level'] is None):
            self.set_status(HTTPStatus.BAD_REQUEST)
            return
        try:
            brightness_level = int(request_data['brightness_level'])
            print("I've started setting the {0}'s brightness
level".format(led.description))
            led.brightness_level = brightness_level
            print("I've finished setting the {0}'s brightness
level".format(led.description))
            response = {
                'id': led.id,
                'description': led.description,
```

```
                    'brightness_level': brightness_level}
            self.set_status(HTTPStatus.OK)
            self.write(response)
        except ValueError as e:
            print("I've failed setting the {0}'s brightness
level".format(led.description))
            self.set_status(HTTPStatus.BAD_REQUEST)
            response = {
                'error': e.args[0]}
            self.write(response)
```

The LedHandler class is a subclass of the tornado.web.RequestHandler superclass. The class overrides the SUPPORTED_METHODS class variable with a tuple that indicates the class just supports the GET and PATCH methods. In addition, the class declares the following two methods, which will be called when the HTTP method with the same name arrives as a request on this HTTP handler:

- get: This method receives the id of the LED whose status has to be retrieved in the id argument. If the received id isn't one of the keys of the drone.leds dictionary, the code calls the self.set_status method with HTTPStatus.NOT_FOUND as an argument to set the status code for the response to HTTP 404 Not Found. Otherwise, the code retrieves the value associated with the key whose value matches id in the drone.leds dictionary and saves the retrieved LightEmittingDiode instance in the led variable. The code prints a message indicating that it started retrieving the LED's brightness level, and saved the value of the led.brightness_level property in the brightness_level variable with a synchronous execution. Then, the code writes a message indicating it finished retrieving the brightness level and generates a response dictionary with the 'id', 'description', and 'brightness_level' keys with their values. Finally, the code calls the self.set_status method with HTTPStatus.OK as an argument to set the status code for the response to HTTP 200 OK, and calls the self.write method with the response dictionary as an argument. Because response is a dictionary, Tornado automatically writes the chunk as JSON and sets the value of the Content-Type header to application/json.

- `patch`: This method receives the `id` of the LED that has to be updated or patched in the `id` argument. As in the previously explained `get` method, the code returns an `HTTP 404 Not Found` if the received `id` doesn't match any of the keys of the `drone.leds` dictionary. Otherwise, the code calls the `tornado.escape.json_decode` method with `self.request.body` as an argument to generate Python objects for the JSON string of the request body and saves the generated dictionary in the `request_data` variable. If the dictionary doesn't include a key named `'brightness_level'`, the code returns an HTTP `400 Bad Request` status code. If there is a key, the code prints a message indicating that it started setting the LED's brightness level, including the description for the LED, and sets the value for the `led.brightness_level` property with a synchronous execution. If the value specified for the `brightness_level` property is not valid, a `ValueError` exception will be caught and the code will return an `HTTP 400 Bad Request` status code and the validation error messages as the response body. Otherwise, the code writes a message indicating it finished setting the LED's brightness value and generates a `response` dictionary with the `'id'`, `'description'`, and `'brightness_level'` keys and their values. Finally, the code calls the `self.set_status` method with `HTTPStatus.OK` as an argument to set the status code for the response to HTTP `200 OK`, and calls the `self.write` method with the `response` dictionary as an argument. Because `response` is a dictionary, Tornado automatically writes the chunk as JSON and sets the value of the `Content-Type` header to `application/json`.

Stay in the `drone_service.py` file in the root folder for the virtual environment (`Tornado01`). Add the following lines to declare an `AltimeterHandler` class, which we will use to represent the altimeter resource. The code file for the sample is included in the `restful_python_2_10_01` folder, in the `Django01/drone_service.py` file:

```
class AltimeterHandler(web.RequestHandler):
    SUPPORTED_METHODS = ("GET")
    ALTIMETER_ID = 1

    def get(self, id):
        if int(id) is not self.__class__.ALTIMETER_ID:
            self.set_status(HTTPStatus.NOT_FOUND)
            return
        unit = self.get_arguments('unit')
        if 'meters' in unit:
            altitude_multiplier = 0.3048
            response_unit = 'meters'
        else:
            altitude_multiplier = 1
```

```
            response_unit = 'feet'
        print("I've started retrieving the altitude")
        altitude = round(drone.altimeter.altitude * altitude_multiplier, 4)
        print("I've finished retrieving the altitude")
        response = {
            'altitude': altitude,
            'unit': response_unit}
        self.set_status(HTTPStatus.OK)
        self.write(response)
```

The `AltimeterHandler` class is a subclass of the `tornado.web.RequestHandler` superclass. The class overrides the `SUPPORTED_METHODS` class variable with a tuple that indicates the class just supports the `GET` method. In addition, the class declares the `get` method, which will be called when the HTTP method with the same name arrives as a request on this HTTP handler.

The `get` method receives the `id` of the altimeter whose altitude has to be retrieved in the `id` argument. If the received `id` doesn't match the value of the `ALTIMETER_ID` class attribute, the code calls the `self.set_status` method with `HTTPStatus.NOT_FOUND` as an argument to set the status code for the response to HTTP `404 Not Found`.

Otherwise, the code calls the `self.get_argument` method with its `name` argument set to `'unit'` to retrieve the value of the `unit` query parameter. If there is no query parameter with this name, the method will return an empty list. If the value of this query parameter matches `'meters'`, the code sets the appropriate value to the `altitude_multiplier` variable to convert an altitude expressed in feet to an altitude expressed in meters, and also sets the value of the `response_unit` variable to `'meters'`. Otherwise, the `altitude_multiplier` variable is set to `1` and `response_unit` is set to the default altitude unit name: `'feet'`.

Then, the code prints a message indicating that it started retrieving the altimeter's altitude, multiplies the value of the `drone.hexacopter.altitude` property by `altitude_multiplier` with a synchronous execution, and saves the result in the `altitude` variable. Then, the code writes a message indicating it finished retrieving the altitude and generates a `response` dictionary with the `'altitude'` key and its value, and the `'unit'` key and the value of the `response_unit` variable.

Finally, the code calls the `self.set_status` method with `HTTPStatus.OK` as an argument to set the status code for the response to HTTP `200 OK` and calls the `self.write` method with the `response` dictionary as an argument. Because `response` is a dictionary, Tornado automatically writes the chunk as JSON and sets the value of the `Content-Type` header to `application/json`.

Mapping URL patterns to request handlers

The following table shows the method of our previously created HTTP handler classes that we want to be executed for each combination of HTTP verb and scope:

HTTP verb	Scope	Class and method
`GET`	Altimeter	`AltimeterHandler.get`
`GET`	Hexacopter	`HexacopterHandler.get`
`PATCH`	Hexacopter	`HexacopterHandler.patch`
`GET`	LED	`LedHandler.get`
`PATCH`	LED	`LedHandler.patch`

If the request results in the invocation of an HTTP handler class with an unsupported HTTP method, Tornado will return a response with the HTTP `405 Method Not Allowed` status code.

Now, we must map URL patterns to our previously coded subclasses of the `RequestHandler` superclass. Stay in the `drone_service.py` file in the root folder for the virtual environment (`Tornado01`). Add the following lines to declare the `Application` class and the __main__ method. The code file for the sample is included in the `restful_python_2_10_01` folder, in the `Django01/drone_service.py` file:

```
class Application(web.Application):
    def __init__(self, **kwargs):
        handlers = [
            (r"/hexacopters/([0-9]+)", HexacopterHandler),
            (r"/leds/([0-9]+)", LedHandler),
            (r"/altimeters/([0-9]+)", AltimeterHandler),
        ]
        super(Application, self).__init__(handlers, **kwargs)


if __name__ == "__main__":
    application = Application()
    port = 8888
    print("Listening at port {0}".format(port))
    application.listen(port)
    tornado_ioloop = ioloop.IOLoop.instance()
    periodic_callback = ioloop.PeriodicCallback(lambda: None, 500)
    periodic_callback.start()
    tornado_ioloop.start()
```

The code declares an `Application` class as a subclass of the `tornado.web.Application` superclass. This class overrides the inherited constructor, that is, the __init__ method. The constructor declares the `handlers` list that maps URL patterns to synchronous request handlers and then calls the inherited constructor with the list as one of its arguments. The `handlers` list is composed of a regular expression (`regexp`) and a `tornado.web.RequestHandler` subclass (`request_class`).

Then, the `main` method creates an instance of the `Application` class and calls the `application.listen` method to build an HTTP server for the application with the defined rules on the specified port. In this case, the code specifies `8888` as the port, saved in the `port` variable, which is the default port for Tornado HTTP servers.

Then, the code registers and starts a periodic callback, named `periodic_callback`, that will be executed every 500 milliseconds by the `IOLoop` to make it possible to use *Ctrl + C* to stop the HTTP server. This code will be useful for the second version of our API. However, we write it now to avoid editing the code later.

Finally, the code calls the `tornado_ioloop.start` method to start the server. This server was created with the previous call to the `application.listen` method.

Making HTTP requests to the Tornado API

Now, we can run the `drone_service.py` script, which launches the development server for Tornado 5.1.1 to compose and send HTTP requests to our unsecured and simple web API. Execute the following command:

```
python drone_service.py
```

The following lines show the output after we execute the previous command. The Tornado HTTP development server is listening on port `8888`:

```
Listening at port 8888
```

With the previous command, we will start the Tornado HTTP server and it will listen on every interface on port `8888`. Thus, if we want to make HTTP requests to our API from other computers or devices connected to our LAN, we don't need any additional configurations.

If you decide to compose and send HTTP requests from other computers or devices connected to the LAN, remember that you have to use the development computer's assigned IP address, instead of localhost. For example, if the computer's assigned IPv4 IP address is `192.168.1.121`, instead of `localhost:8888`, you should use `192.168.1.121:8888`. Of course, you can also use the hostname instead of the IP address. The previously explained configurations are very important because the consumers of our RESTful APIs might use mobile devices, and we will always want to test the apps that make use of our APIs in our development environments.

Working with command-line tools - curl and httpie

We will start composing and sending HTTP requests with the `curl` and HTTPie command-line tools, which we introduced in Chapter 1, *Developing RESTful APIs and Microservices with Flask 1.0.2*, in the section named *Working with command-line tools - curl and httpie*. Make sure you read this section before executing the next examples.

Whenever we compose HTTP requests with the command line, we will use two versions of the same command: the first one with HTTPie and the second one with `curl`. This way, you will be able to use the most convenient for you.

Make sure you leave the Tornado 5.1.1 development server running. Don't close the Terminal or Command Prompt that is running this development server. Open a new Terminal in macOS or Linux, or a Command Prompt in Windows, activate the virtual environment we have been using, and run the following command. We will compose and send an HTTP `PATCH` request to turn on the hexacopter and set its motor speed to 50 RPMs. The code file for the sample is included in the `restful_python_2_10_01` folder, in the `Tornado01/cmd/cmd1101.txt` file:

```
http PATCH ":8888/hexacopters/1" motor_speed_in_rpm=50
```

The following is the equivalent `curl` command. The code file for the sample is included in the `restful_python_2_10_01` folder, in the `Tornado01/cmd/cmd1102.txt` file:

```
curl -iX PATCH -H "Content-Type: application/json" -d
'{"motor_speed_in_rpm":50}' "localhost:8888/hexacopters/1"
```

The previous commands will compose and send the HTTP request `PATCH`
`http://localhost:8888/hexacopters/1` with the following JSON key-value pair:

```
{
    "motor_speed_in_rpm": 50
}
```

The request specifies `/hexacopters/1`, and therefore Tornado will iterate over the list of
tuples with regular expressions and request classes, and will match the
`'/hexacopters/([0-9]+)'` regular expression. Tornado will create an instance of the
`HexacopterHandler` class and run the `HexacopterHandler.patch` method with 1 as the
value for the `id` argument.

As the HTTP verb for the request is `PATCH`, Tornado calls the `patch` method. If the
hexacopter's speed is successfully set, the method returns an HTTP `200 OK` status code and
the key-value pairs with the speed and status for the recently updated hexacopter serialized
to JSON in the response body. The following lines show an example response for the HTTP
request:

```
HTTP/1.1 200 OK
Content-Length: 48
Content-Type: application/json; charset=UTF-8
Date: Tue, 30 Oct 2018 17:01:06 GMT
Server: TornadoServer/5.1.1
{
    "is_turned_on": true,
    "motor_speed_in_rpm": 50
}
```

Now, we will write a command to compose and send an HTTP `GET` request to retrieve the
status and the motor speed for the hexacopter. Run the following command. The code file
for the sample is included in the `restful_python_2_10_01` folder, in the
`Tornado01/cmd/cmd1103.txt` file:

```
http ":8888/hexacopters/1"
```

The following is the equivalent `curl` command. The code file for the sample is included in
the `restful_python_2_10_01` folder, in the `Tornado01/cmd/cmd1104.txt` file:

```
curl -iX GET -H "localhost:8888/hexacopters/1"
```

The previous commands will compose and send the following HTTP request: `GET http://localhost:8888/hexacopters/1`. The request specifies `/hexacopters/1`, and therefore it will match the `'/hexacopters/([0-9]+)'` regular expression and run the `HexacopterHandler.get` method with `1` as the value for the `id` argument. As the HTTP verb for the request is `GET`, Tornado calls the `get` method. The method retrieves the hexacopter's status and generates a JSON response with the key-value pairs.

The following lines show an example response for the HTTP request. The first lines show the HTTP response headers, including the status (`200 OK`) and the content type (`application/json`). After the HTTP response headers, we can see the details for the hexacopter's status in the JSON response:

```
HTTP/1.1 200 OK
Content-Length: 48
Content-Type: application/json; charset=UTF-8
Date: Tue, 30 Oct 2018 17:06:10 GMT
Etag: "172316bfc38ea5a04857465b888cff65c72a228c"
Server: TornadoServer/5.1.1
{
    "is_turned_on": true,
    "motor_speed_in_rpm": 50
}
```

After we run the two requests, we will see the following lines in the window that is running the Tornado HTTP server. The output shows the results of executing the print statements that describe when the code started setting or retrieving information, and when it finished:

```
I've started setting the hexacopter's motor speed
I've finished setting the hexacopter's motor speed
I've started retrieving the hexacopter's status
I've finished retrieving the hexacopter's status
```

The different methods we coded in the request handler classes end up calling `time.sleep` to simulate the operations taking some time with the hexacopter. In this case, our code is running with a synchronous execution, and therefore each time we compose and send a request, the Tornado server is blocked until the operation with the hexacopter finishes and the method sends the response. We will create a new version of this API that will use an asynchronous execution later, and will understand the advantages of Tornado's non-blocking features. However, first, we will understand how the synchronous version of the API works.

The following screenshot shows two Terminal windows side by side on macOS. The Terminal window on the left-hand side is running the Tornado HTTP server and displays the messages printed in the methods that process the HTTP requests. The Terminal window on the right-hand side is running `http` commands to generate the HTTP requests. It is a good idea to use a similar configuration to check the output while we compose and send the HTTP requests:

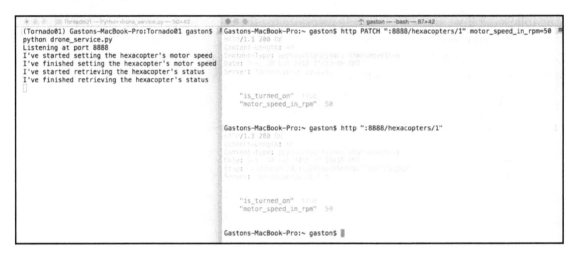

Now, we will write a command to compose and send an HTTP request to retrieve a hexacopter that doesn't exist. Remember that we just have one hexacopter in our drone. Run the following command to try to retrieve the status for a hexacopter with an invalid `id`. We must make sure that the utilities display the headers as part of the response to see the returned status code. The code file for the sample is included in the `restful_python_2_10_01` folder, in the `Tornado01/cmd/cmd1105.txt` file:

```
http ":8888/hexacopters/5"
```

The following is the equivalent `curl` command. The code file for the sample is included in the `restful_python_2_10_01` folder, in the `Tornado01/cmd/cmd1106.txt` file:

```
curl -iX GET "localhost:8888/hexacopters/5"
```

The previous commands will compose and send the following HTTP request: `GET http://localhost:8888/hexacopters/5`. The request is the same as the previous one we have analyzed, with a different number for the `id` parameter. The server will run the `HexacopterHandler.get` method with 5 as the value for the `id` argument. The `id` is not equal to 1, and therefore the code will return an HTTP `404 Not Found` status code. The following lines show an example header response for the HTTP request:

```
HTTP/1.1 404 Not Found
Content-Length: 0
Content-Type: text/html; charset=UTF-8
Date: Tue, 30 Oct 2018 17:22:13 GMT
Server: TornadoServer/5.1.1
```

Now, we will write a command to compose and send an HTTP `GET` request to retrieve the altitude from the altimeter included in the drone, expressed in meters. Run the following command. The code file for the sample is included in the `restful_python_2_10_01` folder, in the `Tornado01/cmd/cmd1107.txt` file:

```
http ":8888/altimeters/1?unit=meters"
```

The following is the equivalent `curl` command. The code file for the sample is included in the `restful_python_2_10_01` folder, in the `Tornado01/cmd/cmd1108.txt` file:

```
curl -iX GET -H "localhost:8888/altimeters/1?unit=meters"
```

The previous commands will compose and send the following HTTP request: `GET http://localhost:8888/altimeters/1?unit=meters`. The request specifies `/altimeters/1`, and therefore it will match the `'/altimeters/([0-9]+)'` regular expression and run the `AltimeterHandler.get` method with 1 as the value for the `id` argument. As the HTTP verb for the request is `GET`, Tornado calls the `get` method. The method will retrieve the value for the unit query parameter, retrieve the altimeter's altitude in feet, convert it to meters, and generate a JSON response with the key-value pairs.

The following lines show an example response for the HTTP request:

```
HTTP/1.1 200 OK
Content-Length: 49
Content-Type: application/json; charset=UTF-8
Date: Tue, 30 Oct 2018 17:35:59 GMT
Etag: "e6bef0812295935473bbef8883a144a7740d4838"
Server: TornadoServer/5.1.1
{
    "altitude": 126.7968,
    "unit": "meters"
}
```

Now, we will write a command to compose and send an HTTP GET request to retrieve the altitude from the altimeter included in the drone, expressed in the default unit: feet. Run the following command. The code file for the sample is included in the restful_python_2_10_01 folder, in the Tornado01/cmd/cmd1109.txt file:

```
http ":8888/altimeters/1"
```

The following is the equivalent curl command. The code file for the sample is included in the restful_python_2_10_01 folder, in the Tornado01/cmd/cmd1110.txt file:

```
curl -iX GET -H "localhost:8888/altimeters/1"
```

The previous commands will compose and send the following HTTP request: GET http://localhost:8888/altimeters/1. The request specifies /altimeters/1, and therefore it will match the '/altimeters/([0-9]+)' regular expression and run the AltimeterHandler.get method with 1 as the value for the id argument. As the HTTP verb for the request is GET, Tornado calls the get method. In this case, there is no unit query parameter, and therefore the method will retrieve the altimeter's altitude in feet and generate a JSON response with the key-value pairs.

The following lines show an example response for the HTTP request:

```
HTTP/1.1 200 OK
Content-Length: 33
Content-Type: application/json; charset=UTF-8
Date: Tue, 30 Oct 2018 17:38:58 GMT
Etag: "985cc8ce1bddf8a96b2a06a76d14faaa5bc03c9b"
Server: TornadoServer/5.1.1
{
    "altitude": 263,
    "unit": "feet"
}
```

Notice that the altitude value is a random number generated each time we require it.

Working with GUI tools - Postman and others

So far, we have been working with two terminal-based or command-line tools to compose and send HTTP requests to our Django development server: cURL and HTTPie. Now, we will work with one of the GUI tools we used when composing and sending HTTP requests to the Flask development server in Chapter 1, *Developing RESTful APIs and Microservices with Flask 1.0.2*. In case you skipped this chapter, make sure you check the installation instructions in the section named *Working with GUI tools - Postman and others*.

Once you launch Postman, make sure you close the modal that provides shortcuts to common tasks. Select the **GET** request in the + new drop-down menu in the upper-left corner of the Postman main window.

Select **GET** in the drop-down menu on the left-hand side of the **Enter request URL** textbox, and enter http://localhost:8888/leds/3 in the textbox on the right-hand side of the drop-down menu.

Then, click **Send** and Postman will display the following information:

- **Status: 200 OK**.
- **Time**: The time it took for the request to be processed.
- **Size**: The response size calculated by adding the body size to the headers size.
- **Body**: The response body with all the notifications formatted as JSON with syntax highlighting. The default view for the response body is the pretty view, and it activate syntax highlighting that makes it easy to read JSON code.

The following screenshot shows the JSON response body in Postman for the HTTP GET request to localhost:8888/leds/3:

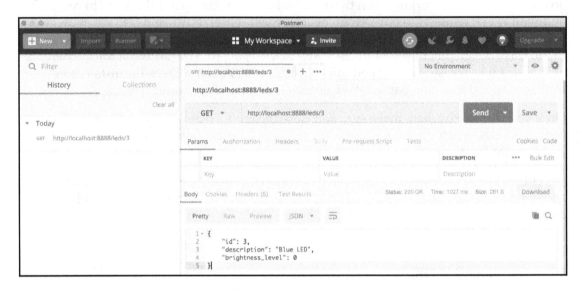

Click on the **Headers (5)** tab at the right-hand side of the **Body** and **Cookies** tabs to read the response headers. The following screenshot shows the layout for the response headers that Postman displays for the previous response. Notice that Postman displays the **Status** on the right-hand side of the response, and doesn't include it as the first line of the headers, as happened when we worked with both the curl and http command-line utilities:

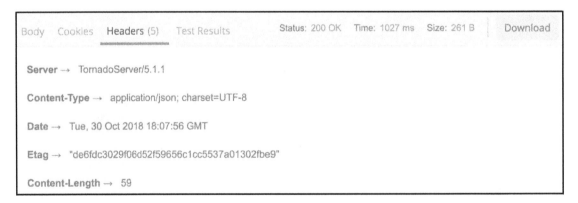

Now, we will compose and send an HTTP request to update the brightness level for an LED, specifically an HTTP PATCH request. Follow these steps:

1. Click on the plus (**+**) button on the right-hand side of the tab that showed the previous request. This way, you will create a new tab.

2. Select **PATCH** in the drop-down menu on the left-hand side of the **Enter request URL** textbox, and enter http://localhost:8888/leds/3 in this textbox at the right-hand side of the drop-down.

3. Click **Body** at the right-hand side of the **Authorization** and **Headers** tabs, within the panel that composes the request.

4. Activate the raw radio button and select **JSON (application/json)** in the drop-down menu on the right-hand side of the binary radio button. Postman will automatically add a **Content-type = application/json** header, and therefore you will notice the **Headers** tab will be renamed to **Headers (1)**, indicating that there is one key-value pair specified for the request headers.

5. Enter the following lines in the textbox below the radio buttons, in the **Body** tab. The code file for the sample is included in the restful_python_2_10_01 folder, in the Tornado01/cmd/cmd1111.txt file:

```
{
    "brightness_level": 64
}
```

The following screenshot shows the request body in Postman:

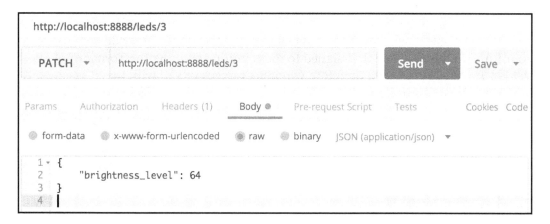

We followed the steps necessary to create an HTTP PATCH request with a JSON body that specifies the necessary key-value pairs to set the new brightness level for the LED whose id is equal to 3. Click **Send** and Postman will display **Status (200 OK)**, the time it took for the request to be processed, and the response body with the recently added game formatted as JSON with syntax highlighting (pretty view). The following screenshot shows the JSON response body in Postman for the HTTP PATCH request in the **Body** tab:

The Tornado HTTP server is listening on every interface on port 8888, and therefore we can also use apps that can compose and send HTTP requests from mobile devices to work with the RESTful API. For example, we can work with the previously introduced iCurlHTTP app on iOS devices, such as the iPad Pro and iPhone. On Android devices, we can work with the previously introduced HTTP Request app.

The following screenshot shows the results of composing and sending the following HTTP request with the iCurlHTTP app: GET http://192.168.1.101:8888/leds/2. Remember that you have to perform the previously explained configurations on your LAN and router to be able to access the Flask development server from other devices connected to your LAN. In this case, the IP assigned to the computer running the Tornado HTTP server is 192.168.1.101, and therefore you must replace this IP with the IP assigned to your development computer:

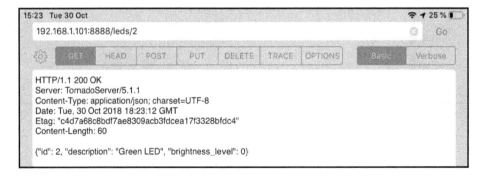

Test your knowledge

Let's see whether you can answer the following questions correctly:

1. Which of the following methods allows us to set the HTTP status code for a response in a subclass of `tornado.web.RequestHandler`?
   1. `self.write_status`
   2. `self.__cls__.write_status_code`
   3. `self.set_satus`

2. Which of the following methods allows us to write the response in a subclass of `tornado.web.RequestHandler`?
   1. `self.write_response`
   2. `self.write`
   3. `self.set_response`

3. The main building blocks for a RESTful API in Tornado are subclasses of which of the following classes?
   1. `tornado.web.GenericHandler`
   2. `tornado.web.RequestHandler`
   3. `tornado.web.IncomingHTTPRequestHandler`

4. If we just want to support the `GET` and `PATCH` methods, we can override the `SUPPORTED_METHODS` class variable with which of the following values?
   1. `("GET", "PATCH")`
   2. `{0: "GET", 1: "PATCH"}`
   3. `{"GET": True, "PATCH": True, "POST": False, "PUT": False}`

5. The list of tuples for the `tornado.Web.Application` constructor is composed of which of the following?
   1. A regular expression (`regexp`) and a `tornado.web.RequestHandler` subclass (`request_class`)
   2. A regular expression (`regexp`) and a `tornado.web.GenericHandler` subclass (`request_class`)
   3. A regular expression (`regexp`) and a `tornado.web.IncomingHTTPRequestHandler` subclass (`request_class`)

6. When we call the `self.write` method with a dictionary as an argument in a request handler, Tornado:
   1. Automatically writes the chunk as JSON but we have to manually set the value of the `Content-Type` header to `application/json`
   2. Requires us to use the `json.dumps` method and set the value of the `Content-Type` header to `application/json`
   3. Automatically writes the chunk as JSON and sets the value of the `Content-Type` header to `application/json`

7. A calls to the `tornado.escape.json_decode` method with `self.request.body` as an argument in a request handler:
   1. Generates Python objects for the JSON string of the request body and returns the generated tuple
   2. Generates Python objects for the JSON string of the request body and returns the generated dictionary
   3. Generates Python objects for the JSON string of the request body and returns the generated list

Summary

In this chapter, we designed a RESTful API to interact with slow sensors and actuators. We defined the requirements for our API and understood the tasks performed by each HTTP method. We set up a virtual environment with Tornado.

We created the classes that represent a drone and wrote code to simulate the slow I/O operations that are called for each HTTP request method. We wrote classes that represent request handlers and process the different HTTP requests, and we configured the URL patterns to route URLs to request handlers and their methods.

Finally, we started the Tornado development server and we used command-line tools to compose and send HTTP requests to our RESTful API, and analyzed how each HTTP request was processed in our code. We also worked with GUI tools to compose and send HTTP requests. We realized that each HTTP request takes some time to provide a response due to the simulation of slow I/O operations.

Now that we understand the basics of Tornado to create RESTful APIs, we will take advantage of the non-blocking features, combined with asynchronous operations in Tornado, in a new version of the API for which we will write units tests, which are the topic of the next chapter.

11
Working with Asynchronous Code, Testing, and Deploying an API with Tornado

In this chapter, we will take advantage of the non-blocking features combined with asynchronous operations in Tornado 5.1.1 in a new version of the API we built in the previous chapter. We will configure, write, and execute unit tests, and learn a few things related to deployment. We will do the following:

- Understand synchronous and asynchronous execution
- Work with asynchronous code
- Refactor code to take advantage of asynchronous decorators
- Map URL patterns to asynchronous and non-blocking request handlers
- Make HTTP requests to the Tornado non-blocking API
- Set up unit tests with `pytest`
- Write the first round of unit tests
- Run unit tests with `pytest` and check testing coverage
- Improve testing coverage
- Understand strategies for deploying Tornado APIs to the cloud

Understanding synchronous and asynchronous execution

In our current version of the RESTful API built with Tornado 5.1.1, each HTTP request is blocking. Hence, whenever the Tornado HTTP server receives an HTTP request, it doesn't start working on any other HTTP requests in the incoming queue until the server sends the response for the first HTTP request is received. The methods we coded in the request handlers are working with a synchronous execution and don't take advantage of the non-blocking features included in Tornado when combined with asynchronous executions.

In order to set the brightness level for the red, green, and blue LEDs, we have to make three HTTP PATCH requests. We will make these requests to understand how our current version of the API processes three incoming requests.

Make sure the Tornado 5.1.1 development server is running. Open three additional Terminals in macOS or Linux, or Command Prompt or Windows PowerShell windows in Windows. Activate the virtual environment in which we have been working for our RESTful API with Tornado in each of the windows. We will run commands in the three windows.

Write the following command in the first window. The command will compose and send an HTTP PATCH request to set the brightness level for the red LED to 255. Write the line in the first window but don't press *Enter* yet, as we will try to launch three commands at almost the same time in three windows. The code file for the sample is included in the restful_python_2_11_01 folder, in the Tornado01/cmd/cmd1201.txt file:

```
http PATCH ":8888/leds/1" brightness_level=255
```

The following is the equivalent curl command. The code file for the sample is included in the restful_python_2_11_01 folder, in the Tornado01/cmd/cmd1202.txt file:

```
curl -iX PATCH -H "Content-Type: application/json" -d
'{"brightness_level":255}' "localhost:8888/leds/1"
```

Now, go to the second window and write the following command. The command will compose and send an HTTP PATCH request to set the brightness level for the green LED to 128. Write the line in the second window but don't press *Enter* yet, as we will try to launch two commands at almost the same time in three windows. The code file for the sample is included in the restful_python_2_11_01 folder, in the Tornado01/cmd/cmd1203.txt file:

```
http PATCH ":8888/leds/2" brightness_level=128
```

The following is the equivalent `curl` command. The code file for the sample is included in the `restful_python_2_11_01` folder, in the `Tornado01/cmd/cmd1204.txt` file:

```
curl -iX PATCH -H "Content-Type: application/json" -d
'{"brightness_level":128}' "localhost:8888/leds/2"
```

Now, go to the third window and write the following command. The command will compose and send an HTTP `PATCH` request to set the brightness level for the blue LED to `64`. Write the line in the third window but don't press *Enter* yet, as we will try to launch two commands at almost the same time in three windows. The code file for the sample is included in the `restful_python_2_11_01` folder, in the `Tornado01/cmd/cmd1205.txt` file:

```
http PATCH ":8888/leds/3" brightness_level=64
```

The following is the equivalent `curl` command. The code file for the sample is included in the `restful_python_2_11_01` folder, in the `Tornado01/cmd/cmd1206.txt` file:

```
curl -iX PATCH -H "Content-Type: application/json" -d
'{"brightness_level":64}' "localhost:8888/leds/3"
```

Now, go to each window, from the first to the third, and press *Enter* quickly in each of them. You will see the following line in the window that is running the Tornado HTTP server for a few seconds:

```
I've started setting the Red LED's brightness level
```

After a few seconds, you will see the following lines, which show the results of executing the print statements that describe when the code finished and then start setting the brightness levels for the LEDs:

```
I've started setting the Red LED's brightness level
I've finished setting the Red LED's brightness level
I've started setting the Green LED's brightness level
I've finished setting the Green LED's brightness level
I've started setting the Blue LED's brightness level
I've finished setting the Blue LED's brightness level
```

It was necessary to wait for the request that changed the brightness level for the red LED to finish before the server could process the HTTP request that changes the brightness level for the green LED. The HTTP request that changes the brightness level for the blue LED had to wait for the other two requests to finish their execution first.

The following screenshot shows four Terminal windows on macOS. The window on the left-hand side is running the Tornado 5.1.1 HTTP server and displays the messages printed in the methods that process the HTTP requests. The three windows on the right run the `http` command to generate the HTTP `PATCH` request that changes the brightness levels for the red, green, and blue LEDs. It is a good idea to use a similar configuration to check the output while we compose and send the HTTP requests, and thus understand how the synchronous execution is working in the current version of the API:

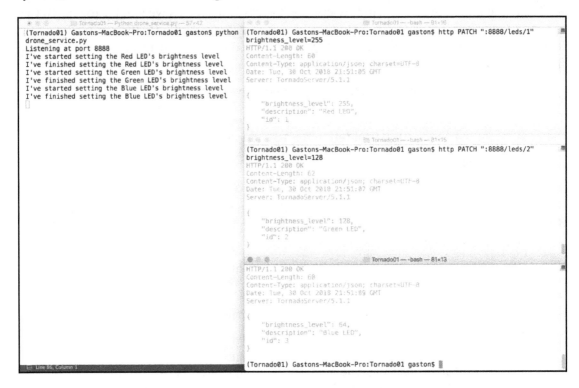

Remember that the different methods we coded in the request handler classes end up calling `time.sleep` to simulate it taking some time for the operations to complete their execution.

Refactoring code to take advantage of asynchronous decorators

As each operation takes some time and blocks the possibility to process other incoming HTTP requests, we will create a new version of this API that will use asynchronous execution, and we will understand the advantages of Tornado's non-blocking features. This way, it will be possible to change the brightness level for the red LED while another request is changing the brightness level for the green LED. Tornado will be able to start processing requests while the I/O operations with the drone take some time to complete.

Make sure you quit the Tornado HTTP server. You just need to press *Ctrl + C* in the Terminal or Command Prompt window in which it is running.

Tornado 5.1.1 provides a generator-based interface that enables us to write asynchronous code in request handlers in a single generator. We don't need to split our methods into multiple methods with callbacks using the `tornado.gen` generator-based interface that Tornado provides to make it easier to work in an asynchronous environment.

The recommended way to write asynchronous code in Tornado is to use coroutines. We will refactor our existing code to use the `@tornado.gen.coroutine` decorator for asynchronous generators in the required methods that process the different HTTP requests in the subclasses of the `RequestHandler` superclass.

 Instead of working with a chain of callbacks, coroutines use the Python `yield` keyword to suspend and resume execution. By using coroutines, our code is going to be as simple to understand and maintain as if we were writing synchronous code.

We will use an instance of the `concurrent.futures.ThreadPoolExecutor` class that provides us with a high-level interface for asynchronously executing callables. Asynchronous execution will be performed with threads. We will also use the `@tornado.concurrent.run_on_executor` decorator to run a synchronous method asynchronously on an executor. In this case, the methods used to get and set data, and provided by the different components of our drone, use synchronous execution. We want them to run with an asynchronous execution.

Create a new Python file named `async_drone_service.py` in the root folder for the virtual environment (`Tornado01`). The following lines show all the necessary imports for the classes that we will create and the code that creates an instance of the `concurrent.futures.ThreadPoolExecutor` class named `thread_pool_executor`. The new lines are highlighted compared with the code in the previous `drone_service.py` file. We will use this instance in the different methods that we will refactor to make asynchronous calls. The code file for the sample is included in the `restful_python_2_11_01` folder, in the `Django01/async_drone_service.py` file:

```python
from http import HTTPStatus
from concurrent.futures import ThreadPoolExecutor
from datetime import date
from tornado import web, escape, ioloop, httpclient, gen
from tornado.concurrent import run_on_executor
from drone import Altimeter, Hexacopter, LightEmittingDiode, Drone


thread_pool_executor = ThreadPoolExecutor()
drone = Drone()
```

Stay in the `async_drone_service.py` file in the root folder for the virtual environment (`Tornado01`). Add the following lines to declare an `AsyncHexacopterHandler` class, which we will use to handle requests for the hexacopter resource with an asynchronous execution. The lines that are added or edited compared with the synchronous version of this handler, named `HexacopterHandler`, are highlighted. The code file for the sample is included in the `restful_python_2_11_01` folder, in the `Django01/async_drone_service.py` file:

```python
class AsyncHexacopterHandler(web.RequestHandler):
    SUPPORTED_METHODS = ("GET", "PATCH")
    HEXACOPTER_ID = 1
    _thread_pool_executor = thread_pool_executor

    @gen.coroutine
    def get(self, id):
        if int(id) is not self.__class__.HEXACOPTER_ID:
            self.set_status(HTTPStatus.NOT_FOUND)
            self.finish()
            return
        print("I've started retrieving the hexacopter's status")
        hexacopter_status = yield
self.retrieve_hexacopter_status()
        print("I've finished retrieving the hexacopter's status")
        response = {
            'motor_speed_in_rpm': hexacopter_status.motor_speed,
```

```
                'is_turned_on': hexacopter_status.is_turned_on,}
            self.set_status(HTTPStatus.OK)
            self.write(response)
            self.finish()

    @run_on_executor(executor="_thread_pool_executor")
    def retrieve_hexacopter_status(self):
        return drone.hexacopter.status
    @gen.coroutine
    def patch(self, id):
        if int(id) is not self.__class__.HEXACOPTER_ID:
            self.set_status(HTTPStatus.NOT_FOUND)
            self.finish()
            return
        request_data = escape.json_decode(self.request.body)
        if ('motor_speed_in_rpm' not in request_data.keys()) or \
            (request_data['motor_speed_in_rpm'] is None):
            self.set_status(HTTPStatus.BAD_REQUEST)
            self.finish()
            return
        try:
            motor_speed = int(request_data['motor_speed_in_rpm'])
            print("I've started setting the hexacopter's motor speed")
            hexacopter_status = yield
self.set_hexacopter_motor_speed(motor_speed)
            print("I've finished setting the hexacopter's motor speed")
            response = {
                'motor_speed_in_rpm': hexacopter_status.motor_speed,
                'is_turned_on': hexacopter_status.is_turned_on,}
            self.set_status(HTTPStatus.OK)
            self.write(response)
            self.finish()
        except ValueError as e:
            print("I've failed setting the hexacopter's motor speed")
            self.set_status(HTTPStatus.BAD_REQUEST)
            response = {
                'error': e.args[0]}
            self.write(response)
            self.finish()

    @run_on_executor(executor="_thread_pool_executor")
    def set_hexacopter_motor_speed(self, motor_speed):
        drone.hexacopter.motor_speed = motor_speed
        hexacopter_status = drone.hexacopter.status
        return hexacopter_status
```

The `AsyncHexacopterHandler` class declares a `_thread_pool_executor` class attribute that saves a reference to the previously created `concurrent.futures.ThreadPoolExecutor` instance. The class declares the following two methods with the `@run_on_executor(executor="_thread_pool_executor")` decorator, which makes a synchronous method run asynchronously with the `concurrent.futures.ThreadPoolExecutor` instance, whose reference is saved in the `_thread_pool_executor` class attribute:

- `retrieve_hexacopter_status`: This method returns the value of the `drone.hexacopter.status` property
- `set_hexacopter_motor_speed`: This method receives the `motor_speed` argument, assigns this value to the `drone.hexacopter.motor_speed` property, and returns the value of the `drone.hexacopter.status` property

We added the `@gen.coroutine` decorator to the `get` and `patch` methods. We added a call to `self.finish` whenever we wanted to finish the HTTP request. It is our responsibility to call this method to finish the response and end the HTTP request when we use the `@gen.coroutine` decorator.

The `get` method uses the following line to retrieve the hexacopter status with a non-blocking and asynchronous execution:

```
hexacopter_status = yield self.retrieve_hexacopter_status()
```

The code uses the `yield` keyword to retrieve the `HexacopterStatus` instance from `Future`, returned by the `self.retrieve_hexacopter_status` method, which runs with an asynchronous execution.

`Future` encapsulates the asynchronous execution of a callable. In this case, `Future` encapsulates the asynchronous execution of the `self.retrieve_hexacopter_status` method.

The next lines for the `get` method didn't require changes, and we only had to add a call to `self.finish` as the last line after we write the response.

The `patch` method uses the following line to set the hexacopter's motor speed with a non-blocking and asynchronous execution:

```
hexacopter_status = yield self.set_hexacopter_motor_speed(motor_speed)
```

The code uses the `yield` keyword to retrieve the `HexacopterStatus` instance from `Future`, returned by `self.set_hexacopter_motor_speed`, which runs with an asynchronous execution. The next lines for `patch` didn't require changes, and we only had to add a call to `self.finish` as the last line after we write the response.

Stay in the `async_drone_service.py` file in the root folder for the virtual environment (`Tornado01`). Add the following lines to declare an `AsyncLedHandler` class, which we will use to represent the LED resources and process requests with an asynchronous execution. The lines that are new or edited, compared to the synchronous version of this handler, named `LedHandler`, are highlighted. The code file for the sample is included in the `restful_python_2_11_01` folder, in the `Django01/async_drone_service.py` file:

```
class AsyncLedHandler(web.RequestHandler):
    SUPPORTED_METHODS = ("GET", "PATCH")
    _thread_pool_executor = thread_pool_executor

    @gen.coroutine
    def get(self, id):
        int_id = int(id)
        if int_id not in drone.leds.keys():
            self.set_status(HTTPStatus.NOT_FOUND)
            self.finish()
            return
        led = drone.leds[int_id]
        print("I've started retrieving {0}'s
status".format(led.description))
        brightness_level = yield self.retrieve_led_brightness_level(led)
        print("I've finished retrieving {0}'s
status".format(led.description))
        response = {
            'id': led.id,
            'description': led.description,
            'brightness_level': brightness_level}
        self.set_status(HTTPStatus.OK)
        self.write(response)
        self.finish()

    @run_on_executor(executor="_thread_pool_executor")
    def retrieve_led_brightness_level(self, led):
        return led.brightness_level

    @gen.coroutine
    def patch(self, id):
        int_id = int(id)
        if int_id not in drone.leds.keys():
            self.set_status(HTTPStatus.NOT_FOUND)
```

```
            self.finish()
            return
        led = drone.leds[int_id]
        request_data = escape.json_decode(self.request.body)
        if ('brightness_level' not in request_data.keys()) or \
            (request_data['brightness_level'] is None):
            self.set_status(HTTPStatus.BAD_REQUEST)
            self.finish()
            return
        try:
            brightness_level = int(request_data['brightness_level'])
            print("I've started setting the {0}'s brightness
level".format(led.description))
            yield self.set_led_brightness_level(led, brightness_level)
            print("I've finished setting the {0}'s brightness
level".format(led.description))
            response = {
                'id': led.id,
                'description': led.description,
                'brightness_level': brightness_level}
            self.set_status(HTTPStatus.OK)
            self.write(response)
            self.finish()
        except ValueError as e:
            print("I've failed setting the {0}'s brightness
level".format(led.description))
            self.set_status(HTTPStatus.BAD_REQUEST)
            response = {
                'error': e.args[0]}
            self.write(response)
            self.finish()

    @run_on_executor(executor="_thread_pool_executor")
    def set_led_brightness_level(self, led, brightness_level):
        led.brightness_level = brightness_level
```

The `AsyncLedHandler` class declares a `_thread_pool_executor` class attribute, which
saves a reference to the previously created `concurrent.futures.ThreadPoolExecutor`
instance. The class has the following two methods with the
`@run_on_executor(executor="_thread_pool_executor")` decorator, which makes
each synchronous method run asynchronously with the `ThreadPoolExecutor` instance,
whose reference is saved in the `_thread_pool_executor` class attribute:

- `retrieve_led_brightness_level`: This method receives a
  `LightEmittingDiode` instance in the `led` argument and returns the value of the
  `led.brightness_level` property.

- `set_led_brightness_level`: This method receives a `LightEmittingDiode` instance in the `led` argument and the `brightness_level` argument. The code assigns the received brightness level to the `led.brightness_level` property.

We added the `@gen.coroutine` decorator to the `get` and `patch` methods. In addition, we added a call to `self.finish` whenever we wanted to finish the HTTP request.

The `get` method uses the following line to retrieve the LED's brightness level with a non-blocking and asynchronous execution:

```
brightness_level = yield self.retrieve_led_brightness_level(led)
```

The code uses the `yield` keyword to retrieve `int` from `Future` returned by `self.retrieve_led_brightness_level`, which runs with an asynchronous execution. The next lines for the `get` method didn't require changes, and we only had to add a call to `self.finish` as the last line after we wrote the response.

The `patch` method uses the following line to set the brightness level for a LED with a non-blocking and asynchronous execution:

```
yield self.set_led_brightness_level(led, brightness_level)
```

The code uses the `yield` keyword to call `self.set_led_brightness_level` with an asynchronous execution. The next lines didn't require changes, and we only had to add a call to `self.finish` as the last line after we write the response.

Stay in the `async_drone_service.py` file in the root folder for the virtual environment (`Tornado01`). Add the following lines to declare an `AsyncAltimeterHandler` class that we will use to represent the altimeter resource and process the `get` request with an asynchronous execution. The lines that are new or edited, compared to the synchronous version of this handler named `AltimeterHandler`, are highlighted. The code file for the sample is included in the `restful_python_2_11_01` folder, in the `Django01/async_drone_service.py` file:

```
class AsyncAltimeterHandler(web.RequestHandler):
    SUPPORTED_METHODS = ("GET")
    ALTIMETER_ID = 1
    _thread_pool_executor = thread_pool_executor

    @gen.coroutine
    def get(self, id):
        if int(id) is not self.__class__.ALTIMETER_ID:
            self.set_status(HTTPStatus.NOT_FOUND)
            self.finish()
```

```
        return
    unit = self.get_arguments(name='unit')
    if 'meters' in unit:
        altitude_multiplier = 0.3048
        response_unit = 'meters'
    else:
        altitude_multiplier = 1
        response_unit = 'feet'
    print("I've started retrieving the altitude")
    altitude_in_feet = yield self.retrieve_altitude_in_feet()
    altitude = round(altitude_in_feet * altitude_multiplier, 4)
    print("I've finished retrieving the altitude")
    response = {
        'altitude': altitude,
        'unit': response_unit}
    self.set_status(HTTPStatus.OK)
    self.write(response)
    self.finish()

@run_on_executor(executor="_thread_pool_executor")
def retrieve_altitude_in_feet(self):
    return drone.altimeter.altitude
```

The `AsyncAltimeterHandler` class declares a `_thread_pool_executor` class attribute, which saves a reference to the previously created `ThreadPoolExecutor` instance. The class declares the `retrieve_altitude_in_feet` method with the `@run_on_executor(executor="_thread_pool_executor")` decorator, which makes the synchronous method run asynchronously with the `ThreadPoolExecutor` instance, whose reference is saved in the `_thread_pool_executor` class attribute. The `retrieve_altitude` method returns the value of the `drone.altimeter.altitude` property.

We added the `@gen.coroutine` decorator to the `get` method. In addition, we added a call to `self.finish` whenever we wanted to finish the HTTP request.

The `get` method uses the following line to retrieve the altimeter's altitude value, expressed in feet, with a non-blocking and asynchronous execution:

```
altitude_in_feet = yield self.retrieve_altitude_in_feet()
```

The code uses the `yield` keyword to retrieve `int` from `Future` returned by `self.retrieve_altitude_in_feet`, which runs with an asynchronous execution. The next line multiplies the `altitude_in_feet` variable by the value stored in the `altitude_multiplier` variable and rounds the result to four decimal places. The next lines didn't require changes, and we only had to add a call to `self.finish` as the last line after we write the response.

Mapping URL patterns to asynchronous request handlers

Stay in the `async_drone_service.py` file in the root folder for the virtual environment (`Tornado01`). Add the following lines to map URL patterns to our previously coded subclasses of the `RequestHandler` superclass, which provide us with asynchronous methods for our request handlers. The following lines create the main entry point for the application, initialize it with the URL patterns for the API, and start listening for requests. The lines that are new or edited, compared to the synchronous version, are highlighted. The code file for the sample is included in the `restful_python_2_11_01` folder, in the `Django01/async_drone_service.py` file:

```python
class Application(web.Application):
    def __init__(self, **kwargs):
        handlers = [
            (r"/hexacopters/([0-9]+)", AsyncHexacopterHandler),
            (r"/leds/([0-9]+)", AsyncLedHandler),
            (r"/altimeters/([0-9]+)", AsyncAltimeterHandler),
        ]
        super(Application, self).__init__(handlers, **kwargs)


if __name__ == "__main__":
    application = Application()
    port = 8888
    print("Listening at port {0}".format(port))
    application.listen(port)
    tornado_ioloop = ioloop.IOLoop.instance()
    periodic_callback = ioloop.PeriodicCallback(lambda: None, 500)
    periodic_callback.start()
    tornado_ioloop.start()
```

The code creates an instance of `tornado.web.Application`, named `application`, with the collection of request handlers that make up the web application. We just changed the name of the handlers for the new names that have the `Async` prefix.

Making HTTP requests to the Tornado non-blocking API

Now, we can run the `drone_service.py` script, which launches the development server for Tornado 5.1.1 to our new version of the web API that uses the non-blocking features of Tornado, combined with an asynchronous execution. Make sure that the `drone_service.py` script is not running anymore. Execute the following command:

```
python async_drone_service.py
```

The following line shows the output after we execute the previous command. The Tornado HTTP development server is listening at port `8888`:

```
Listening at port 8888
```

In our new version of the API, each HTTP request is non-blocking. Thus, whenever the Tornado HTTP server receives an HTTP request and makes an asynchronous call, it is able to start working on any other HTTP requests in the incoming queue before the server sends the response that the first HTTP request is received. The methods we coded in the request handlers work with an asynchronous execution and take advantage of the non-blocking features included in Tornado, combined with asynchronous execution.

In our previous example, we executed three HTTP `PATCH` requests to set the brightness levels for the red, green, and blue LEDs. We will run them again with the same Windows configurations we used before to understand how our new version of the API processes three incoming requests.

Use the history features for the Terminal, Command Prompt, or Windows PowerShell window to enter the commands again in each window that executed the previous HTTP `PATCH` request. As we did before, do not press *Enter* yet, just leave the commands written.

Now, go to each window that has the commands to compose and send the HTTP `PATCH` request, from the first to the third window and press *Enter* quickly in each of them. You will see the following lines in the window that is running the Tornado HTTP server:

```
I've started setting the Red LED's brightness level
I've started setting the Green LED's brightness level
I've started setting the Blue LED's brightness level
```

Then, you will see the following lines, which show the results of executing the print statements that describe when the code finished setting the brightness level for the three LEDs:

```
I've finished setting the Red LED's brightness level
I've finished setting the Green LED's brightness level
I've finished setting the Blue LED's brightness level
```

The server could start processing the request that changes the brightness level for the green LED before the request that changes the brightness level of the red LED finishes its execution. In addition, the server could start processing the request that changes the brightness level for the blue LED before the other two requests finish their execution.

The following screenshot shows four Terminal windows on macOS. The window on the left-hand side is running the Tornado 5.1.1 HTTP server and displays the messages printed in the methods that process the HTTP requests. The three windows on the right run the `http` command to generate the HTTP `PATCH` request that changes the brightness level for the red, green, and blue LEDs. It is a good idea to use a similar configuration to check the output while we compose and send the HTTP requests and understand how the asynchronous execution works on the new version of the API:

Each operation takes some time but doesn't block the possibility of processing other incoming HTTP requests, thanks to the changes we made to the API to take advantage of asynchronous execution. This way, it is possible to change the brightness level for the red LED while another request is changing the brightness level for the green LED. Tornado is able to start processing requests while the I/O operations with the drone take some time to complete.

Setting up unit tests with pytest

Make sure you quit the Django development server. You just need to press *Ctrl + C* in the Terminal or Command Prompt window in which it is running.

Now, we will install many additional packages to be able to easily run tests and measure their code coverage. Make sure you have activated the virtual environment that we created in the previous chapter, named `Tornado01`. After you activate the virtual environment, it is time to run many commands that will be the same for macOS, Linux, and Windows.

Now, we will edit the existing `requirements.txt` file to specify the additional packages that our application requires to be installed on any supported platform. This way, it will be extremely easy to repeat the installation of the specified packages with their versions in any new virtual environment.

Use your favorite editor to edit the existing text file, named `requirements.txt`, within the root folder for the virtual environment. Add the following lines after the last line to declare the additional packages that we require. The code file for the sample is included in the `restful_python_2_11_01` folder, in the `Tornado01/requirements.txt` file:

```
pytest==3.9.3
coverage==4.5.1
pytest-cov==2.6.0
pytest-tornasync==0.5.0
```

Each additional line added to the `requirements.txt` file indicates the package and the version that need to be installed.

The following table summarizes the packages and the version numbers that we specified as additional requirements to the previously included packages:

Package name	Version to be installed
pytest	4.0.2
coverage	4.5.2
pytest-cov	2.6.0
pytest-tornasync	0.5.0

We will install the following Python packages in our virtual environment:

- pytest: This is a very popular Python unit test framework that makes testing easy and reduces boilerplate code.
- coverage: This tool measures code coverage of Python programs and we will use it to determine which parts of the code are being executed by unit tests and which parts aren't.
- pytest-cov: This plugin for pytest makes it easy to produce coverage reports that use the coverage tool under the hood and provides some additional features.
- pytest-tornasync: This plugin for pytest provides fixtures to make it easier to test Tornado asynchronous code with pytest.

Now, we must run the following command on macOS, Linux, or Windows to install the additional packages and the versions outlined in the previous table with pip, using the recently edited requirements.txt file. Make sure you are located in the folder that has the requirements.txt file before running the command:

```
pip install -r requirements.txt
```

The last lines for the output will indicate whether all the new packages and their dependencies have been successfully installed. If you downloaded the source code for the example and you didn't work with the previous version of the API, pip will also install the other packages included in the requirements.txt file:

```
Installing collected packages: pytest, coverage, pytest-cov, pytest-tornasync
Successfully installed coverage-4.5.2 pytest-4.0.2 pytest-cov-2.6.0 pytest-tornasync-0.5.0
```

Create a new `setup.cfg` file in the root folder for the virtual environment (`Tornado01`). The following lines show the code that specifies the desired configuration for `pytest` and the `coverage` tools. The code file for the sample is included in the `restful_python_2_11_01` folder, in the `Tornado01/setup.cfg` file:

```
[tool:pytest]
testpaths = tests.py

[coverage:run]
branch = True
source =
    drone
    async_drone_service
```

The `tool:pytest` section specifies the configuration for `pytest`. The `testpaths` setting assigns the `tests.py` value to indicate that the tests are located in the `tests.py` file.

The `coverage:run` section specifies the configuration for the `coverage` tool. The `branch` setting is set to `True` to enable branch coverage measurement in addition to the default statement coverage. The `source` setting specifies the modules that we want to be considered for coverage measurement. We just want to include the `drone` and `async_drone_service` modules.

In this case, we won't be using configuration files for each environment. However, in more complex applications, you will definitely want to use configuration files.

Writing the first round of unit tests

Now, we will write the first round of unit tests. Specifically, we will write unit tests related to the LED resources. Test fixtures provide a fixed baseline to enable us to reliably and repeatedly execute tests. Pytest makes it easy to declare a test fixture function by marking a function with the `@pytest.fixture` decorator. Then, whenever we use the fixture function name as an argument in a test function declaration, `pytest` will make the fixture function provide the fixture object.

The `pytest-tornasync` plugin provides us with many fixtures that we will use to easily write tests for our Tornado API. In order to work with this plugin, we must declare a fixture function, named `app`, that returns a `tornado.web.Application` instance. In our case, this fixture function will return an instance of the `Application` class, which maps the URL patterns to asynchronous and non-blocking request handlers. We don't need to specify an `app` as an argument for the test functions, because the `pytest-tornadoasync` plugin will use the `app` fixture under the hood in other fixtures, such as the `http_server_client` fixture, which we will use to create an asynchronous HTTP client to compose and send HTTP requests in our tests.

Create a new `tests.py` file within the virtual environment's root folder (`Tornado01`). Add the following lines, which declare many `import` statements, the `app` fixture, and the `test_set_and_get_leds_brightness_levels` test function. The code file for the sample is included in the `restful_python_2_11_01` folder, in the `Tornado01/tests.py` file:

```python
from async_drone_service import Application
from http import HTTPStatus
import json
import pytest
from tornado import escape
from tornado.httpclient import HTTPClientError


@pytest.fixture
def app():
    application = Application(debug=False)
    return application


async def test_set_and_get_leds_brightness_levels(http_server_client):
    """
    Ensure we can set and get the brightness levels for the three LEDs
    """
    for led_id in range(1, 4):
        patch_args = {'brightness_level': led_id * 60}
        patch_response = await http_server_client.fetch(
            '/leds/{}'.format(led_id),
            method='PATCH',
            body=json.dumps(patch_args))
        assert patch_response.code == HTTPStatus.OK
        get_response = await http_server_client.fetch(
            '/leds/{}'.format(led_id),
            method='GET')
```

```
        assert get_response.code == HTTPStatus.OK
        get_response_data = escape.json_decode(get_response.body)
        assert 'brightness_level' in get_response_data.keys()
        assert get_response_data['brightness_level'] == \
            patch_args['brightness_level']
```

First, the code declares the app fixture function, which creates an instance of the Application class, defined in the async_drone_service module with the debug argument set to False, and returns the instance.

The test_set_and_get_leds_brightness_levels asynchronous method tests whether we can set and get the brightness levels for the red, green, and blue LEDs. The code composes and sends three HTTP PATCH methods to set new brightness level values for the LEDs whose IDs are equal to 1, 2, and 3. The code sets a different brightness level for each LED. Notice that the method is declared with the async keyword before def to indicate that the method is an asynchronous method, that is, a coroutine.

The method uses the test client received in the http_server_client argument, which provides an asynchronous HTTP client for tests and calls its fetch method to compose and send the HTTP PATCH requests. http_server_client fetches the app fixture that we defined.

Notice that the call to this method uses the await keyword to obtain the result of the coroutine execution. The code calls json.dumps with the dictionary to be sent as the body of an argument for the fetch method.

Then, the code uses the http_server_client.fetch method again with the await keyword to compose and send HTTP GET methods to retrieve the brightness level values for the LEDs whose brightness values have been modified. The code uses tornado.escape.json_decode to convert the bytes in the response body to a Python dictionary. The method uses assert to check for the following expected results for each LED:

- The status_code for the HTTP PATCH response is HTTP 200 OK (HTTPStatus.OK)
- The status_code for the HTTP GET response is HTTP 200 OK (HTTPStatus.OK)

- The response body for the HTTP GET response includes a key named brigthness_level
- The value for the brightness_level key in the HTTP GET response matches the brightness level set to the LED

Running unit tests with pytest and checking testing coverage

Now, we will use the pytest command to run tests and measure their code coverage. Make sure you run the command in the Terminal or Command Prompt window in which you have activated the virtual environment, and that you are located within its root folder (Tornado01). Run the following command:

```
pytest --cov -v
```

The test runner will execute all the functions defined in tests.py that start with the test_ prefix, and will display the results. We use the -v option to instruct pytest to print the test function names and statuses in verbose mode. The --cov option turns on test coverage report generation with the use of the pytest-cov plugin.

The following lines show the sample output:

```
============================================= test session starts
=============================================
platform darwin -- Python 3.7.1, pytest-4.0.2, py-1.7.0, pluggy-0.8.0 --
/Users/gaston/HillarPythonREST2/Tornado01/bin/python3
cachedir: .pytest_cache
rootdir: /Users/gaston/HillarPythonREST2/Tornado01, inifile:
setup.cfg
plugins: tornasync-0.5.0, cov-2.6.0
collected 1 item
tests.py::test_set_and_get_leds_brightness_levels PASSED
[100%]
---------- coverage: platform darwin, python 3.6.6-final-0 -----------
-
Name                      Stmts   Miss Branch BrPart   Cover
----------------------------------------------------------------
async_drone_service.py      141     81     20      4     40%
drone.py                     63     23     10      3     59%
----------------------------------------------------------------
TOTAL                       204    104     30      7     46%
```

The output provides details that the test runner discovered and executed one test, which passed. The output displays the module and function names for each method in the `test_views` module that started with the `test_` prefix and represented a test to be executed.

The test code coverage measurement report provided by the `coverage` package, in combination with the `pytest-cov` plugin, uses the code analysis tools and the tracing hooks included in the Python standard library to determine which lines of code are executable and which of these lines have been executed. The report provides a table with the columns we examined in Chapter 4, *Testing and Deploying an API in a Microservice with Flask*, in the section named *Running unit tests with pytest and checking testing coverage*.

We definitely have a very low coverage for the `async_drone_service.py` and `drone.py` modules, based on the measurements shown in the report. In fact, we just wrote one test related to LEDs, and therefore it makes sense that the coverage has to be improved. We didn't create tests related to other hexacopter resources.

Now, run the `coverage` command with the `-m` command-line option to display the line numbers of the missing statements in a new `Missing` column:

```
coverage report -m
```

The command will use the information from the last execution and will display the missing statements and the missing branches. The next lines show a sample output that corresponds to the previous execution of the unit tests. A dash (–) is used to indicate a range of lines that were missed. For example, `107-109` means that lines `107` and `109` were missing statements. A dash followed by a greater than sign (–>) indicates that the branch from the line before –> to the line after it was missed. For example, `61->62` means that the branch from line `61` to line `62` was missed:

```
Name                      Stmts   Miss Branch BrPart   Cover   Missing
-------------------------------------------------------------------------
async_drone_service.py      141     81     20      4     40%    20-32, 36,
40-67, 71-73, 84-86, 107-109, 114-116, 129-135, 148-168, 172, 186-193,
83->84, 106->107, 112->114, 185->186
drone.py                     63     23     10      3     59%    7-8, 21,
25-31, 35, 39-40, 60, 62, 70-71, 88-93, 59->60, 61->62, 87->88
-------------------------------------------------------------------------
TOTAL                       204    104     30      7     46%
```

Now, run the following command to get annotated HTML listings detailing missed lines. The command won't produce any output:

```
coverage html
```

Open the `index.html` HTML file generated in the `htmlcov` folder with your web browser. The following screenshot shows an example report coverage generated in HTML format:

Coverage report: 46%						filter...
Module ↓	*statements*	*missing*	*excluded*	*branches*	*partial*	*coverage*
async_drone_service.py	141	81	0	20	4	40%
drone.py	63	23	0	10	3	59%
Total	**204**	**104**	**0**	**30**	**7**	**46%**

coverage.py v4.5.1, created at 2018-10-31 15:06

Click or tap `async_drone_service.py` and the web browser will render a web page that displays the statements that were run, the missing ones, the excluded, and the partially executed with different colors. We can click or tap on the **run**, **missing**, **excluded**, and **partial** buttons to show or hide the background color that represents the status for each line of code. By default, the missing lines of code will be displayed with a pink background, and those partially executed will be displayed with a yellow background. Thus, we must write unit tests that target these lines of code to improve our test coverage.

The following screenshot shows the buttons with the summary:

Coverage for **async_drone_service.py** : 40%

141 statements	60 run	81 missing	0 excluded	4 partial

```python
1   from http import HTTPStatus
2   from concurrent.futures import ThreadPoolExecutor
3   from datetime import date
4   from tornado import web, escape, ioloop, httpclient, gen
5   from tornado.concurrent import run_on_executor
6   from drone import Altimeter, Hexacopter, LightEmittingDiode, Drone
7
8
9   thread_pool_executor = ThreadPoolExecutor()
10  drone = Drone()
11
12
13  class AsyncHexacopterHandler(web.RequestHandler):
14      SUPPORTED_METHODS = ("GET", "PATCH")
15      HEXACOPTER_ID = 1
16      _thread_pool_executor = thread_pool_executor
17
18      @gen.coroutine
19      def get(self, id):
20          if int(id) is not self.__class__.HEXACOPTER_ID:
21              self.set_status(HTTPStatus.NOT_FOUND)
22              self.finish()
23              return
24          print("I've started retrieving the hexacopter's status")
25          hexacopter_status = yield self.retrieve_hexacopter_status()
26          print("I've finished retrieving the hexacopter's status")
27          response = {
28              'motor_speed_in_rpm': hexacopter_status.motor_speed,
29              'is_turned_on': hexacopter_status.is_turned_on,}
30          self.set_status(HTTPStatus.OK)
31          self.write(response)
32          self.finish()
33
34      @run_on_executor(executor="_thread_pool_executor")
35      def retrieve_hexacopter_status(self):
36          return drone.hexacopter.status
37
38      @gen.coroutine
39      def patch(self, id):
40          if int(id) is not self.__class__.HEXACOPTER_ID:
41              self.set_status(HTTPStatus.NOT_FOUND)
```

The next screenshot shows the highlighted missing lines and the partially evaluated branches for some lines of code in the `async_drone_service.py` module:

```
103    @gen.coroutine
104    def patch(self, id):
105        int_id = int(id)
106        if int_id not in drone.leds.keys():                                    106→107
107            self.set_status(HTTPStatus.NOT_FOUND)
108            self.finish()
109            return
110        led = drone.leds[int_id]
111        request_data = escape.json_decode(self.request.body)
112        if ('brightness_level' not in request_data.keys()) or \               112→114
113            (request_data['brightness_level'] is None):
114            self.set_status(HTTPStatus.BAD_REQUEST)
115            self.finish()
116            return
117        try:
118            brightness_level = int(request_data['brightness_level'])
119            print("I've started setting the {0}'s brightness level".format(led.description))
120            yield self.set_led_brightness_level(led, brightness_level)
121            print("I've finished setting the {0}'s brightness level".format(led.description))
122            response = {
123                'id': led.id,
124                'description': led.description,
125                'brightness_level': brightness_level}
126            self.set_status(HTTPStatus.OK)
127            self.write(response)
128            self.finish()
129        except ValueError as e:
130            print("I've failed setting the {0}'s brightness level".format(led.description))
131            self.set_status(HTTPStatus.BAD_REQUEST)
132            response = {
133                'error': e.args[0]}
134            self.write(response)
135            self.finish()
136
```

Improving testing coverage

Now, we will write additional unit tests to improve the testing coverage. Specifically, we will write unit tests related to the hexacopter motor and the altimeter.

Open the `tests.py` file in the root folder for the virtual environment (`Tornado01`). Insert the following lines after the last line. The code file for the sample is included in the `restful_python_2_11_02` folder, in the `Django01/tests.py` file:

```python
async def
test_set_and_get_hexacopter_motor_speed(http_server_client):
    """
    Ensure we can set and get the hexacopter's motor speed
    """
    patch_args = {'motor_speed_in_rpm': 200}
    patch_response = await http_server_client.fetch(
        '/hexacopters/1',
        method='PATCH',
        body=json.dumps(patch_args))
    assert patch_response.code == HTTPStatus.OK
    get_response = await http_server_client.fetch(
        '/hexacopters/1',
        method='GET')
    assert get_response.code == HTTPStatus.OK
    get_response_data = escape.json_decode(get_response.body)
    assert 'motor_speed_in_rpm' in get_response_data.keys()
    assert 'is_turned_on' in get_response_data.keys()
    assert get_response_data['motor_speed_in_rpm'] ==
patch_args['motor_speed_in_rpm']
    assert get_response_data['is_turned_on']


async def
test_get_altimeter_altitude_in_feet(http_server_client):
    """
    Ensure we can get the altimeter's altitude in feet
    """
    get_response = await http_server_client.fetch(
        '/altimeters/1',
        method='GET')
    assert get_response.code == HTTPStatus.OK
    get_response_data = escape.json_decode(get_response.body)
    assert 'altitude' in get_response_data.keys()
    assert 'unit' in get_response_data.keys()
    assert get_response_data['altitude'] >= 0
    assert get_response_data['altitude'] <= 3000
    assert get_response_data['unit'] == 'feet'


async def
test_get_altimeter_altitude_in_meters(http_server_client):
    """
    Ensure we can get the altimeter's altitude in meters
```

```
"""
get_response = await http_server_client.fetch(
    '/altimeters/1?unit=meters',
    method='GET')
assert get_response.code == HTTPStatus.OK
get_response_data = escape.json_decode(get_response.body)
assert 'altitude' in get_response_data.keys()
assert 'unit' in get_response_data.keys()
assert get_response_data['altitude'] >= 0
assert get_response_data['altitude'] <= 914.4
assert get_response_data['unit'] == 'meters'
```

The previous code added the following three test functions, whose names start with the test_ prefix and who receive the http_server_client argument to use this test fixture:

- test_set_and_get_hexacopter_motor_speed: This test function tests whether we can set and get the hexacopter's motor speed
- test_get_altimeter_altitude_in_feet: This test function tests whether we can retrieve the altitude value from the altimeter, expressed in feet
- test_get_altimeter_altitude_in_meters: This test function tests whether we can retrieve the altitude value from the altimeter, expressed in meters

We just coded a few tests related to the hexacopter and the altimeter in order to improve test coverage and note the impact on the test coverage report.

Now, we will use the pytest command to run tests and measure their code coverage. Make sure you run the command in the Terminal or Command Prompt window in which you have activated the virtual environment, and that you are located within its root folder (Tornado01). Run the following command:

```
pytest --cov -s
```

The following lines show the sample output:

```
=============================================== test session starts
===============================================
platform darwin -- Python 3.7.1 pytest-4.0.2, py-1.7.0, pluggy-0.8.0 --
/Users/gaston/HillarPythonREST2/Tornado01/bin/python3
cachedir: .pytest_cache
rootdir: /Users/gaston/HillarPythonREST2/Tornado01, inifile:
setup.cfg
plugins: tornasync-0.5.0, cov-2.6.0
collected 4 items
tests.py::test_set_and_get_leds_brightness_levels PASSED
[ 25%]
tests.py::test_set_and_get_hexacopter_motor_speed PASSED
```

```
[ 50%]
tests.py::test_get_altimeter_altitude_in_feet PASSED
[ 75%]
tests.py::test_get_altimeter_altitude_in_meters PASSED
[100%]
---------- coverage: platform darwin, python 3.7.1-final-0 -----------
Name                      Stmts   Miss Branch BrPart   Cover
----------------------------------------------------------------
async_drone_service.py      142     41     20      8     69%
drone.py                     63     10     10      5     79%
----------------------------------------------------------------
TOTAL                       205     51     30     13     72%
```

The output provided details indicating that the test runner executed four tests and all of them passed. The test code coverage measurement report provided by the coverage package increased the Cover percentage of the async_drone_service.py module from 40% to 69%. In addition, the Cover percentage of the drone.py module increased from 59% in the previous run to 79%. The new tests we wrote executed additional code in different modules, and therefore there is an important impact in the coverage report. The total coverage increased from 46% to 72%.

If we take a look at the missing statements, we will notice that we aren't testing scenarios where validations fail. Now, we will write additional unit tests to improve the testing coverage further. Specifically, we will write unit tests to make sure that we cannot set invalid brightness levels for the LEDs, we cannot set invalid motor speeds for the hexacopter, and that we receive an HTTP 404 Not Found status code when we try to access a resource that doesn't exist.

Open the tests.py file in the root folder for the virtual environment (Tornado01). Insert the following lines after the last line. The code file for the sample is included in the restful_python_2_11_03 folder, in the Django01/tests.py file:

```
async def test_set_invalid_brightness_level(http_server_client):
    """
    Ensure we cannot set an invalid brightness level for a LED
    """
    patch_args_led_1 = {'brightness_level': 256}
    try:
        patch_response_led_1 = await http_server_client.fetch(
            '/leds/1',
            method='PATCH',
            body=json.dumps(patch_args_led_1))
    except HTTPClientError as err:
        assert err.code == HTTPStatus.BAD_REQUEST
    patch_args_led_2 = {'brightness_level': -256}
    try:
```

```
            patch_response_led_2 = await http_server_client.fetch(
                '/leds/2',
                method='PATCH',
                body=json.dumps(patch_args_led_2))
    except HTTPClientError as err:
        assert err.code == HTTPStatus.BAD_REQUEST
    patch_args_led_3 = {'brightness_level': 512}
    try:
            patch_response_led_3 = await http_server_client.fetch(
                '/leds/3',
                method='PATCH',
                body=json.dumps(patch_args_led_3))
    except HTTPClientError as err:
        assert err.code == HTTPStatus.BAD_REQUEST


async def
test_set_brightness_level_invalid_led_id(http_server_client):
    """
    Ensure we cannot set the brightness level for an invalid LED id
    """
    patch_args_led_1 = {'brightness_level': 128}
    try:
            patch_response_led_1 = await http_server_client.fetch(
                '/leds/100',
                method='PATCH',
                body=json.dumps(patch_args_led_1))
    except HTTPClientError as err:
        assert err.code == HTTPStatus.NOT_FOUND


async def
test_get_brightness_level_invalid_led_id(http_server_client):
    """
    Ensure we cannot get the brightness level for an invalid LED id
    """
    try:
            patch_response_led_1 = await http_server_client.fetch(
                '/leds/100',
                method='GET')
    except HTTPClientError as err:
        assert err.code == HTTPStatus.NOT_FOUND
```

The previous code added the following three test functions, whose names start with the `test_` prefix and receive the `http_server_client` argument to use this test fixture:

- `test_set_invalid_brightness_level`: This test function makes sure that we cannot set an invalid brightness level for an LED through an HTTP `PATCH` request. In this method, many `try...except` blocks capture an `HTTPClientError` exception as `err` and use `assert` to make sure the `err.code` attribute matches `HTTPStatus.BAD_REQUEST`. This way, the test makes sure that each HTTP `PATCH` request generates an HTTP `400 Bad Request` status code.
- `test_set_brightness_level_invalid_led_id`: This test function makes sure that we cannot set the brightness level for an invalid LED `id` through an HTTP `PATCH` request.
- `test_get_brightness_level_invalid_led_id`: This test function makes sure that we cannot get the brightness level for an invalid LED `id` through an HTTP `GET` request.

In the last two methods, a `try...except` block captures an `HTTPClientError` exception as `err`. The `except` block uses `assert` to make sure the `err.code` attribute matches `HTTPStatus.NOT_FOUND`. This way, the test makes sure that the HTTP `PATCH` and HTTP `GET` requests to generate an HTTP `404 Not Found` status code.

 When an HTTP request is unsuccessful, the `http_server_client.fetch` method raises a `tornado.httpclient.HTTPClientError` exception and the status code is available in the `code` attribute for the instance.

Stay in the `tests.py` file in the root folder for the virtual environment (`Tornado01`). Insert the following lines after the last line. The code file for the sample is included in the `restful_python_2_11_03` folder, in the `Django01/tests.py` file:

```python
async def test_set_invalid_motor_speed(http_server_client):
    """
    Ensure we cannot set an invalid motor speed for the hexacopter
    """
    patch_args_hexacopter_1 = {'motor_speed': 89000}
    try:
        patch_response_hexacopter_1 = await http_server_client.fetch(
            '/hexacopters/1',
            method='PATCH',
            body=json.dumps(patch_args_hexacopter_1))
    except HTTPClientError as err:
        assert err.code == HTTPStatus.BAD_REQUEST
    patch_args_hexacopter_2 = {'motor_speed': -78600}
```

```python
    try:
        patch_response_hexacopter_2 = await http_server_client.fetch(
            '/hexacopters/1',
            method='PATCH',
            body=json.dumps(patch_args_hexacopter_2))
    except HTTPClientError as err:
        assert err.code == HTTPStatus.BAD_REQUEST
    patch_args_hexacopter_3 = {'motor_speed': 8900}
    try:
        patch_response_hexacopter_3 = await http_server_client.fetch(
            '/hexacopters/1',
            method='PATCH',
            body=json.dumps(patch_args_hexacopter_3))
    except HTTPClientError as err:
        assert err.code == HTTPStatus.BAD_REQUEST


async def test_set_motor_speed_invalid_hexacopter_id(http_server_client):
    """
    Ensure we cannot set the motor speed for an invalid hexacopter id
    """
    patch_args_hexacopter_1 = {'motor_speed': 128}
    try:
        patch_response_hexacopter_1 = await http_server_client.fetch(
            '/hexacopters/100',
            method='PATCH',
            body=json.dumps(patch_args_hexacopter_1))
    except HTTPClientError as err:
        assert err.code == HTTPStatus.NOT_FOUND


async def test_get_motor_speed_invalid_hexacopter_id(http_server_client):
    """
    Ensure we cannot get the motor speed for an invalid hexacopter id
    """
    try:
        patch_response_hexacopter_1 = await http_server_client.fetch(
            '/hexacopters/5',
            method='GET')
    except HTTPClientError as err:
        assert err.code == HTTPStatus.NOT_FOUND


async def test_get_altimeter_altitude_invalid_altimeter_id(http_server_clie
nt):
    """
    Ensure we cannot get the altimeter's altitude for an invalid altimeter
id
```

```
"""
try:
    get_response = await http_server_client.fetch(
        '/altimeters/5',
        method='GET')
except HTTPClientError as err:
    assert err.code == HTTPStatus.NOT_FOUND
```

The previous code added the following four test functions, whose names start with the `test_` prefix and receive the `http_server_client` argument to use this test fixture:

- `test_set_invalid_brightness_level`: This test function makes sure that we cannot set an invalid brightness level for the LED through an HTTP `PATCH` request
- `test_set_motor_speed_invalid_hexacopter_id`: This test function makes sure that we cannot set the motor speed for an invalid hexacopter `id` through an HTTP `PATCH` request
- `test_get_motor_speed_invalid_hexacopter_id`: This test function makes sure that we cannot get the motor speed for an invalid hexacopter `id`
- `test_get_altimeter_altitude_invalid_altimeter_id`: This test function makes sure that we cannot get the altitude value for an invalid altimeter `id`

We coded many additional tests that will make sure that all the validations work as expected. Now, we will use the `pytest` command again to run the tests and measure their code coverage. Make sure you run the command in the Terminal or Command Prompt window in which you have activated the virtual environment, and that you are located within its root folder (`Tornado01`). Run the following command:

```
pytest --cov -v
```

The following lines show the sample output:

```
=============================================== test session starts
================================================
platform darwin -- Python 3.7.1, pytest-4.0.2, py-1.7.0, pluggy-0.8.0 --
/Users/gaston/HillarPythonREST2/Tornado01/bin/python3
cachedir: .pytest_cache
rootdir: /Users/gaston/HillarPythonREST2/Tornado01, inifile:
setup.cfg
plugins: tornasync-0.5.0, cov-2.6.0
collected 11 items
tests.py::test_set_and_get_leds_brightness_levels PASSED
[  9%]
tests.py::test_set_and_get_hexacopter_motor_speed PASSED
[ 18%]
```

```
tests.py::test_get_altimeter_altitude_in_feet PASSED
[ 27%]
tests.py::test_get_altimeter_altitude_in_meters PASSED
[ 36%]
tests.py::test_set_invalid_brightness_level PASSED
[ 45%]
tests.py::test_set_brightness_level_invalid_led_id PASSED
[ 54%]
tests.py::test_get_brightness_level_invalid_led_id PASSED
[ 63%]
tests.py::test_set_invalid_motor_speed PASSED
[ 72%]
tests.py::test_set_motor_speed_invalid_hexacopter_id PASSED
[ 81%]
tests.py::test_get_motor_speed_invalid_hexacopter_id PASSED
[ 90%]
tests.py::test_get_altimeter_altitude_invalid_altimeter_id PASSED
[100%]
------------ coverage: platform darwin, python 3.7.1-final-0 -----------
```

Name	Stmts	Miss	Branch	BrPart	Cover
async_drone_service.py	142	17	20	2	87%
drone.py	63	8	10	3	85%
TOTAL	205	25	30	5	86%

The output provided details indicating that the test runner executed 11 tests and all of them passed. The test code coverage measurement report provided by the coverage package increased the Cover percentage of the async_drone_service.py module from 69% to 87%. In addition, the Cover percentage of the drone.py module increased from 79% in the previous run to 85%. The new tests we wrote executed additional code in different modules, and therefore there is an important impact in the coverage report. The total coverage increased from 72% to 86%.

Understanding strategies for deploying Tornado APIs to the cloud

Tornado supplies its own HTTP server, and therefore it can run without a WSGI container. However, some cloud providers, such as Google App Engine, only enable the running of Tornado in a WSGI-only environment. When Tornado runs in a WSGI-only environment, it doesn't support asynchronous operations. Hence, we must take into account this important limitation when selecting our cloud platform for Tornado.

We must make sure that the API runs under HTTPS in production environments. In addition, we have to make sure we add some authentication and throttling policies. Our Tornado sample is a simple RESTful API that provides some features we can use as a baseline to generate a more complex and secure API.

It is convenient to use a different configuration file for production. However, another approach, which is becoming extremely popular, especially for cloud-native applications, is to store configuration in the environment. If we want to deploy cloud-native RESTful web services and follow the guidelines established in the Twelve-Factor App Methodology, we should store config in the environment.

Each platform includes detailed instructions for deploying our application. All of them will require us to generate the `requirements.txt` file, which lists the application dependencies together with their versions. This way, the platforms will be able to install all the necessary dependencies listed in the file. We have been updating this file each time we needed to install a new package in our virtual environment. However, it is a good idea to run the following `pip freeze` within the root folder of our virtual environment, `Tornado01`, to generate the final `requirements.txt` file:

```
pip freeze > requirements.txt
```

The following lines show the contents of a sample generated `requirements.txt` file. Notice that the generated file also includes all the dependencies that were installed by the packages we specified in the original `requirements.txt` file:

```
atomicwrites==1.2.1
attrs==18.2.0
certifi==2018.10.15
chardet==3.0.4
coverage==4.5.2
httpie==1.0.2
idna==2.7
more-itertools==4.3.0
pluggy==0.8.0
py==1.7.0
Pygments==2.2.0
pytest==4.0.2
pytest-cov==2.6.0
pytest-tornasync==0.5.0
requests==2.20.0
six==1.11.0
tornado==5.1.1
urllib3==1.24
```

Test your knowledge

Let's see whether you can answer the following questions correctly:

1. `Future` does which of the following?
    1. Encapsulates the asynchronous execution of a callable
    2. Encapsulates the synchronous execution of a callable
    3. Runs an asynchronous method synchronously on the executor specified as an argument

2. The `concurrent.futures.ThreadPoolExecutor` class provides us with which of the following?
    1. A high-level interface for synchronously executing callables
    2. A high-level interface for asynchronously executing callables
    3. A high-level interface for composing HTTP requests

3. The `@tornado.concurrent.run_on_executor` decorator allows us to do which of the following?
    1. Run an asynchronous method synchronously on an executor
    2. Run an asynchronous method on an executor without generating `Future`
    3. Run a synchronous method asynchronously on an executor

4. The recommended way to write asynchronous code in Tornado is to use which of the following?
    1. Coroutines
    2. Chained callbacks
    3. Subroutines

5. Which of the following fixtures, defined by the `pytest-tornasync` `pytest` plugin, provide an asynchronous HTTP client for tests?
    1. `tornado_client`
    2. `http_client`
    3. `http_server_client`

6. If we want to convert the bytes in a JSON response body into a Python dictionary, we can use which of the following functions?
   1. `tornado.escape.json_decode`
   2. `tornado.escape.byte_decode`
   3. `tornado.escape.response_body_decode`

Summary

In this chapter, we understood the difference between synchronous and asynchronous execution. We created a new version of the RESTful API that takes advantage of the non-blocking features in Tornado, combined with an asynchronous execution. We improved the scalability of our existing API and made it possible to start executing other requests while waiting for slow I/O operations with sensors and actuators. We avoided splitting our methods into multiple methods with callbacks by using the `tornado.gen` generator-based interface that Tornado provides, to make it easier to work in an asynchronous environment.

Then, we set up a testing environment. We installed `pytest`, along with many plugins, to make it easy to discover and execute unit tests. We wrote the first round of unit tests, measured test coverage, and then wrote additional unit tests to improve that test coverage. We created all the necessary tests to have coverage of a nice amount of lines of code.

We built RESTful web services with Django, Flask, Pyramid, and Tornado. We chose the most appropriate framework for each case. We learned how to design a RESTful API from scratch, and to run all the necessary tests to make sure that our API works without issues as we release new versions. We learned that we could encapsulate RESTful APIs in microservices and deploy them to the dozens of available modern cloud platforms. Now, we are ready to create RESTful APIs with any of the web frameworks with which we have been working throughout this book.

Assessment

Chapter 1

1. A command-line HTTP client written in Python that makes it easy to compose and send HTTP requests
2. Resources built on top of Flask pluggable views
3. `patch`
4. `put`
5. `post`
6. `get`
7. A RESTful resource
8. Apply the field filtering and output formatting specified in `notification_fields` to the appropriate instance

Chapter 2

1. `flask run -h 0.0.0.0`
2. A library that uses the Alembic package to handle SQLAlchemy database migrations for Flask applications
3. A lightweight library for converting complex datatypes to and from native Python datatypes
4. An ORM
5. Registers a method to invoke before deserializing an object
6. Takes the instance or collection of instances passed as an argument and applies the field filtering and output formatting specified in the `Schema` subclass to the instance or collection of instances
7. The field will nest a single `Schema` or a collection of `Schema` based on the value for the `many` argument

Chapter 3

1. PUT
2. PATCH
3. 535,000
4. A proxy that allows us to store on this whatever we want to share for one request only
5. A password hashing framework that supports more than 30 schemes
6. Makes this function become the callback that `Flask-HTTPAuth` will use to verify the password for a specific user
7. All the methods declared in the resource will have the `auth.login_required` decorator applied to them
8. `page_number = request.args.get('page', 1, type=int)`

Chapter 4

1. `@pytest.fixture`
2. `test_`
3. `coverage report -m`
4. A unit test framework that makes testing easy and reduces boilerplate code
5. Measures the code coverage of Python programs

Chapter 5

1. `python manage.py startapp recipes`
2. `'django-rest-framework'`
3. Is integrated with Django
4. Mediators between the model instances and Python primitives
5. Route URLs to views
6. Python primitives and HTTP requests and responses
7. A `Game` class as a subclass of the `django.db.models.Model` superclass

Chapter 6

1. A wrapper that converts a function-based view into a subclass of the `rest_framework.views.APIView` class
2. `Form` and `ModelForm` classes
3. `SlugRelatedField`
4. `HyperlinkedRelatedField`
5. Generates human-friendly HTML output for each resource whenever the request specifies `text/html` as the value for the `Content-type` key in the request header

Chapter 7

1. `title = django.db.models.CharField(max_length=250, unique=True)`
2. `title = django.db.models.CharField(max_length=250, unique=False)`
3. `DEFAULT_PAGINATION_CLASS`
4. `rest_framework.pagination.LimitOffsetPagination`
5. Provides an HTTP basic authentication against username and password
6. Works with Django's session framework for authentication
7. `DEFAULT_AUTHENTICATION_CLASSES`

Chapter 8

1. `client`
2. `@pytest.mark.django_db`
3. Limits the rate of requests for specific parts of the API identified with the value assigned to the `throttle_scope` property
4. Limits the rate of requests that a specific user can make
5. Provides field filtering capabilities
6. Provides single query parameter-based searching capabilities and it is based on the Django admin's search function
7. `filterset_class`

Chapter 9

1. Python objects such as functions, classes, and instances that implement a `__call__` method
2. `pyramid.request.Request`
3. `status_code`
4. `HTTPCreated`
5. `json_body`

Chapter 10

1. `self.set_satus`
2. `self.write`
3. `tornado.web.RequestHandler`
4. `("GET", "PATCH")`
5. A regular expression (`regexp`) and a `tornado.web.IncomingHTTPRequestHandler` subclass (`request_class`)
6. Automatically writes the chunk as JSON and sets the value of the `Content-Type` header to `application/json`
7. Generates Python objects for the JSON string of the request body and returns the generated dictionary

Chapter 11

1. Encapsulates the asynchronous execution of a callable
2. A high-level interface for asynchronously executing callables
3. Run a synchronous method asynchronously on an executor
4. Coroutines
5. `http_server_client`
6. `tornado.escape.json_decode`

Other Books You May Enjoy

If you enjoyed this book, you may be interested in these other books by Packt:

Hands-On Data Structures and Algorithms with Python - Second Edition
Dr. Basant Agarwal, Benjamin Baka

ISBN: 978-1-78899-557-3

- Understand object representation, attribute binding, and data encapsulation
- Gain a solid understanding of Python data structures using algorithms
- Study algorithms using examples with pictorial representation
- Learn complex algorithms through easy explanation, implementing Python
- Build sophisticated and efficient data applications in Python
- Understand common programming algorithms used in Python data science
- Write efficient and robust code in Python 3.7

Learn Python Programming - Second Edition
Fabrizio Romano

ISBN: 978-1-78899-666-2

- Get Python up and running on Windows, Mac, and Linux
- Explore fundamental concepts of coding using data structures and control flow
- Write elegant, reusable, and efficient code in any situation
- Understand when to use the functional or OOP approach
- Cover the basics of security and concurrent/asynchronous programming
- Create bulletproof, reliable software by writing tests
- Build a simple website in Django
- Fetch, clean, and manipulate data

Leave a review - let other readers know what you think

Please share your thoughts on this book with others by leaving a review on the site that you bought it from. If you purchased the book from Amazon, please leave us an honest review on this book's Amazon page. This is vital so that other potential readers can see and use your unbiased opinion to make purchasing decisions, we can understand what our customers think about our products, and our authors can see your feedback on the title that they have worked with Packt to create. It will only take a few minutes of your time, but is valuable to other potential customers, our authors, and Packt. Thank you!

Index

210, 212, 214, 216

I

iCurlHTTP
  reference 54
Integrated Development Environment (IDE) 51
Internet of Things (IoT) 9

J

JavaScript Object Notation (JSON) 181

L

Light-Emitting Diode (LED) 403
lightweight virtual environments
  working with 14, 15, 16, 17, 18, 20

M

Marshmallow schema
  creating, serialize SurfboardMetricModel model
    382, 383
  creating, to deserialize SurfboardMetricModel
    model 382, 383
  creating, to validate SurfboardMetricModel model
    382, 383
microservices 13
migrations
  default value, setting for required field 315, 317,
    319
  executing 87, 88, 90
  executing, for user table generation 139, 140,
    142
  running 252, 254
miles per hour (MPH) 370
model serializers
  using, to eliminate duplicate code 224, 225
models
  creating, with relationships 68, 70
  relationships, declaring with 245, 247, 248, 249,
    250
  security-related data, adding 307, 308, 309, 310
  unique constraints, adding 286, 288, 290, 291
  unique constraints, improving 106, 107, 108,
    110, 111, 113

N

NotificationModel class
  creating 24

O

object-level permissions
  customized permission class, creating for 311,
    312
Object-Relational Mapping (ORM) 10, 69, 179,
  370
Organic Light Emitting Diode (OLED) 10

P

packages
  installing, with requirements.txt file 63, 64, 65
pagination classes
  customizing 301, 302, 303, 304
pagination features
  adding 121, 122, 124, 126
pagination
  advantage 293, 296, 298, 300
PATCH method
  used, for updating single field for resource 292,
    293
permissions 304, 306, 307
PostgreSQL 10.5 database
  configuring 67
  creating 65, 67
  interaction, by designing RESTful API 60
  reference 65
PostgreSQL database
  contents, verifying 91, 92, 255, 256
  creating, for testing 151
  first round of unit test, writing 155, 159, 161
  related resources, creating 93, 94, 95, 97, 99,
    101
  related resources, retrieving 93, 94, 95, 97, 99,
    101
PostgreSQL
  creating, for testing 152
  packages, installing with requirements.txt file
    250, 251
Postman app
  reference 46
PUT method

W

Web Server Gateway Interface (WSGI) 175, 365